Studies in Celtic History XLIII

THE LEGACY OF GILDAS

STUDIES IN CELTIC HISTORY

ISSN 0261-9865

General editors
Dauvit Broun
Máire Ní Mhaonaigh
Huw Pryce

Studies in Celtic History aims to provide a forum for new research into all aspects of the history of Celtic-speaking peoples throughout the whole of the medieval period. The term 'history' is understood broadly: any study, regardless of discipline, which advances our knowledge and understanding of the history of Celtic-speaking peoples will be considered. Studies of primary sources, and of new methods of exploiting such sources, are encouraged.

Founded by Professor David Dumville, the series was relaunched under new editorship in 1997. Proposals or queries may be sent directly to the editors at the addresses given below; all submissions will receive prompt and informed consideration before being sent to expert readers.

Professor Dauvit Broun
Dauvit.broun@glasgow.ac.uk

Professor Máire Ní Mhaonaigh
mnm21@cam.ac.uk

Professor Huw Pryce
a.h.pryce@bangor.ac.uk

For titles already published in this series
see the end of this volume

THE LEGACY OF GILDAS

CONSTRUCTIONS OF AUTHORITY IN THE EARLY MEDIEVAL WEST

STEPHEN J. JOYCE

THE BOYDELL PRESS

© Stephen J. Joyce 2022

All Rights Reserved. Except as permitted under current legislation no part of this work may be photocopied, stored in a retrieval system, published, performed in public, adapted, broadcast, transmitted, recorded or reproduced in any form or by any means, without the prior permission of the copyright owner

The right of Stephen J. Joyce to be identified as the author of this work has been asserted in accordance with sections 77 and 78 of the Copyright, Designs and Patents Act 1988

First published 2022
The Boydell Press, Woodbridge
Paperback edition 2026

ISBN 978-1-78327-672-1 (Hardback)
ISBN 978-1-83765-382-9 (Paperback)

The Boydell Press is an imprint of Boydell & Brewer Ltd
and of Boydell & Brewer Inc.
website: www.boydellandbrewer.com

Our Authorised Representative for product safety in the EU is Easy Access System Europe – Mustamäe tee 50, 10621 Tallinn, Estonia, *gpsr.requests@easproject.com*

A catalogue record of this publication is available from the British Library

The publisher has no responsibility for the continued existence or accuracy of URLs for external or third-party internet websites referred to in this book, and does not guarantee that any content on such websites is, or will remain, accurate or appropriate

CONTENTS

FIGURES

PREFACE AND ACKNOWLEDGEMENTS

This monograph is the result of my long-held interest in the histories and legends associated with the British Isles in the opaque period following the decline and fall of the western Roman empire. Working from a theological and literary perspective, I have attempted to illuminate aspects of this 'dark age' through the lens of the Bible and a 'thick description' of select textual witnesses. The former methodology has been aided by the collective wisdom held at Monash University; the latter methodology has been supported by the digitisation of medieval texts and the development of search engines and textual comparison software to complement these digitised collections.

There can be no doubt that the most important influence on this book has been Professor Constant Mews. Significant other influences include Associate Professor Lisa Bailey, Professor Megan Cassidy-Welch, Professor Peter Howard, Professor Bronwen Neil, Dr Lynette Olson, and Professor Jonathan Wooding. Special thanks to Emeritus Professor John Crossley for his comments, to Sonia Kretschmar for the artwork, and to Caroline Palmer for steering the publication process. I am also indebted to specialist scholars for support and advice: Associate Professor Doru Costache, Dr Cornel Dora, Dr Chris Doyle, Associate Professor Geoffrey Dunn, Associate Professor Roy Flechner, Associate Professor Andrew Gillett, Dr Julianna Grigg, Dr Anne Holloway, Professor Mark Humphries, Dr Edwin Hustwit, Associate Professor Jonathan Jarrett, Dr Luca Larpi, Professor Rosamond McKitterick, Dr Sven Meeder, Dr Kathleen Neal, Dr Sigbjørn Sønnesyn, Dr Clare Stancliffe, Dr Carol Williams, Professor Ian Wood, and the anonymous peer reviewers.

This book was facilitated by an Australian Government Research Training Program Scholarship and an Australian Academy of the Humanities Publication Subsidy. I dedicate it to my late mother, Margaret, to my father, Jim, and to my wife, Michelle.

Stephen J. Joyce

ABBREVIATIONS

AA	*Auctores Antiquissimi*
CCCC 279	Cambridge, Corpus Christi College, 279
CCSL	*Corpus Christianorum Series Latina*
CSEL	*Corpus Scriptorum Ecclesiasticorum Latinorum*
De excidio	*De excidio Britanniae*
Epistola	*Epistola ad milites Corotici*
fragmenta	*fragmenta Gildae*
Hibernensis	*Collectio canonum Hibernensis*
Historia ecclesiastica	*Historia ecclesiastica gentis Anglorum*
MGH	*Monumenta Germaniae Historica*
PL	*Patrologia Latina*
SC	*Sources chrétiennes*
SRM	*Scriptores rerum Merovingicarum*
Turonensis	*Collectio canonum Turonensis*
Vita Germani	*Vita Germani episcopi Autissiodorensis*

INTRODUCTION

This book seeks to refine the image of Gildas, a key figure of authority in the early medieval British church. It does so by examining his self-image as presented in surviving works variously dated to the fifth or sixth centuries, and subsequent images as developed by the reception of these works – the legacy of Gildas – up to the early eighth century. The purpose of this investigation is to clarify and reconcile these often-conflicting depictions in order to better understand Gildas. This reconciliation is important because the way we perceive Gildas – a rare beacon in a 'dark age' – is inextricably bound up in the way we perceive the Christian culture of the British Isles in the opaque period following the decline and fall of the western Roman empire.[1] A Gildas that shines more brightly, this book argues, shines more light on the early Insular church and its place within the continental church.[2]

When describing the Christian culture of Britain and Ireland in the fifth and sixth centuries, Gildas is an exceptional figure. This is not because of the particularity of his historical and religious vision, but rather because he is the only remotely contemporary Insular voice narrating a pivotal shift in the history of the British Isles – the period when the Roman province of *Britannia* and the political entities of the Picts and Scots began to evolve into the medieval nations of England, Scotland, Wales, and Ireland. The detail of this significant shift, bedevilled by enigmatic material evidence and limited textual sources, is not well understood. Gildas is, thus, an essential witness, and the way in which his historical and religious vision has been received by scholars has profoundly shaped perceptions of this hugely important, yet poorly documented, transition.

Gildas's unique history of the Christian culture of *Britannia* forms a discrete section in his most notable surviving text, the *De excidio Britanniae* or the *Ruin of Britain*.[3] An open letter in three parts, Gildas denounces contemporary secular and church leaders of the former Roman province of *Britannia* in the context of corruption, civil strife, and partition with pagan powers. In briefly narrating the history of the Britons from the coming of the Romans (as the providential messengers of Christ) to an immediate political and spiritual crisis, Gildas presents, as a pointed

1 This book will use the geographic term 'British Isles' interchangeably with the equivalent term 'Britain and Ireland' to describe those islands sometimes referred to as the Atlantic archipelago. I acknowledge that these geographic terms may have problematic political and cultural associations. This book will also use the sometimes problematically applied metaphor 'dark age' to represent the lack of contemporaneous accounts describing events in the British Isles in the period *ca* 450–600, particularly as it relates to Bede's presentation of the past. On this, see Chapter 1.

2 This book will refer to a capitalised 'Insular' as having an origin in the British Isles. A lower-case 'insular' will refer to its meaning as culturally inward-looking. The 'continent' will represent both continental Europe and the area influenced by Roman Christianity, thus also encompassing North Africa and the Middle East.

3 For Gildas's *De excidio Britanniae*: see *Gildas* (ed. Winterbottom, 87–142, trans., 13–79). Winterbottom's use of the title *De excidio Britonum* has been set aside for the more widely used title *De excidio Britanniae*.

prelude, his historical vision of a Christian nation where past triumphs and calamities are attached to the moral choices of her people. This visceral vision of divine judgement, inspired by the Old Testament and Israel, is remarkably fluid. Generally devoid of chronological anchors, Gildas's 'providential history', difficult to date precisely, is susceptible to different readings. This is particularly so with his account of the *adventus Saxonum*, the belligerent arrival of the Germanic peoples subsequently known as the English in Britain.[4] Welsh grievances relating to Gildas's reports of the ruthless dispossession of the Britons have been countered by English observations of his portrayal of a weak and sinful people unfit to hold the island.[5] Open to interpretation, the *De excidio Britanniae* (*De excidio*) is an opaque text on which later historical, religious, and national agendas have often been projected.

The same can be said for Gildas himself. While the image of Gildas as a historian might dominate the way in which modern scholars have interacted with him, his history of *Britannia* does not dominate his surviving works. This emphasis on Gildas's 'judgemental' history has tended to gloss over other, more positive, aspects of his contributions to Insular culture. The other sections of the *De excidio*, presenting both criticisms of and advice for Christian secular and church leaders in the manner of a 'mirror for princes', are often set aside. So, too, are fragments of a personal letter cited in Insular canon law collections.[6] Yet the transition between these two works – from the critical 'voice in the wilderness' to intimate ecclesiastical advice – points to a significant evolution in his authority. While the image of Gildas as a 'doleful historian' – promoted by the English scholar, Bede (*ca* 673–735) – implies an impotent chronicler lamenting inevitable decline, the image of Gildas as a significant contributor to the Christian culture of the British Isles – remembered particularly in Ireland – implies a doyen engaged in successful political and ecclesiastical reform.[7] This 'dislocation' has resulted in a variety of Insular images. Gildas is remembered differently by the English, the Welsh, the Irish (as *Scotti* or Scots), and, in a continental setting, the Bretons.[8] His image varies depending on whether he is seen as originating from the north or south of Britain, whether he is active in the fifth or sixth centuries, and whether he is viewed as a cleric or monk, as a historian or canon lawyer, or as a polemicist or moderator. In brief, much depends on whether he is seen as a failure or a success. It is particularly this last point – the image of Gildas as an effective authority and its reciprocal impact on our views of the Insular church – that this book investigates.

[4] Descriptors for these Germanic peoples shift significantly in the period under investigation: this book will use the term 'Saxons' when discussing the *adventus Saxonum* as described by Gildas; 'Anglo-Saxons' when discussing the *adventus Anglorum sive Saxonum* as described by Bede; and 'English' when discussing these peoples more broadly, as also influenced by Bede.

[5] On opposing English and Welsh interpretations of Gildas in the eighth and ninth centuries, see, briefly, Charles-Edwards, *Wales and the Britons*, 446–7. For more on this, see Chapter 2.

[6] For the *fragmenta Gildae*, see *Gildas* (ed. Winterbottom, 143–5, trans., 80–2). For the relationship between the *fragmenta Gildae* and Insular canon law collections, see Sharpe, 'Gildas as a Father of the Church'.

[7] Bede, *Historia ecclesiastica*, I.22 (edd. Colgrave & Mynors, 68–9): 'quae historicus eorum Gildas flebili sermone describit' [which Gildas their own historian describes in doleful words]. For convenience, this will be the edition used in this book. The latest critical edition is Latin-Italian. See *Beda: Storia degli Inglesi* (ed. Lapidge & trans. Chiesa). For an overview of Irish images of Gildas, see Chapter 2.

[8] What the Picts may have thought of Gildas is, at the time of publication, still lost to history.

The malleability of Gildas's image in the face of historical, religious, and national agendas is, perhaps, best seen in debates over the evolution of the Christian culture of Britain and Ireland in the early medieval period. Following Bede's influential narrative of English conversion from paganism and 'Insular Christianity' to Roman orthodoxy in his *Historia ecclesiastica gentis Anglorum* or the *Ecclesiastical History of the English People*, the modern era tended to stress religious tensions between the Insular church and the continental Roman church, as exemplified by fierce disputes over the correct tonsure and the correct calculation of the lunar festival of Easter. This perception of a dissident and idiosyncratic Insular church dominated by monasticism and affected by heresy and schism powerfully shaped attitudes to the rare voices surviving from this period. In this context, Gildas was fashioned into a 'dark-age Insular monk', an obtuse and polemical moraliser disconnected from classical learning and continental orthodoxy.[9] In the contemporary era, reassessments of Gildas's works on their own terms have revealed that this image is highly problematic. A seminal study published in 1984 reframed Gildas as an ecclesiastic actively connected to continental classical tradition and Insular church reform.[10] However, while Gildas has been reconnected to continental influences, arguments still remain that Gildas had no influence *on* the continent.[11] This book seeks to further expand our understanding of Gildas's impact.

Building on this reframed image, Gildas emerges as a figure of significant authority. The Irish *peregrinus* Columbanus (*ca* 543–615), the founder of several monasteries in Gaul and Italy, spoke of Gildas as an *auctor* or authority when communicating with Pope Gregory the Great (*r.* 590–604).[12] The Irish compilers of the *Collectio canonum Hibernensis* (*Hibernensis*) named him alongside church fathers in their comprehensive manual of canon law *ca* 669–748.[13] Bede, as we have seen, referred to Gildas when assembling his *Historia ecclesiastica gentis Anglorum* (*Historia ecclesiastica*) *ca* 731. The different ways in which Gildas has been invoked links contrasting Insular and continental attitudes toward authority within Christian society in these centuries. Analysis of this reception – the legacy of Gildas – will unpack new perspectives on the early Insular church and its relationship to the continent.

9 On this, see Chapter 1.

10 Lapidge & Dumville (edd.), *Gildas*.

11 For instance, Wright, 'Columbanus's *Epistulae*', 86, and Stancliffe, 'The Thirteen Sermons', 180, argue that the *De excidio* appears to be unknown on the continent outside Brittany and had no impact on the continent contemporary to its publication.

12 For instance, Columbanus, *Epistulae*, I.6 (ed. Walker, 8–9): 'simoniacos et Gildas auctor pestes scripsit eos' [Gildas the writer set them down as simoniacs and plagues].

13 *The Hibernensis*, I.16 (ed. Flechner, 15, trans., 488): 'Gildas ait: Habent quippe sacerdotes et episcopi terribilem iudicem, cui pertinet et non nobis, de illis in utroque seculo iudicare' [Gildas said: Indeed, *sacerdotes* and bishops have a terrible judge, to whom it belongs, and not us, to judge them in both worlds]. I would like to thank Dr Flechner for access to his page-proofs prepared for the Dublin Institute for Advanced Studies. References are to his recently published edition with the Catholic University of America Press. The question of whether the *Hibernensis* was compiled by one person, as the prologue implies, or more than one person is set aside for the general term 'compilers'. For a discussion of the problematic identification of the compilers as Ruben of Dairinis (*ob. ca* 725) and Cú Chuimne of Iona (*ob. ca* 747), see *The Hibernensis* (ed. Flechner, 53*–9*). See also Flechner, *Making Laws for a Christian Society*, 13–16, where a firmer case is made. For dating, see Chapter 1, 18.

This book explores how Gildas and his legacy influenced perceptions of authority in the early medieval West. In connecting Gildas to Columbanus and Gregory the Great, and subsequently, in select ways, to the compilers of the *Hibernensis* and to Bede, this legacy will be established within a wider context. I shall argue that contestations over religious traditions within the early Insular church were not idiosyncratic but reflected broader tensions over innovations in authority as a Roman Christian *imperium* evolved into a succession of medieval Christian kingdoms. As one of the earliest *auctores* to define and defend Christian kingship, Gildas deserves to be seen as a significant contributor to the political development of the medieval West.

So, what can we currently say about Gildas? Like many early medieval Insular figures, he is difficult to place. While he is one of only two identifiable Insular authors describing the British Isles in the fifth century, his relative obscurity is in stark contrast to the continued celebration of the other enigmatic critic of corrupt authority, the apostle to Ireland, Bishop Patrick (*ob. ca* 461 or 493).[14] This disjuncture in reception is all the more surprising when we consider the significance of their surviving works. Patrick's *Confessio* and *Epistola ad milites Corotici* (*Epistola*), open letters dated to the fifth century, place him within the Roman Christian literary conventions of his time.[15] Gildas's *De excidio*, an open letter dated to the fifth or sixth centuries, provides the earliest surviving instances of several medieval literary conventions.[16] The *De excidio* is the earliest surviving text to construct a 'national' history (as *Britannia*) of a former Roman province.[17] Gildas is the first author to identify a post-Roman *gens* or 'nation' (the *Britones*) as a chosen people of God.[18] The *De excidio* is possibly the earliest surviving work describing the legal expectations, in a scriptural sense, of the authority of Christian kings and bishops, the emerging polity

[14] Patrick is known, in part, for his excommunication of the secular leader, Coroticus, for the crimes of murder, theft, and slavery. For a recent introduction to Patrick and his attitudes toward authority, see Flechner, *Saint Patrick Retold*, 1–28. For further discussion, see Chapter 1. While other potentially Insular texts do survive from the fifth century, such as those attributed to a Bishop Fastidius, they are discourses on a Christian life rather than descriptive in a secular or historical sense. On Fastidius, see Rees, *Pelagius*, 15–16. Other surviving works by authors with a formative education in the British Isles and active in the fifth century, such as those by the controversial theologian, Pelagius (*fl. ca* 390–418), and Bishop Faustus of Riez (*ob. ca* 490), are written in a continental context.

[15] For Patrick's letters, see *Liber Epistolarum* (ed. Howlett): *Epistola* (ed. Howlett, 25–39); *Confessio* (ed. Howlett, 52–93). For Patrick's literary conventions as relating to those of Augustine of Hippo, see Swan, *The Experience of God*, 62. For dating, see Chapter 1, 14, n. 2.

[16] Christopher Snyder has noted various scholarly positions on the dating of the *De excidio* in a useful table: David Dumville (*ca* 550), Michael Lapidge (pre-500), Thomas O'Sullivan (*ca* 515–20), Michael Herren (*ca* 500), Nicholas Higham (*ca* 479–84), Michael Jones (post-500). See Snyder, *The Britons*, 123. For more on dating, see Chapter 1, 14, n. 2.

[17] Thompson, 'Gildas and the History of Britain', 208, notes that Gildas was 'the first man in the entire west to write a provincial history'. Jones, *The End of Roman Britain*, 123, notes that this 'must have been a conscious rhetorical innovation'.

[18] Howlett, *Insular Inscriptions*, 29, notes that '[n]o-one before Gildas had identified a single Christian people as *praesens Israel*, but that is what Gildas called the Britons… In the psychology of self-definition of the Britons it would be hard to overstate the importance of this idea.' O'Loughlin, *Gildas and the Scriptures*, 25, also notes his originality: 'The perception of his people as a distinct baptised nation marks an important break in the history of theology. This focus on his own *populus*… means that we can treat Gildas as the first medieval theologian.'

of post-Roman western Europe.[19] Despite these innovations, Gildas's reputation as a 'difficult' historian, first established by the Anglo-Norman William of Newburgh (*ca* 1136–1198), lingers.[20]

This uncertain reputation has influenced interpretations of Gildas's other surviving works: he is almost certainly the author of a letter mentioned by Columbanus to a British and/or Irish ecclesiastic, Finnian (*ob. ca* 549 or 579), fragments of which are preserved as the so-called *fragmenta Gildae* (*fragmenta*) in a variety of seventh- and/or eighth-century Insular canon collections, most notably the *Hibernensis*.[21] A preface on penance, the *Praefatio Gildae de poenitentia*, is ascribed to him.[22] Also assigned to him are two hymns, the *Lorica Gildae* and the *Oratio Rythmica*.[23] These attributed works have, for brevity, been set aside from detailed analysis in favour of the *De excidio* and the fragments of the letter to Finnian. The effect of Gildas's lingering reputation as an unreliable witness is that he continues to 'languish' in the hands of specialists of early medieval Britain, Ireland, and Brittany, though with some additional notoriety from within non-specialist circles attempting to historicise King Arthur (to whom Gildas is obliquely connected by a ninth-century Welsh history, the *Historia Brittonum*, and directly connected by a twelfth-century Welsh life, both outside the detailed scope of this book).[24]

19 The *De excidio* as potentially the earliest surviving medieval *speculum principum* is an argument put forward in this book. The 'revolutionary' nature of the text as it relates to kingship has been noted by Brooks, 'Gildas's *De excidio*', 1 and 10, but in the context of a failed 'outburst'. This book will argue that Gildas's *De excidio* is a 'mirror for princes' with significant influence.

20 On William of Newburgh, see Chapter 2, 41. While specialists in the history of the early medieval Insular church have moved away from regarding Gildas as 'difficult', this impression still appears in a wider context. See, for instance, Merrills, *History and Geography*, 278, who describes aspects of Gildas's historical vision as 'famously obtuse'.

21 Columbanus, *Epistulae*, I.7 (ed. Walker, 8–9): 'Vennianus auctor Gildam de his interrogavit, et elegantissime ille rescripsit' [Finnian the writer questioned Gildas about them, and he sent a most polished reply]. Sharpe, 'Gildas as a Father of the Church', argues, against Michael Winterbottom's *fragmenta epistularum*, that all the fragments, thematically cohesive, come from the letter to Finnian mentioned by Columbanus. For the purposes of this book, I will relate the fragments solely to Gildas's letter to Finnian. Finnian is variously identified as that of Clonard, *ob. ca* 549, or of Moville, *ob. ca* 579. For a brief overview of the enigmatic figure(s) of Finnian, see Yorke, *The Conversion of Britain*, 112–13, and Dunn, 'Paradigms of Penance', 19–20. For an argument for a British origin for Finnian and a singular Finnian, see Dumville, 'Gildas and Uinniau'; updated in Dumville, 'The Colophon'. For an argument that this Finnian was an Irish figure in Britain before becoming identified with both Clonard and Moville, see Ó Riain, 'Finnio and Winniau'. For the preservation of the *fragmenta* in Irish canon collections, see Chapter 5.

22 For the *Praefatio Gildae de poenitentia*, see *Gildas* (ed. Winterbottom, 146–7, trans., 84–6). Recent scholarship has attributed the *Praefatio Gildae* to an author other than Gildas (as author of the *De excidio*). See Herren, 'Gildas and Early British Monasticism', 70. For an argument affirming the attribution of the *Praefatio Gildae* to Gildas, see Mews & Joyce, 'The Preface of Gildas'.

23 For the *Lorica*, see *Gildas* (ed. Williams, 304–13). For the *Oratio Rhythmica*, see Gildas, *Oratio Rhythmica* (ed. Meyer). Recent scholarship has attributed the *Lorica* and the *Oratio Rhythmica* to authors other than Gildas (as author of the *De excidio*). See again Herren, 'Gildas and Early British Monasticism', 65–6. The *Lorica* is most often connected to the Irish monk Laidcenn or Lathcen (*ob. ca* 661) in the manuscript tradition: see *The Hisperica Famina II* (ed. Herren, 42–5). Herren subsequently edits an edition of the *Lorica* as the *Lorica of Laidcenn* in the same volume, 76–89.

24 The *Historia Brittonum* mentions Arthur in connection to the battle of Badon Hill, a siege mentioned by Gildas. See Gildas, *De excidio*, XXVI.1 (ed. Winterbottom, 98, trans., 28): 'obsessionis

There is also significant uncertainty over when Gildas was historically active. He is identified in a possibly contemporaneous entry in the *Chronicle of Ireland* as having died in 570.[25] Yet in his *On the Antiquity of the Church at Glastonbury*, William of Malmesbury (*ca* 1095–1143) records a death in 512 and reports that he is buried 'in the old church before the altar'.[26] There are also similarly conflicting details in the two surviving *vitae*: one Breton and dating to the ninth century with an eleventh-century addition; the other, as mentioned, Welsh and dating to the twelfth century.[27] These details also record a figure active in the fifth and sixth centuries.[28] The result is scholarly indecision about when Gildas wrote the *De excidio*, with a variety of positions ranging from *ca* 479 (based on interpretations of the context of the *De excidio*) to *ca* 550 (respecting the reports of his death in the annals).[29] These differing benchmarks have exerted a considerable impact on constructing chronological narratives for Britain and Ireland in the early medieval period. While Gildas's historical context is not the core concern of this book, unpacking his legacy and its relationship to authority in the British Isles and on the continent will suggest new

Badonici montis' [the siege of Badon Hill]; *The Historia Brittonum*, LVI (ed. Morris, 35, trans., 76): 'Duodecimum fuit bellum in monte Badonis, in quo corruerunt in uno die nongenti sexaginta viri de uno impetu Arthur' [The twelfth battle was on Badon Hill and in it nine hundred and sixty men fell in one day, from a single charge of Arthur's]. Caradog of Llancarfan's life of Gildas mentions Gildas as a contemporary of King Arthur. See Caradog of Llancarfan, *Vita Gildae*, V (trans. Williams, *Two Lives*, 90–1): 'Contemporaneus Gildas vir sanctissimus fuit Arturi regis totius maioris Britanniae' [St Gildas was the contemporary of Arthur, the king of the whole of Britain]. For an overview of attempts to historicise King Arthur, see Halsall, *Worlds of Arthur*.

25 *The Chronicle of Ireland* (trans. Charles-Edwards, 108). For a brief introduction, see *The Chronicle of Ireland* (trans. Charles-Edwards, 1–3). For more detail on Gildas in the Irish and Welsh annals, see Chapter 2, 36–7. This book will set aside the arguments over whether the reconstructed *Chronicle of Ireland* represents a continuously updated chronicle begun in the late sixth century, can only be regarded as relating to a final form in the early tenth century, or is a putative text that never historically existed. As such, entries in the *Chronicle of Ireland* dating from the late sixth century will be flagged as 'possibly contemporaneous'. On these arguments, see Flechner, 'The Chronicle of Ireland'.

26 William of Malmesbury, *De Antiquitate Glastonie Ecclesiae*, VII (ed. Scott, 54): 'Nam, sicut a maioribus accepimus, Gildas, neque insulsus neque infacetus historicus, cui Britanni debent si quid noticie inter ceteras gentes habent, multum annorum ibi exegit loci sanctitudine captus. Ibique anno domini DXII de medio factus, in uetusta ecclesia ante altare est sepultus' [For, as we have learnt from our elders, Gildas, a historian who was neither boring nor boorish and to whom the Britons owe what knowledge they have as a people, spent many years there because of the holiness of the place. And in the year 512 he was taken from their midst and buried in the old church before the altar]. Translation is my own. The old church at Glastonbury was destroyed by fire *ca* 1184. William was certainly at Glastonbury *ca* 1129. This report implies that he was witness to a cult of Gildas at Glastonbury. This connection to Glastonbury is supported by the Welsh *vita*. The editor, John Scott, has argued that the last sentence of the entry is an interpolation as it is not repeated in William's (earlier, but subsequently revised) *Gestis regum Anglorum*. See William of Malmesbury, *De Antiquitate Glastonie Ecclesiae* (ed. Scott, 23–4 and 188, n. 27).

27 Both lives can be found conveniently in *Two Lives* (trans. Williams): Caradog of Llancarfan, *Vita Gildae* (trans. Williams, 84–103); Monk of Ruys, *Vita Gildae* (trans. Williams, 12–79). While Lapidge & Sharpe, *Bibliography*, 250, following the 1909 edition by Ferdinand Lot, date the Breton life to the eleventh century, Hugh Williams, following the 1898 edition by Theodor Mommsen, argues that the Breton life is predominantly a ninth-century text with an eleventh-century addition. See *Two Lives* (trans. Williams, 7–10). For the 1909 edition of the Breton life, see Lot, 'Mélanges d'histoire bretonne'. For further comment, see Chapter 2, 39–40.

28 See Chapter 2, 42–3, for more detail.

29 See above, n. 16. For an expansion on dating, see Chapter 1, 14, n. 2.

narratives for the period under study, particularly as they relate to Gildas, Columbanus, and the *Hibernensis*.[30]

The two works of Gildas tracked in the period under examination – the *De excidio* and the fragments of his letter to Finnian – reveal different aspects of his authority. The *De excidio*, an open letter critical of contemporary secular and church leaders, is a persuasive claim to authority in the tradition of the Old Testament prophets. While Gildas does not directly mention his rank or status in the *De excidio*, he does speak of belonging to the clerical orders (*ordo noster*), at the same time criticising those clerics who mock the precepts of holy men (*praecepta sanctorum*), suggesting an association with monasticism.[31] The *fragmenta*, on the other hand, advise tolerance and respect for secular, church, and monastic leaders, and suggest a Gildas who has attained a significant position of authority, probably post-dating the claims in the *De excidio*.[32] What we have, then, are two works concerned with the abuse of authority that adopt different tones: one prophetic, as in the *De excidio*, which affirms the right of subordinate 'holy men' to censure their secular and church leaders; and the other pastoral, as in the letter to Finnian, which adopts the tone of a spiritual master supportive of the need for leadership, order, and discipline, yet voicing concern about the impact of religious zeal and excessive excommunication on church unity.[33]

The abbot and priest, Columbanus, seeing no contradiction in these constructions of authority, adopted both in his letter to Gregory the Great in which he defended Insular approaches to the calculation of the date of Easter.[34] Subsequently, the compilers of the *Hibernensis* called on the authority of Gildas, as represented by his

30 This book will propose a date for the *De excidio* in the late fifth century and suggest new contexts for Columbanus and the *Hibernensis*. On the *De excidio*, see Chapter 2, 51–2, and Conclusion, 158. For Columbanus and the *Hibernensis*, see Chapters 4 and 5, respectively.

31 Gildas, *De excidio*, LXV.1 (ed. Winterbottom, 118, trans., 51): 'si non tantos talesque malitiae episcoporum vel ceterorum sacerdotum aut clericorum in nostro quoque ordine erigi adversus deum vidissem montes' [if I did not see such great mountains of wickedness raised against God by bishops and clerics of my order also]; LXVI.4 (ed. Winterbottom, 119, trans., 52–3); 'ad praecepta sanctorum, si aliquando dumtaxat audierint, quae ab illis saepissime audienda erant, oscitantes ac stupidos' [They yawn stupidly at the precepts of holy men – if they ever do hear them: though they should constantly]. Gildas's clerical and monastic status is discussed further in Chapter 3. For the purposes of this book, monasticism will be generally regarded as a lay movement. Monasticism as a distinct order post-dates the period under study. The early medieval sources themselves are ambiguous on how monks were differentiated from the secular clerical and lay orders. See Bailey, *Religious Worlds*, 21–52, for a discussion of the complex hierarchical relationship between monks, religious clergy, secular clergy, and the laity in a Gallic situation. While Bailey utilises the term 'ascetic' to cover those in any order who advocate or support an ascetic life, this book will attempt to differentiate between ascetics in a formal religious life (monks), and supporters and practitioners of asceticism in secular clerical and lay orders (ascetics).

32 Most notably seen in Gildas's support in his *fragmenta* for princes, bishops, and abbots. This point is also made in Stancliffe, 'Columbanus and Shunning', 128. See Chapter 5, 112–17, for a discussion.

33 On excommunication, see Appendix, 159–62. See also Joyce, 'Attitudes to Excommunication'.

34 Columbanus, *Epistulae*, I.6 (ed. Walker, 8–9): (alluding to the *De excidio*) 'Ceterum de episcopis illis quid iudicas, interrogo, qui contra canones ordinantur, id est quaestu; simoniacos et Gildas auctor pestes scripsit eos' [Concerning those bishops, however, who ordain uncanonically, that is for hire, I ask what you decree; Gildas the writer set them down as simoniacs and plagues]; I.7 (ed. Walker, 8–9): (referring to the letter to Finnian) 'Vennianus auctor Gildam de his interrogavit, et elegantissime ille rescripsit' [Finnian the writer questioned Gildas about them, and he sent a most polished reply].

letter to Finnian, to support episcopal authority and to discipline those who continued to express their support for a non-Roman tonsure.[35] Bede's *Historia ecclesiastica* cemented the Insular Easter and tonsure controversy as an expression of Irish and Pictish isolation and British insularity, a controversy Bede connected, in part, to the crimes of British secular and church leaders reported by Gildas in his *De excidio*.[36] Gildas, however, never mentions an Easter or tonsure controversy. While the Insular Easter controversy has been much examined as a contest over its calculation, this book will examine its liturgical significance in the early medieval period as the preferred festival for both baptism and ordination, and the notion that a 'false Easter' would lead to 'false Christians' and 'false clerics' in the image of the first heretic, Simon Magus.[37] The use of the image of Simon Magus to criticise corrupt clerical authority (as for Gildas and Columbanus), or to criticise independence from Rome (as for the *Hibernensis* and Bede), reflects a marked continuity with the legacy of Gildas.

Building on the premise that the conflict within Britain and Ireland over religious practice reflects a wider conflict over the structuring of institutional authority, this book will examine the legacy of Gildas within the contests over uniformity in religious practice represented by the Insular Easter controversy (and the associated controversy over the Insular tonsure). As such, I investigate the ways in which the memory of Gildas was invoked to shape continuing debates over authority up to the resolution of the Insular Easter controversy in an Irish and Pictish context in the

35 The reference to Gildas on the tonsure is not regarded as authentic. See *The Hibernensis*, LI.6 (ed. Flechner, 409–10, trans., 781): 'Gildas ait: Britones toto mundo contrarii, moribus Romanis inimici, non solum in missa, sed etiam in tonsura, cum Iudeis umbrae futurorum seruientes, quam ueritati. Pascha cum Iudaeis XIIII luna celebrantes' [Gildas said: The Britons are in opposition to the whole world, enemies of Roman customs, not only in respect to mass, but also to tonsure, together with the Jews they worship the shadows of future things more than truth. They celebrate Easter with the Jews on the fourteenth moon]. On this, see Chapter 5, 123–7.

36 On Irish (and by association Pictish) isolation, see Bede, *Historia ecclesiastica*, III.4 (edd. Colgrave & Mynors, 224–5): 'Verum qualiscumque fuerit ipse… in tempore quidem summae festiuitatis dubios circulos sequentes, utpote quibus longe ultra orbem positis nemo synodalia paschalis obseruantiae decreta porrexerat' [It is true that they used tables of doubtful accuracy in fixing the date of the chief festival, since they were so far away at the ends of the earth that there was none to bring them the decrees of the synods concerning the observance of Easter]. On British insularity, see Bede, *Historia ecclesiastica*, I.22 (edd. Colgrave & Mynors, 68–9): 'Qui inter alia inenarrabilum scelerum facta, quae historicus eorum Gildas flebili sermone describit, et hoc addebant, ut numquam genti Saxonum sive Anglorum, secum Brittaniam incolenti uerbum fidei praedicando committerent' [To other unspeakable crimes, which Gildas their own historian describes in doleful words, was added this crime, that they never preached the faith to the Saxons or Angles who inhabited Britain with them]; II.2 (edd. Colgrave & Mynors, 134–7): 'Non enim paschae diem dominicum suo tempore sed a quarta decima usque ad uicesimam lunam obseruabant, quae conputatio LXXXIIII annorum circulo continetur; sed et alia plurima unitati ecclesiasticae contraria faciebant' [They did not keep Easter Sunday at the proper time, but from the fourteenth to the twentieth day of the lunar month; this reckoning is based on an 84-year cycle. They did other things too which were not in keeping with the unity of the church].

37 For an overview of the Easter controversy from the perspective of the history of its calculation and controversies over judaising, see *Bede: The Reckoning of Time* (trans. Wallis, xxxiv–lxiii). On the significance of Pentecost (as related to the date of Easter) on clerical ordination, see Reynolds, *Clerical Orders*, XI, 4–5. Simon Magus or Simon the Magician, first appearing in Acts 8.9–24, was condemned by Peter for offering money to become an apostle. Subsequent apocryphal texts explore clashes between Peter and Simon over Simon's claims to authority within the church. For more on Simon Magus, see Ferreiro, *Simon Magus*. The attachment of a false Easter to the image of Simon Magus will be explored in Chapter 4.

first half of the eighth century. The verifiable authors that draw directly on Gildas in this period are, as mentioned, Columbanus (specifically his *Epistulae*), the compilers of the *Hibernensis* (and two earlier versions), and Bede (specifically his *Historia ecclesiastica* and, as will be argued, his *Epistula ad Ecgbertvm*). A close reading of these select texts will examine the way he is utilised by these authors.[38] One of Gildas's innovations is helpful in this regard: his use of the Bible to construct a 'legal' corrective for kings and clerics in his *De excidio* is highly individual, and there are biblical phrases he cites in this context that are entirely original.[39] The subsequent use of the *De excidio* as a florilegium of scripture for the edification of kings and bishops is, thus, a means to gain insight into Insular debates in a way that may not be immediately obvious. Further, the subtle shaping of the authority of Gildas by opposing sides of these divisive debates offers a unique window on points of commonality.

This method of 'thick description' is not without its issues.[40] The process of attempting to unravel how authority was characterised in the British Isles through a close reading of select primary sources will inevitably lead, given the extended chronological and geographic range, to superficial representations of other complex contexts, particularly in relation to the situation on the continent. Notwithstanding these issues, the intention is to establish the evolving images of the authority of Gildas up to the eighth century and to situate these representations within the tensions described by Bede. These images and tensions will subsequently be situated within the wider context of the evolution of political and ecclesiastical authority in the early medieval West. The outcome will be to propose new ways of approaching Britain and Ireland in the early medieval period.

The approach taken in this book is, thus, to examine the legacy of Gildas on its own terms up to the second quarter of the eighth century. Chapter 1 charts the evolution in the modern era of the historiographical arguments for discontinuity or continuity as they relate to the Christian culture of the British Isles in the period under study. These arguments go back to Bede's presentation of the end of the western Roman empire and the coming of Augustine of Canterbury, an account that has promoted the perception of a dark age in Britain prior to the seventh century. This exploration of narratives for Britain and Ireland in the early medieval period emphasises the continuing and problematic respect given to Bede's account, and its impact on the historiography of both the period under study and Gildas himself.

Chapter 2 gives an overview of the *De excidio* and the fragments of the letter to Finnian (*fragmenta Gildae*) as they relate to contextualising Gildas. Subsequently, attention is given to the way in which the themes of the *De excidio* and the letter to Finnian were remembered by authors in the medieval period. This establishes the evolution of multiple images that have led to uncertainty over his context. Some representations, I argue, are shaped by the discrete modes of authority expressed in the *De excidio* and the *fragmenta*. Other representations potentially relate to memories

38 The methodology will rely on close textual comparison utilising *Factotum*, developed by Monash University, with subsequent investigations into the origins and influence of key phrases and key biblical citations via digitised Latin text databases such as Brepols's *Library of Latin Texts*, University of Zurich's *Corpus Corporum*, and *MGH*. Unique Latin phrases shared by authors will be highlighted **in bold**. On the development of *Factotum*, see Zahora *et al.*, 'Deconstructing Bricolage'.

39 This book will use the Douay-Rheims translation of the Vulgate, unless otherwise stated.

40 On 'thick description' as an interpretive methodology for understanding social discourse, see Geertz, 'Thick Description'. Geertz stresses the importance of context when observing and describing complex cultural interactions.

of two discrete religious figures active in the fifth and sixth centuries. Subsequently, in resituating the images of Gildas within the concerns presented in fifth-century works describing Britain and Ireland, this chapter will offer a fresh interpretation of the context of the *De excidio* as a response to ongoing Insular and continental arguments over authority in the late fifth century.

Chapter 3 explores Gildas's legitimation of his criticisms of secular and episcopal authority in the prophetic tradition through his select use of patristic authors in the *De excidio*. His patristic choices are detailed, emphasising the significant influence of monastic figures such as Jerome (*ca* 347–420), John Cassian (*ca* 360–435), and Salvian of Marseilles (*ca* 400–80), the latter pair representing a Gallic monastic culture cautious about the episcopal authority of Augustine of Hippo (*ca* 354–430). As such, Gildas drew on, defended, and further developed an ascetic tradition that placed a complementary role of *speculator* or watchman within monasticism and looked to the Old Testament and Israel for political models of authority.

Chapter 4 explores Columbanus's criticisms of episcopal authority in a continental context, criticisms that drew directly on the authority of Gildas. Focusing on simony, this chapter demonstrates how Columbanus used and adapted the *De excidio* to shape a perspective that intimately connected the heretical image of Simon Magus to a 'false Easter' and notions of 'false baptism' and 'false ordination'. Subsequently the impact of this Insular view of simony is made explicit in a continental setting, particularly in its influence on Pope Gregory the Great and his elevation of simony to heresy. This chapter reveals that Columbanus and Gregory, sometimes described as antipathetic, shared similar traditions and offers evidence that Gildas, via Columbanus, may have influenced the pastoral mission of Gregory the Great.

Chapter 5 expands on Gildas's contribution to canon law in an Irish context via his letter to Finnian. Through an examination of Gildas's influence, both direct and indirect, this chapter argues that the compilers of the *Hibernensis* utilised the authority of Gildas to promote conformity on the issue of the non-Roman tonsure – an independence from Roman authority that had become aligned to the image of Simon Magus. Within this contested readjustment of ecclesiastical traditions in Ireland, the authority of Gildas as a father of the Insular church was transmuted from that of a critic of bishops in the prophetic tradition to a respected monastic voice supporting episcopal authority, as represented by the Apostle to Ireland, Patrick.

Chapter 6 explores Bede's evolving use of Gildas's *De excidio* in his construction of two histories in chronicle form, the *Chronica minora* (*ca* 716) and the *Chronica maiora* (*ca* 725), and his subsequent historical narrative for the Christian culture of Britain from an English perspective, the *Historia ecclesiastica* (*ca* 731). I also demonstrate Gildas's influence on Bede's subsequent and singular instance of public criticism, his letter to Bishop Ecgbert (*ca* 734). Charting Bede's growing respect for Gildas, this chapter argues that Bede directly invoked Gildas as a providential historian (*historicus*) to construct a new handbook for kings and bishops with his *Historia ecclesiastica*, but one that strengthened the working relationship of kings and bishops by positive example rather than 'negative' criticism.

Finally, Gildas's impact on the shaping of authority within Insular and continental debates will be surveyed in order to suggest new perspectives on the evolution of political and ecclesiastical authority in the early medieval West. In the process, Gildas and his legacy will be recontextualised. While the Insular church may have been at variance with the authority of Rome on some issues, this merely reflected similar contestations over the authority of Rome on the continent in this period. Indeed, rather than representing an idiosyncratic Christianity, or a disjointed beneficiary of continental orthodoxy and stability, I argue that the Christian culture of Britain and Ireland, as represented by Gildas, contributed in a significant way to wider deliberations over the structuring of political and ecclesiastical authority in the early medieval West.

In order to begin this investigation, Gildas's influence on contemporary narratives describing political rupture in the British Isles in the early medieval period will be explored. This exploration will situate Gildas's vision of *Britannia* within the limited sources that have framed historical approaches to the end of western Roman imperial authority and the beginnings of the medieval nations of England, Scotland, Wales, and Ireland.

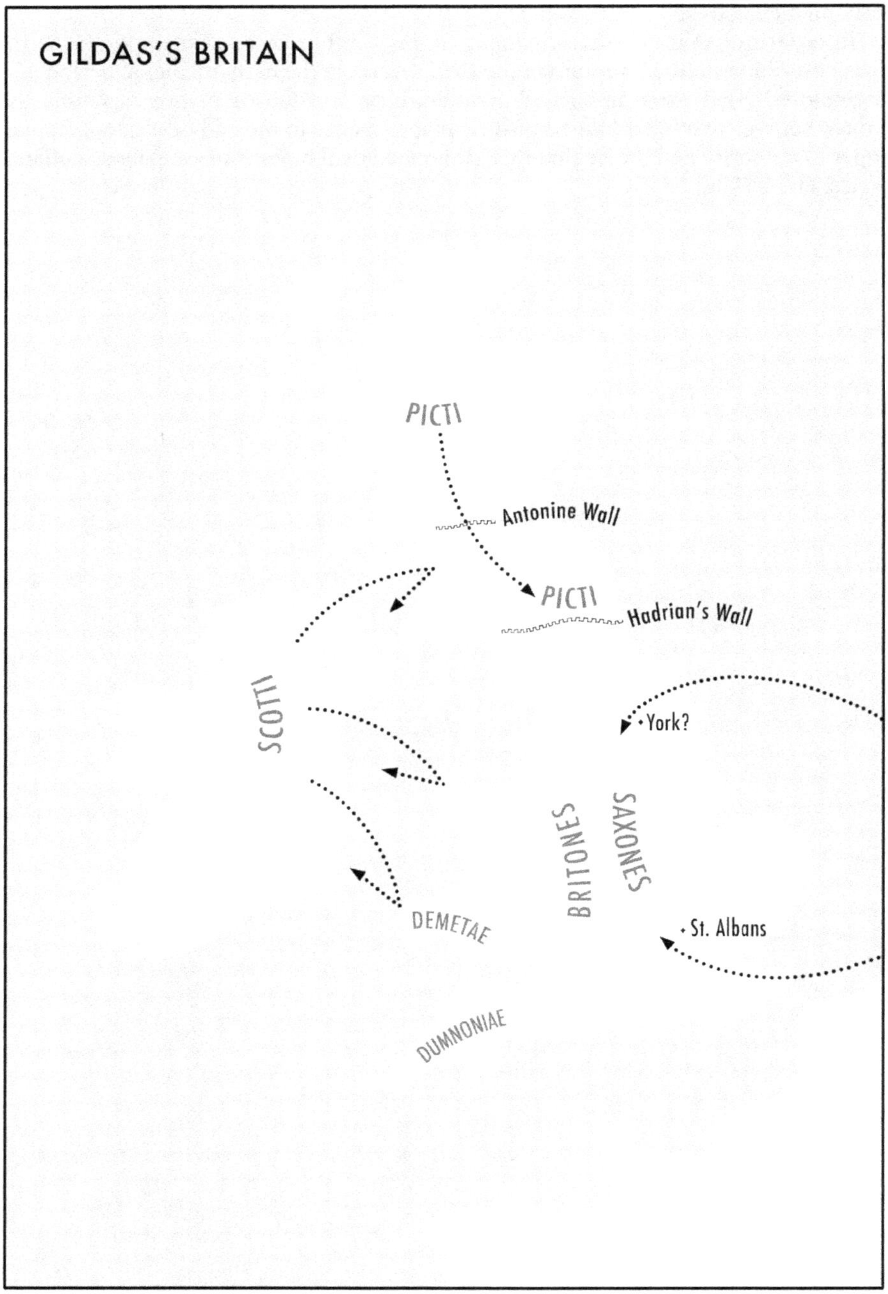

Gildas's (limited) description of Britain as interpreted from his De excidio.

1

NARRATIVES FOR EARLY MEDIEVAL BRITAIN AND IRELAND

Political rupture is often articulated as a significant factor shaping the evolution of early medieval Christian culture in the British Isles. This is particularly so in relation to the fifth and sixth centuries, a period informed by the profound restructuring engendered by the end of Roman imperial authority, internal and external migration, and the beginnings of what would become England, Wales, Scotland, and Ireland. This period, sometimes referred to as a 'dark age' due to a dearth of surviving written sources, is often associated with notions of political fragmentation and ecclesiastical disorganisation as explanations for its 'idiosyncratic' Christian culture when compared to the continent. The problem is compounded by the uncertain contexts and disconnects between Gildas's *De excidio* and the other surviving texts describing this dark age, namely Patrick's *Confessio* and *Epistola*, and, from a continental perspective, the *Vita Germani episcopi Autissiodorensis* or the *Life of Bishop Germanus of Auxerre* by the Gallo-Roman aristocrat, perhaps priest, Constantius of Lyon (*ca* 410–90).[1] The lack of connection between these texts has contributed to a historiography emphasising disintegration and ongoing fragmentation in Britain in the fifth and sixth centuries.

This chapter reviews the narratives fashioned for the British Isles in the period described by Gildas and subsequently by Bede. It discusses the problems of disconnection associated with the early sources, with the result that the Irish *peregrinus*, Columbanus (*ca* 543–615), is often presented as an 'exotic' religious personality on the continent. It also addresses the select way Gildas is used in the Irish conciliar collection, the *Hibernensis* (*ca* 669–748), and Bede's *Historia ecclesiastica* (*ca* 731). Detailing the problems associated with the paucity of Bede's account of the history of the Insular church *ca* 450–600, I argue that his construction of a dark age is a literary device in a providential history, an observation that nuances his status as an authority for early medieval Britain. The subsequent influence of Bede's account on modern historiography will be examined, exploring how his providential construction of a dark age still subtly impacts historical narratives for the British Isles, and our views of Gildas himself.

1 For Constantius's *Vita Germani*, see *Vie de St. Germain* (ed. Borius). For a brief introduction to the *Vita Germani* and Constantius of Lyon, see van Egmond, *Conversing with the Saints*, 25–36. See also Wood, 'The End of Roman Britain', 9–17. A notable attempt to utilise the *Vita Germani* as a historical source for fifth-century Britain is Thompson, *Saint Germanus of Auxerre*, though not without criticism. See, for example, Harries, 'E. A. Thompson'. For a more nuanced approach to the *Vita Germani* as a historical source, see Higham, 'Constantius'.

Disconnected sources: Britain and Ireland in the early medieval period

The lack of sources that describe the transition from the Roman province of *Britannia* (and the neighbouring political entities of the Picts and Scots) to the beginnings of medieval 'kingdoms' has long contributed to contested narratives for Britain and Ireland in the early medieval period. Of the surviving sources that describe events in the fifth century, for instance, there are only three identifiable Insular texts, namely Patrick's *Confessio* and *Epistola*, assigned various dates in fifth-century Ireland, and Gildas's *De excidio*, dated variously to a late fifth- or sixth-century Britain.[2] From a continental perspective, only one text narrates events in the British Isles in this period: Constantius of Lyon's *Vita Germani episcopi Autissiodorensis* (*Vita Germani*), dated to late fifth-century Gaul, with the Gallic bishop Germanus of Auxerre active in Britain against the influence of the controversial theologian, Pelagius (*fl. ca* 390–418), in the second quarter of the fifth century.[3] These texts describing the Christian culture of the British Isles, however, only add to the ambiguity. Brief summations of their narratives, as supported by entries in continental chronicles, are placed in a traditional chronological order below, although scholars are divided on precise dates:[4]

2 The dating of Patrick's surviving works is problematic: Sharpe, 'Martyrs and Local Saints', 81, estimates Patrick as writing *ca* 430–80; Jones, *The End of Roman Britain*, 112, has Patrick as either late fourth century to the mid-fifth century (to *ca* 457), or totally fifth century (to *ca* 493), reflecting the various reports in the Irish annals; O'Sullivan, *The* De Excidio, 127–8, favours a Patrick active around the early to mid-fifth century; David Dumville and a number of other scholars argue for a totally fifth-century Patrick (to *ca* 493) in Dumville *et al.*, *Saint Patrick 493–1993*, particularly 29–33. The dating of Gildas's *De excidio* is equally problematic. As already stated, Snyder, *The Britons*, 123, notes various scholarly positions on the dating of *De excidio* from 479–550 in a useful table: Dumville, 'Gildas and Maelgwn' (*ca* 550); Lapidge, 'Gildas's Education', 49 (pre-500); O'Sullivan, *The* De Excidio, 178–80 (*ca* 515–20); Herren & Brown, *Christ in Celtic Christianity*, 27–8 (*ca* 500); Higham, *The English Conquest*, 137 (*ca* 479–84); and Jones, *The End of Roman Britain*, 45, n. 20 (post-500). This lack of consensus amongst specialists in early medieval Britain and Ireland has tended to reinforce a dating of the *De excidio* to the second quarter of the sixth century, as supported by reports for the death of Gildas *ca* 570 in the Irish and Welsh annals. Accordingly, Snyder dates the *De excidio* to *ca* 530. A notable defender of this orthodox dating is Stancliffe, 'The Thirteen Sermons', 177–81, who dates the *De excidio* conservatively to *ca* 513–88 with a preference for *ca* 530–44. Sharpe, 'Martyrs and Local Saints', 82, while following the orthodox dating, notes that it is difficult to defend any particular date for the *De excidio*. As noted previously, this book will argue for a date in the late fifth century. See Conclusion, 158.

3 See Sharpe, 'Martyrs and Local Saints', 115–16, n. 165, for a discussion of the dating of the *Vita Germani*. See also Gillett, *Envoys and Political Communication*, 278–82. The *Vita Germani* is generally dated to *ca* 480, though Sharpe proposes an earlier date *ca* 460–70. On a biography of the controversial British or Irish monk and 'arch-heresiarch', Pelagius, see Rees, *Pelagius*. Bonner, *The Myth of Pelagianism*, has recently questioned the heretical status of Pelagius and the existence of Pelagianism. Her positioning of fifth-century sources critical of Pelagius and Pelagianism as reflecting 'a grand conspiracy' is problematic: see Brown, 'The Myth of Pelagianism'. As such, Bonner's argument will be set aside in this book. The term 'Pelagianism' will be utilised to identify that strain of thought that emphasised the importance of the human will in leading a sinless life against an evolving orthodoxy that emphasised the necessary intervention of divine grace in a life impossible without sin. For further discussion on Pelagianism, see Chapter 2, 48–51.

4 Insular annal entries for the fifth century are not regarded as contemporaneous and are set aside from this brief analysis. On this, see Chapter 2. The approximates dates for Patrick's writing activities reflect those of Sharpe, 'Martyrs and Local Saints', 81.

1. [*ca* 430–80] In his *Confessio*, the Briton Patrick, missionary to Ireland, describes a British and/or Irish church with Roman ecclesiastical structures. As a bishop with responsibilities in Ireland, he issues a letter of excommunication to a Roman Christian, perhaps British, military leader, Coroticus (*Epistola*), asserting the right of episcopal authority to censure secular authority. A papal mission to Britain by Bishop Germanus, responding to the influence of Pelagianism, is assigned to the year 429.[5] A papal mission to Ireland by Bishop Palladius, responding to requests for formal ecclesiastical ties, is dated to the year 431.[6] Patrick makes no mention of Pelagius, Germanus, Palladius, or Gildas.

2. [*ca* 480] Constantius's *Vita Germani* describes a flourishing British church at the time of its publication in the late fifth century.[7] This flourishing church is known through two interventions, supported by the Gallic church, of the Roman aristocrat and bishop, Germanus of Auxerre, against the activities of followers of Pelagius.[8] Constantius, however, makes no mention of Palladius, Patrick, or Gildas.

3. [*ca* 479–550] Gildas's *De excidio* describes a Britain partitioned with pagan Saxons and Picts, and denounces a corrupt British church where bishops either collude with or fail to censure corrupt secular authorities.[9] The political

[5] Prosper of Aquitaine (*ca* 390–455) reports a visit by Germanus to Britain to combat Pelagianism in 429. Prosper, *Epitoma Chronicorum* (ed. Mommsen, *Chronica*, I, 472): Year 429, 'Agricola pelagianus, Seueriani episcopi pelagiani filius, ecclesias Britanniae dogmatis sui insinuatione corrumpit. sed ad insinuationem Palladii diaconi papa Caelestinus Germanum Autisiodorensem episopum uice sua mittit' [Agricola the Pelagian, son of the Pelagian bishop Severianus, corrupted the churches of Britannia by his underhand ways. But at the instance of Palladius the deacon, Pope Celestine sent Germanus, Bishop of Auxerre, to act on his behalf]. Translation, Thomas, *Christianity in Roman Britain*, 301. Prosper reports papal authority for this mission rather than the authority of the Gallic church as described by Constantius.

[6] Prosper reports a papal mission to Ireland by Bishop Palladius in 431. Prosper, *Epitoma Chronicorum* (ed. Mommsen, *Chronica*, I, 473): Year 431, 'ad Scottos in Christum credentes ordinatus a papa Caelestino Palladius primus episcopus mittitur' [Pope Celestine sent Palladius, ordained as their first bishop, to the Irish believers in Christ]. See also Prosper, *Contra Collatorem*, XXI.2 (ed. Migne): 'pontifex Coelestinus… et ordinato Scotis episcopo, dum Romanam insulam studet servare catholicam, fecit etiam barbaram Christianam' [Pope Celestine… for having ordained a bishop for the Irish, while he was careful to keep the Roman island Catholic, he also made the non-Roman one Christian]. Translations, Thomas, *Christianity in Roman Britain*, 300–1. The latter work was written in the context of ongoing debates over Pelagianism.

[7] Constantius, *Vita Germani*, V.27 (ed. Borius, 172): 'ut in illis locis etiam nunc fides intemerata perduret' [even now the faith is persisting intact in those parts]. Translations, unless otherwise stated, are from Hoare, 'Constantius'. This textual evidence for a thriving British church *ca* 480 has been challenged from an archaeological perspective. On this, see below, 23–5. However, recent archaeological evidence appears to confirm medieval reports of early Christian activity at Glastonbury. See Avalon Marshes, 'Earliest Monastery in the British Isles Discovered', for radio-carbon evidence of monastic activity at Beckery, one mile from Glastonbury, in the fifth or early sixth centuries.

[8] See Constantius, *Vita Germani*, III.12–18 (ed. Borius, 144–59), for the first visit, and V.25–27 (ed. Borius, 171–3), for the second visit. The first visit, as reported by Prosper, is dated to 429. The second visit is related by the *Vita Germani* to within a year of Germanus's death, variously dated from *ca* 437–48. See Gillett, *Envoys and Political Communication*, 278–82.

[9] Gildas implies that the Scots are not settled as a distinct political entity in Britain at the time of publication. See Chapter 2, 32, n. 4.

success of the Saxons is noted in contemporary continental chronicles.[10] In constructing a providential history of Britain from the arrival of the Romans to his present day to support his criticisms of kings and bishops in the prophetic traditions of the Old Testament, Gildas makes no mention of Pelagius, Germanus, Palladius, or Patrick.

The narratives, all describing events in the fifth century, do not appear to support each other. The failure of these sources to mutually corroborate significant religious actors in this period has reinforced perceptions of tension between the Christian culture of the British Isles and that of the continent, perceptions that contribute to the concept of an idiosyncratic Insular church.

This 'idiosyncrasy' is further compounded when we re-enter a period where the survivability of sources increases and the sources themselves become more reliable. Around 590, the Irish abbot and priest, Columbanus, embarked on a religious exile or *peregrinatio* to the continent. The religious traditions with which he arrived appeared to be different from those practised in Gaul and Italy. Columbanus emphasised a different form of penance to that promoted by Gallic bishops; Columbanus celebrated Easter on a different date to that designated by Rome; Columbanus was comfortable in his role as a junior criticising the behaviour of kings and bishops.[11] One might suppose that these were Insular variations in traditions or innovations, but Columbanus, in a critical letter nominally addressed to Pope Boniface IV (*r.* 608–15) and alluding to the papal mission of Palladius, was adamant he represented the universal church:

> For all we Irish, inhabitants of the world's edge, are disciples of Saints Peter and Paul and of all the disciples who wrote the sacred canon by the Holy Ghost, and we accept nothing outside the evangelical and apostolic teaching; none has been a heretic, none a Judaizer, none a schismatic; but the Catholic Faith, as it was delivered by you first, who are the successors of the holy apostles, is maintained unbroken.[12]

[10] See *Chronica Gallica a. CCCCLII* (ed. Mommsen, *Chronica*, I, 660): year XVIII, 'Britanniae usque ad hoc tempus variis cladibus eventibusque latae in dicionem Saxonum rediguntur' [Britain, suffering up to this time from various disasters and torments, is reduced to the authority of the Saxons]. The year is generally assigned to 441/442. See also 'The Gallic Chronicle of 452' (ed. Burgess, 79–80): year XVIII, 'Brittanniae usque ad hoc tempus uariis cladibus euentibusque laceratae in ditionem saxonum rediguntur'. This event is repeated in *Chronica Gallica a. DXI* (ed. Mommsen, *Chronica*, I, 661): year XVI, 'Britanniae a Romanis amissae in dicionem Saxonum cedunt' [Britain, lost to the Romans, falls into the hands of the Saxons], but is assigned to the year 440. See also 'The Gallic Chronicle of 511' (ed. Burgess, 97): year XVI, 'Brithanniae a Romanis amissae in ditionem Saxonum cedunt'. Translations are my own. These dates contradict interpretations of the *De excidio* that argue for a Saxon success *ca* 446–54. On this, see 18–22. For a discussion of these continental records, see Wood, 'The End of Roman Britain'. Wood potentially connects the *Gallic Chronicle of 452* to the noted British-educated former abbot of the influential Gallic monastery of Lérins, subsequently bishop of Riez, Faustus (*ca* 400–95). See Wood, 'Continuity or Calamity?', 14. For further discussion of the chronicles, see Muhlberger, 'Looking Back from Mid-Century'.

[11] For a summation of the career of Columbanus, see Bullough, 'The Career of Columbanus'. For a caution on the arguments behind the dating of his career and on the 'exotic' nature of some of his religious practices, see Chapter 4.

[12] Columbanus, *Epistulae*, V.3 (ed. Walker, 38–9): 'Nos enim sanctorum Petri et Pauli et omnium discipulorum divinum canonem spiritu sancto scribentium discipuli sumus, toti Iberi, ultimi habitatores mundi, nihil extra evangelicam et apostolicam doctrinam recipientes; nullus hereticus, nullus Iudaeus, nullus schismaticus fuit; sed fides catholica, sicut a vobis primum, sanctorum

In doing so, he called on his namesake, the Old Testament Prophet Jonah, placing himself within that tradition:

> I am called Jonah in Hebrew, Peristera in Greek, Columba in Latin, yet so much is my birth-right in the idiom of your language, though I use the ancient Hebrew name of Jonah.[13]

Significantly, Columbanus, while not mentioning Patrick or Germanus, is our earliest secure witness to Gildas. In a letter to Pope Gregory the Great *ca* 600, he cited the authority of Gildas to criticise simony in the Gallic church, and referred to a letter sent by Gildas to Finnian to offer a solution to the problem of monks who broke their communal vows to seek a more religious life:

> Concerning those bishops, however, who ordain uncanonically, that is for hire, I ask what you decree; Gildas the writer set them down as simoniacs and plagues.[14]

> What is to be done about those monks who, for the sake of God, and inflamed by the desire for a more perfect life, impugn their vows, leave the places of their first profession, and against their abbots' will, impelled by monastic fervour, either relapse or flee to the deserts. Finnian the writer questioned Gildas about them, and he sent a most polished reply.[15]

In addressing the pope, Columbanus called on the authority of Gildas. He did so in ways that suggest that Gregory was aware of that authority.[16] Written responses from Gregory, if there were any, have not survived. A more tangible 'response' to Columbanus's entry into continental affairs *ca* 590 may have been Gregory's intervention in the Christian culture of the British Isles in 597, led by the abbot and priest, Augustine (*ob. ca* 604), subsequently ordained bishop of Canterbury.[17]

After Columbanus's death *ca* 615, uniformity on the celebration of Easter became an important issue for Roman clerical authority both on the continent and in Britain and Ireland. The controversy became intimately linked with uniformity over the Roman tonsure. This assertion of authority had failed to persuade detractors at two assemblies held in this period: the Synod of Mag Léne in Ireland *ca* 630, and

videlicet apostolorum successoribus, tradita est, inconcussa tenetur'. Whether this letter was sent to Boniface IV will be examined in Chapter 4.

13 Columbanus, *Epistulae*, V.16 (ed. Walker, 54–5): 'mihi Ionae hebraice, Peristerae graece, Columbae latine, potius tantum vestrae idiomate linguae nancto, licet prisco utor hebraeo nomine'.

14 Columbanus, *Epistulae*, I.6 (ed. Walker, 8–9): 'Ceterum de episcopis illis quid iudicas, interrogo, qui contra canones ordinantur, id est quaestu; simoniacos et Gildas auctor pestes scripsit eos'.

15 Columbanus, *Epistulae*, I.7 (ed. Walker, 8–9): 'quid faciendum est de monachis illis, qui pro Dei intuitu et vitae perfectioris desiderio accensi, contra vota venientes primae conversionis loca relinquunt, et invitis abbatibus, fervore monachorum cogente, aut laxantur aut ad deserta fugiunt. Vennianus auctor Gildam de his interrogavit, et elegantissime ille rescripsit'.

16 Evidence that Gregory was probably aware of the authority of Gildas will be examined in Chapter 4.

17 While Augustine's mission had a focus on the conversion of the English, it also had, perhaps evolving, ambitions for the diocese of Britain (and perhaps Ireland). On Augustine's ordination to bishop, Gregory granted him the pallium, nominally placing the British (and perhaps Irish) bishops under the authority of Canterbury and Rome. See Gregory's letter as recorded by Bede, *Historia ecclesiastica*, I.29 (edd. Colgrave & Mynors, 104–6).

the Northumbrian royal council known as the Synod of Whitby in Britain *ca* 664.[18] Against the backdrop of these turbulent contestations, the authority of Gildas, as drawn from his letter to Finnian, was reported in a collection of Irish canon law, the *Collectio canonum Hibernensis* (*Hibernensis*). Compiled between the last quarter of the seventh century and the first half of the eighth century, the *Hibernensis* cited both Gildas and Patrick among many church fathers, including Pelagius, identified here as an authority rather than as a heretic.[19] It did not cite Palladius or Germanus, nor did it name significant Irish monastic figures such as Columba (*ca* 521–97), the apostle to the northern Picts.[20] Rather than emphasising the Easter controversy, it linked Gildas and Patrick to a range of issues including the Insular tonsure, not an issue mentioned by Gildas or Columbanus.[21] This select use of Gildas to support rather than criticise episcopal authority contrasted with that of Columbanus.

Gregory the Great's mission to convert the English was the cornerstone of Bede's *Historia ecclesiastica gentis Anglorum* completed *ca* 731. In scrupulously constructing a history of Britain and Ireland that supported the authority of the Roman church and the decision of the Synod of Whitby on the contentious issues of Easter and the tonsure, Bede drew together the narrative sources in a way that has also contributed to uncertainty. He was the first author to place Palladius, Pelagius, Germanus, and Gildas within a historical narrative describing Britain in the fifth and sixth centuries. However, Bede neither mentioned Patrick nor referred to his works.

The failure of these early sources to support a common narrative, combined with uncertainty over their contexts, has resulted in a historiographical emphasis on Bede as the earliest reliable witness to the history of Britain in the early medieval period. In order to investigate this problematic emphasis, we need to briefly examine how Bede's vision has shaped our perceptions of the past.

Continuity or rupture: problems with Bede

The conflicting narratives for early medieval Britain and Ireland were tackled, but not ultimately resolved, by Bede in his *Historia ecclesiastica*. Bede's *ur*-history of the Insular church from a Northumbrian or English perspective failed to completely unify the identifiable witnesses for the fifth and sixth centuries. Patrick was not mentioned, and Bede's linear narrative reduced the late fifth and sixth centuries to a

[18] For Mag Léne, see, briefly, Charles-Edwards, *Early Christian Ireland*, 276–7; for Whitby, see, briefly, Charles-Edwards, *Wales and the Britons*, 396–7.

[19] Flechner dates the *Hibernensis* conservatively to 669–748, with a historical argument for 716–47. See *The Hibernensis* (ed. Flechner, 61*). For an example of a citation of Pelagius in the *Hibernensis*, see *The Hibernensis*, XXVI.13 (ed. Flechner, 175, trans., 602): 'Pilagius ait: Plerique etiam contra se calumniantur, cur in presenti Deus non reddit, non intellegentes quod, si ita fieret, nullus pene hominum remansiset, nec umquam de iniustis fierent iustii' [Pelagius said: Many even protest to their own injury, 'Why does God not punish at once?', not understanding that if it were so, hardly anyone would have remained, nor ever would any of the unrighteous have become righteous].

[20] Bede notes Columba as missionary to the northern Picts. See Bede, *Historia ecclesiastica*, III.4 (edd. Colgrave & Mynors, 220–2). For more on Columba, see below, 24–5.

[21] For example, citing Patrick, *The Hibernensis*, LI.7 (ed. Flechner, 410, trans., 781): 'De excommonicandis clericis, qui non tondentur tonsura Romana' [That clerics who are not tonsured in the Roman manner must be excommunicated].

single paragraph referring the reader to Gildas's *De excidio*.[22] Bede thus marked out a period from around 450 (and the *adventus* of the English) to around 600 (and the *adventus* of Augustine of Canterbury) with a notable silence.

This literary construction of a 150-year dark age in Book I alerts us to Bede's structuring of his *Historia ecclesiastica*. The conversion of *Britannia* is taken from the *Liber Pontificalis* and placed in the reign of Emperor Marcus Verus beginning in the year 156.[23] The descriptions of the British martyr Alban and the Diocletianic Persecutions are placed in a ten-year period prior to the end of Diocletian's reign, datable to 296–305.[24] The *adventus* of the Anglo-Saxons and the end of the western Roman empire occur in a ten-year interval from 446–55. The transition from Book I (and the *adventus* of Augustine to Canterbury in 596) to Book II (and the death of Pope Gregory the Great in 605) repeats the ten-year interval and the 150-year period. The subsequent four books of the *Historia ecclesiastica* (II–V) cover thirty-year periods or so up to around 725, followed by a contemporary analysis (725–31) and a conjecture from Bede of what the next age will bring for the English.

The structure of a 150-year period (directly related to ten-year intervals), subdivided into thirty-year periods, appears to be derived from a solar calendar. Bede's *De temporum ratione* details this solar calendar and its uses, together with the lunar calendar, in calculating the correct date of Easter:

[22] The narrative breaks at Bede's description of the end of the western Roman empire in *Historia ecclesiastica*, I.21 (edd. Colgrave & Mynors, 64–7), dated by Bede to 455; to a brief overview of *Britannia* in *Historia ecclesiastica*, I.22 (edd. Colgrave & Mynors, 67–9), one that refers to Gildas's *De excidio*; to a resumption of the narrative with Augustine's mission to Canterbury in *Historia ecclesiastica*, I.23 (edd. Colgrave & Mynors, 69–71), dated by Bede to 596.

[23] Bede, *Historia ecclesiastica*, I.4 (edd. Colgrave & Mynors, 24–5): 'Anno ab incarnatione Domini centesimo quinquagesimo sexto Marcus Antoninus Uerus quartus decimus ab Augusto regnum cum Aurelio Commodo fratre suscepit. Quorum temporibus cum Eleuther uir sanctus pontificatui Romanae ecclesiae praeesset, misit ad eum Lucius Brittaniarum rex epistolam, obsecrans ut per eius mandatum Christianus efficeretur' [In the year of Our Lord 156 Marcus Antoninus Verus was made emperor together with his brother Aurelius Commodus. He was the fourteenth after Augustus. In their time, while a holy man named Eleutherius was bishop of the church of Rome, Lucius, a king of Britain, sent him a letter praying him that he might be made a Christian by a rescript from him]. For the *Liber Pontificalis*, see *Le Liber Pontificalis*, I, XIIII (ed. Duchesne, 136): 'ELEUTHER, natione Grecus, ex patre Habundio, de oppido Nicopoli, sedit ann. XV m. III d. II. Fuit autem temporibus Antonini et Commodi, usque Paterno et Bradua. Hic accepit epistula a Lucio, Brittanio rege, ut christianus efficeretur per eius mandatum' [ELEUTHER, born in Greece, son of Abundius, from the town of Nicopolis, held the see 15 years 3 months 2 days. He was bishop in the time of Antoninus and Commodus to the (consulship) of Paternus (Maternus) and Bradua. He received a letter from Lucius, a British king, who wanted to become a Christian at his order]. Translations, unless otherwise stated, come from *The Book of Pontiffs* (trans. Davis). Gildas appears to place the arrival of Christianity in *Britannia* in the reign of Tiberius (14–37). See Gildas, *De excidio*, VIII (ed. Winterbottom, 91, trans., 18): 'tempore, ut scimus, summo Tiberii Caesaris, quo absque ullo impedimento eius propagabatur religio' [This happened first, as we know, in the last years of the emperor Tiberius, at a time when Christ's religion was being propagated without hindrance].

[24] Bede, *Historia ecclesiastica*, I.6 (edd. Colgrave & Mynors, 28–9): 'Interea Diocletianus in Oriente, Maximianus Herculius in Occidente uastari ecclesias... praeceperunt... per x annos' [Meanwhile Diocletian in the east and Maximianus Herculius in the west ordered the churches to be laid waste... for ten years]. Bede follows Gildas's conjecture that the martyrdom of Alban occurred during the persecutions of Diocletian. See Gildas, *De excidio*, X (ed. Winterbottom, 92).

> Because anyone who has memorized the cycle of the Sun and Moon… ought to remember that the same solar concurrents will follow in 30 years as will come next year, and in 60 years from now as will come in four years, and in 120 years from now as will come in eight years, and in 150 years from now as in ten years, and the others in a like manner.[25]

There is also another detail that may have influenced Bede's use of a 150-year structuring of the *Historia ecclesiastica*, drawn from Gildas. In his *De excidio*, Gildas announces the arrival of the Saxons within a pagan prophecy also structured around 150-year periods:

> Then a pack of cubs burst forth from the lair of the barbarian lioness, coming in three keels, as they call warships in their language. The winds were favourable; favourable too the omens and auguries, which prophesied, according to a sure portent among them, that they would live for three hundred years in the land towards which their prows were directed, and that for half the time, a hundred and fifty years, they would repeatedly lay it waste.[26]

This prophecy supported Bede's providential construction of a dark age from the *adventus* of the Saxons to the conversion of the English, a period defined by constant and debilitating warfare.[27] Further, it added to Bede's concerns for the future, for the prophecy was inconclusive about what might happen to the English subsequent to a 300-year period in Britain. This period, if we accept Bede's structuring, was imminent (746–55). He issues a veiled warning about its end: 'What the result will be, a later generation will discover.'[28]

25 Bede, *De temporum ratione liber*, LV (ed. Jones): 'quia… qui solis et lunae circulum memoriter tenet… meminisse debet easdem concurrentes solis tricesimo abhinc anno quas et proximo secuturas, easdem sexagesimo quas et quarto, easdem nonagesimo quas et sexto, easdem centesimo uicesimo quas et octauo, easdem centesimo quinquagesimo quas et decimo, et caeteras in hunc modum esse redituras'. The translation is from *Bede: The Reckoning of Time* (trans. Wallis, 137–8). This use of a solar calendar is subtly supported by Bede's use of a 150-year period from the founding of Iona to its acceptance of the Roman Easter (565–715) in *Historia ecclesiastica*, III.4; the difference of some 40 years between the 'Insular' solar period and his 'orthodox' solar period possibly points to computational differences concerning epacts. See *Bede: The Reckoning of Time* (trans. Wallis, 138).

26 Gildas, *De excidio*, XXIII.3 (ed. Winterbottom, 97, trans., 26): 'Tum erumpens grex catulorum de cubili laeanae barbarae, tribus, ut lingua eius exprimitur, cyulis, nostra longis navibus, secundis velis omine auguriisque, quibus vaticinabatur, certo apud eum praesagio, quod ter centum annis patriam, cui proras librabat, insideret, centum vero quinquaginta, hoc est dimidio temporis, saepius vastaret'.

27 Both Alex Woolf and Karen George regard the pagan prophecy reported in the *De excidio* as a later interpolation. See Woolf, 'An Interpolation'; George, *Gildas's* De Excidio, 40–1. Woolf notes the 150/300-year prophecy, and proposes that the gloss, tied in with the *adventus* of both the Saxons and Augustine, originated in Canterbury *ca* 672–747. However, as Bede appears to be influenced by this passage, it may have been incorporated earlier, perhaps as contemporary support for Augustine of Canterbury's mission. On a potential connection between this pagan prophecy and the mission of Augustine, see Howlett, 'The prophecy of Saxon occupation'. For more on the eschatological influence of Gildas's pagan prophecy on Bede, see Escalona, 'Un futuro innombrable'.

28 Bede, *Historia ecclesiastica*, V.23 (edd. Colgrave & Mynors, 560–1): 'Quae res quem sit habitura finem, posterior aetas uidebit'.

The selection and structuring of sources in Bede's 'vital and highly contrived prelude' is significant.[29] While Bede clearly acknowledges Gildas's *De excidio*, he does not use Gildas's letter to Finnian. Mining Constantius's *Vita Germani* for important narrative material, he does not refer to Patrick's *Confessio* and *Epistola*, nor does Patrick – a figure much discussed in Ireland in Bede's lifetime – appear in his historical narrative.[30] He does not mention other surviving Insular sources, primarily penitential in form, attributed to Gildas, Finnian, and the patron saint of Wales, David (*ca* 500–89).[31] There are records of two Irish synods attributed to Patrick (*Synodus I Patricii*; *Synodus II Patricii*), as well as of two sixth-century British synods, *Sinodus Aquilonalis Britaniae* (Synod of North Britain) and *Sinodus Luci Victorie* (Synod of the Grove of Victory).[32] These texts demonstrate memories of significant attention to church discipline in the British Isles in the fifth and/or sixth centuries, and all circulated in some form in seventh- and/or eighth-century Ireland.[33] The seventh-century life of Columbanus and the seventh- or early eighth-century life of the British bishop, Samson (*ca* 485–565), detail an Insular church actively engaged with the continent in the sixth century.[34] Yet Columbanus is named only once in the *Historia ecclesiastica*, in a letter reported by Bede in Book II and outside his dark age; Samson not at all.[35] While it is possible that Bede did not have access to these sources, it seems more probable, given the depth and breadth of his scholarship, that

29 Wallace-Hadrill, *Bede's Ecclesiastical History*, 6. Miller, 'Bede's Use of Gildas', 255–6, notes Bede's selection and restructuring of the sources in the context of his reporting of the visits of Germanus. Bede deftly elides and places the two reported missions from the *Vita Germani* after his report of the *adventus Saxonum* (dated by Bede to 449) and prior to his report of the death of Emperor Valentinian (dated by Bede to 455). The missions of Germanus are thus 'placed' within the providential ten-year window from 446–55. This is despite Bede having access to the continental chronicle that reports the first mission for the year 429. For more discussion, see Chapter 6.

30 On the debates over Patrick in Ireland contemporary to Bede's lifetime, see Flechner, *St Patrick Retold*, 183–205.

31 *The Irish Penitentials* (ed. Bieler): *Praefatio Gildae de Poenitentia* (ed. Bieler, 60–7); *Excerpta Quedam de Libro Dauidis* (ed. Bieler, 70–3); *Penitentialis Vinniani* (ed. Bieler, 74–95).

32 *The Irish Penitentials* (ed. Bieler): *Synodus I S. Patricii* (ed. Bieler, 54–9); *Sinodus Aquilonalis Britaniae* (ed. Bieler, 66–7); *Sinodus Luci Victorie* (ed. Bieler, 68–9); *Synodus II S. Patricii* (ed. Bieler, 184–97). On the problematic ascription and contexts of the Patrician synods, see Chapter 5, 111–12.

33 On this, see Mews & Joyce, 'The Preface of Gildas'. The *Synodus II Patricii*, elements of which are also referred to as being from the *Synodus Romana*, is commonly held to be a seventh-century text, though it may be older. Its attribution to Patrick, perhaps as early as the eighth century, indicates that it was thought to be older than the seventh century. On the Patrician synods, see Chapter 5.

34 On the seventh-century *Vita Columbani*, see Chapter 4. For the *Vita Samsonis*, see *La Vie ancienne de saint Samson* (ed. Flobert). Flobert dates the *vita* to the middle of the eighth century at 115. However, Sharpe, 'Martyrs and Local Saints', 84–5, advocates a seventh-century dating for the work. Jonathan Wooding prefers a dating of the life around the last decades of the seventh century and the first decade of the eighth century: see Wooding, 'The Representation', 139–40.

35 For Bede's mention of Columbanus within a letter from Bishops Laurentius, Mellitus, and Justus to the Scots, see Bede, *Historia ecclesiastica*, II.4 (ed. Colgrave & Mynors, 146–7): 'Scottos uero per Daganum espiscopum in hanc, quam superius memorauimus, insulam, et Columbanum abbatem in Gallis uenientem nihil discrepare a Brettonibus in eorum conuersatione didicimus' [But now we have learned from Bishop Dagan when he came to this island and from Abbot Columban when he came to Gaul that the Irish did not differ from the Britons in their way of life].

he may have set such sources aside in favour of those that supported his structuring of history.[36] His conception of a 150-year dark age demonstrated the providential outcome of a Christian culture cut off from the civilising apostolic power of Rome.[37] Like the Saxon prophecy recorded in the *De excidio*, Bede presented the island of Britain as a wasteland.

The second period of the Saxon prophecy, on the other hand, was set aside by Bede for the evolution of the English as a chosen people tied directly to the apostolic authority of Rome. While Bede had pointedly referred to Gildas's description of a failed church subordinated to worldly secular orders, he subsequently argued that a reassertion of clerical authority in the seventh century, led by Rome, had saved the English from paganism and error and revitalised the isolated Irish and Pictish churches. Integral to Bede's vision of an Insular church restored by Rome was the papal mission of Augustine of Canterbury. Crucial to reasserting this authority was the establishment of a uniform Easter and tonsure.[38] Bede charts the protracted acceptance of the Roman Easter and the Roman tonsure in the British Isles diligently and with enthusiasm: by 731 and the publication of the *Historia ecclesiastica*, only the insular Britons still resisted the universal church.

It is clear the *Historia ecclesiastica* was structured to serve a providential purpose. In solely referring to the *De excidio*, Bede framed his 150-year dark age with Gildas's descriptions of sin, civil war, and partition. Bede's account continues to promote themes of disintegration and fragmentation in early medieval Britain. These themes, reinforced by Bede's caricatures of isolation and insularity, have profoundly influenced narratives from the fifth to the seventh centuries, as well as approaches to Gildas himself.

Historiography of the Christian culture in early medieval Britain and Ireland

By the nineteenth century, scholars had settled upon a straightforward narrative for the evolution of the Christian culture of the British Isles in the early medieval period,

[36] While arguments over whether Bede set specific sources aside or whether he did not have access to those sources are both from silence, the former is more probable given the context of Bede's scholarship. Bede's debts to Irish learning, for instance, have been demonstrated by several scholars. On an Irish influence on Bede's *computus*, for example, see Ó Cróinín, 'The Irish Provenance'. It is unlikely, given Bede's networks and interests, that he was unaware of the significant debates over Patrick and the impact of these nominally fifth- and sixth-century Insular sources or, indeed, their authors, in shaping the literary output in Ireland in his lifetime. This observation is not intended as an attack on Bede's integrity, rather noting that he, like Gildas, shaped his history for the moral edification of his present rather than as a comprehensive contemporary vision of the past. For more on Bede's intentions in writing his *Historia ecclesiastica*, see Chapter 6.

[37] While Bede does refer to some sources for the period *ca* 450–600 in Books II–V, these references are placed outside his overarching historical narrative and are, in a sense, presented as contextual asides that do not interfere with his 'providential' structuring.

[38] For instance, at Augustine's Oak (*ca* 603): Bede, *Historia ecclesiastica*, II.2 (edd. Colgrave & Mynors, 138–9): 'ut pascha suo tempore celebretis' [to keep Easter at the proper time]. Also, on the calling of the Synod of Whitby (*ca* 664); III.25 (edd. Colgrave & Mynors, 298–9): 'Mota ergo ibi quaestione de pascha uel tonsura uel aliis rebus ecclesiasticis… synodus fieri' [When this question of Easter and of the tonsure and other ecclesiastical matters was raised, it was decided to hold a council].

a narrative profoundly influenced by Bede. It was understood that the Roman empire had abandoned its province of *Britannia* at the beginning of the fifth century; *Britannia* was quickly overrun by the pagan tribes of Angles, Saxons, Jutes, and Frisians (subsequently referred to as the Anglo-Saxons or English), leaving a Christian 'Celtic fringe' in western and northern Britain which continued to evangelise Ireland.[39] Thus the discontinuity of the 'fall of the Roman empire' created an inward-looking church which, cut off from the influence of continental Christianity, evolved into a distinctive 'Celtic Christianity', characterised by a preference for monastic authority over episcopal authority and different approaches to significant Christian traditions such as the calculation of the date for the lunar festival of Easter.[40] This picture was reinforced by interpretations of the identifiable Insular texts that described Britain and Ireland in this turbulent period: Patrick's *Confessio* and *Epistola*, and Gildas's *De excidio*.

With the improvements in the early twentieth century in the assessment of archaeological evidence, it became clear that the Anglo-Saxon 'invasion' of *Britannia* was neither swift nor simple. On top of this, the absence of precisely datable archaeological evidence of Christian culture in the sub-Roman period immediately after the withdrawal of the Romans pointed to the extinction of Christianity prior to a post-Roman reintroduction as evidenced by the writings of Patrick and Gildas. Scholars such as Hugh Williams (initially), Victor Nash-Williams, Ralegh Radford, and William Frend argued that the 'Celtic church' owed nothing to the influence of Roman Christianity, instead looking to a second conversion of the western Isles sometime in the later fifth century and emanating from monasteries in Gaul, perhaps even monasteries in the east.[41] This discontinuity in the Christianity of Britain and Ireland, subsequently reintroduced and circulated via western seaways in a monastic form independent of episcopal authority, reinforced the regional isolation and distinctiveness of the Celtic fringe. By the second half of the twentieth century, contrary assertions from scholars such as Jocelyn Toynbee and Charles Thomas argued that the Insular church was in ecclesiastical continuity with the broader Roman church.[42] Richard Sharpe agreed, pointing out that any 'monastic inspiration' from the continent would recognise and defer to episcopal authority.[43]

The dominant role of monasticism in the Christian culture of early medieval Ireland has seen an emphasis on a specifically Irish context in shaping an idiosyncratic Insular Christianity. Influenced by reports in the *Catalogus sanctorum Hiberniae* of an age of saintly bishops followed by an age of saintly abbots, Nora Chadwick posited a regional and cultural discontinuity caused by a lack of urban centres, and hence

39 As an example, see Zimmer, *The Celtic Church*, 6–7.

40 On the idealisation of a distinctive Celtic Christianity (against that of an English Christianity) over the past 1300 years, see Bradley, *Celtic Christianity*. For English reactions to Celtic Christianity, see Jones, 'England Against the Celtic Fringe'.

41 Williams, *Some Aspects*, 55–132 (though he did oscillate on this point: his final work, *Christianity in Early Britain*, published after his death in 1912, favoured continuity); Nash-Williams, *The Early Christian Monuments*, 4; Radford, 'Christian Origins in Britain'; Frend, 'Ecclesia Britannica', 143. In this section, I follow the survey given in Sharpe, 'Martyrs and Local Saints', 85–105. This trajectory has also been laid out, from a Welsh perspective, by Edwards, 'Perspectives on Conversion in Wales', 98–103.

42 Toynbee, 'Christianity in Roman Britain', 24; Thomas, *Britain and Ireland*, 84. The perspectives of Toynbee and Thomas, as they relate to Frend, are laid out in more detail in Watts, *Christians and Pagans*, 8–24.

43 Sharpe, 'Martyrs and Local Saints', 99–100.

episcopal centres, which encouraged a distinctive Christian culture to evolve around monastic foundations.[44] Kathleen Hughes argued against this urban discontinuity, pointing out that the pastoral needs of the Irish were mainly served by conventional ecclesiastical structures.[45] She maintained that the subsequent evolution of this distinctive 'monastic' Christian culture in Ireland, as evidenced by the preponderance of abbot-bishops, was influenced by a growing preference of secular authorities for the spiritual authority resident in monastic foundations against that of ecclesiastical foundations. Richard Sharpe subsequently argued that the episcopal hierarchy of Ireland had not been supplanted by abbots and that the case for an emphasis on monastic authority had been overstated.[46] His intervention on behalf of continuity between the Christian culture of the British Isles and that of the continent, and against the notion of a Celtic church, has seen support from the academy.[47] Work by Westley Follett on Irish monasticism has reinforced Sharpe's sense of connectivity and continuity: Irish Christian culture was not profoundly disconnected from Christian culture on the continent nor did it evolve in a non-traditional way.[48] Scholarship on surviving early medieval Irish religious texts, such as the *Hibernensis*, has also seen growing support for connection and continuity, placing these texts within the wider context of western Europe rather than within an insular Celtic fringe.[49] However, even within this broad continuity, local exceptionalism, particularly as it relates to perceptions of national identity in England and Ireland, continues to be hotly debated.[50]

The recent emphasis on a fundamental continuity of Christian culture within Britain and Ireland over these centuries still does not come to terms with the idiosyncratic approaches to ecclesiastical authority, evident in Bede's description of the monastery of Iona, where a bishop was subject to an abbot's authority:

> This island always has an abbot for its ruler who is a priest, to whose authority the whole kingdom, including even bishops, have to be subject. This unusual arrangement follows the example of their first teacher, who was not a bishop but a priest and monk.[51]

Iona's first teacher was Columba, who embarked on the distinctive Insular practice of *peregrinatio* or religious exile from his homeland in Ireland *ca* 563 to establish a monastery on the island of Iona, located off the coast of modern-day western Scotland. It was Columba's monks that converted Bede's Northumbria and supplied it

44 Chadwick, *The Age of the Saints*, 17–35; *Catalogus sanctorum Hiberniae* (ed. Grosjean). For more on the *Catalogus sanctorum Hiberniae*, see Chapter 2, 37.

45 Hughes, *The Church in Early Irish Society*.

46 Sharpe, 'Some Problems Concerning the Organization of the Church'.

47 For instance, Davies, 'The Myth of the Celtic Church'. See also, supporting Sharpe, Etchingham, *Church Organisation in Ireland*. However, it must be noted, there is still significant opposition to this position: see Ó Cróinín, 'Review'.

48 Follett, *Céli Dé in Ireland*.

49 O'Loughlin, 'The Latin Sources'.

50 For instance, see O'Hara, '17.03.08, Flechner and Meeder'. Here the reviewer criticises the editors' presentation of the Irish as a form of racism. A history of the heated debate from an Irish perspective, as described by the terms 'nativist', 'revisionist', and 'post-revisionist', is touched upon by Flechner, 'Conversion in Ireland', 45–6.

51 Bede, *Historia ecclesiastica*, III.4 (edd. Colgrave & Mynors, 222–5): 'Habere autem solet ipsa insula rectorem semper abbatem presbyterum, cuius iuri et omnis prouincia, et ipsi etiam episcopi ordine inusitato debeant esse subiecti, iuxta exemplum primi doctoris illius, qui non episcopus, sed presbyter extitit et monachus'.

with its first bishops. A number of scholars, following Bede's sympathetic description of the 'isolated' Irish, have tended to set aside differences between the Christianity embodied by Iona and that represented by the papal mission of Augustine to Canterbury. Marilyn Dunn, in her study on western monasticism, suggests that cases of inverted authority, as observed by Bede, may simply be misleading.[52] Similarly, the vitriolic debate over Easter, as witnessed by the significant failures of the Synods of Mag Léne and Whitby to enforce consensus, is not investigated as a significant pastoral conflict over the impact of an incorrect date on the veracity of connected liturgical rites, but as a rather remote, albeit passionate, contest over *computus*.[53] This perspective tends to describe differences within a paradigm of continuity occasionally marred by an intense defence of local religious traditions.

Some scholars continue to emphasise this fragmentated approach to authority as symptomatic of a discontinuity with the continental church. Dorothy Watts, drawing on material evidence, continues to present a historical perspective that Insular Christianity was profoundly weakened by a pagan revival and the withdrawal of Roman imperial authority, only regaining traction with the arrival of Augustine of Canterbury.[54] Michael Herren and Shirley Brown, exploring various early medieval Insular texts and images, argue that the 'common Celtic Church', preserved by relative isolation, was sympathetic to the controversial teachings of Pelagius.[55] Karen George, in her study on Gildas's *De excidio*, posits a British church influenced by a continued attachment to a theological perspective cautious of Augustine of Hippo's teachings and caricatured in the early modern era as 'semi-Pelagian'.[56] These investigations into divergence, whether material or doctrinal, stand in stark contrast to the cultured orthodoxy proclaimed by Columbanus in his letter to Pope Boniface.[57] However, Herren and Brown have made a strong case that the Insular Easter controversy was not a debate over *computus* but over the fundamental issue of authority or *magisterium*, particularly as it relates to the authority of the scriptures against that of the apostolic succession.[58]

The issue of secular authority in early medieval Britain and Ireland is also opaque. This period saw the, sometimes traumatic, evolution of political power from imperial authority and its attached public offices to that of *gens*-based or regionally defined Christian kingship intimately connected to diocesan bishops, a process to which Gildas was an early witness.[59] Within this transition, the *ad hoc* nature

52 Dunn, *The Emergence of Monasticism*, 147–8.

53 For instance, Yorke, *The Conversion of Britain*, 115–18; in an Irish context, see Charles-Edwards, *Early Christian Ireland*, 391–415. The emphasis is, in a sense, on the correct calculation rather than on how an incorrect calculation might impact the vicissitude of liturgical rites connected to Easter in this period. See Chapter 4 for Columbanus's views of the impact of an incorrect Easter (and associated festivals) on baptism and ordination.

54 See Watts, *Christians and Pagans*; Watts, *Religion in Late Roman Britain*. In this context, Patrick and Gildas are witnesses to an Insular church struggling for relevancy.

55 Herren & Brown, *Christ in Celtic Christianity*, 1–9. For an overview of Herren & Brown's 'defensive' return to 'discontinuity', see Márkus, 'Pelagianism and the "Common Celtic Church"'.

56 George, *Gildas's* De Excidio, 127–32.

57 Columbanus, *Epistulae*, V.3 (ed. Walker, 38).

58 Herren & Brown, *Christ in Celtic Christianity*, 64. The point is also made by Charles-Edwards, *Early Christian Ireland*, 412–15.

59 Gildas, *De excidio*, XXI.4 (ed. Winterbottom, 96, trans. 24): 'Ungebantur reges non per deum sed qui ceteris crudeliores exstarent, et paulo post ab unctoribus non pro veri examinatione trucidabantur aliis electis trucioribus' [Kings were anointed not in God's name, but as being crueller

of monasticism evolved from charismatic leaders and their followers to a series of organised and regulated institutions, institutions that also claimed, as with kings and bishops, 'the *magisterium* of tradition'.[60] While the evolution of Christian kingship and episcopal authority in the early medieval period has received scholarly attention, the historiography on the influence of monasticism on this political transition remains relatively scarce.[61] Tensions between the charisma of 'holy men' and the institutional authority of kings and bishops have been well explored since the seminal study of Peter Brown on the holy man in Late Antiquity.[62] However, the institutional claims of monasticism to edify the authority of kings and bishops remain relatively unstudied. Recent works by James Bruce and Michael Enright in the context of the British Isles, specifically on the *Vita Columbae* written by the abbot of Iona, Adomnán (*ca* 624–704), have investigated and established Adomnán's construction of Columba – a senior monastic figure intimately connected to the edification of kings and bishops – as a prophet in the tradition of the Old Testament.[63] However, these studies have not sought to contextualise this singular construction of a monk as prophet within a wider tradition exemplified by Gildas and Columbanus in the British Isles and on the continent.[64] Further to this, the origins of medieval kingship, whether barbarian, pre-Christian, or something else, remain obscure.[65]

than the rest; before long they would be killed, with no enquiry into the truth, by those who anointed them, and others still crueller chosen to replace them]. This mention of the anointing of kings chronologically precedes Gildas's description of the *adventus Saxonum*, generally placed around the middle of the fifth century. Gildas notes two of the five tyrants are directly related to the *Dumnonii* (Constantine) and the *Demetae* (Vortipor). A detailed assessment of Gildas's vision of authority in Britain is given by Dumville, 'The Idea of Government in Sub-Roman Britain'. Dumville relates potential *tyranni* to tribes and *ciuitates*, often tribal centres.

60 Leyser, *Authority and Asceticism*, 171.

61 For kingship, see Sawyer & Wood (edd.), *Early Medieval Kingship*; Myers, *Medieval Kingship*; Canning, *A History of Medieval Political Thought*; Oakley, *Empty Bottles of Gentilism*. For papal authority, see Sessa, *The Formation of Papal Authority*; Demacopoulos, *The Invention of Peter*. For an overview of episcopal authority, see Rapp, *Holy Bishops in Late Antiquity*.

62 See Brown, 'The Rise and Function of the Holy Man'. On the impact of Brown's work, see Howard-Johnson & Hayward (edd.), *The Cult of Saints*, 1–26.

63 Enright, *Prophecy and Kingship*; Bruce, *Prophecy, Miracles, Angels*. For the *Vita Columbae*, see *Adomnán's Life of Columba* (edd. Anderson & Anderson). See also Michael Enright's earlier monograph, *Iona, Tara, and Soissons*. This study does seek to connect monasticism and kingship both in an Insular and continental context but focuses on a period later than that of Gildas and Columbanus.

64 For example, Albrecht Diem's study of Jonas of Bobbio's *Vita Columbani*, utilising the theoretical framework developed by Max Weber, follows the tension between the 'pure charisma' of the holy man (as a founder of monasteries), and the 'routinization' required by the monastic foundation. He makes a good case that Jonas constructed the *Vita Columbani* to edify the institutional charisma of the monastery. However, he does not investigate the possibility that the 'pure charisma' of Columbanus himself may have been developed within an institutional setting. See Diem, 'Monks, Kings'.

65 Henry Myers, for instance, posits a dual origin from Germanic and Roman models. See Myers, *Medieval Kingship*, 1–14. For problems in discerning origins for medieval kingship in a pre-Christian Germanic past, see Halsall, *Barbarian Migrations*, 121–4. At 313, Halsall points out that Gildas's mention of the anointing of Christian kings chronologically precedes that of Visigothic Spain, making the western British rulers possibly the first to legitimate kingship within Old Testament conventions. Recent studies have moved away from pagan origins toward biblical inspiration, but often from a continental perspective that reinforces a disconnected British

This dearth of research into prophetic authority within the early medieval period does not necessarily just lie with historians. Prophetic authority within this period has also been neglected by historians of theology who have traditionally posited that it ended with the apostles in the first century, or with the heresy of Montanism (a heresy that emphasised prophetic authority) in the second century.[66] This has been challenged in recent scholarship from a 'non-cessationist' position, but generally only in the context of the reassertion of prophecy in the nineteenth and twentieth centuries as evidenced, among others, in the Pentecostal churches.[67] The result has been a historiographical propensity to see prophecy as a literary genre derived from the Bible, not as a claim to authority within the church.[68] As James Bruce points out, it is improbable that the received tradition in which Adomnán wrote was just a literary genre, or that was he alone in this tradition.[69] The claims to prophetic authority described in Adomnán's literary reconstruction of Columba, revealed by Gildas in his *De excidio*, and invoked by Columbanus in his communication with the papacy, points to an entrenchment of prophetic authority within monasticism, a distinct claim unexamined within the historiography covering the Christian culture of the British Isles and the continent from the fifth to the eight centuries.

This evolution in the historiography of the Christian culture of Britain and Ireland in the early medieval period is reflected in the evolution of the historiography of Gildas himself. The image of Gildas as a 'dark-age Celtic monk' – monastically educated, isolated from classical tradition and continental orthodoxy, and writing in an unwieldy 'Insular Latin' prose – dominated historiography until the middle of the twentieth century. It was Owen Chadwick who first proposed that Gildas established himself, not as a monk, but as a cleric, most probably a deacon, making his criticisms of the clerical and secular orders less remote.[70] François Kerlouégan's seminal analysis of the *De excidio* subsequently identified Gildas's Latin (and, therefore, his intended audience's Latin) as classical rather than Insular.[71] A new edition of the *De excidio* by Michael Winterbottom affirmed Gildas's Latin as classical.[72] In the same

Isles. Thus Gildas, an early witness to Christian kingship, is not mentioned. See Hen, 'The Christianisation of Kingship'; Goosman, 'The Long-haired Kings'.

66 See, for instance, Farnell, 'The Current Debate'.

67 For example, Grudem, *The Gift of Prophecy*. A recent exception is Hvidt, *Christian Prophecy*, who does focus on medieval prophecy. However, early medieval prophecy is not covered.

68 For example, when Peter Brown touches on Gildas's descriptions of the Britons as an erring people of Israel and himself as their Jeremiah, he does not comment on the wider religious and political implications of Gildas's claims on behalf of himself and the Britons. See Brown, *The Rise of Western Christendom*, 92–3. Victoria Flood charts recent scholarly interest in medieval prophecy as a literary genre. See Flood, *Prophecy, Politics and Place*, 1–3.

69 Bruce, *Prophecy, Miracles, Angels*, 223.

70 Chadwick, 'Gildas and the Monastic Order'. Owen Chadwick suggests Gildas's strong emphasis on ordination rites identifies him as a deacon. Gildas's status as a deacon has been confirmed most recently by Thomas O'Loughlin: see O'Loughlin, *Gildas and the Scriptures,* 24–5. O'Loughlin notes how Gildas is careful to offer both episcopal and diaconal examples of good and bad clerical behaviour. For the possible monastic status of Gildas, see Wright, 'Gildas's Reading', 136, 160. A more succinct case is made in Chapter 3. Gildas's position as a deacon and monk at the time of publishing the *De excidio* does not, of course, preclude a subsequent ordination to the priesthood or a rise to a position of abbot, as remembered in a variety of later texts. See Chapter 2.

71 Kerlouégan, 'Le Latin'; Kerlouégan, *Le De excidio*.

72 *Gildas* (ed. Winterbottom, 6–7, and 10, n. 8).

year, Thomas O'Sullivan confirmed the textual unity of the *De excidio*.[73] Scholars subsequently expanded Gildas's limited reading with more continental influences.[74] Most recently, Thomas O'Loughlin, in his study of Gildas's original use of the scriptures, has confirmed Gildas's claim to prophetic authority.[75] This presents a picture of Gildas, not as a 'dark-age Celtic monk', but as an ascetic cleric presenting a powerful public critique, shaped by biblical prophecy, and written from within an organised church still influenced by respect for *romanitas*. His image, and that of the Insular church he represents, can no longer be seen as difficult and disconnected.

[73] O'Sullivan, *The* De Excidio, 5–22, and 48–76. O'Sullivan was writing against a tradition revisited in the first half of the twentieth century that divided the *De excidio* into two discrete works – the *Epistola Gildae* and the *Excidium Gildae* – by two different authors.

[74] For instance, Lapidge & Dumville (edd.), *Gildas*; Wright, *History and Literature*.

[75] O'Loughlin, *Gildas and the Scriptures*, 25. See Chapter 2, 34–5, for more detail.

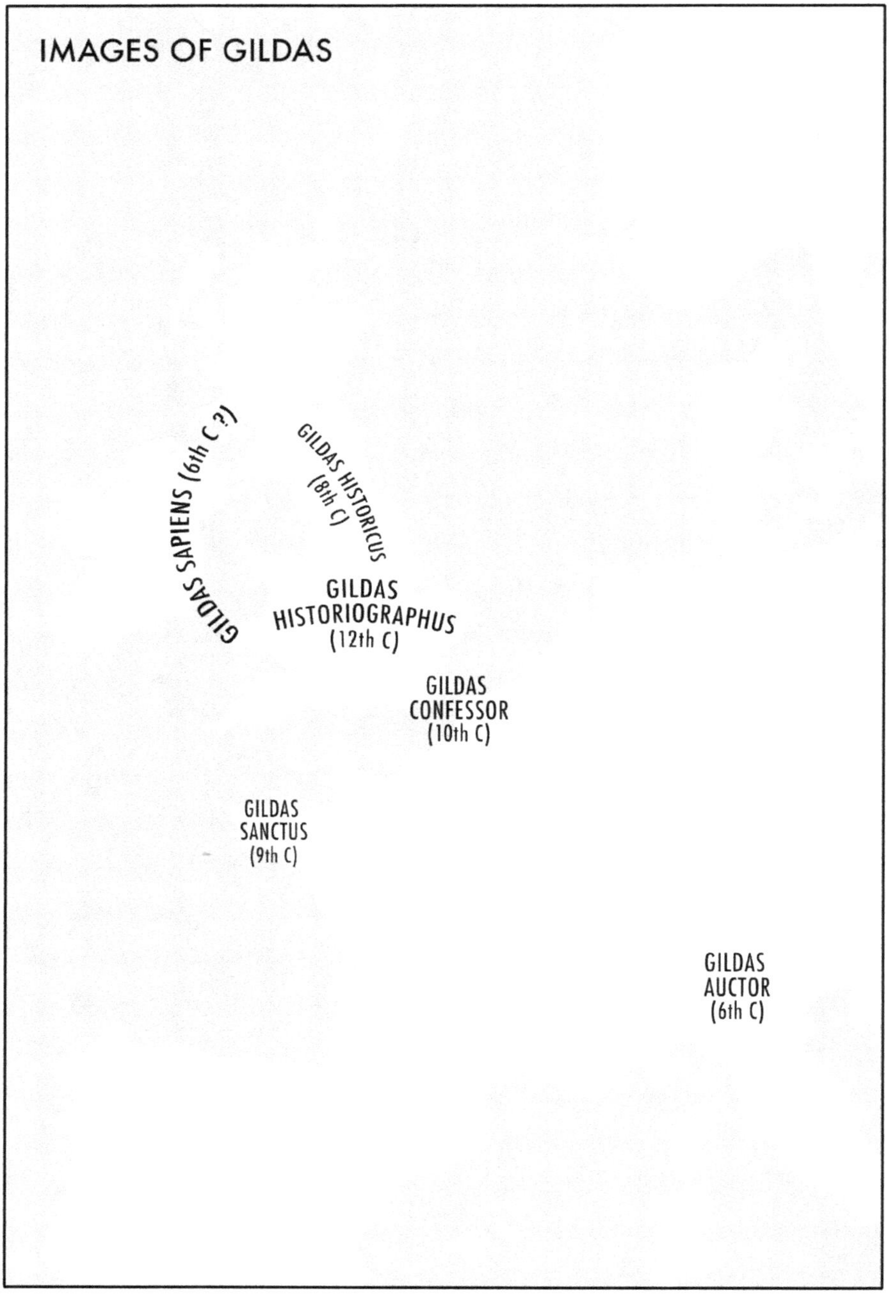

Regional representations of Gildas from the sixth to the twelfth centuries.

2

IMAGES OF GILDAS

Bede's construction of a 'dark age' in Book I of his *Historia ecclesiastica* placed significant weight on Gildas as the chief witness for the period *ca* 450–600. Gildas's providential history of *Britannia* and his immediate criticisms of its leaders remains a unique window on the transition from Roman province to the beginning of medieval kingdoms. The problem, even in Bede's time, was Gildas's reluctance to synchronise his history with other sources: datable events were set aside for a providential overview where historical outcomes were related to the moral choices of a people. The result, from a modern perspective, is that the *De excidio* responds to a crisis at any point between 479 and 550, effectively making its immediate context indeterminable: Gildas's vision of Britain inhabits the entirety of Bede's dark age like a spectre. Scholarly attempts to rationalise a useful outcome, in a historical sense, have ultimately agreed to place the *De excidio* around the middle point of Bede's dark age, *ca* 530. Uneasily situated, the date of Gildas's intervention presents an ongoing conundrum.

This chapter seeks to explore Gildas's context through his many images. Gildas's self-image will be analysed via the *De excidio* and the fragments of his letter to Finnian. Subsequently, I will investigate the way in which the themes of these texts were remembered by authors up to the twelfth century. This will highlight a variety of images of Gildas that have led to uncertainty over his context. I will argue that two of these images – Gildas *Historicus* and Gildas *Sapiens* – are modelled on the two discrete modes of authority found in the *De excidio* and the *fragmenta*: that of providential historian, as formulated primarily in England through an emphasis on the *De excidio*; and that of a canonist, as remembered in Ireland through an emphasis on the letter to Finnian. Other representations possibly relate to memories of two discrete religious figures with the same name active in the fifth and sixth centuries. Subsequently returning to the interrelationship between Gildas's *De excidio*, Patrick's *Confessio* and *Epistola*, and Constantius's *Vita Germani*, I will offer a context for Gildas's intervention as a response to a crisis of authority in the late fifth century.

Gildas on himself

Of the surviving works attributed to Gildas, only those referred to by Columbanus, the *De excidio* and the letter to Finnian (surviving as the *fragmenta Gildae*), are most probably written by him.[1] Of these, the most significant text, in both a literary and a historical sense, is the *De excidio*.

1 Sharpe notes Gildas as confirmed author solely of the *De excidio* and the *Epistola ad Vinniauum* (as the *fragmenta*); see Sharpe, *A Handlist*, 149.

Gildas's *De excidio Britanniae* is one of the earliest surviving Insular accounts of the Christian culture of the British Isles in the fifth and/or sixth centuries.[2] Variously dated from 479 to 550, it contains a fierce denunciation of the sins of contemporary rulers and churchmen.[3] Gildas, addressing a moral and political crisis in Britain, calls for the spiritual and physical restoration of his divided *patria* through obedience to God's law. Written as an open letter in three discrete sections, the *De excidio* begins with a personal preface outlining his reasons for writing, followed by a brief history of Britain from the Roman invasion and the arrival of Christianity to his own day (Book I). The history is structured to reinforce divine punishment for sin through historical *exempla* and by overt comparison with the Old Testament *historia* of God's chosen people, Israel. This providential journey is relatively simple to follow, in a historical sense, up to the last quarter of the fourth century and the rise of the British-based imperial usurper, subsequently western Roman emperor, Magnus Maximus (*r.* 383–8). Its historical detail becomes obscure, however, when Gildas enters the fifth century and narrates a providential journey of political independence, civil war, and political fragmentation. Despite its ambiguity, the text remains the earliest narrative detailing the arrival of the English (or Anglo-Saxons) in Britain.

Gildas laments a land divided: pagan Picts have claimed British lands in the north; pagan Saxons have claimed British lands in the east; Christian Britons are warring among themselves in the west.[4] He presents a *divortium* or border, probably militarised, as existing between British and Saxon controlled areas as defined by *urbs Legionum* (perhaps York) and *Verulamium* (St Albans), and between British and

2 Only seven complete or partial manuscript witnesses for the *De excidio* survive: Reims, Bibliothèque Carnegie, Ms 414, 78r–79v (s. IX–X, perhaps from Brittany); London, British Library, Cotton Vitellius A.VI, ff. 1r–37v (s. X, perhaps from Canterbury); Cambridge, University Library, Ff.I.27, ff. 1r–7v (s. XII, perhaps from Durham); Avranches, Bibliothèque Municipale, Ms 162, ff. 48r–63v (s. XII, from Mont Saint-Michel, Normandy); Copenhagen, Det Kongelige Bibliotek, Courtenaykompendiet, 2011/5, 133–189 (s. XIV, from Breamore Abbey or Glastonbury Abbey); Cambridge, University Library, Dd.I.17, ff. 83r–93v (s. XIV–XV, perhaps from Glastonbury Abbey); Paris, Bibliothèque Nationale de France, lat. 6235, f. 7 (s. XVI, perhaps from Lincolnshire). See Larpi, *Prolegomena*, 20–30. There are, of course, indirect witnesses, such as Bede's *Historia ecclesiastica*. On these, see Larpi, *Prolegomena*, 31–88. See Chapter 5, 112–14, for the manuscript tradition for the *fragmenta*.

3 For dating, see Chapter 1, 14, n. 2.

4 Gildas appears to suggest that the Irish (as Scots), allies of the Picts, are 'pirates' or raiders, and are not actively settled as a distinct political entity in Britain at the time of publication. While they were involved with the Picts in seizing lands in the north, they subsequently return to Ireland after a truce brought about by a significant British victory. Gildas, *De excidio*, XIX.1 (ed. Winterbottom, 95, trans., 23): 'tetri Scottorum Pictorumque greges… extremamque terrae partem pro indigenis muro tenus capessunt' [the foul hordes of Scots and Picts… seized the whole of the extreme north of the island from its inhabitants, right up to the wall]; XX.3 (ed. Winterbottom, 95, trans., 24): 'Et tum primum inimicis… strages dabant' [now for the first time they inflicted a massacre on them]; XXI.1–2 (ed. Winterbottom, 95, trans., 24): 'Revertuntur ergo impudentes grassatores Hiberni domos, post non longum temporis reversuri. Picti in extrema parte insulae tunc primum et deinceps requieverunt… In talibus itaque indutiis' [So the impudent Irish pirates returned home (though they were shortly to return); and for the first time the Picts in the far end of the island kept quiet from now on… So in this period of truce…]. If the miraculous British victory against Picts and Scots reported by Gildas is the equivalent of the miraculous British victory against Picts and Saxons narrated in the *Vita Germani*, then the year is 429.

Pictish controlled areas as possibly defined by Hadrian's Wall.[5] Gildas describes the Britain he knows as dominated by moral depravity and material affluence. Drawing on the authority of the Bible, he names and shames five Christian, presumably British, kings or 'tyrants' for their immorality and idolatry (Book II).[6] Again drawing on the authority of the Bible, he shames the unnamed clergy of the British church for a lack of moral leadership, for fornication, greed, and corruption, and for illegitimacy and simony (Book III). It is worth visiting, albeit briefly, a selection of Gildas's rhetoric:

> Britain has kings, but they are tyrants; she has judges, but they are wicked. They often plunder and terrorize – the innocent; they defend and protect – the guilty and thieving. They have many wives – whores and adulteresses. They constantly swear – false oaths; they make vows – but almost at once tell lies. They wage wars – civil and unjust.[7]

> Britain has priests, but they are fools; very many ministers, but they are shameless; clerics, but they are treacherous grabbers. They are called shepherds, but they are wolves all ready to slaughter souls. They do not look to the good of their people, but to the filling of their own bellies.[8]

[5] Gildas, *De excidio*, X.2 (ed. Winterbottom, 92, trans., 19): '[Sanctorum martyrum] nunc corporum sepulturae et passionum loca, si non lugubri divortio barbarorum quam plurima ob scelera nostra civibus adimerentur, non minimum intuentium mentibus ardorem divinae caritatis incuterent: sanctum Albanum Verolamiensem, Aaron et Iulium Legionum urbis cives ceterosque utriusque sexus diversis in locis summa magnanimitate in acie Christi perstantes dico' [(The holy martyrs's) graves and the places where they suffered would now have the greatest effect in instilling the blaze of divine charity in the mind of the beholders, were it not that our citizens, thanks to our sins, have been deprived of them by the unhappy partition with the barbarians. I refer to St. Alban of Verulam, Aaron and Julius, citizens of Caerleon, and the others of both sexes who, in different places, displayed the highest spirit in the battle-line of Christ]. For an identification of *urbs Legionum* with York, see Field, 'Gildas and the City of Legions'. As noted by Field, other favoured sites are Caerleon (as translated by Winterbottom) and Chester. Caerleon does have a claim to being *urbs Legionum* on the basis of medieval reports of a local shrine to Aaron and Julius. See Seaman, 'Julius and Aaron'. However, both Caerleon and Chester appear to be under the control of British kings at the time Gildas is writing, and the point must be made that the remains of martyrs are notoriously transportable. There also appears to be no material evidence to support 'barbarian' control of Caerleon or Chester in the dates assigned to Gildas's text. On the archaeology of partition in a Saxon context and the problems modelling the *adventus Saxonum* from an archaeological perspective, see Härke, 'Anglo-Saxon Immigration and Ethnogenesis'. Charles-Edwards, *Wales and the Britons*, 210, notes that the Picts probably formed as a confederation of British peoples beyond the Antonine Wall in the third century: Gildas's indication that they subsequently seized British lands up to the wall in the fifth century and continued to hold them in whole or in part after a negotiated truce implies the possibility of a new border at Hadrian's Wall. A military border at Hadrian's Wall is also strongly implied by Gildas's descriptions of 'high towers' and the 'high wall'. See *De excidio XIX*. For more on Gildas's geographical understanding of the island of Britain, see Chapter 6.

[6] The tyrants are named as Constantine, Vortipor, Aurelius Caninus, Cuneglasus, and Maglocunus. For a discussion of the named tyrants see O'Sullivan, *The* De Excidio, 87–133, and Dumville, 'Gildas and Maelgwn'.

[7] Gildas, *De excidio*, XXVII.1 (ed. Winterbottom, 99, trans., 29): 'Reges habet Britannia, sed tyrannos; iudices habet, sed impios; saepe praedantes et concutientes, sed innocentes; vindicantes et patrocinantes, sed reos et latrones; quam plurimas coniuges habentes, sed scortas et adulterantes; crebro iurantes, sed periurantes; voventes, sed continuo propemodum mentientes; belligerantes, sed civilia et iniusta bella agentes'.

[8] Gildas, *De excidio*, LXVI.1 (ed. Winterbottom, 118, trans., 52): 'Sacerdotes habet Britannia, sed insipientes; quam plurimos ministros, sed impudentes; clericos, sed raptores subdolos; pastores,

Even in translation, Gildas's criticisms, underscored by thesis and antithesis, thunder from the page.

The candour of Gildas's invective was shaped by fears of an impending political and spiritual catastrophe as buttressed by biblical revelation. For Gildas, the future had been laid out in the past: partitioned Britain mirrored the partitioned kingdoms of Israel and Judah prior to the destruction of Judah and Jerusalem by the Babylonians.[9] It was this biblical revelation, drawn from Jeremiah, which was the cornerstone of his warnings to contemporary Christians.[10] Gildas, thus, shaped his critique of secular and spiritual authority within the prophetic traditions of the Old Testament. In doing so, as noted by Thomas O'Loughlin, he claimed the status of prophet:

> as Isaiah, Jeremiah and Hosea, and many others were in Israel, and as the *sancti uates* were in the first churches, so Gildas is in Britain in his time.[11]

Thomas Charles-Edwards has similarly confirmed Gildas's status as a prophet when speaking about his historical perspective:

> When Gildas thought of prophecy, this is not what we usually mean by the term, namely prediction of future events. His was fundamentally an Old Testament conception of prophet, someone who, guided by God, declared to his people their current spiritual state… The only reason why the future was relevant at all was that God's judgement might visit future reward or punishment on present virtue or sin. The present was the primary concern of the prophet, but informed by a belief in a divine judgement that expressed itself within history, not just the end of time… In his own time, Gildas was rightly both prophet and historian.[12]

The success, in some form, of Gildas's claim to prophetic authority is demonstrated by the subsequent utilisation of extracts from his letter to Finnian within collections of canon law in an Irish context.[13] Here, however, the emphasis is not on denunciations in the manner of an Old Testament prophet, but on advice in relation to pastoral authority. The *fragmenta Gildae* consist of eight fragments assigned to Gildas and two fragments attributed to Gildas.[14] Fragments one and seven oppose the excessive use of excommunication in a clerical and monastic context (see Appendix); fragments two and three warn against excessive fasting in a clerical, monastic, and secular context; fragments four and five suggest a pragmatic approach to monastic discipline; fragments six and nine counsel against judgementalism in a clerical, monastic, and secular context; and fragments eight and ten are Gildasian sayings.[15] While not offering information on Gildas himself, the *fragmenta* are notable for the

ut dicuntur, sed occisioni animarum lupos paratos, quippe non commoda plebi providentes, sed proprii plenitudinem ventris quaerentes'. This section draws from Ezekiel 34 and John 10.12. See O'Loughlin, *Gildas and the Scriptures*, 258.

9 See Joyce, 'Gildas and His Prophecy for Britain'.

10 Nicholas Higham and Karen George have noted Gildas's affiliation with Jeremiah: see Higham, *The English Conquest*, 67–89; George, *Gildas's* De Excidio, 29–41. For further discussion, see Chapter 3, 57–8.

11 O'Loughlin, *Gildas and the Scriptures*, 25.

12 Charles-Edwards, *Wales and the Britons*, 204.

13 Sharpe, 'Gildas as a Father of the Church'.

14 For discussion, see Chapter 5.

15 For more detail on the *fragmenta*, see Joyce, 'Attitudes to Excommunication'.

fact that they present Gildas as an advisor on clerical, monastic, and secular matters. They imply that the claim to prophetic authority in the *De excidio* elevated Gildas to the status of a spiritual master, advising ecclesiastical figures such as Finnian on the interpretation of scriptural and canon law as it pertained to discipline within the wider Insular church.[16]

Despite these significant claims to authority, we know little about Gildas himself. The *De excidio* is barren in personal detail. Gildas tells us he was forty-three years old at the time of publication and that he was a cleric.[17] He alludes to the fact that he was a deacon and that he may also be a monk.[18] He tells us through his use of language and rhetoric that he was well educated and, by implication, a member of the Romano-British elite.[19] The precision with which he uses Latin implies that he might have had a secular career or a period of training for a secular career.[20] He appears to support a *romanitas* that situates Britain as a *natio* amongst *nationes* and not directly dependent on Roman imperial authority.[21] The way he describes his Britain suggests a geographical position at the time of publication somewhere in the south-west.[22]

16 While it is possible that the letter to Finnian may precede the *De excidio*, Gildas is adamant, at the age of forty-three, that he been silent for ten or more years, making it unlikely. See Gildas, *De excidio*, II (ed. Winterbottom, 87, trans., 13): 'silui, fateor… spatio bilustri temporis vel eo amplius praetereuntis' [I kept silent… as the space of ten years or more passed by]. Stancliffe, 'Columbanus and Shunning', 127, also argues that the letter to Finnian is from a later period than the *De excidio*.

17 Gildas, *De excidio*, XXVI.1 (ed. Winterbottom, 98, trans., 28): 'quique quadragesimus quartus (ut novi) orditur annus mense iam uno emenso, qui et meae nativitatis est' [That was the year of my birth; as I know, one month of the forty-fourth year since then has already passed]; LXV.1 (ed. Winterbottom, 118, trans., 51): 'si non tantos talesque malitiae episcoporum vel ceterorum sacerdotum aut clericorum in nostro quoque ordine erigi adversus deum vidissem montes' [if I did not see such great mountains of wickedness raised against God by bishops and other priests and clerics of my order also].

18 See Chapter 1, 27, n. 70.

19 Lapidge, 'Gildas's Education', 34–5.

20 Lapidge, 'Gildas's Education', 46–7. Lapidge notes that Gildas's classical education implies an education for a secular career. Gildas's relatively junior clerical status at the age of forty-three also implies some form of secular career prior to entering the clerical orders. See Chapter 3, 61. His precision in the use of Latin hints that it may have been a military career. See Chapter 3, 65.

21 Gildas, *De excidio*, XXV1.4 (ed. Winterbottom, 99, trans., 29): 'Quippe quid celabunt cives quae non solum norunt sed exprobrant iam in circuitu nationes?' [Indeed, why should their countrymen conceal what surrounding nations are aware of and reprove?]

22 For a discussion of Gildas's locality, see Higham, *The English Conquest*, 90–117. Higham makes a reasonable case for Gildas writing somewhere in the south-west. This location is supported more broadly by Sharpe, 'Martyrs and Local Saints', 108. Thompson, 'Gildas and the History of Britain', 225, has made a case for Gildas writing in the north-west, in the region of Cheshire or Lancashire. Thompson's position has been supported by Breeze, 'Where was Gildas Born?'. However, one of the most immediate criticisms expressed by Gildas is levelled at Constantine of Dumnonia (Devon and Cornwall), reinforcing the argument for the south-west: not only does Gildas denounce Constantine for pedicide, but he appears to be aware of Constantine's immediate situation. Gildas is clearly close to the political situation in Dumnonia. See Gildas, *De excidio*, XXVIII.1 (ed. Winterbottom, 99, trans., 29): 'Cuius tam nefandi piaculi non ignarus est inmundae leaenae Damnoniae tyrannicus catulus Constantinus. Hoc anno… facturum… latera regiorum tenerrima puerorum vel praecordia crudeliter' [This unspeakable sin is not unknown to Constantine, tyrant whelp of the filthy lioness of Dumnonia. This very year… he most cruelly tore at the tender sides and vitals of two royal youths]; XXIX.1 (ed. Winterbottom, 100, trans., 30): 'quasi praesentem arguo, quem adhuc superesse non nescio' [I know full well you are alive,

Like the *De excidio*, the *fragmenta* imply a pragmatic and inclusive attitude towards human weakness, but one fearful of divine judgement for recalcitrance.[23] In order to flesh out what we know about Gildas, we need to look at how he was remembered.

Images of Gildas in the early medieval period

The earliest secure witness to Gildas is the letter to Pope Gregory the Great *ca.* 600 in which Columbanus refers to him as author of the *De excidio* and the letter to Finnian.[24] Columbanus, an Irishman living in Gaul and Italy, describes Gildas as an *auctor* or authority on Christian matters, implying that he was known to Gregory the Great in Rome.[25] This early witness is potentially reinforced by references to Gildas within the various Irish annals, possibly set down as early as the late sixth century, but deriving from a lost common source that can be firmly dated no earlier than the tenth century.[26] Here he is remembered as dying between 567 and 577, in one instance under the title of *sapiens*, another under the title of *episcopus*.[27] A death in 570 is also reported in the Welsh annals, likely incorporating material from earlier Welsh and Irish chronicles but similarly set down in a source that can only be securely dated to

and I charge you as though you were present]. If Gildas's 'forty-fourth year and one month' refers to a publication one month into a new year, then the immediacy of 'hoc anno' is even more compelling. For further discussion of Gildas's 'forty-fourth year', see below, 46–8.

23 See Sharpe, 'Gildas as a Father of the Church', 197.

24 See Introduction, 7.

25 Columbanus, *Epistulae*, I.6 (ed. Walker, 8–9): 'simoniacos et Gildas auctor pestes scripsit eos' [Gildas the writer set them down as simoniacs and plagues]. For an expansion on the argument concerning Gregory the Great, see Chapter 4.

26 See Thornton, *Kings, Chronologies, and Genealogies*, 11–14. Bannerman, 'Notes on the Scottish Entries' and Smyth, 'The Earliest Irish Annals' both argue for the earliest contemporaneous entries preserved in the Irish annals being set down by Columba in Iona post *ca* 563 in what is known as the *Iona Chronicle*, a probable source for Bede. The *Iona Chronicle* has been reconstructed as part of the putative source for the later annals, the *Chronicle of Ireland*. On the *Chronicle of Ireland*, see Introduction, 6. On the debates over the origins and reliability of the Irish annals, see Mc Carthy, 'The Origin of the Latercus Paschal Cycle', 37–44; Evans, *The Present and the Past in Medieval Irish Chronicles*, 1–6; Ó Cróinín, *Early Medieval Ireland*, 8–14.

27 The *Chronicle of Ireland* reports a possibly contemporaneous obit for Gildas in 570. See *The Chronicle of Ireland* (trans. Charles-Edwards, 108). The reliability of this obit for Gildas is briefly discussed in Charles-Edwards, *Wales and the Britons*, 215–16, where he notes it as worthy of attention, but not conclusive. *The Annals of Ulster* report an obit of Gillas, identified as Gildas, in 570 and 577 (AU570.3, AU577.6), and *The Annals of Inisfallen* report an obit for a Bishop Gildas (*Gilldais epscoip*) in 567 (AI567.1). See *The Annals of Ulster* (edd. Mac Airt & Mac Niocaill); *The Annals of Inisfallen* (ed. Mac Airt). The Inisfallen entry implies a different Gildas, as Gildas, author of the *De excidio*, is not remembered as a bishop in his *vitae*. *The Annals of Tigernach* report an obit for Gillas in 569 (AT569.3): see 'The Annals of Tigernach' (ed. Stokes). *The Book of Leinster* reports an obit for Gildas *Sapiens* in 570. See 'Annals from the Book of Leinster', in *The Tripartite Life of Patrick*, II (ed. Stokes, 512–29, 515). On the synchronising of the various Irish annals, see Mc Carthy, *Chronological Synchronisation*.

the tenth century.[28] This tradition likewise describes Gildas as *sapiens*, reporting a visit to Ireland in 565.[29]

Gildas's name is cited, along with elements of his letter to Finnian (*fragmenta*), in an Insular or Insular-influenced canon collection (*Incipiunt capitula canonica*), compiled perhaps as early as the first quarter of the seventh century.[30] This letter to Finnian, along with Gildas's name, is subsequently quoted more fully as a continuous text within another Insular canon collection (*Collectio canonum Turonensis*), perhaps compiled in Ireland in the second quarter of the seventh century.[31] Also at this time, substantial elements of the preface on penance attributed to Gildas are copied into the *Penitential of Cummian*, presumably by the same Irish scholar, Cummian (*ob. ca* 661), who wrote a learned treatise on the date of Easter *ca* 632.[32] Sometime in the last quarter of the seventh century or the first half of the eighth century, fragments of Gildas's letter to Finnian are incorporated, along with several instances of his name, within the highly influential Irish canon collection, the *Collectio canonum Hibernensis*.[33] In the last quarter of the seventh century, the literary styles of the *De excidio* influence the Canterbury school of Archbishop Theodore (*ob. ca* 690) and Abbot Hadrian (*ob. ca* 710), and the works of the abbot and bishop, Aldhelm of Malmesbury (*ob. ca* 709).[34] By 700, we can already see the development of distinct English and Irish lines of transmission for the *De excidio* and the letter to Finnian.

In the eighth century, Gildas is remembered in the *Catalogue of the Saints of Ireland* (*ca* 730), along with David and Cadog (*fl.* sixth century), as one of the *sancti viri* who brought the liturgy from Britain to Ireland.[35] Around the same time in a Northumbrian context, Gildas is remembered in *Willibrord's Calendar* (*ca* 728) for

[28] The *Harleian Chronicle*, a mid-tenth-century recension of a St Davids chronicle written down *ca* 1100, reports an obit for Gildas in 570 (a126.1). See *Annales Cambriae: The A Text* (transcr. Gough-Cooper, 5). On dating and Irish influence, see Guy, 'The Origins', 25–45; Dumville, 'Gildas and Maelgwn', 54.

[29] The *Breviate Chronicle*, a late thirteenth-century recension of a St Davids chronicle, reports an obit for Gildas, *britonum sapientissimus*, in 570 (b598.1), and a visit to Ireland in 565 (b593.1). See *Annales Cambriae: The B Text* (transcr. Gough-Cooper, 24–5). The *Cottonian Chronicle*, also a late thirteenth-century recension of a St Davids chronicle, reports an obit for Gildas *Sapiens* (cw128.6). See *Annales Cambriae: The C Text* (transcr. Gough-Cooper, 10). A later hand dates this entry to 512. On these chronicles, see Gough-Cooper, 'Meet the Ancestors?'

[30] See Chapter 5.

[31] See Chapter 5.

[32] For the *Penitential of Cummian*, see *Paenitentiale Cummeani* (ed. Bieler, 108–35). On Cummian as potentially an abbot and bishop, see Bieler (ed.), *The Irish Penitentials*, 6. For Cummian's letter on Easter, see Ó Cróinín & Walsh (edd.), *Cummian's Letter*. Winterbottom, 'The Preface', 286, n. 38, observes that Cummian's letter is modelled on the preface to Gildas's *De excidio*.

[33] See Chapter 5.

[34] For the School of Canterbury, see Hardison, 'Words, Meanings, and Readings'. For Aldhelm, see O'Sullivan, *The* De Excidio, 63–5.

[35] *Catalogus sanctorum Hiberniae* (ed. Grosjean, 206): '[Secundus vero ordo sanctorum] ritum celebrandi missam acceperunt a sanctis viris de Britannia, scilicet a sancto David et sancto Gilda et a sancto Doco' [The second order of saints accepted their ritual of the Mass from holy men of Britain: St David and St Gildas and St Doc]. Translation, de Paor, *Saint Patrick's World*, 225–6. While the editor, Grosjean, argues for a dating to the ninth or tenth centuries, Graff, 'A Note on the Divisions of Time', has made a compelling case that the text should be dated to the second quarter of the eighth century.

the feast day of 29 January under the title of *sapiens*.[36] Bede draws on the *De excidio* in his *Historia ecclesiastica* (*ca* 731) and is the first person to refer to Gildas as *historicus*, a designation not taken up again until the twelfth century. Subsequently, in a continental context, the Northumbrian scholar Alcuin (*ca* 735–804) refers to Gildas as *Brittonum sapientissimus* in two letters to Canterbury and Kent, dated *ca* 793 and *ca* 797 respectively.[37]

In the ninth century, the *Stowe Missal* (*ca* 800) remembers Gildas as a *sacerdos* in an Irish context.[38] The *Martyrology of Tallaght* (*ca* 830), an Irish text derived from a Northumbrian source, and the related *Martyrology of Oengus* (*ca* 830), also from Ireland, remember Gildas as *episcopus* on the feast day of 29 January, but also potentially record a second feast day for a Gildas on 28 September, a detail picked up by an English calendar in the tenth century.[39] In a Welsh context, the *Historia Brittonum* (*ca* 830) constructs a history of the Britons using Gildas's *De excidio*, but does not mention his name.[40]

Hagiographies going back to at least the ninth century also begin to record the memory of Gildas.[41] In Ireland, the Latin *Life of Saint Brendan* (perhaps eighth or ninth century) records a meeting of Brendan with Gildas, describing him as *sanctissimus.*[42] The Irish *Life of Finnian* (perhaps ninth or tenth century) – supporting

[36] *The Calendar of Willibrord* (ed. Wilson, 20): 'Gildas Sapientis' [Gildas the Wise]. In the following section, unless otherwise stated, translations are my own.

[37] Alcuin, *Epistolae*, XVII (ed. Dümmler, *Karolini aevi II*, 47): 'Legitur vero in libro Gildi Brettonum sapientissimi' [As it is truly read in the book of Gildas, the wisest of Britons]; Alcuin, *Epistolae*, CXXIX (ed. Dümmler, *Karolini aevi II*, 192): 'Discite Gyldum Brittonem sapientissimum' [Study Gildas, the wisest of Britons].

[38] *The Stowe Missal*, II (ed. Warner, 16): 'Item et sacerdotum… Gilde' [and likewise the priests… Gildas].

[39] *Martyrology of Tallagh* (ed. Kelly, *Calendar*, xi–xlii, xiv): 29 January, 'Gilde Eps. et sapiens' [Bishop Gildas the Wise]. *The Martyrology of Oengus* (ed. & trans., Stokes, 38): 29 January, 'Áin epscoip ro rádius, ron-snádat diar n-dílius, Hipolitus, Paulus, Gillas, Constantínus' [Splendid (are) the bishops I have mentioned may they protect us to our possession! Hippolytus, Paulus, Gildas, Constantinus]; (ed. Stokes, 197, trans., 197): 28 September, 'Dá Fhindio geldai' [The two bright Findios]. The entry and potential interpretation of *geldai* as Gillas/Gildas is discussed by Stokes on 213. This interpretation is picked up by Ó Riain, 'Gildas', 35. While the etymology of the name of Gildas is not part of the scope of this book, these entries do suggest that the name may be a play on 'bright/geldai' or 'servant/gillas'. I would like to thank Dr Julianna Grigg for this suggestion. The *Martyrology of Donegal* records a feast day for a Gildas on 4 November. See *Martyrology of Donegal* (ed. Kelly, *Calendar*, 34). For the English calendar, see below, 39.

[40] For dating, see *The Historia Brittonum* (ed. Dumville, 3).

[41] The dating of 'early medieval' Irish Latin lives (*vitae*) and Irish vernacular lives (*bethada*), only preserved in high medieval or early modern manuscripts, is highly problematic and ranges from the seventh to the fourteenth centuries. Pádraig Ó Riain is sceptical of early dates for Irish hagiography, conceding only early dates in the seventh century to select *vitae* of Patrick, Brigid, and Columba. The remaining hagiography largely belongs, in his estimation, to intense activity in the twelfth century. See Ó Riain, *Dictionary of Irish Saints*, 39–40. Sharpe, *Medieval Irish Saints' Lives*, 384–9, on the other hand, has proposed that certain *vitae* derive from the period 650–890, reducing the period of 'hagiographic inactivity' to the tenth and eleventh centuries. It is this period he conjectures for the *bethada* but acknowledges that they have been neglected by the academy. Kathleen Hughes argues that some *bethada* are more primitive than the equivalent *vitae* and date as early as the ninth century. See below, n. 43.

[42] *Vita Prima Sancti Brendani* (ed. Plummer, *Vitae*, I.141): 'Audiens enim famam sanctissimi Gilde, uiri scilicet magne uirtutis, assumptis secum uiris religiosis, properauit uisitare illum' [For hearing of the fame of the most holy Gildas, certainly a man of great virtue, and taking with him

the connections of both Columbanus and the *Catalogue of the Saints of Ireland* – records a dispute between Gildas and David mediated by Finnian and Cathmael (Cadog), describing Gildas as a *sui* or seer.[43] In Brittany, the first life of Gildas by an anonymous monk of Ruys is written *ca* 880, describing his noble birth in north Britain and his death in Brittany on the feast day of 29 January.[44] It describes Gildas (also Gildasius) as a *beatus*, a *presbyter*, and an *abbas*, and quotes sections of his *De excidio*.[45] Two other Breton lives written around the same time – of Saint Winwaloe and Saint Paul of Leon – describe Gildas as a *sanctus* and a wise writer, notably of canon law.[46]

In the tenth century in a Frankish context, the *Rheims Litanies* remember Gildas as a *confessor*.[47] This is replicated in English calendars of the period, with 29 January recording the feast day of Gildas as a *confessor*.[48] One calendar from south-west

religious men, he hurried to visit him]. Sharpe, *Medieval Irish Saints' Lives*, 24, notes that the dating of this life is extremely uncertain. The *vita* of Saint Brendan in the Salmanticensis collection also has a similar phrase: see *Vita altera S. Brendani* (ed. Heist, *Vitae*, 329): 'Sanctissimi autem viri nomine Gilde fama accitus, per maria terrasque ipsum adivit' [For attracted from afar by the fame of the holy man named Gildas, he brought himself by land and sea to him]. For the dating of elements of the Salmanticensis collection to as early as the eighth century, see Charles-Edwards, 'The Northern Lectionary'.

43 'Betha Fhindein Clúana h-Eraird' (ed. Stokes, *Lives*, 75–6, trans., 222): 'Fuair tri suithe ara cind annsin .i. Dabid & Gillas & Cathmael a n-anmanna. Rob e fath a comthinoil annsin, cosnum cennachta & apdaine innsi Bretan etir dís díbh .i. etir Dabid & Gillas' [There he found before him three sages named David, Gildas, and Cathmael. This was the cause of their being gathered together there – a contention for the headship and abbacy of the island of Britain between two of them, that is between David and Gildas]. Hughes, 'The Historical Value', 371–2, argues that the *betha* of Finnian can be dated to the ninth or tenth century. The incident is repeated in the later *vitae* of Finnian, dated by Hughes to the Anglo-Norman period in Ireland.

44 Monk of Ruys, *Vita Gildae*, XXX (trans. Williams, 58–9): 'redditit spiritum quarto kalendas Februarii' [he gave up the ghost on the 29th of January]. For details of his birth and death, see below, 42–3. For the dating of the *vita*, see *Two Lives* (trans. Williams, 7–10). Williams's further linguistic argument concerning the consonant change from *w-* to *gu-* for Werocus/Guerecus from the ninth-century section to the eleventh-century addition is convincing. This argument was not noticed by the subsequent editor, Ferdinand Lot, who argued for a single author in the eleventh century despite also having the consonant change in his edition. See *Two Lives* (trans. Williams, 45–7, n. 2). See also Jackson, *Language and History*, 41–2.

45 Monk of Ruys, *Vita Gildae*, III (trans. Williams, 16–17): 'Beatus autem Gildas, qui et Gildasius' [Now, the blessed Gildas, who is also called Gildasius]; VIII (trans. Williams, 26–7): 'et presbyteratus fungeretur officio' [and was discharging the duties of a presbyter]; XVIII (trans. Williams, 40–1): 'Licet vero abbatis locum teneret' [Although, indeed, he held the office of an abbot]. For excerpts from the *De excidio*, see Monk of Ruys, *Vita Gildae*, I (trans. Williams, 14); XIX (trans. Williams, 42–4).

46 Uurdisten, *Vita Sancti Winwaloei* (ed. de la Borderie, *Cartulaire*, 8): 'qui haec plenius scire voluerit legat sanctum Gyldam' [any who wish to fully know these things should read Saint Gildas]. Wormonoc, *Vita S. Pauli* (ed. Plaine, 215): 'Sanctum Gyldam, cuius sagacitate(m) ingenii industria(m)que legendi atque in sacris canonum libris peritia(m) liber ille artificiosa compositur instructione quem Ormestam Britanniae vocant' [Saint Gildas, whose innate wisdom, industry in reading, and expertise in the sacred books of the canons is indeed declared in that book, crafted with instruction, known as the Prophecy of Britain].

47 *The Rheims Litanies* (ed. Stokes, *The Tripartite*, II.502): 'De confessoribus… S. Gilda' [Concerning the confessors… Saint Gildas].

48 Ten pre-1100 English calendars mention Gildas on the feast-day of 29 January. See Jankulak & Wooding, 'The Cult of Saint Gildas', 29.

Britain records a second feast day for Gildas on 28 September.[49] In the eleventh century in the aftermath of Viking raids, the Breton *Life of Gildas* is appended with Gildas's miraculous involvement in the rebuilding of the monastery at Ruys, and Wulfstan, Archbishop of York (*r.* 1002–1023), invokes Gildas as a *þeodwita*, a wise man or historian, perhaps prophet.[50] In a Welsh context, the *Life of Cadog* (end of eleventh century), a saint linked to Gildas since the eighth century, describes Gildas as *scolasticus* and *scriptor optimus*, and the *Life of David* (*ca* 1092), a saint also linked to Gildas since the eighth century, refers to him as *sanctus*.[51] The *Life of David* also appears to cite elements of David's monastic rule, elements criticised in Gildas's letter to Finnian, supporting the tension between Gildas and David related in the Irish *Life of Finnian*.[52] In Normandy, a chronicle compiled at Mont Saint-Michel, probably from earlier material, records the birth of Saint Gildas in 421.[53]

The twelfth century sees a resurgence in interest in Gildas. In an Anglo-Norman context, William of Malmesbury describes Gildas as *historicus* in his *History of the English Kings* (*ca* 1126).[54] An addition to the same entry in William's *The Early History of Glastonbury* (*ca* 1129–39) assigns his death to 512 and burial at Glastonbury 'in the old church before the altar'.[55] Around the same time in a Welsh

49 [29 January], 'Gylde confessoris' [Gildas the confessor]; 28 September, 'Gylde confessoris' [Gildas the confessor]. See *A Pre-Conquest English Prayer-Book* (ed. Muir, 3, 11).

50 The destruction of the monastery at Ruys in the early tenth century by Vikings/Normans saw relics associated with Gildas taken to the region of Berry in the diocese of Bourges. An eleventh-century manuscript leaf (bound into a sixteenth-century manuscript) lists works at the library of the Abbey of Our Saviour and Gildas in Berry, perhaps originally from the monastery at Ruys, including a 'Textum sancti Gildasii' [The text of Saint Gildasius]. See Kohler, 'Inventaire'. While Kohler identifies this text as Gildas's Bible, it is probably his *De excidio*. These relics were returned to the town of Saint-Gildas-de-Rhuys sometime after the French Revolution, but their provenance is uncertain. For Wulfstan, see Lionarons, *The Homiletic Writings*, 152: 'An þeodwita waes on Brytta tidum Gildas hatte' [There was a wise man of the nation in the time of the Britons called Gildas].

51 Lifris of Llancarfan, *Vita S. Cadoci* (edd. Wade-Evans & Lloyd, *Vitae*, 84–5): 'quidam Britannus, egregius scolasticus, et scriptor optimus, nomine Gildas, filius Cau, callidus artifex' [a certain Briton, an excellent scholar, and a very good writer, Gildas by name, son of Caw, a skilful craftsman]. Rhygyfarch, *Life of St David* (edd. Sharpe & Davis, 112–13): 'quam predicabat sanctus Gildas, Cau filius, in tempore regis Triphuni' [which St Gildas, son of Caw, was preaching in the time of King Tryffin].

52 A point first picked up by Morris, 'The Dates of the Celtic Saints', 349–50 and 384–5. This is covered in detail in Dumville, *Saint David of Wales*.

53 *Aliud chronicon S. Michaelis* (ed. Migne): Year 421, 'Natus est S. Gildas. His diebus fuit Artus rex Britannorum fortis, et facetus' [Saint Gildas is born. In those days King Arthur of the Britons was strong and accomplished]. The chronicle ends in the year 1056.

54 William of Malmesbury, *Gesta Regvm Anglorum*, I, XX.1 (edd. Mynors *et al.*, 804): 'Nam, sicut a maioribus accepimus, Gildas, neque insulsus neque infacetus historicus, cui Britanni debent si quid notitiae inter ceteras gentes habent, multum annorum ibi exegit loci sanctitudine captus' [For, as we have learnt from our elders, Gildas, a historian who was neither boring nor boorish and to whom the Britons owe what knowledge they have as a people, spent many years there because of the holiness of the place].

55 William of Malmesbury, *De Antiquitate Glastonie Ecclesiae*, I (ed. Scott, 54): 'nam, sicut a maioribus accepimus, Gildas, neque insulsus neque infacetus historicus, cui Britanni debent si quid noticie inter ceteras gentes habent, multum annorum ibi exegit loci sanctitudine captus. Ibique anno domini DXII de medio factus, in uetusta ecclesia ante altare est sepultus' [For, as we have learnt from our elders, Gildas, a historian who was neither boorish nor boring and to whom the Britons owe what knowledge they have as a people, spent many years there because of the

context *ca* 1130, Caradog of Llancarfan writes the second life of Gildas, describing a noble birth in north Britain and a burial at Glastonbury: Gildas is called *sapientissimus doctor*, *sanctissimus venerabilis historiographus*, and *heremita.*[56] In Brittany, Peter Abelard (*ca* 1079–1142), abbot of the monastery dedicated to Gildas at Ruys, writes a hymn to Gildas describing him as *sanctus*.[57] A few years later *ca* 1136, the Cambro-Norman or Welsh cleric, Geoffrey of Monmouth (*ca* 1095–1155), writes his *History of the Kings of Britain*, a work that draws directly on the *De excidio* and describes Gildas as *hystoricus*.[58] The Welsh lives of Saint Teilo, Saint Oudoceus, and Saint Illtud, compiled around the middle of the twelfth century, also present Gildas as *historiographus* and *sapiens*.[59] Welsh genealogies, probably drawing from earlier material, begin to mention his name within aristocratic lineages.[60] His name is subsequently attached to twelfth-century recensions of the ninth-century Welsh text, the *Historia Brittonum*.[61] By the end of the twelfth century, the Cambro-Norman archdeacon, Gerald of Wales (*ca* 1146–1223), identifies Gildas as *scriptor* and *sanctus*, while the Anglo-Norman canon, William of Newburgh (*ca* 1136–98), describes him as *historiographus*, noting that his writings are rare and difficult.[62]

holiness of the place. And in the year 512 he was taken from their midst and buried in the old church before the altar].

56 Caradog of Llancarfan, *Vita Gildae*, III (trans. Williams, 84–5): 'Religio sapientissimi doctoris' [The religion of the very wise teacher]; VI (trans. Williams, 92–3): 'sanctissimus Gildas venerabilis historiographus' [the most holy Gildas, the venerable historian]; XII (trans. Williams, 100–1): 'religiosissimus Gildas heremitariam iterum vitam colere' [the most devout Gildas desired to live a hermit's life]. For the details of his birth and death, see below, 42–3.

57 Abelard, *De sancto Gilda* (edd. Blume & Dreves, *Analecta*, 214–5): 'De sancto Gilda' [Concerning Saint Gildas]. I would like to thank Dr Carol Williams for drawing this to my attention.

58 Geoffrey of Monmouth, *The History of the Kings of Britain*, I.22 (ed. & trans. Reeve & Wright, 30–1): 'Quam contentionem quia Gildas hystoricus satis prolixe tractauit'[Since their argument has been discussed in length by the historian Gildas]. The ethnicity of Geoffrey is much debated. For a recent overview, see Smith, 'Introduction and Biography'.

59 *De Vita Sancti Teilavi Landauensis* (edd. Evans & Rhys, *The Text*, 100): 'Siquis autem inde plenius scire desiderat: inhistoria Gildae britannorum historiografi repperiet' [If any wish to know more fully of those times, he can learn from the history of Gildas, historian of the Britons]. *Incipit uita beati Ovdocei* (edd. Evans & Rhys, *The Text*, 138): 'ecce uir bonus & iustus & totius britanniae historiographus Gildas sapiens ut inhistoriis nominator, qui eo tempore conuersabatur in insula Echni ducens anchoritalem uitam' [behold, when calling on history, the good and honest man and historian of all Britain, Gildas the Wise, who in that time lived the life of an anchorite on the island of Echni]. *Vita sancti Illtuti* (edd. Wade-Evans & Lloyd, *Vitae*, 222–3): 'qui legatus erat Gildae historiographi' [who was a messenger of Gildas the historian].

60 *Bonedd y Saint* (ed. Bartrum, *Early Welsh*, 63): 'Gildas m. Caw' [Gildas son of Caw]; (ed. Bartrum, *Early Welsh*, 66): 'Gildas ab Kaw' [Gildas son of Caw]. For dating to the twelfth century, see Bartrum (ed.), *Early Welsh*, 51. See also Lewis, '*Bonedd Y Saint*', 139, n. 2. These details are reflected in both the ninth-century Breton life and the twelfth-century Welsh life.

61 For more information on the pseudo-Gildas recensions of the *Historia Brittonum*, see Dumville, '"Nennius" and the *Historia Brittonum*'.

62 Gerald of Wales, *Descriptio Kambriae* (ed. Dimock, *Giraldi*, 158): 'Prae aliis itaque Britanniae scriptoribus solus mihi Gildas… imitabilis esse videtur' [to me, out of all the writers of Britain, only Gildas appears worthy of imitation]; (ed. Dimock, *Giraldi*, 208): 'Gildas, qui vir sanctus erat et de gente eadem' [Gildas, who was a sainted man and of that people]. William of Newburgh, *The History of English Affairs*, I.2 (edd. Walsh & Kennedy, 28–9): 'Habuit autem gens Britonum ante nostrum Bedam proprium historiographum Gildam, quod et Beda testatur quaedam ejus verba suis litteris inserens, sicut ipse probavi cum ante annos aliquot in ejusdem Gildae librum legendum incidissem. cum enim sermone sit admodum impolitus atque insipidus,

It is clear these representations of Gildas evolved both geographically and in time within the context of the images of authority represented by the *De excidio* and the *fragmenta*. In an Irish context, one that sets aside Columbanus's image of *auctor*, Gildas is primarily remembered as *sapiens* and occasionally situated as a senior cleric, reflecting memories of his letter to Finnian, a work that made a significant contribution to canon law. In an early northern English context, Gildas is also remembered, following Ireland, as *sapiens*, with Bede's designation of Gildas as *historicus*, an image drawn solely from the *De excidio*, appearing to be a distinct innovation. The Breton context, supported by several centres for his cult, is primarily hagiographical, emphasising Gildas as *sanctus*.[63] In southern English and Frankish contexts – perhaps linked – Gildas is a *confessor*, a defender of the faith, nominally of low clerical status or a monk. In a later Welsh or Cambro-Norman context, one which appears to combine Irish, English, and Breton traditions, Gildas is remembered as *sapiens*, *historiographus*, and *sanctus* in a monastic setting. The contemporary Anglo-Norman context, however, following Bede, stresses Gildas as *historiographus*. It is this particularly 'English' perspective of a 'difficult' historian that came to dominate scholarly perceptions in the modern period and continues to have influence.

There may also have been more than one notable figure named Gildas, as preserved in the memories of two feast days, 29 January and 28 September. The narratives of the two *Vitae Gildae* also hint at a conflation of two figures named Gildas, reporting events that appear to take place in both the second half of the fifth century and the second half of the sixth century. Their more detailed descriptions of Gildas place his *gens* in the north of Britain and locate his career in Britain, Ireland, and Gaul, but differ in their narratives and the location of his final resting place.[64]

The older of the two surviving lives of Gildas, from Brittany, describes Gildas as born in north Britain and educated in south Wales.[65] It places Gildas in his thirtieth

paucis eum vel transcribere vel habere curantibus, raro invenitur' [The race of Britons had their own historian before our Bede in the person of Gildas, as Bede attests when he includes some of his words in his writings. I proved this to my satisfaction when some years ago I came across this same Gildas's book for reading purposes. Since his language is unpolished and lacks flavour, few people have bothered to transcribe or possess it, and so it is rarely found].

63 See Jankulak & Wooding, 'The Cult of Saint Gildas'. Gildas's cult is not remembered widely in Britain or Ireland, except for a late tradition attached to Glastonbury and its surrounding areas.

64 The *vitae* appear to be independent of each other in terms of narrative. Both are interpreted to claim a descent for Gildas from the Strathclyde region in northern Britain: Monk of Ruys, *Vita Gildae*, I (trans. Williams, 12–13): 'Beatus Gildas Arecluta fertilissima regione oriundus' [St Gildas, born in the very fertile district of Arecluta]; Caradog of Llancarfan, *Vita Gildae*, I (trans. Williams, 84–5): 'Nau fuit rex Scotiae nobilissimus regum aquilonalium, qui XXIIII filios habuit victores bellicosos, quorum unus nominabatur Gildas' [Nau, king of Scotia, was the noblest of the kings of the north. He had twenty-four sons, victorious warriors. One of these was named Gildas]. See Monk of Ruys, *Vita Gildae* (trans. Williams, 12, n. 1), for a discussion relating *Arecluta* to the River Clyde in modern Scotland. The Breton *vita* appears to place Gildas's death on the island of *Horata*, identified as the island of Houat off the south coast of Brittany (but also implies the possibility of Gildas's oratory at Mount Coetlann in the district of St Demetrius, identified as Plozévet in Brittany); the Welsh *vita* places Gildas's death in the region of Glastonbury in Britain. On this, see below, 43. For a standard biography, see John Morris's introduction to Winterbottom's edition; *Gildas* (ed. Winterbottom, 3). For a more cautious approach to the biographic material, see Kerlouégan, 'Gildas [St Gildas] (fl. 5th–6th cent.)'.

65 For the location of Gildas's education, see Monk of Ruys, *Vita Gildae*, V (trans. Williams, 22–3): 'Quae insula usque in hodiernum diem Lanna Hilduti vocitatur' [That island is called, up to this

year in north Gaul in the reign of the pagan Frank, Childeric (*r. ca* 458–81).[66] It reports that he joined the clerical orders as a priest, preaching in north Britain and, at the invitation of Saint Brigid (*ob. ca* 525) and King Ainmericus (*ob. ca* 569), in Ireland.[67] Returning from a pilgrimage to Rome, Gildas founded the monastery of Ruys in Brittany where he wrote the *De excidio*, interacted with the Breton rulers Conomerus (*fl. ca* 540) and Count Werocus (*ob. ca* 550), and adopted a son (also named Gildas), before dying from illness.[68] The later Welsh *vita* does not accord Gildas formal clerical or monastic status, describing him as a preacher, a hermit, and a *doctor*, and a contemporary of Cadog and King Arthur.[69] It reports that he wrote the *De excidio* at Glastonbury and that he was buried at Glastonbury, a geographical location also suggested by the internal logic of the *De excidio*, the testimony of William of Malmesbury, and potentially by archaeology.[70]

day, Llanilltud]. Llanilltud is the modern town of Llantwit Major in Glamorgan, South Wales.

66 Monk of Ruys, *Vita Gildae*, XVI (trans. Williams, 36–9): 'Erat autem tunc temporis parva res regum regnique Francorum. Childericus enim eo tempore Merovei filius gentilium errori deditus imperabat Francis, quod ex gestis veterum prudens lector cognoscere potest. Sanctus igitur Gildas triginta habens annos venit ad quandam insulam, quae in Reuvisii pagi prospectu sita est, ibique aliquamdiu solitariam duxit vitam' [At that time, however, the resources of the kings and kingdom of the Franks were small. For in those days, as any wise reader can learn from the histories of the ancients, it was Childericus, the son of Meroveus, a man devoted to the error of the heathen, that was ruling over the Franks. St Gildas, therefore, in the thirtieth year of his age, came to some island which lay in sight of the district of Reuvisium, and there, for a considerable time, spent a solitary life].

67 Monk of Ruys, *Vita Gildae*, VIII (trans. Williams, 26–7): 'Igitur cum ad sacros ordines promotus esset et presbyteratus fungeretur officio, audiens quod gentes, quae aquilonalem plagam Britanniae insulae incolebant, adhuc gentili errore detinerentur' [When, therefore, he had been promoted to holy orders, and was discharging the duties of a presbyter, he heard that the people who inhabited the northern region of the island of Britain were still held back by pagan error]; X (trans. Williams, 28–9): 'Audiens autem beata Brigidda, quae ipso tempore insignis erat in Hibernensi manens insula et monasterio virginum praeerat abbatissa, virgo praeclara, famam beati Gildae misit ad eum nuntium' [Now St Bridget, an illustrious virgin, who dwelt and flourished at that time in the island of Hibernia, and presided as abbess over a nunnery, on hearing of the renown of St Gildas, sent a messenger to him]; XI (trans. Williams, 28–9): 'Eo tempore regnabat Ainmericus rex per totam Hiberniam' [At that time, all Hibernia was governed by king Ainmericus].

68 Monk of Ruys, *Vita Gildae*, XX (trans. Williams, 44–7): 'Erat ergo in illis diebus quidam tyrannus nomine Conomerus… At ipse praefatus tyrannus… misit ad quendam principem… nomine Werocum' [Now there lived in those days… a certain tyrant whose name was Conomorus… the aforesaid tyrant personally sent… to some prince called Werocus]; XXV (trans. Williams, 50–1): '[Gildas] qui iussit puerulum baptizari nomenque suum ei imponere fecit' [(Gildas) ordered the child to be baptised, and to be called after his own name]; XXX (trans. Williams, 56–7): 'quamvis invalescente morbo iam iamque vir sanctus deficere videretur' [as his illness was increasing, he seemed already to be failing].

69 Caradog of Llancarfan, *Vita Gildae*, IV (trans. Williams, 86–7): 'praedicatur erat clarissimus per tria regna Britanniae' [He was the most renowned preacher throughout the three kingdoms of Britain]; V (trans. Williams, 90–1): 'Contemporaneus Gildas vir sanctissimus fuit Arturi regis totius maioris Britanniae' [St Gildas was the contemporary of Arthur, the king of the whole of Britain]; VIII (trans. Williams, 94–5): 'Cadocus abbas Nancarbanensis ecclesiae rogavit Gildam doctorem' [Cadoc, the abbot of the church of Nancarban, asked the teacher Gildas]; XII (trans. Williams, 100–1): 'religiosissimus Gildas heremitariam iterum vitam colere' [the most devout Gildas desired to live again a hermit's life].

70 Caradog of Llancarfan, *Vita Gildae*, X (trans. Williams, 98–9): 'ibi [Glastonia] scripsit historias de regibus Britanniae' [It was there (Glastonbury) that he wrote the history of the kings

In the seventeenth century, Thomas Gale identified four images of Gildas when he published his edition of the *De excidio*: Gildas *Sapiens*, Gildas *Historicus*, Gildas *Albanius*, and Gildas *Badonicus*.[71] While the first pair, as we have seen, clearly relate to the distinct modes of authority expressed by Gildas in his *De excidio* (*historicus*) and his letter to Finnian (*sapiens*), the second pair indicate that in the seventeenth century two other images of Gildas were still recalled: Gildas *Albanius*, named for the reports locating his *gens* in north Britain or *Alba* as reported in the *vitae*; and Gildas *Badonicus*, named for his birth in the year of the siege of *mons Badonicus* as interpreted from the *De excidio*.[72] The former figure was identified as the Gildas whom William of Malmesbury says died in 512 and was buried at Glastonbury, as supported by reports in the Welsh *vita*. The latter figure was identified as the Gildas who wrote the *De excidio* and the *fragmenta* and died *ca* 570 in Brittany, as supported by reports in the Breton *vita* and the Irish and Welsh annals. Scholarly opposition to multiple images of Gildas in the modern period, as exemplified by Gale who published his edition under the sole image of Gildas *Sapiens*, gradually influenced the merging of the authorial image of Gildas *Sapiens* with the historical image of Gildas *Badonicus* and the abandonment of other representations.

This position was reinforced in the nineteenth century by Theodor Mommsen who edited the *De excidio* and the *fragmenta* (along with the attributed preface on penance and the *vitae*) in 1898, and their subsequent translation into English (with notes) by Hugh Williams in 1899.[73] In this perspective, Gildas *Sapiens* was dated to *ca* 500–70. The subtle impact of reassigning the image of Gildas *Sapiens* from the *fragmenta* to the *De excidio* has been to continue to reinforce the English image of Gildas as a providential historian rather than the Irish image of Gildas as a significant contributor to canon law. This attitude continues to bedevil an understanding of Gildas's context.

Contextualising modern images: problems with chronology

Modern treatments of Gildas continue to contribute to his representation as a problematic historian.[74] The apparent 'opacity' of the *De excidio*, shaped by biblical prophecy

of Britain]; XIII (trans. Williams, 100–1): 'faceret deferri corpus suum ad abbatiam Glastonie' [to cause his body to be borne to the abbey of Glastonia]. As noted in Chapter 1, radio-carbon evidence for a recently discovered monastic community just a mile from Glastonbury Abbey, at Beckery Chapel, places activity in the fifth or early sixth century.

71 Gale, *Historiae Britannicae,* preface: 'Gildas Historicus, Albanius, Badonicus, Sapiens, tot enim innotuit titulis' [Gildas Historicus, Albanius, Badonicus, Sapiens, he is known by all these titles].

72 Gildas, *De excidio*, XXVI (ed. Winterbottom, 98, trans., 28): 'usque ad annum obsessionis Badonici montis… quique quadragesimus quartus (ut novi) orditur annus mense iam uno emenso, qui et meae nativitatis est' [This lasted right up till the year of the siege of Badon Hill… That was the year of my birth; as I know, one month of the forty-fourth year since then has already passed]. For a discussion of this interpretation, see below, 45–7.

73 Gildas, *De excidio* (ed. Mommsen, *Chronica*, III, 1–110); *Gildas* (ed. Williams). Mommsen accords his edition of the *De excidio* to Gildas *Sapiens*; Williams, perhaps the first to settle on a more prosaic modern image, merely accords his translation to Gildas. He differs from Mommsen in including the attributed *Lorica Gildae*.

74 A recent example is Susan Oosthuizen, who describes Gildas's *De excidio* as a book 'never intended as a history'. See Oosthuizen, *The Emergence*, 22. See also Coumert, 'Gildas', 34, who situates Gildas in a 'world that has lost its reference points'.

and open to fluid interpretation, has, in a sense, 'delegitimised' his historical intent under the scrutiny of subsequent generations. He is often interpreted as an unreliable historian whose historical choices are merely shaped to enhance his message of providential judgement for sin. This gives no credit either to Gildas or to his audience of church and secular leaders, clerics and aristocrats who represented significant education and power. He is unlikely to have legitimated his plea for obedience to God's law within a providential *schema* shaped by the obvious manipulation of historical events that lay within the living memory of his audience.[75] Most notable, in this context, are criticisms levelled at Gildas for the narrative error in his placement of his (now lost) source, the *Epistula ad Agitium*, a plea for Roman assistance identified as relating to the third consulship (446–54) of the western Roman *magister militum*, Aetius (*ca* 391–454), and framed by Bede as a response to the *adventus Saxonum*.[76] Gildas places this plea prior to the *adventus Saxonum* (as 'an enemy much more savage than the first'), and as a response to attacks by Picts and Scots (as the 'two plundering races'):

> But before I make good my promise, I shall try, God willing, to say a little about the situation of Britain; about her obstinacy, subjection, and rebellion, her second subjection and harsh servitude; about religion, persecution, the holy martyrs, diverse heresies, tyrants, **two plundering races**; about a defence and a further devastation; about hunger, **about the letter to Aëtius**, about victory, crimes, enemies suddenly announced, a memorable plague, a council, **an enemy much more savage than the first**, the destruction of cities; about those who survived, and about the final victory of our country that has been granted to our times by the will of God.[77]

While recent, more critical approaches to Bede's manipulation of these events in his *Historia ecclesiastica* have nuanced his authorial intentions, they have not diminished his status as a preferred authority.[78] Gildas, on the other hand, writing within

[75] A point made by McKee, 'Gildas: Lessons from History'.

[76] Gildas, *De excidio*, XX.1 (ed. Winterbottom, 95, trans., 23): 'Igitur rursum miserae mittentes epistolas reliquiae ad Agitium Romanae potestatis virum, hoc modo loquentes: "Agitio ter consuli gemitus Britannorum."' [So the miserable remnants sent off a letter again, this time to the Roman commander Aëtius, in the following terms: 'To Aëtius, thrice consul, the groans of the British']. Karen George discusses the chronological problems of Gildas's historical narrative: see George, *Gildas's* De Excidio, 48–52. Included in this discussion is Gildas's other notable error, his dating of the construction of the Antonine Wall and Hadrian's Wall to the late fourth/early fifth century. While mistaken, as the original walls date to the second century, Gildas may be recalling a substantial reconstruction in the late fourth century. See Hingley, *Hadrian's Wall*, 47. For an overview of the narrative problems created by the common identification and dating of Gildas's described historical event (and source) – the letter to Agitius – with the third consulship of Aetius (446–54), see Higham, *The English Conquest*, 120–37.

[77] Gildas, *De excidio*, II (ed. Winterbottom, 16, 89): 'Sed ante promissum deo volente pauca de situ, de contumacia, de subiectione, de rebellione, item de subiectione ac diro famulatu, de religione, de persecutione, de sanctis martyribus, de diversis haeresibus, de tyrannis, **de duabus gentibus vastatricibus**, de defensione itemque vastatione, de secunda ultione tertiaque vastatione, de fame, **de epistolis ad Agitium**, de victoria, de sceleribus, de nuntiatis subito hostibus, de famosa peste, de consilio, **de saeviore multo primis hoste**, de urbium subversione, de reliquiis, de postrema patriae victoria, quae temporibus nostris dei nutu donata est, dicere conamur'. Emphasis is mine.

[78] For a general overview of recent critical approaches to Bede's *Historia ecclesiastica*, and reactions to these approaches, see Goffart, 'Bede's History in a Harsher Climate'. On Bede's restructuring of the events recorded by Gildas, see Miller, 'Bede's Use of Gildas'.

living memory of these events (no matter where we might place the *De excidio* chronologically within the accepted range of 479–550), continues to sustain criticism for his 'notorious chronological confusion'.[79] Attempts to construct narratives from Gildas's *De excidio* for Britain in the fifth and/or sixth centuries continue to be tangled with interpretations of Bede's *Historia ecclesiastica.* This problematic distrust of Gildas combined with continued respect for Bede – both, ironically, providential historians – is further problematised by the retrospective alignment made possible by surviving copies of the *Historia ecclesiastica* dating earlier than surviving copies of Bede's sources, notably Gildas's *De excidio.*[80] Attempts to illuminate Bede's dark age with sources that have been possibly interpolated by Bede's vision are in danger of circularity. This is exemplified with the struggle to contextualise modern images of Gildas.

The surviving Welsh and Irish annals, drawing on sources that can be firmly dated no earlier than the tenth century, report the death of Gildas around 570.[81] While these entries may reflect an accurate retrospective memory or even a contemporaneous record, they may also be influenced by a reading of Bede's *Historia ecclesiastica.* Bede's understanding of Gildas's notoriously opaque *quadragesimus quartus annus* passage is worth highlighting, along with Gildas's original:

> [Bede] From that time on, first the Britons won and then the enemy were victorious until the year of the siege of Mount Badon, when the Britons slaughtered no small number of their foes about forty-four years after their arrival in Britain.[82]

> [Gildas] From then on victory went now to our countrymen, now to their enemies: so that in this people the Lord could make trial (as he tends to) of his latter-day Israel to see whether it loves him or not. This lasted right up till the siege of Badon Hill, pretty well the last defeat of the villains, and certainly not the least. That was the year of my birth; as I know, one month of the forty-fourth year since then has already passed.[83]

Bede's reading of the forty-fourth year as relating to *ex eo tempore* and, in his interpretation, the *adventus Saxonum* as correlating with the third consulship of Aetius (446–54), places the siege of Badon Hill *ca* 489–97. A direct reading of the *quadragesimus quartus annus* passage from the *De excidio* can interpret the siege of Badon Hill as relating to the year of Gildas's birth. The effect of a combination of these readings is to place both the siege of Badon Hill and Gildas's birth in the same year in the last decade of the fifth century, with the implication that the *De excidio*

[79] George, *Gildas's* De Excidio, 48.

[80] For a surviving manuscript tradition of the *Historia ecclesiastica* dating back to the eighth century, see Bede, *Historia ecclesiastica* (edd. Colgrave & Mynors, xlii–xlvi). The earliest surviving manuscript of the *De excidio* dates to the ninth or tenth century. See above, 32, n. 2.

[81] See above, 36–7.

[82] Bede, *Historia ecclesiastica*, I.16 (edd. Colgrave & Mynors, 54–5): 'Et ex eo tempore nunc ciues nunc hostes uincebant usque ad annum obsessionis Badonici montis, quando non minimas eisdem hostibus strages dabant, quadragesimo circiter et quarto anno aduentus eorum in Brittaniam'.

[83] Gildas, *De excidio*, XXVI.1 (ed. Winterbottom, 98, trans., 28): 'Ex eo tempore nunc cives, nunc hostes, vincebant, ut in ista gente experiretur dominus solito more praesentem Israelem, utrum diligat eum an non: usque ad annum obsessionis Badonici montis, novissimaeque ferme de furciferis non minimae stragis, quique quadragesimus quartus (ut novi) orditur annus mense iam uno emenso, qui et meae nativitatis est'.

was written *ca* 540 (in Gildas's forty-fourth year) followed by a death *ca* 570. The chronology reinforces an annal entry that may have been constructed or adjusted in the same way. This problematic combination of readings, effectively doubling up Gildas's 'forty-fourth year' to present some ninety years between the *adventus* and the publication of the *De excidio*, still consciously and subconsciously influences modern scholarship.[84]

The annalistic tradition also raises difficulties when we turn to dating Gildas's letter to Finnian and Patrick's *Confessio* and *Epistola*. Based on entries originally attached to Easter tables, they were potentially constructed at a time when the controversy over Easter had been solved, but from material drawn from controversial Easter tables. The thirty-odd year discrepancy that is reported for Patrick (*ob. ca* 461 or 493) and Finnian (*ob. ca* 549 or 579), a discrepancy that potentially duplicates these figures, hints at problems interpreting two Christian solar dating schemes relating the Roman kalends to Easter tables: one from the fifth century, the *Anno Passionis* (A.P.) calendar, celebrating the first year as being from Christ's death and resurrection (i.e. A.P. 1, equivalent to A.D. 28–34); the other from the sixth century, the *Anno Domini* (A.D.) calendar, celebrating the first year as being from Christ's birth (i.e. A.D. 1).[85]

The Insular annals describing the British Isles in the early medieval period, while worthy of consideration, are not conclusive. The texts of Gildas and Patrick, difficult to date precisely, need to be contextualised in order to be placed within a chronology. But here, once again, existing interpretations are shaped by tradition: David Dumville's subsequent attempt to build a chronology of Britain purely from a

84 Various scholarly approaches to the 'quadragesimus quartus annus' passage are outlined in detail up to 1978 by O'Sullivan, *The* De excidio, 134–57. For a more up-to-date discussion, see Larpi, *Prolegomena*, 7–11. Dumville, 'The Chronology', 83–4, places Badon Hill *ca* 500 (presumably consciously of subconsciously following Bede), and Gildas's *De excidio ca* 545 (following Gildas). On this, see below. Charles-Edwards, *Wales and the Britons*, 217, following a similar trajectory, places Badon Hill *ca* 480s/90s (presumably consciously or subconsciously following Bede), and places Gildas's *De excidio ca* 530x545 (following Gildas). A rare voice unpicking this duplication of Bede/Gildas is Wood, 'The End of Roman Britain', 23, where he favours Bede's interpretation of Gildas's text over modern interpretations of Gildas's text. In this case, he places Gildas's birth in the year of the victory of Ambrosius Aurelianus (reported at *De excidio XXV*) and combines the publication of the *De excidio* with the siege of Badon Hill, placing these contemporaneous events as early as *ca* 485. For nuanced support of Wood's position, see Joyce, 'A New Source'.

85 For examples on Patrick, see *The Annals of Ulster* (edd. Mac Airt & Mac Niocaill), AU457.2: 'Quies senis Patricii, ut alii libri dicunt' [Repose of the elder Patrick, as some books state]; AU461.2: 'Hic alii quietem Patrici dicunt' [Here some record the repose of Patrick]; AU492.1: 'Dicunt Scoiti hic Patricium archiepiscopum defunctum fore' [The Irish state here that Patrick the Archbishop died]; AU493.4: 'Patricius archiapostulus archiepiscopus et apostolus Scotorum quieuit 16 kl. Aprilis, .c.xx. anno etatis sue, .lx. autem quo uenit ad Hiberniam anno ad babtistandos Scotos' [Patrick, arch-apostle, or archbishop and apostle of the Irish, rested on the 16th of the Kalends of April in the 120th year of his age, in the 60th year after he had come to Ireland to baptize the Irish]. For examples on Finnian, see *The Annals of Ulster* (edd. Mac Airt & Mac Niocaill), AU549.3: 'Mortalitas magna in qua isti pausant: Finnio maccu Telduib' [A great mortality in which these rested: Finnia moccu Telduib]; AU579.1: 'Quies Uinniani episcopi, m. nepotis Fiatach' [Repose of bishop Finnian moccu Fiatach]. For the potential problems in relating A.P. to A.D., see Storey, 'The Frankish Annals', 86–8. While the issue of A.P. and A.D. might favour the later dates, we cannot be certain that A.D. dates were not subsequently perceived as A.P. dates, and converted erroneously. Victorius's passion date is A.D. 28; Bede's is A.D. 34. See Ohashi, '"Sexta aetas"', 58–9.

contextual analysis of Book I of the *De excidio* simply results in the same chronology as supported by the annals, one based on a possible duplication of the *quadragesimus quartus annus* passage and an acceptance of Gildas's error in his placing of the letter to Aetius.[86] It is worth setting out a brief version of Dumville's chronology:

446x454	The *miserae reliquiae* appeal by letter to Agitius-Aëtius, *ter consul*
ca 500+	Battle of Mount Badon. Slaughter of the Saxons.
ca 500 x *ca* 545	Gildas's lifetime. Up to his 44th year, that of writing.

The fixation on *Agitius ter consul* as a genuine historical detail, rather than, say, as a subsequent interpolation identifying Agitius as Aetius, or as an erroneous scribal rendition of a third delivery (*agere*) of a request for military assistance from British *consiliari*, continues to contribute to the 'demonising' of Gildas's historical reputation.[87]

The favoured modern image of a sixth-century Gildas is, thus, a chronological construct created, in part, to help explicate the contexts of the Insular texts that fall within Bede's dark age, namely Patrick's *Confessio* and *Epistola*, and Gildas's *De excidio* and *fragmenta*, particularly as they relate to continental texts such as Constantius's *Vita Germani*. However, as mentioned in Chapter 1, the interrelationship between these texts within this chronology is problematic: they do not support each other's historical vision. Scholars, following the example of Dumville, have consequently continued to examine these texts through relating them to developments in the history of theology and literary culture as well as in archaeology.

Images of authority: towards new narratives

The main attempts to resolve these chronological questions in recent years have been to contextualise the sources under discussion through an examination of the doctrinal images projected by their authors. The fifth century saw a fundamental theological argument between Bishop Augustine of Hippo (supported by Jerome) and the Irish or British monk Pelagius (supported by the priest Caelestius (*fl. ca* 390–430)) over the role of divine will and human agency in salvation, a conflict replicated in Gaul and Britain.[88] Augustine's victory over Pelagius and Caelestius through anathemas issued and confirmed in 418 and 431, supported by Germanus's victories in a British context in 429 and *ca* 437–48, emphasised the more intangible role of faith and divine grace in salvation over a Pelagian position, possibly caricatured, that assured salvation through obedience to the divine precepts and attention to good deeds.[89]

86 Dumville, 'The Chronology', 83.

87 The *De excidio* is unlikely to be perfectly preserved, even in Bede's time: Gildas's Saxon prophecy, possibly influential on Bede, is potentially an interpolation. See Chapter 1, 20. The letter to Aetius is the third British request for Roman aid in Gildas's providential history. The *ter consul* as a potential interpolation is explored by Jones, 'The Appeal to Aetius', but in a context where he proposes another figure, Aegidius (*fl. ca* 456–65), as the Agitius mentioned by Gildas.

88 On Augustine's struggle with Pelagius see Brown, *Augustine of Hippo*, 340–53. See also Rees, *Pelagius*, 1–7.

89 Pelagianism was anathematised at the Council of Carthage in 418. See *Concilium Carthaginense a. 418*, in *Concilia Africae 345–525* (ed. Munier, 69–77). The decision was subsequently confirmed at the First Council of Ephesus in 431, canons I and IV. See *Concilium Universale*

A subsequent radical interpretation of Augustine's position that deemed only faith as significant to salvation (an interpretation known as 'predestinarianism') provoked a response reemphasising the consequences of inaction and sin. Championed principally in Gaul by monastic writers such as John Cassian (*ob. ca* 435), this response emphasised both faith and deeds as significant to salvation, a position anachronistically and pejoratively termed 'semi-Pelagian' in the early modern period but effectively a moderating and unifying endeavour to reframe traditional teachings in light of the fractious doctrinal debates between Augustine and Pelagius and their supporters.[90] This view was dominant in Gaul *ca* 473–4 when the Synods of Arles and Lyon condemned predestinarianism.[91] Augustine's teachings were re-emphasised in a Gallic context some two generations later at the Second Council of Orange in 529, where the bishops affirmed the significance of divine grace in salvation, but denied predestinarianism.[92]

Thus, we have, in a sketch, a period in Britain around the first quarter of the fifth century in which the teachings of Pelagius (*ob. ca* 418) appear to be influential. This was then followed by a turbulent period in Britain around the second quarter of the fifth century, as exemplified by the interventions of Germanus of Auxerre (*ob. ca* 437–48), in which Pelagian thought was directly challenged. In the second half of the fifth century and the first quarter of the sixth century, a compromise period followed, potentially reflecting activity in Gaul, tempering the more radical aspects of Pelagian and Augustinian thought, as represented by the influence of the teachings of Cassian. This view, influential on Insular monasticism, would continue to be persuasive in the sixth century alongside the efforts of Gallic bishops to further refine orthodox doctrine from an Augustinian perspective. It is important to note that both perspectives, critical of each other on the interpretation of some finer points of doctrine, were considered orthodox in the sixth century: the monk Columbanus may have had his clerical detractors, but none publicly accused him of heresy.

While the Insular annal entries describing the fifth and sixth centuries continue to frame a disconnect between Germanus, Patrick, and Gildas, analyses of their representative texts suggest a shared context. Notably, in the case of the *Confessio* and *Epistola*, is Patrick's emphasis on grace in defence of his role as a bishop.[93] A

Ephesenum Anno 431 (ed. Schwartz, *Acta*, I.5.1, 27–8). As noted earlier, Bonner, *The Myth of Pelagianism*, will be set aside. For a more nuanced approach to the history of Pelagianism, one that accepts the historical record on Pelagianism but investigates the complexities of 'orthodoxy' as an evolving construct rather than a monolithic constant, see Markus, 'The Legacy of Pelagius'.

90 On anachronistic attempts to situate Cassian within 'semi-Pelagianism' rather than as a gifted exponent of contemporary orthodoxy, see Cassiday, *Tradition and Theology*. For a study of 'semi-Pelagianism', see Weaver, *Divine Grace*.

91 As reported in Bishop Faustus of Riez's letter to the errant priest Lucidus. See Faustus of Riez, *Epistula Ad Lucidum* (ed. Engelbrecht, *Epistolae*, 161–4).

92 Pelagian thought was once again condemned at the Second Council of Orange in 529, under the auspices of the former monk, Bishop Caesarius of Arles (*ob. ca* 542), who was influenced by both Augustine and Cassian. See *Concilium Arausicanum a. 529* (ed. de Clercq, *Concilia*, 55–62). While the canons can be seen to be critical of elements of Cassianic thought, Cassian is not named and continued to be held in esteem, albeit in a nuanced fashion, in the sixth century: see Stewart, *Cassian the Monk*, 24–5. On the unusual nature of the Second Council of Orange, and an assessment of its canons and impact, see Mathisen, 'Caesarius of Arles'.

93 For example, Patrick, *Confessio*, I (ed. Howlett, 52–3): 'Unde autem tacere non possum neque expedit quidem tanta beneficia et tantum gratiam quam mihi Dominus praestare dignatus est'

theologically uncontroversial defence utilising both grace and predestination implies that Patrick aligned himself with the preaching of Germanus in the brief window, paralleling developments in Gaul, which embraced Augustinian thought.[94] Alison Bonner's innovative work on Patrick's routine use of an unreconstructed form of Augustinian theology, while acutely aware of the controversy over dating, appears to promote the traditional dating of his texts to the middle of the fifth century and his death *ca* 461.[95]

Studies of the apparent doctrinal positions taken in the *Vita Germani* and the *De excidio*, on the other hand, continue to be influenced by assumptions framed by traditional contexts. Constantius, in emphasising Germanus's defeat of Pelagianism in Britain, is assumed to have sympathies with Augustine's teachings on grace; Gildas, in being silent on Germanus's visits to Britain, is assumed to have sympathies with Pelagius's teachings on deeds.[96] However, both narratives appear to place themselves against a backdrop where grace and deeds are equally significant, making their doctrinal contexts less certain. While Gildas does not emphasise doctrinal heresy, and his *De excidio* inhabits a religious landscape dominated by habitual sin, he does pause briefly to emphasise the importance of grace and deeds in his preface:

> I knew the Lord was merciful, but I feared his judgement too. I praised his graciousness, but I was afraid of the reward of every man according to his deeds.[97]

Similarly, Constantius, while describing Germanus as a conduit for miraculous grace in his correction of the followers of Pelagius, also emphasises his deeds:

> But He who was calling him to glory hastened his journey; the Lord was inviting the tired hero to receive the reward of his laborious days.[98]

Gildas and Constantius, in identifying different threats to the church, appear to emphasise both grace and deeds, but in a prosaic fashion, without attention to the finer doctrinal arguments of either Pelagius or Augustine.[99] In this instance, atten-

[Whence moreover I cannot be silent, nor assuredly is it expedient, about such great benefits and such great grace, which the Lord has deigned to supply to me].

94 Patrick, *Epistola*, II (ed. Howlett, 28–9), specifically uses the word 'predestined': 'Partem habeo cum his quos aduocauit et praedestinauit euangelium praedicare in persecutionibus non paruis usque ad extremum terrae' [I have a part with those whom He has called to (Him) and predestined to proclaim the Gospel among not insignificant persecutions as far as the remote part of land].

95 See Bonner, 'Was Patrick Influenced', 602–7.

96 For a brief review of these positions, see George, *Gildas's* De excidio, 110–13, and 119–20. On 113, she describes Constantius as a supporter of Augustinian doctrine; on 129, she describes Gildas as someone concerned with aspects of Augustine's doctrine on grace.

97 Gildas, *De excidio*, I.11 (ed. Winterbottom, 88, trans, 14): 'Sciebam misericordiam domini, sed et iudicium timebam; laudabam gratiam, sed redditionem unicuique secundum opera sua verebar'. Gildas's mention of grace and deeds is just prior to his mention of the 'predestinarian' heresy of the Nicolaitans.

98 Constantius, *Vita Germani*, VII.42 (ed. Borius, 198): 'Accelerabat transitum qui uocabat ad gloriam et fessum eroam laboribus Dominus inuitabat ad praemia'. For the debate over the year of Germanus's death (the year in which his second visit to Britain took place according to his *vita*), see Sharpe, 'Martyrs and Local Saints', 80, n. 22.

99 As with Gildas's *De excidio* and *fragmenta*, there appears to be no discernible influence of Augustine on the *Vita Germani* that I can detect by a direct comparison with the works of Augustine.

tion given to contextualising their indistinct doctrinal images has served, rather, to disguise a more fundamental theme linking their works: that of the role of episcopal authority and its relationship to secular authority.[100] This perspective, one that combines with the anxieties of Patrick, hints at the possibility that Patrick, Constantius, and Gildas shared similar concerns about authority, although they responded in different ways.

This shared context is supported by other studies. Arguments that Gildas's literary culture is profoundly classical have contributed to uncertainty over the dating of the *De excidio*, now placed anywhere between 479 and 550.[101] This uncertainty aligns with continental sources and archaeological evidence that have moved Bede's *adventus Saxonum* from the third consulship of Aetius (446–54) back to *ca* 440–2 (as an *adventus* in a political sense), and potentially as far back as the 420s (as an *adventus* in a physical sense).[102] The fluidity of the dates assigned to Patrick's *Confessio* and *Epistola* and Gildas's *De excidio*, as they relate to Constantius's *Vita Germani*, has resulted in an unsatisfactory return to a chronology possibly influenced by a duplicate reading of the *quadragesimus quartus annus* passage, an acceptance of Gildas as an unreliable historian, and an inconclusive Insular annalistic tradition. Once again, this draws attention to Gildas's notable silence on Pelagius, Patrick, and Germanus in his providential history. However, if we set aside Bede's emphasis on the problematic historical detail of *Agitius ter consul* in his providential structuring of the *Historia ecclesiastica*, we are left with the historical traditions that Bede represents: in the early eighth century there was a perspective that Gildas's *quadragesimus quartus annus* – and, therefore, his birth – related not to the siege of Badon Hill but to the *adventus Saxonum*, a period also connected to the episcopal interventions of Germanus. Bede's representation of the past suggests a context for Gildas's *De excidio* in the late fifth century, an argument also put forward by Ian Wood.[103]

An emphasis on the relationship between episcopal and secular authority in the *De excidio* and the *Vita Germani* raises the possibility that these texts may be addressing a similar context evident in Patrick's *Confessio* and *Epistola*.[104] If, following Bede's singular reading of the *quadragesimus quartus annus* passage, we place these uniquely historical texts within contemporary debates in the fifth century, their

This is curious if Constantius's sole purpose was to refute Pelagius. Gildas's doctrinal position is further explored in Chapter 3.

[100] Ian Wood notes the *Vita Germani* as a 'handbook for bishops'. See Wood, 'The End of Roman Britain', 9.

[101] For literary analyses, see Lapidge & Dumville (edd.), *Gildas*; Wright, *History and Literature*.

[102] From an archaeological perspective, see Dark, *Britain and the End*, 48–9, where the dating of the *adventus* can be drawn back as early as *ca* 420. Michael Jones posits that the *adventus Saxonum*, defined in keeping with British and English traditions of an original, identifiable settlement leading to permanent independent kingdoms, must be dated on the basis of continental evidence to between 410 and 441/2. See Jones, *The End of Roman Britain*, 42. Jones's end dates are influenced by the *Gallic Chronicle of 452*. See Chapter 1, 15–16.

[103] Wood, 'The End of Roman Britain', 23.

[104] For the dating of the *Vita Germani*, see Chapter 1, 14, n. 3. Sharpe remains an outlier, but his observation that the *Vita Germani* was written earlier than *ca* 480, perhaps *ca* 470 or earlier, does not mitigate against a publication date *ca* 480. The manuscript for the *Vita Germani* was circulated for a period prior to publication.

similarities and differences offer a new approach.[105] It is worth returning to a new version of the *schema* from Chapter 1:

1. [*ca* 450] In his *Confessio*, Patrick defends his appointment to episcopal office against charges of corruption, describing an Insular church enforcing church discipline. As a bishop with ecclesiastical responsibilities in Ireland, he issues a letter of excommunication to a British secular leader Coroticus (*Epistola*) in response to a political and ecclesiastical crisis engendered by Christians enslaving Christians.
2. [*ca* 480] Gildas's *De excidio* describes a sinful Britain partitioned with pagan Saxons and Picts and denounces a British church where worldly bishops collude with tyrannical kings. In linking this political and ecclesiastical crisis to endemic sin, but singularly avoiding calls for excommunication, Gildas advocates a return to a 'golden-age' in cooperative Christian governance around the middle of the fifth century, as chastened by the Saxon rebellion and informed by a model of authority inspired by the Old Testament.[106]
3. [*ca* 480] Constantius's *Vita Germani* describes a flourishing British church known through two interventions, supported by the Gallic church, of the ascetic Roman aristocrat, bishop, and imperial agent, Germanus of Auxerre, against the heresy of Pelagius. In emphasising Germanus's episcopal role in saving Britain through debate, example, and a judicious use of excommunication, Constantius, singularly not referring to British kings, connects Britain's contemporary fortunes to a 'golden-age' in Christian imperial governance around the middle of the fifth century, as represented by the western Roman emperor, Valentinian III (*r.* 425–55), and his devoutly Christian mother, Empress Galla Placidia (*ob.* 450).[107]

The key texts describing the Christian culture of the British Isles in the fifth century appear to represent debates over the structuring of authority.

105 Gildas's unique approach to history is noted in the Introduction. Andrew Gillett has pointed out Constantius's unique literary style creates the 'illusion of historicity': see Gillett, *Envoys and Political Communication*, 125.

106 Gildas, *De excidio*, XXVI.2–3 (ed. Winterbottom, 98–9, trans, 28): 'Haesit etenim tam desperati insulae excidii insperatique mentio auxilii memoriae eorum qui utriusque miraculi testes extitere: et ob hoc reges, publici, privati, sacerdotes, ecclesiastici, suum quique ordinem servarunt' [For the remembrance of so desperate a blow to the island and of such unlooked for recovery stuck in the minds of those who witnessed both wonders. That was why kings, public and private persons, priests and churchmen, kept to their own station]. If we can date the Saxon rebellion to the early 440s, then an 'unlooked for recovery' could be placed *ca* 450.

107 For the judicious use of excommunication, see Constantius, *Vita Germani*, V.26 (ed. Borius, 170–2): 'Recognoscit populum in ea qua reliquerat credulitate durantem, intelligunt culpam esse paucorum, inquirunt auctores inuentosque condemnant' [(Germanus) could see that the people as a whole had persevered in the faith in which he had left them and the bishops realised that the fallings-away had been the work only of a few. These were identified and formally condemned]. For the piety of Valentinian and Placidia, see Constantius, *Vita Germani*, VII.35 (ed. Borius, 188): 'Regebat etiam Romanum imperium Placidia regina cum filio Valentiniano iam iuuene. Qui ita fidem catholicam diligebant ut, cum omnibus imperarent, Dei famulis sublimi humilitate seruirent' [The Empress Placidia reigned over the Roman Empire jointly with her son Valentinian, who was still a young man. They loved the Catholic faith so well that, though rulers of all, they obeyed with the deepest humility the servants of God].

Gildas constructed a providential history of Britain as a foundation to his prophetic claim as an authority on church law. In order to explore new perspectives on the evolution of the Christian culture of the British Isles in the early medieval period, it is important to unpack Gildas's claim to authority and his descriptions of the legal expectations of secular and ecclesiastical authority in his *De excidio*. The authority on which Gildas himself drew to buttress his claim needs to be examined. It is to Gildas's denunciation of a wasteland of sin caused by worldly kings and submissive clerics that we now turn.

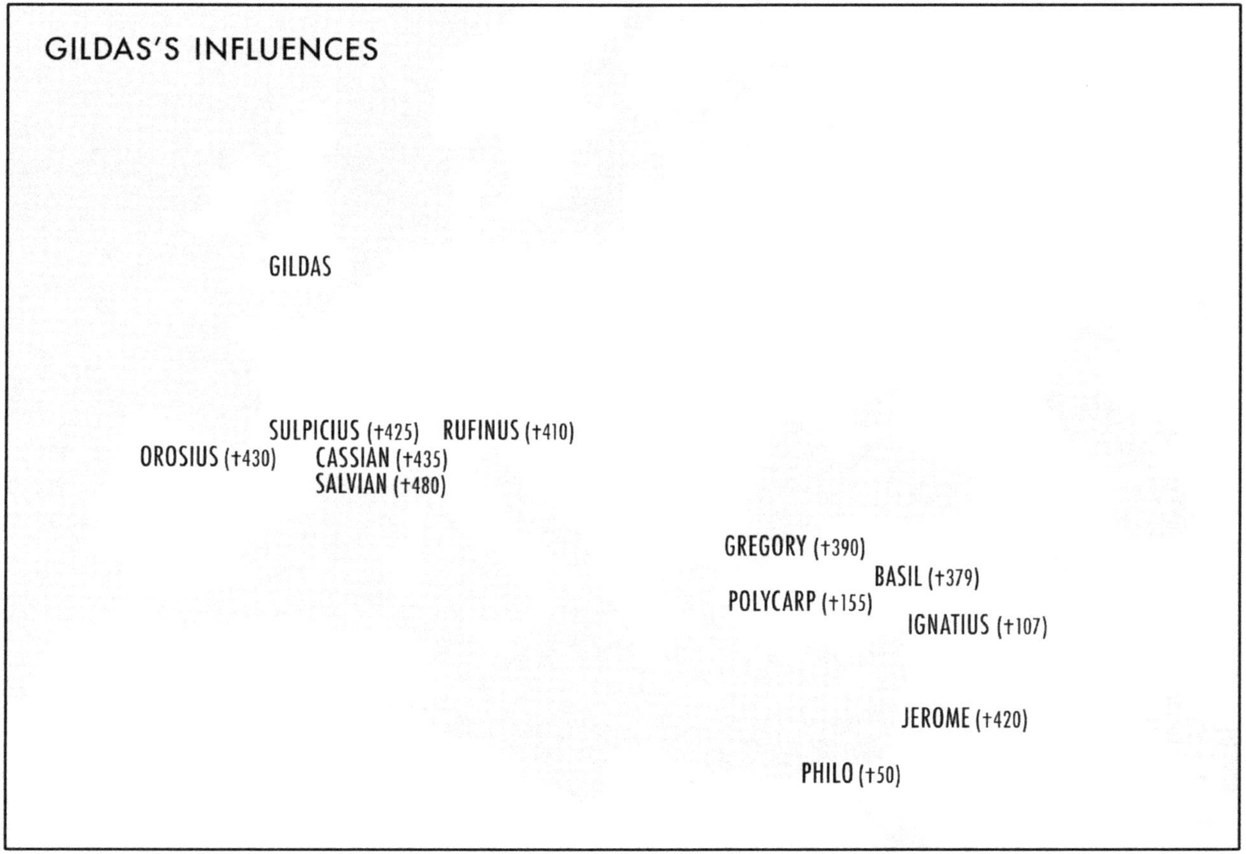

Regional distribution of church authorities drawn on by Gildas in his writing.

3

GILDAS'S *DE EXCIDIO* – AUTHORITY AND THE MONASTIC IDEAL

Bede's representation of Gildas as a 'doleful historian' created an emphasis on the *De excidio* that has overshadowed the contribution of the letter to Finnian. The outcome has been a preference for the polemical and judgemental image drawn from the *De excidio*, one that overlooks the moderate and judicious image remembered in the *fragmenta*. This preferred aspect has, in turn, subtly legitimised Bede's construction of a dark age *ca* 450–600, perpetuating notions of disorganisation and fragmentation in the Insular church. The image of Gildas *Historicus*, upheld by Bede as the most significant witness to a political and ecclesiastical rupture in Britain in the fifth and sixth centuries, has cultivated an understanding of the *De excidio* as a negative and unsuccessful intervention.

Yet clearly, from an Irish perspective, the image of Gildas *Sapiens* as an expert in canon law implies a memory of the *De excidio* as a positive and successful intervention that established Gildas as an authority. The *De excidio* of Gildas *Sapiens* emphasises his immediate concerns: the providential history of Book I foregrounds the divine favour contingent on accepting his plea for a return to proper Christian governance; Books II and III detail the discrepancies between the contemporary behaviours of kings and clerics and biblical expectations, simultaneously criticising and legitimising these roles as crucial to good Christian governance. The immediate problem for Gildas was how to defend his model of authority without having the formal standing in which to articulate it. He makes clear the challenge he faced:

> What, you wretch (I say to myself), have you, like some important and eminent teacher, been given the task of standing up against the blows of so violent a torrent, against the rope of congenital sins that has been stretched far and wide for so many years together? Look after what is committed to your trust, and keep silent. Otherwise it is like saying to the foot: Keep watch, and to the hand: Speak. Britain has her governors, she has her watchmen. Why should *you* stutter out your ineptitudes?[1]

Gildas's criticisms of his seniors were forged from an acknowledged position outside the established order. To make these criticisms meaningful, he had to establish

[1] Gildas, *De excidio*, I.14 (ed. Winterbottom, 88–9, trans., 15): 'Quid? (mihimet aio) tibine, miser, veluti conspicuo ac summo doctori talis cura committitur ut obstes ictibus tam violenti torrentis, et contra hunc inolitorum scelerum funem per tot annorum spatia ininterrupte lateque protractum? Serves depositum tibi creditum et taceas. Alioquin hoc est dixisse pedi: speculare et manui: fare. Habet Britannia rectores, habet speculatores. Quid tu nugando mutire disponis?' Charles-Edwards, *Wales and the Britons*, 206, argues that Gildas is stating, via a modesty trope, that he is a *doctor*. However, this interpretation appears to contradict the sense of this passage. If Gildas was a *doctor* and already one of the *rectores* or *speculatores* of *Britannia*, he would not need to debate his authority to speak out.

his credentials. How Gildas constructed his credentials is crucial to understanding his intervention.

In establishing his authority to speak out, Gildas looked to a select vision of the present and the past. Setting aside the historiographical and biblical inspirations for the *De excidio*, this chapter examines Gildas's place within the Insular church and the significant monastic figures, namely Jerome (*ca* 347–420) and John Cassian (*ca* 360–435), whom Gildas used to shape his perspective on contemporary authority in *Britannia*. Rather than attempting to define Gildas solely by arguments framed by his silences, it explores the model of authority he puts forward in his *De excidio*.[2] In doing so, I argue that Gildas drew primarily on his status as a monk to legitimate his intervention. In doing so, he appended Cassian's interpretation of Jerome – one that defined the monastery as the educational foundation for both the 'holy man' and the cleric – to a model of authority based on the biblical image of the kingdom of Israel, one that included kings. In stressing the 'holy man' as a complementary authority to kings and clerics, Gildas emphasised the monastery as a complementary institution to the secular aristocracies and the church; each institution, in its own way, the provider of governors (*rectores*) and watchmen (*speculatores*) to the orders that made up Gildas's *Britannia*.

Returning to Gildas's *De excidio*

Gildas was constantly aware in his *De excidio* that he stood outside the established order. Unlike Constantius, he had no commission to write, nor does he refer to any patron.[3] His oblique reference to his status as a cleric implies this role was not significant enough to attach any meaningful authority to his voice alone.[4] The only other traction he may have had was his possible position as an aristocrat, but he does not invoke this. In constructing his highly innovative *De excidio*, Gildas would only look within *Britannia*'s shared culture of *romanitas* to the divine authority of the Bible and the interpretive authority of the church fathers to buttress his right to criticise his seniors.

Gildas set about crafting the *De excidio* as an *epistola*, rhetorically structured into three discrete sections or books.[5] Book I begins with a lengthy preface (*praefatio*) establishing the tone and motive for writing, followed by a brief providential history (*historia*) of Britain that overtly mirrors that of biblical Israel and provides the providential context for his intervention. Book II contains a targeted admonition of five

2 This chapter draws on material already published: see Joyce, 'Contested Origins'. I would like to thank the *Journal of the Australian Early Medieval Association* for permission.

3 Gildas only refers to a past debt that needs to be repaid. See Gildas, *De excidio*, I.16 (ed. Winterbottom, 89, trans., 16): 'persolvo debitum multo tempore antea exactum' [I now pay the debt so long ago incurred]. Constantius's patrons for his *Vita Germani* are the bishops Patiens of Lyon (*ob. ca* 480) and Censurius of Auxerre (*ob. ca* 486).

4 Gildas refers to his clerical status at Gildas, *De excidio*, LXV.1 (ed. Winterbottom, 118, trans., 51): 'episcoporum vel ceterorum sacerdotum aut clericorum in nostro quoque ordine' [by bishops and other priests and clerics of my order also]. For more on this, see below, 61–2.

5 O'Sullivan, *The* De Excidio, 2–3, has a table describing the basic structuring of Gildas's *epistola*. Lapidge, 'Gildas's Education', 41–2, has a legal structuring of the *De excidio* according to the rhetorical conventions of *romanitas*. See also Howlett, *The Celtic Latin Tradition*, 73. Howlett offers a different structure from Lapidge, but not in a way that undermines the basic argument of a rhetorical structuring of the *De excidio*.

corrupt contemporary kings followed by biblical passages applicable to both wicked and good rulers.[6] Book III contains a general admonition of corrupt contemporary clergy followed by biblical passages applicable to both unworthy and worthy priests. It ends in a brief conclusion (*epilogus*) calling for repentance and obedience to God's Law.

In his open letter, Gildas describes a *Britannia* fragmented by civil war and sin. Addressing this moral and political crisis, he calls for the spiritual and physical restoration of his divided homeland through obedience to God's Law. His letter is addressed to those he deems to be legitimately appointed to defend its secular and spiritual welfare; the remaining Christian secular and church leaders within *Britannia*, the majority probably based in west Britain. Gildas legitimates his immediate criticisms of these secular and church leaders within the rhetorical conventions of *romanitas* and the 'divine' conventions of the Bible. These leaders clearly had the education to, at least, recognise these cultural legitimations.

Gildas's emphasis was on divine punishment as a just retribution for sinful deeds: *sed redditionem unicuique secundum opera sua verebar*, 'but I was afraid of the reward for every man according to his deeds'.[7] This emphasis, predicated on a personal revelation linking this phrase from Matthew 16.27 and Romans 2.6 to Jeremiah 50.29, supported Gildas's identification of a divided Britain with a divided Israel prior to the fall of Judah and Jerusalem to the Babylonians.[8] In declaring that he 'saw how clearly the men of our day have increasingly put care aside, as though there was nothing to fear', Gildas drew directly on the description of biblical Israel as laid out in Jeremiah 3.6–11: Israel was divided into two kingdoms, Judah and Israel; these two kingdoms were, in turn, unfaithful (poor Jews) and faithless (idolaters); God instructed Jeremiah to warn unfaithful Judah but they ignored his warnings, with God, preferring faithless Israel, abandoning and destroying unfaithful Judah.[9] The revelation for Gildas was clear. Directly equating Christian Britain with unfaithful

6 The tyrants are named as Constantine, Vortipor, Aurelius Caninus, Cuneglasus, and Maglocunus. For a discussion of the named tyrants, see O'Sullivan, *The* De Excidio, 87–133, and Dumville, 'Gildas and Maelgwn'.

7 Gildas, *De excidio*, I.11 (ed. Winterbottom, 88, trans., 14). Both David Howlett and Karen George have noted Gildas's *praefatio* is defined by a symmetrical repetition that emphasises this biblical phrase. See Howlett, *Celtic Latin Tradition*, 72–81; George, *Gildas's* De Excidio, 46.

8 Gildas's notes a personal revelation connecting the Old and New Testaments at Gildas, *De excidio*, I.7 (ed. Winterbottom, 88, trans., 14): 'Ista ego et multa alia veluti speculum quoddam vitae nostrae in scripturis veteribus intuens, convertebar etiam ad novas, et ibi legebam clarius quae mihi forsitan antea obscura fuerant, cessante umbra ac veritate firmius inlucescente' [I gazed on these things and many others in the Old Testament as though on a mirror reflecting our own life; then I turned to the New Testament also, and read there more clearly what had previously, perhaps, been dark to me: the shadow passed away, and the truth shone forth more boldly]. The following section links themes from Matthew, Paul, and Jeremiah. See Joyce, 'Gildas and His Prophecy for Britain', 41–5. Gildas describes Britain as *praesens Israel* at Gildas, *De excidio*, XXVI.1 (ed. Winterbottom, 98, trans., 28): 'ut in ista gente experiretur dominus solito more praesentum Israelem' [so that in this people the Lord could make trial (as he tends to) of his latter-day Israel].

9 Gildas, *De excidio*, I.12 (ed. Winterbottom, 88, trans., 15): 'Videbam e regione quantum securitatis hominibus nostri temporis, ac si non esset quod timeretur, increverat'. Most notably at Jeremiah 3.8: 'quia pro eo quod moechata esset aversatrix Israel, dimisissem eam, et dedissem ei libellum repudii: et non timuit praevaricatrix Juda soror ejus, sed abiit, et fornicata est etiam ipsa' [That because the rebellious Israel had played the harlot, I had put her away, and had given her a bill of divorce: yet her treacherous sister Juda was not afraid, but went and played the harlot also herself].

Judah, and pagan Britain with faithless Israel, Gildas anticipated two outcomes: obedience to God's Law would result in the reunification of *Britannia* under the royal house of west Britain (as Judah); continued disobedience would result in the abandonment of the Britons by God and the establishment of a new covenant with the pagan peoples in the east and north.[10]

In denouncing his contemporary generation of ruthless secular leaders and corrupt church leaders within the prophetic tradition, Gildas took a risk, not only personally, but in credibility. Gildas drew on an array of legitimations in constructing his message: his use of the legal conventions of *romanitas* via his Latinity and rhetorical structures; his use of biblical *exempla*, exegesis, and styles; his construction from historical sources of a narrative history that emphasised a providential judgment for sin.[11] These legitimations were reinforced by the profound monastic influences of the biblical scholar, Jerome, the reformer, John Cassian, and the moraliser, Salvian.[12] Other profound influences, in a historiographic sense, were the monk, Rufinus of Aquileia (*ca* 340–410), and his translation and updating of the *Historia ecclesiastica* by Bishop Eusebius of Caesarea (*ca* 260–340), and the ascetic priest, Orosius of Braga (*ca* 375–420), disciple of Augustine of Hippo and author of the *Historia adversum paganos*.[13] Ascetics directly influenced by monasticism clearly lay at the heart of Gildas's vision for Britain. In attacking secular and church leaders dominated by worldly values, Gildas was articulating these monastic authorities as an answer to corruption within the church and the wider community. Significantly, he was also using these patristic authorities to buttress his claim to prophecy. That Gildas himself subsequently became revered by a later generation as a spiritual authority implies that his intervention – as legitimated by these authorities – was accepted in some form by the audience he was addressing.[14]

Gildas's emphasis on divine punishment based on deeds appears to place him within a monastic tradition that emphasised sin and *praesens iudicium*, or 'judgement in the here and now', and distanced itself from a clerical perspective that contrasted faith with the threat of heresy. The historical absence of the episcopal authority of Germanus and his struggles against the heresy of Pelagianism in Gildas's providential history is matched, in this sense, by Gildas's silence on the episcopal authority of

10 See Joyce, 'Gildas and His Prophecy for Britain', 41–5. Indeed, the connection made between the tyrants and the Kings of Judah is direct in the case of Vortipor: see Gildas, *De excidio*, XXXI.1 (ed. Winterbottom, 101, trans., 31): 'boni regis nequam fili, ut Ezechiae Manasses' [bad son of a good king (like Manasseh son of Hezekiah)].

11 See, for example, Lapidge, 'Gildas's Education'; Howlett, *The Celtic Latin Tradition*, 72–81.

12 For a study of Gildas's patristic influences, see Kerlouégan, *Le De excidio*; Wright, 'Gildas's Reading', 152, has a useful table.

13 See Wright, 'Gildas's Reading', 146–50 for Rufinus, and 144–6 for Orosius. For an overview of Eusebian political theology and its impact on the West, see Oakley, *Empty Bottles of Gentilism*, 89–98 and 112–17. On Orosius's relationship with asceticism, see, briefly, Markus, *The End of Ancient Christianity*, 66. A more oblique influence may well be the fourth-century, heavily Christianised, Latin translation and adaptation of the *Jewish Wars* by the Jewish historian Flavius Josephus (*ca* 37–100), travelling under the title *De Excidio Hierosolymitano* and attributed to the Christian historian Hegesippus (*ca* 110–180). On this text, see Pollard, 'The *De excidio* of "Hegesippus"'. In this context, Gildas would be drawing on a Judaeo-Christian historiographical lineage.

14 See Sharpe, 'Gildas as a Father of the Church', 193–4. Sharpe notes, based on the evidence of Columbanus's letter to Gregory, that Gildas was asked for advice on a matter of church discipline and came to be regarded as an authority amongst the 'Celtic Churches'.

the church father, Augustine of Hippo.[15] Gildas's position as a cleric who primarily draws on monastic authority when addressing the kings and clerics of his *patria* in the prophetic tradition is, thus, significant. Setting aside both Gildas's use of the Bible (as covered most recently by Thomas O'Loughlin) and his use of the historiographical leitmotifs of Rufinus and Orosius (as covered by Robert Hanning and Neil Wright), we need to elucidate Gildas's relationship with monasticism.[16]

Gildas and monasticism

In order to clarify Gildas's relationship with monasticism it is important to contextualise the cultural influences underpinning his criticisms of the secular and church leaders of Britain. That the *De excidio* is a product of 'a mind well-versed in the Latin library tradition' is evident from the seminal work of François Kerlouégan, Michael Winterbottom, Michael Lapidge, and Neil Wright, who all established Gildas's Late Latin credentials.[17] Kerlouégan himself concluded that Gildas's prose was not a unique and bizarre example of Insular Latin, but rather closely allied to the style of mid to late fifth-century Christian rhetoricians such as the aristocrat and bishop, Sidonius Apollinaris (*ca* 430–89), in Gaul.[18] This cultural link to fifth-century Gaul is reinforced by the influence on the *De excidio* of the monk and priest, Salvian of Marseilles, whose *De gubernatione Dei* (*ca* 440), and its representation of the Roman empire as a 'failed Israel' beset by sin, provides the closest literary parallel to the *De excidio*.[19] The influence of Salvian is further reinforced when we see that, in emphasising the phrase from Jeremiah 50.29, Gildas recalls the last biblical quote of *De gubernatione Dei* where Salvian relates the Vandal invasion of Roman Africa to divine punishment for sin.[20] Salvian, a former monk of the influential monastery of Lérins, was a generational contemporary of John Cassian, also based in Marseilles. Cassian's two works – *Institutes* (*ca* 420) and *Conferences* (*ca* 426–30) – profoundly

15 See below, 64–5 for a discussion on this point.

16 O'Loughlin, *Gildas and the Scriptures*; Hanning, *The Vision of History*; Wright, 'Did Gildas Read Orosius?'; Wright, 'Gildas's Prose Style'.

17 Wright, 'Gildas's Prose Style', 107–8; Kerlouégan, 'Le Latin', 151–76; *Gildas* (ed. Winterbottom, 5–9); Lapidge, 'Gildas's Education'.

18 Kerlouégan, 'Le Latin', 156.

19 See Hanning, *The Vision of History*, 46–8; O'Sullivan, *The* De Excidio, 60–1. *De gubernatione dei* is generally dated from internal evidence to the first half of the 440s. See Lambert, 'The Uses of Decay', 115, n. 1.

20 Salvian, *De gubernatione Dei*, VIII, V.25 (ed. Lagarrigue): 'Iustus ergo est dominus et iustum iudicium suum; quae enim, ut scriptum est, seminarunt, haec et metunt, ut uere uideatur de improbitate illius gentis dixisse dominus: Reddite ei secundum opus suum; iuxta omnia quae fecit facite illi, quia contra dominum erecta est' [So God is just and his judgments are righteous, for, as the Scripture says: 'What men have sowed, that shall they also reap'. God seems to have referred to the wickedness of the people of Africa, when he said: 'Recompense her according to her work; according to all that she hath done do unto her; for she hath been proud against the Lord']. Translations, unless otherwise stated, are from Salvian, *On the Government of God* (trans. Sanford). The work ends abruptly and is either unfinished or incomplete. Gildas, *De excidio*, I.11 (ed. Winterbottom, 88, trans., 14): 'Sciebam misericordiam domini, sed et iudicium timebam; laudabam gratiam, sed redditionem unicuique secundum opera sua verebar' [I knew the Lord was merciful, but I feared his judgement too. I praised his graciousness, but I was afraid of the reward for every man according to his deeds]. Salvian appears to the only patristic author quoting this phrase from Jeremiah.

shaped monasticism in western Europe.[21] The influence of Cassian on Gildas's *De excidio* is also profound.[22] This nexus centred on southern Gaul – on Marseilles in particular – is supported by Gildas's use of the works of the Gallic ascetic aristocrat, perhaps later monk of Marseilles, Sulpicius Severus (*ca* 363–425).[23] This network can also be directly linked to Jerome. It was Bishop Proculus of Marseilles (*r.* 381–428), personally favoured by Jerome, who had originally invited Cassian from the east to institute monastic reform.[24] Wright notes that Jerome is the only Great Latin Father drawn on by Gildas.[25]

It is significant that Gildas's primary influences are mostly monks, and that all are located within a specific monastic network linking southern Gaul to the eastern church in the fifth century. Clerical authority is present in the *De excidio*, as represented by the *exempla* of the eastern bishops, Ignatius of Antioch (*ca* 35–107), Polycarp of Smyrna (*ca* 69–155), and Basil of Caesarea (*ca* 329–79), but there is a notable absence of the authority of western bishops, particularly of the church fathers and bishops, Hilary of Poitiers (*ca* 310–67), Ambrose of Milan (*ca* 340–97), and Augustine of Hippo.[26] While Gildas is clearly framing his criticisms within a particular cultural mindset, it is equally clear that Gildas is criticising kings and

[21] For more detail on Cassian and his works, see 69. For a study of the influence of Lerinian monasticism, as influenced by Cassian, see Leyser, '"This Sainted Isle"'. It is perhaps significant in this context, that Salvian is described by the Gallic priest, Gennadius of Marseilles (*ob. ca.* 496), in his continuation of Jerome's *De uiris illustribus*, as a teacher of bishops or 'magister episcoporum'. See Gennadius, *De uiris illustribus* (ed. Richardson, 84).

[22] See Wright, 'Gildas's Reading', 136–40.

[23] Alban Butler reports a tradition that Sulpicius Severus, author of the *Vita Martini*, became a monk of Marseilles in later life. See Butler, *The Lives of the Fathers*, I, 379–80. For Gildas's use of Sulpicius Severus, see Wright, 'Gildas's Reading', 151.

[24] Jerome, *Epistulae*, 56, CXXV.20 (ed. Hilberg, 141): 'habes ibi sanctum doctissimumque pontificem proculum, qui uiua et praesenti uoce nostras scidulas superet' [In Proculus you have a reverend and most learned prelate, able by the sound of his voice to do more for you than I with my written sheets]. Translations of Jerome's letters, unless otherwise stated, come from 'Letters of St Jerome' (trans. Fremantle *et al.*). On this connection, see Rousseau, *Ascetics, Authority and the Church*, 174–5. If we accept Rousseau's timeline for Cassian's life, then Cassian's possible presence at the Council of Diospolis in 415 (the Council, led by Bishop John II of Jerusalem, which returned Pelagius to communion with the church) connects him to the anti-Pelagian group present: Jerome, Orosius, and two disciples of Martin of Tours, the former Gallic bishops, Lazarus and Heros, both under the protection of Proculus. What we can see then, in Cassian's arrival in Marseilles *ca* 415 under the auspices of Proculus, is the coalescing of the ascetic influences of Jerome, Orosius (representing Augustine), and the disciples of Martin, all tempered by the dispute at Diospolis between John II and Jerome over Pelagius and clerical authority over the monastic life. For an argument that the Cassian located in Antioch by Rousseau is not the Cassian of Marseilles, see Dunn, 'Cassian in Syria?' On the ecclesiastical situation in Gaul at the time, see Mathisen, *Ecclesiastical Factionalism*, 27–43.

[25] Wright, 'Gildas's Prose Style', 108.

[26] Kerlouégan, *Le De Excidio*, 78. Of the only named clerics that are pointed out as *exempla* for the British church in the *De excidio* – Ignatius of Antioch, Polycarp of Smyrna, and Basil of Caesarea – all are bishops in the east. Wright has detected that Gildas may also have drawn on Rufinus's translations of the writings of Gregory of Nazianzus (*ca* 329–90), also an eastern bishop. See Wright, 'Rufinus, Gregory of Nazianzus, and Gildas', 12–35. This silence on western bishops in the work of a cleric based in the west is curious: it implies that Gildas aligned his vision of the British church with the eastern church, and begs the question whether he was writing into a dispute or schism with Rome. There is a schism within the date range ascribed to the *De excidio*, that of the Acacian schism from 484 to 519.

bishops from within an Insular church intimate with the wider Christian culture of the continent.

What then is Gildas's position within the church he criticises? Gildas wrote against his church from within the clerical orders.[27] As Thomas O'Loughlin has argued, following Owen Chadwick, he was a deacon whose clerical roles involved scriptural study and pastoral care.[28] Whether he had also embraced the ascetic life in a formal sense (as a monk) is no longer regarded as certain. It used to be maintained that he was a monk, but his classical education, as Lapidge has argued, is unlikely to have been in a monastic setting.[29] His relatively junior clerical status at the age of 43 implies a secular career prior to joining the church or possibly entering the monastic life.[30] While there is no reason why he could not have been a deacon and a monk, both Neil Wright and Michael Herren argue for a purely clerical position, supported by a view that Gildas's overriding concern is the reform of the clergy and that he totally neglects monasticism in his *De excidio*.[31] But monasticism, as Gildas describes it, is influential in Britain. He denounces two significant representatives of monasticism: the former abbot, now 'tyrant', Constantine, and the former monk, now 'tyrant', Maglocunus, indicating that monasticism already had significant traction but, like the clerical orders, was also overly influenced by worldly secular elites.[32]

It is, perhaps, his use of Cassian that provides the best support for Gildas as an active member of a monastic community when writing the *De excidio*. Firstly, Cassian's works offered a pastoral model of monasticism, a model that supported radical developments in southern Gaul in the first half of the fifth century which saw monks increasingly take clerical office within a Gallic church also beset by corruption.[33] Secondly, Gildas's specific use of Cassian's phrasing implies he was a coenobitic

27 Gildas indicates he is a cleric at Gildas, *De excidio*, LXV.1 (ed. Winterbottom, 118, trans., 51): 'episcoporum vel ceterorum sacerdotum aut clericorum in nostro quoque ordine' [by bishops and other priests and clerics of my order also].

28 For Gildas as a deacon, see Chadwick, 'Gildas and the Monastic Order'. See also O'Loughlin, *Gildas and the Scriptures*, 24–5.

29 Lapidge, 'Gildas's Education'. For a former position on Gildas solely as a monk, see *Gildas* (ed. Williams, 160, n. 3).

30 Gildas identifies himself as being in his forty-fourth year at Gildas, *De excidio*, XXVI.1 (ed. Winterbottom, 98, trans., 28): 'quique quadragesimus quartus (ut novi) orditur annus mense iam uno emenso, qui et meae nativitatis est' [That was the year of my birth, as I know, one month of the forty-fourth year since then has already passed].

31 Wright, 'Gildas's Reading', 160–1; Herren, 'Gildas and Early British Monasticism', 75.

32 Gildas, *De excidio*, XXVIII.1 (ed. Winterbottom, 99, trans., 29): 'tyrannicus catulus Constantinus. Hoc anno, post horribile iuramenti sacramentum, quo se devinxit nequaquam dolos civibus… facturum… sub sancti abbatis amphibalo, latera regiorum tenerrima puerorum vel praecordia crudeliter duum' [Constantine, tyrant whelp, …this very year he bound himself by dreadful oath not to work his wiles on our countrymen… then…in the habit of a holy abbot, he most cruelly tore at the tender sides and vitals of two royal youths]; XXXIV.1 (ed. Winterbottom, 102, trans., 33): 'dein popularis aurae cognitioni proferens, monachum sine ullo infidelitatis, ut aiebas' [then, publishing it to the knowledge of the public breeze, you vowed to be a monk forever]. This point is also picked up by Marilyn Dunn. See Dunn, 'Paradigms of Penance', 20–1.

33 Rousseau notes that Cassian aligned the hopes and ideals of the monk with the pastoral opportunities of the church. See Rousseau, *Ascetics, Authority and the Church*, 2. Robert Markus also comments that Cassian turned asceticism into something that could be appropriated by the clergy. See Markus, *The End of Ancient Christianity*, 191. For a brief discussion of the movement of monks into the clerical orders of the Gallic church, see Markus, *The End of Ancient Christianity*, 199–202.

or communal monk at the time of writing the *De excidio*. In his transition from his attack on the 'tyrants' to his attack on the church, Gildas takes time to apologise to those good Christians who will be caught up in his attack. In doing so, Gildas echoes Cassian's hope of becoming a solitary monk or anchorite:

> [Gildas] Sed mihi quaeso, ut iam in superioribus dixi, ab his veniam impertiri quorum **vitam** non solum laudo verum etiam cunctis mundi opidus praefero, **cuiusque me**, si fieri possit, ante mortis diem **esse** aliquamdiu **participem opto** et sitio.[34]

> [Cassian] secundum anachoretarum, qui prius in coenobiis instituti iamque in actuali conversatione perfecti solitudinis elegere secreta: **cuius professionis nos quoque optamus esse participes**.[35]

One of Cassian's fundamental monastic reforms was that the status of anchorite could only be achieved after serving as a monk in a coenobitic community.[36] It is probable, therefore, that Gildas could only express a tangible hope to become an anchorite if he was already a coenobite.[37]

This Cassianic influence on Gildas, that the solitary life could only be gained after serving within a communal monastery and with the authority of its abbot, is reinforced by the witness of Columbanus, who, writing around 600 to Gregory the Great, alludes to Gildas's position on the matter:

> What is to be done about those monks who, for the sake of God, and inflamed by the desire for a more perfect life, impugn their vows, leave the places of their first profession, and against their abbots' will, impelled by monastic fervour, either relapse or flee to the deserts? Finnian the writer questioned Gildas about them, and he sent a most polished reply.[38]

Further, Gildas's dependence on the patristic authority of Jerome reinforces a monastic slant to his perspective.[39] Gildas's spiritual legacy – as demonstrated by attributed

[34] Gildas, *De excidio*, LXV.2 (ed. Winterbottom, 118, trans., 52): 'But, as I have said earlier, I beg to be forgiven by those whose life I praise and indeed prefer to all the riches of the world. If it may be so, **I desire** and thirst **to be a participant in that life** for a time before I die'.

[35] Cassian, *Collationes*, XVIII.4 (ed. Petschenig, 509): 'The second is that of the anchorites, who were first trained in the Coenobium and then being made perfect in practical life chose the recesses of the desert: **and in this order we also hope to gain a place**.' Translations, unless otherwise stated, come from 'The Conferences' (trans. Gibson). See also Wright, 'Gildas's Reading', 136.

[36] On this, see Markus, *The End of Ancient Christianity*, 182–3.

[37] This is against the position held by Neil Wright. See Wright, 'Gildas's Reading', 160–1.

[38] Columbanus, *Epistulae*, I.7 (ed. Walker, 8–9): 'quid faciendum est de monachis illis, qui pro Dei intuitu et vitae perfectioris desiderio accensi, contra vota venientes primae conversionis loca relinquunt, et invitis abbatibus, fervore monachorum cogente, aut laxantur aut ad deserta fugiunt. Vennianus auctor Gildam de his interrogavit, et elegantissime ille rescripsit'. The authority of abbots in relation to the adjustment of coenobitic vows is also affirmed in the letter to Finnian. See Gildas, *Fragmenta*, V (ed. Winterbottom, 144–5).

[39] Gildas's draws on Jerome's *De uiris illustribus*, selected *Epistulae*, *Vita Malchi*, and *Vita Pauli*. For Jerome's influence on Gildas, see Wright, 'Gildas's Reading', 141–4. For further comment, see below, 63–9.

works addressing a monastic context – builds on memories of his agency in establishing and organising monastic life in Britain and Ireland.[40]

This monastic perspective appears to be crucial to understanding Gildas's select use of patristic authorities to buttress his prophetic denunciation of Britain. Unlike the Bible – from which Gildas constructs a rhetorical case against the kings and clergy with two separate and sequential scans through the Old and New Testaments – and the historiographic works of Rufinus and Orosius – which are generally used to support his providential history of Britain – Gildas sprinkles Jerome and Cassian throughout his work in a non-linear way, suggesting that selected works of Jerome and Cassian were close to his mind or hand at the time the *De excidio* was being written.[41] Clearly both Jerome and Cassian were significant in Gildas's conception of himself as a legitimate critic in the prophetic tradition.

Gildas and Jerome

Jerome took up the monastic life *ca* 372 at the age of twenty-seven. Following a pilgrimage to the east and to Jerusalem, he spent two or three years as an anchorite in the wilderness. A move to Antioch saw Jerome ordained as a priest and take up a life as a scholar. His growing reputation resulted in a call to Rome in 382 under the favour of Pope Damasus (*r. ca* 366–84), where he embarked on a revision of the Latin text of the New Testament. Subsequently falling out of favour, Jerome moved back to the east, finally settling in a monastery in Bethlehem. From there, he revised the Latin text of the Old Testament and compiled commentaries on the Old Testament prophets. He was a noted ally of Augustine against heresy and a prolific supporter of the monastic life via his many letters.[42]

Building on the work of François Kerlouégan, Neil Wright notes that Gildas knew Jerome's *De uiris illustribus*, the *Vita Pauli*, and some of his *Epistulae*.[43] Of Jerome's letters, *Epistula 14* (to Heliodorus, a monk, dated to 373 or 374) and *Epistula 133* (to Ctesiphon, dated to 415) were certainly known by Gildas. Of the remainder, Gildas was probably aware of *Epistula 1* (to Innocent, dated to 374), *Epistula 58* (to Paulinus of Nola, dated to 395), *Epistula 60* (to Heliodorus, now bishop, dated to 396), *Epistula 125* (to Rusticus, a monk, dated to 411), *Epistula 127* (to Principia, dated to 412), and *Epistula 130* (to Demetrias, dated to 414).

In discussions of Gildas's use of Jerome's letters, the most debated has been the letter to Ctesiphon. In the opening of his *historia*, Gildas draws on both this letter to Ctesiphon and Jerome's *De uiris illustribus* when quoting the anti-Christian

40 Follett, *Céli Dé in Ireland*, 32 and 85.

41 In his criticisms of kings and clergy, Gildas generally lays out his biblical citations in the order they are bound in his Bible, strongly suggesting he is methodically moving from beginning to end in each case. For a list of biblical citations in the *De excidio*, see *Gildas* (ed. Winterbottom, 156–9). For Gildas's use of the Bible, see also O'Loughlin, *Gildas and the Scriptures*, 81. For an analysis of Gildas's non-linear use of Cassian, see Joyce, *Gildas*. For a list of works, see Wright, 'Gildas's Reading', 152.

42 For a summation of the life of Jerome, see Kelly, *Jerome*. For an overview of the impact of Jerome's letters, see Cain, *The Letters of Jerome*.

43 See Wright, 'Gildas's Reading', 141–4. Wright's work on Jerome's influence on Gildas's phrasing has been amended by a search of Brepol's *Library of Latin Texts*. Only selected phrases unique to Jerome and Gildas are examined. Jerome's *Preface to Jeremiah* has been set aside as part of the Vulgate.

philosopher, Porphyry (*ca* 234–305), and his description of Britain as 'a province fertile of tyrants':

> [Gildas] ita ut **Porphyrius rabidus** orientalis **adversus ecclesiam canis** dementiae suae ac vanitatis stilo hoc etiam adnecteret: '**Britannia**', inquiens, '**fertilis provincia tyrannorum**'.[44]

> [Jerome] quod solet nobis obicere contubernalis uester **porphyrius** - qua ratione clemens et misericors deus ab adam usque ad moysen et a moysi usque ad aduentum christi passus sit uniuersas gentes perire ignorantia legis et mandatorum dei. neque enim **britanni, fertilis prouincia tyrannorum**, et scythiae gentes omnesque usque ad oceanum per circuitum barbarae nationes moysen prophetasque cognouerant.[45]

> [Jerome] discant igitur celsus, **porphyrius**, iulianus, **rabidi aduersum christum canes**.[46]

Interpretations of Gildas's misunderstanding of Jerome's passage (as relating to his citing of Jerome as a 'direct quote' of Porphyry) have been used as an attack on Gildas's capacity as a historian and a Latinist, buttressing a representation of Gildas as disconnected and poorly read.[47] However, the charge that he misquoted Jerome's ambiguous text, ably set aside by Wright, has often obscured the fact that Ctesiphon was writing to Jerome for advice on the teachings of Pelagius.[48] Arguments that have seen Gildas simply not knowing about Pelagius, nor of his doctrinal struggles with Augustine, cannot stand against Gildas's use of Jerome's letter to Ctesiphon.[49]

Gildas's silence on Germanus's mission to Britain to combat Pelagianism thus appears profound. From this profound silence and interpretations of his use of quotations from the works of unnamed British authorities, probably clerics, arguments have been put forward that Gildas was sympathetic to the teachings of Pelagius.[50]

44 Gildas, *De excidio*, IV.3 (ed. Winterbottom, 90, trans., 17): 'in fact **Porphyry, the "mad dog"** of the east **who vents** his fury **on the church**, has this to add to his crazy and meaningless writings: **"Britain is a province fertile of tyrants"**.'

45 Jerome, *Epistulae*, 56, CXXXIII.9 (ed. Hilberg, 255): 'Or lastly make your own the favorite cavil of your associate **Porphyry**, and ask how God can be described as pitiful and of great mercy when from Adam to Moses and from Moses to the coming of Christ He has suffered all nations to die in ignorance of the Law and of His commandments. **For Britain, that province so fertile in despots**, the Scythian tribes, and all the barbarians round about as far as the ocean were alike without knowledge of Moses and the prophets'.

46 Jerome, *De uiris illustribus* (ed. Richardson, *prologus*): 'Let Celsus, **Porphyry**, and Julian learn, **rabid as they are against Christ**'. Translations, unless otherwise stated, come from *De Viris Illustribus* (trans. Richardson).

47 Thompson, 'Gildas and the History of Britain', 209–10.

48 Wright, 'Gildas's Prose Style', 108–9.

49 Hugh Williams made this point forcibly in his edition of the *De excidio*: see *Gildas* (ed. Williams, 17–18, n. 4). For arguments that Gildas knew nothing of Pelagius, see *Gildas* (ed. Winterbottom, 153, n. 38.2); Morris, 'Pelagian Literature', 56.

50 See, for instance, Davies, 'The Church in Wales', 140. Gildas quotes from two unnamed authors, probably British clerics: Gildas, *De excidio*, XCII.3 (ed. Winterbottom, 133, trans., 69): 'sicut bene quidam nostrorum ait: "optabiliter cupimus ut hostes ecclesiae sint nostri quoque absque ullo foedere hostes, et amici ac defensores nostri non solum foederati sed etiam patres ac domini habeantur"' [One of us is right to say: 'We greatly desire that the enemies of the church be our enemies also, with no kind of alliance, and that her friends and protectors be not only our allies but our fathers and masters too']; XXXVIII.2 (ed. Winterbottom, 105, trans., 37): 'quia, ut bene

However, Karen George's study of Gildas's *De excidio* has shown, on the slender doctrinal evidence in the text, that the *De excidio* is probably addressing issues with predestination. Rather than seeing Gildas as influenced by the teachings of Pelagius, she argues that Gildas is more concerned with interpretations of the teachings of Augustine subsequent to his death *ca* 430, reflecting a position taken by the monastically influenced clergy of the Gallic church in the latter half of the fifth century and the first quarter of the sixth century.[51]

Gildas's use of Jerome's letter to Ctesiphon is largely historiographical, in the sense that he uses it to underscore his providential history of Britain as disobedient and sinful. However, Gildas's use of Jerome's letter to the monk Heliodorus offers the opportunity to see how he uses Jerome in an exhortatory way: first, when addressing himself in his *praefatio*; then when addressing the church in his *epilogus*. Jerome's letter to Heliodorus, written when he was a young man *ca* 373, is an exhortation to the ex-soldier Heliodorus to give up his ambitions for clerical orders and, once again, take up the monastic life: Heliodorus had returned home to Italy rather than accompany Jerome to the desert. In laying out the advantages of the secluded and contemplative monastic life, Jerome describes the responsibilities and pitfalls of the urban and active clerical life. Replete with military metaphors, as would appeal to an ex-soldier, the letter serves as a model exhortation to join the monastic life, but also, undoubtedly, as a model exhortation to remain in the monastic life. According to Wright's survey, it is the letter most alluded to by Gildas, perhaps indicative, if we assume a later clerical and monastic calling for Gildas, of an earlier military career that may have attracted him to the rhetorical style of the letter.[52]

Gildas calls on Jerome's letter to Heliodorus twice from the same section: these imitations serve to bookend the *De excidio*, appearing in the *praefatio* and the *epilogus*. The first imitation, significantly in the past tense, contrasts the apostles Peter

quidam nostrum ait, non agitur de qualitate peccati, sed de transgressione mandati' [As one of us well says, it is not a question of the nature of the offence, but of the breaking of an order]. This last phrase is usually attributed to Pelagius via his letter, *De virginitate*. Karen George, however, is probably correct in her assessment that this phrase is drawn from the anonymous 'Pelagian' letter, *Epistola de malis doctoribus et operibus fidei et de iudicio futuro*, not only in a thematic sense in its focus on bad teaching, but also in its specific influence on Gildas's arguments. See George, *Gildas's* De excidio, 71–3. The attribution of the *Epistola de malis doctoribus* to Sixtus, martyr and bishop, has seen it attributed to both Pope Sixtus II (who was a martyr, but from the third century, prior to the Pelagian controversy) and Pope Sixtus III (who was not a martyr, but was contemporary to the Pelagian controversy in the fifth century). See Rees, *Pelagius*, 16 and 212–14, for a discussion of the dating and possible authors. A candidate might be the otherwise unknown Sixtus mentioned by Augustine of Canterbury to Pope Gregory as a local British martyr and saint in a letter dated *ca* 600: Richard Sharpe conjectures that this martyr cult of Sixtus was, perhaps, at Chichester, Silchester, or Winchester. See Sharpe, 'Martyrs and Local Saints', 123–4. A local bishop, unknown to Rome, martyred in the south, and writing within a context where the arguments between the supporters of Pelagius and the supporters of Augustine were still current (as alluded to in the letter), could possibly have been martyred as a result of the Saxon rebellion described by Gildas, one generally dated to around the middle of the fifth century. It is possible that Gildas is then drawing on this local martyrdom for legitimation, rather than the modern perception of the author's 'Pelagianism'.

51 George, *Gildas's* De excidio, 127.

52 See Wright, 'Gildas's Reading', 141–3. Gildas consistently uses Late Latin military descriptors with precision. See Morris, *The Age of Arthur*, 132: 'foederati' [allies bound by treaty], 'annona' [supplies], 'hospites' [billeted troops], 'praepositi' [commanders], 'consilium' [council], 'consiliari' [advisors], and 'cuneus' [formation].

and Judas, and the deacons Stephen and Nicolas, emphasising the proper order for exalted and fallen clerics:

> [Gildas] merito beatissimum dicebam **Petrum** ob Christi integram confessionem, at **Iudam** infelicissimum propter cupiditatis amorem, **Stephanum** gloriosum ob martyrii palmam, sed **Nicolaum** miserum propter immundae haeresos notam.[53]

> [Jerome] adtendis **petrum**, sed et **iudam** considera. **stephanum** suspicis, sed et **nicolaum** respice.[54]

The second imitation is to emphasise that appearance – in a sense, status – is not enough in itself to deflect the judgement of God:

> [Gildas] **Nec sibi quisquam** sacerdotum **de corporis mundi** solum conscientia **supplaudat**.[55]

> [Jerome] **nec sibi quisquam de corporis** tantum **mundi** castitate **supplaudat**.[56]

If we place Gildas's use of Jerome into the context of the letter to Heliodorus, Gildas's attack on the clergy of the British church becomes more defined: not all bishops are true bishops; clerical rank does not make a man a Christian; and, most tellingly, though a priest can intercede for a fallen monk, who can intercede for a fallen priest?[57] The question of who could intercede for a fallen priest would clearly be uppermost in Gildas's mind, certainly prior to his composition of the *De excidio*. Jerome leaves his rhetorical question unanswered. In doing so, he implies two possible answers: the first, that the dangers inherent in the burden of clerical office preclude intercession for a fallen cleric; the second, perhaps more subtle, is that the monk or 'holy man' has the responsibility to intercede for the fallen priest.[58] This second inference is supported within the section by Jerome's *exempla* of the pagan centurion, Cornelius, the child, Daniel, the farmer, Amos, and the shepherd, David,

[53] Gildas, *De excidio*, I.11 (ed. Winterbottom, 88, trans., 14): 'I used to say that it was right that **Peter** was most blessed because he wholly confessed Christ, **Judas** most wretched because he loved greed: **Stephen** glorious because of his martyr's palm, **Nicholas** unhappy because of the stain of his foul heresy'.

[54] Jerome, *Epistulae*, 54, XIV.9 (ed. Hilberg, 57): 'You consider **Peter**; mark **Judas** as well. You notice **Stephen**; look also on **Nicolas**'.

[55] Gildas, *De excidio*, CX.1 (ed. Winterbotton, 141, trans., 79): '**Nor should any** priest **applaud himself** solely **because** he is conscious that **his own body is pure**'.

[56] Jerome, *Epistulae*, 54, XIV.9 (ed. Hilberg, 58): '**No man need pride himself… on** merely **physical chastity**'.

[57] Jerome, *Epistulae*, 54, XIV.9 (ed. Hilberg, 57–9): 'non omnes episcopi episcopi… non facit ecclesiastica dignitas christianum… monachus si ceciderit, rogabit pro eo sacerdos; pro sacerdotis lapsu quis rogaturus est?' [Not all bishops are bishops… For it is not ecclesiastical rank that makes a man Christian… If a monk fall, a priest shall intercede for him; but who shall intercede for a fallen priest?]

[58] The view that priests and bishops face a terrible burden is mirrored in Gildas's *fragmenta*: 'Habent quippe sacerdotes et episcopi terribilem iudicem, cui pertinet, non nobis, de illis in utroque saeculo iudicare' [For priests and bishops have a terrible judge; it is his task, not ours, to judge them in both worlds]. See Gildas, *Fragmenta*, V (ed. Winterbottom, 145, trans., 82).

who, as men or boys without religious status, were divinely inspired to edify their elders.[59] For someone like Gildas, whose world view, influenced by the Old Testament, saw God acting within history, a lack of status, supported by the example of Jerome, was not a barrier to being called by God to save the priesthood of the church.

This debate within Gildas, over whether to speak out or not, is clearly laid out in his *praefatio*.[60] In his *historia*, he once again turns to Jerome's exhortatory letter to Heliodorus when describing the invasions of his *patria* by pagan Picts and Scots:

> [Gildas] terminos rumpunt caeduntque omnia et **quaeque obvia** maturam ceu segetem **metunt** calcant transeunt.[61]
>
> [Jerome] ecce bis acutus gladius ex regis ore procedens **obuia quaeque metit**.[62]

The phrase, a unique elision by Jerome of Revelation 19.15 and the classical poet, Vergil, is used by Gildas to connect the destruction of Britain with the Last Judgement.[63] But the context of Jerome's letter is, again, far more personal. In exhorting Heliodorus to give up the luxury of clerical office and rejoin the monastic life of the desert, we can see here a plea to Gildas to give up the luxury of clerical silence:

> What keeps you, effeminate soldier, in your father's house? Where are your ramparts and trenches? When have you spent a winter in the field? Lo, the trumpet sounds from heaven! Lo, the Leader comes with clouds! He is armed to subdue the world, and out of His mouth proceeds a two-edged sword to mow down all that encounters it. But as for you, what will you do?[64]

The superior calling for Jerome is the ascetic life of the monk: it is only from this position of true humility that God can call his 'soldiers' to the status that is defined by duty or the active life.

This point of view, emphasising merit over seniority and influenced by Matthew 20.16 – 'so shall the last be first, and the first last' – is reinforced in another imitation

[59] Jerome, *Epistulae*, 54, XIV.9 (ed. Hilberg, 58): 'cornelius centurio adhuc ethnicus dono spiritus sancti inundatur; presbyteros danihel puer iudicat; amos ruborum mora destringens repente propheta est; dauid pastor adlegitur in regem; minimum discipulum iesus amat plurimum' [The centurion Cornelius was still a heathen when he was cleansed by the gift of the Holy Spirit. Daniel was but a child when he judged his elders. Amos was stripping mulberry bushes when, in a moment, he was made a prophet. David was only a shepherd when he was chosen to be king. And the least of His disciples was the one Jesus loved the most].

[60] Most notably at Gildas, *De excidio*, I.15 (ed. Winterbottom, 89), where Gildas uses the story of Balaam's Ass to make the point that even an ass can be called by God to edify his senior.

[61] Gildas, *De excidio*, XVI (ed. Winterbottom, 94, trans., 21): 'They went trampling over everything that stood in their path, **cutting it down** like ripe corn'.

[62] Jerome, *Epistulae*, 54, XIV.2 (ed. Hilberg, 46): 'Lo… out of [the Leader's] mouth proceeds a two-edged sword **to mow down all** that encounters it'.

[63] See Perkins, 'Biblical Allusion', 97–8.

[64] Jerome, *Epistulae*, 54, XIV.2 (ed. Hilberg, 46): 'quid facis in paterna domo, delicate miles? ubi uallum, ubi fossa, ubi hiemps acta sub pellibus? ecce de caelo tuba canit, ecce cum nubibus debellaturus orbem imperator armatus egreditur, ecce bis acutus gladius ex regis ore procedens obuia quaeque metit: et tu mihi ... ?' For Gildas's silence of 'ten years or more' prior to the publication of the *De excidio*, see Gildas, *De excidio*, I.2 (ed. Winterbottom, 87): 'silui, fateor… spatio bilustri temporis vel eo amplius praetereuntis' [I kept silent… as the space of ten years or more passed by].

by Gildas noted by Wright, this time from Jerome's letter to the ascetic aristocrat Paulinus of Nola (*ca* 354–431) on the question of whether Paulinus should also take up clerical orders.[65] Jerome's use of Matthew 20.16 to describe the former 'persecutor' and apostle Paul as the highest in merit, despite being last in the apostolic order, is twisted by Gildas to both criticise and offer hope to the tyrant and former monk, Maglocunus, who, though last on Gildas's list of kings, is the most evil:

> [Gildas] Quid tu enim, insularis draco, multorum tyrannorum depulsor tam regno quam etiam vita supra dictorum, **novissime** stilo, **prime in** malo?[66]

> [Jerome] paulus apostolus in uas electionis de persecutore mutatus **nouissimus** in ordine, **primus in** meritis est.[67]

Like the letter to Heliodorus, this section in the letter to Paulinus also emphasises that junior merit can edify seniority and, once again, mentions the example of a young Daniel judging his elders.[68]

The example of Daniel, along with those of Cornelius, Amos, and David, all point to juniors being granted authority to edify their seniors through a direct prophetic experience or through an appointed prophet. Jerome's letter to Paulinus, like that to Heliodorus, once again exhorts his addressee to keep faith with the secluded monastic life rather than take up the urban clerical life, but, taking a step further, Jerome also outlines the biblical models for the clerical and monastic life. The clerical life is modelled on the apostles, but the monastic life is modelled on the Old Testament prophets and the ascetic communities that supported them, the *filii prophetarum* or the sons of the prophets:

> And, to come to our own case, let bishops and presbyters take for their examples the apostles or their companions; and as they hold the rank which these once held, let them endeavour to exhibit the same excellence. And last of all, let us monks take as the patterns which we are to follow the lives of Paul, of Antony, of Julian, of Hilarion, of the Macarii. And to go back to the authority of scripture, we have our masters in Elijah and Elisha, and our leaders in the sons of the prophets; who lived in fields and solitary places and made themselves tents by the waters of Jordan.[69]

[65] Wright, 'Gildas's Reading', 142.

[66] Gildas, *De excidio*, XXXIII.1 (ed. Winterbottom, 102, trans., 32): 'What of you, dragon of the island, you who have removed many of these tyrants from their country and even their life? You are **last** in my list, **but first** in evil'.

[67] Jerome, *Epistulae*, 54, LVIII.1 (ed. Hilberg, 528): 'The apostle Paul, that chosen vessel framed out of a persecutor, **though last** in the apostolic order **is first** in merit'.

[68] Jerome, *Epistulae,* 54, LVIII.1 (ed. Hilberg, 528): 'et danihel adhuc puer et longaeuos iudicat, atque inpudicos senes aetas lasciua condemnat' [And, as a boy, Daniel judges old men and in the flower of youth condemns the incontinence of age].

[69] Jerome, *Epistulae*, 54, LVIII.5 (ed. Hilberg, 533): 'et ut ad nostra ueniamus, episcopi et presbyteri habeant in exemplum apostolos et apostolicos uiros, quorum honorem possidentes habere nitantur et meritum. nos autem habemus propositi nostri principes paulos, antonios, iulianos, macarios; et ut ad scripturarum auctoritatem redeam, noster princeps helias, noster helisaeus, nostri duces filii prophetarum, qui habitabant in agris et solitudine et faciebant sibi tabernacula propter fluenta iordanis'. The *filii prophetarum* are first mentioned at I Samuel 10.5. For a study of the Old Testament sons of the prophets, see Price, 'The Schools'.

Gildas's prophetic vocation, following his use of Jerome, appears to be legitimised by a monastic tradition that emphasises that the humble will be called by God from the contemplative life, when necessary, to edify or replace, in the prophetic tradition, their worldly seniors. This emphasis on the monastic life as a legitimation for the edification of secular and church leaders appears to be fundamental to Gildas's mindset. The influence of Jerome is matched by the influence of John Cassian, and again, as with Jerome, Gildas appears to be fixated with the biblical legitimacy of monasticism.

Gildas and Cassian

John Cassian was integral to the movement of the eastern ascetic tradition to the west. A student of the monk and theologian, Evagrius Ponticus (*ca* 345–399), he was a refugee from the Origenistic controversy in Alexandria *ca* 400.[70] Cassian fled first to the patriarch of Constantinople, John Chrysostom (*ca* 349–407), where he was ordained a deacon, and then, with the exile of Chrysostom, he fled to Rome *ca* 404, where he presented himself to Pope Innocent I (*r.* 401–17). Sometime around 415, he founded two monasteries at Marseilles in southern Gaul. Cassian's move to Gaul was crucial in restoring credibility to a 'rogue' ascetic movement beset by scandal.[71]

Drawing on his personal experience of the desert fathers and adapting their philosophies to a Gallic context, Cassian constructed two texts for the purpose of structuring and edifying the monastic movement: *De institutis coenobiorum et de octo principalium uitiorum remediis* or *Institutes* (*ca* 420), and *Collationes patrum in scetica eremo* or *Conferences* (*ca* 426–30).[72] Wright's study reveals the influence of both these works on Gildas through his use of imitations and echoes of Cassian's Latin phrasing.[73] As noted above, Gildas imitated Cassian's phrasing when expressing his desire to become a solitary monk or anchorite. Significantly around a quarter of the total imitations and echoes detected by Wright in the *De excidio* come from *Conferences XVIII*, 'Conference of the Abbot Piamun; on the three sorts of monks'. The origins of monasticism had a clear hold on Gildas's imagination when composing the *De excidio*.

In *Conferences XVIII*, just as in Jerome's letter to Heliodorus, Cassian utilises the examples of Judas and Nicolas to emphasise that the church has always had fallen clerics. In his attack on the British clergy, Gildas draws on Cassian when he revisits the proper order for exalted and fallen clerics as influenced by Jerome and stated in his *praefatio* in the past tense. Commenting in the present tense, Gildas stresses the enormity of the current crisis in the British church. The *ordo* is inverted – Judas stands in Peter's place, as Nicolas stands in Stephen's:

70 The Origenistic controversy at the end of the fourth century – fuelled, perhaps, by the translations of Origen's works from Greek into Latin by Rufinus – saw elements of the third-century theologian's teaching criticised for doctrinal deviation. Origen's translated works, for instance, influenced Pelagius. For a discussion of Pelagius's reception of Origen's writings, see Scheck, *Origen*, 83–5. For a general overview, see Clark, *The Origenist Controversy*.

71 For a brief account of Cassian's elusive life, see Rousseau, *Ascetics, Authority, and the Church*, 169–76. See also Stewart, *Cassian the Monk*, 3–26. On the significance of Cassian's intervention in Gaul, see Leyser, *Authority and Asceticism*, 34–5.

72 On the literary styles and purpose of the *Institutes* and *Conferences*, see Stewart, *Cassian the Monk*, 27–39.

73 Wright, 'Gildas's Reading', 136–40.

[Gildas] **Iudam** quodammodo in Petri cathedra... ac **Nicolaum** in loco Stephani martyris statuunt **immundae haereseos adinventorem**.[74]

[Cassian] denique si uel Satanan inter angelos uel **Iudam** inter apostolos uel **Nicolaum prauissimae haereseos inuentorem** inter diaconos reminiscamur electos.[75]

Cassian's answer to the problem of fallen clerics was the example of the journey of Paphnutius from coenobitic monk to a semi-anchoritic abbot and priest, clearly setting aside Jerome's insistence of a clear delineation between monk and cleric.[76] For Cassian, as represented by Paphnutius, the monastery provided the firm foundation for both clerical office and the life of the coenobite and the anchorite.[77] This idea of a firm foundation being the source of divine authority is picked up by Gildas in his *epilogus* where he reminds the clergy of their vows. This section is also influenced by Jerome's letter to Heliodorus.[78] Gildas, like Cassian, recalls Christ's parable of the wise and foolish builders (Matthew 7.24–7), but uses Cassian's distinctly non-scriptural phrasing:

[Gildas] in aedificando domo **arenarum pendulae mobilitati** dominus non cooperetur.[79]

[Cassian] quae uero in **harenarum pendula mobilitate** constructa est statim fuisse conlapsam.[80]

For Cassian, doubtful foundations relate to weakness, weaknesses that can only be overcome with patience, tranquillity, and humility. Gildas, too, utilises the house built on sand as a metaphor for a church built on poor behaviour. He offers a firm foundation as a foil to a foolish priesthood: Peter, the rock on which the church was built, is the model for all true priests.[81]

74 Gildas, *De excidio*, LXVII.4 (ed. Winterbottom, 119–20, trans., 54): 'In a sense, placing **Judas**... in the seat of Peter, **and that contriver of a filthy heresy, Nicholas**, in the place of the martyr Stephen.'

75 Cassian, *Collationes*, XVIII.16 (ed. Petschenig, 528): 'Finally if we bear in mind that Satan was chosen among the angels, and **Judas** among the apostles, **and Nicholas the author of a detestable heresy** among the deacons.'

76 The tale of the abbot and priest Paphnutius is in the proceeding chapter. The last sentence emphasises Cassian's attachment of virtue to a good foundation. See Cassian, *Collationes*, XVIII.15 (ed. Petschenig, 526): 'si igitur ad culmen uirtutum eius uolumus peruenire, talia nobis exordiorum fundamenta iacienda sunt' [If then we want to attain to his height of virtue, we must lay the same foundation to begin with]. On Cassian's development of the example of Paphnutius over the course of writing the *Conferences*, see Rousseau, *Ascetics, Authority, and the Church*, 179–80.

77 On Cassian's emphasis on the example of the abbot as a fitting mediator for divine influence, see Rousseau, *Ascetics, Authority, and the Church*, 233–4.

78 The similarities between Gildas, *De excidio*, CVI–CVII (ed. Winterbottom, 138–40), and Jerome, *Epistulae*, 54, XIV.8 (ed. Hilberg, 55) are pronounced.

79 Gildas, *De excidio*, CIX.4 (ed. Winterbottom, 141, trans., 78–9): 'The Lord does not assist... in building their house **on the doubtful shifting of sands**.'

80 Cassian, *Collationes*, XVIII.13 (ed. Petschenig, 520): 'While [the house] which was built **on the shifting and moving sand** at once collapsed.'

81 Gildas, *De excidio*, CIX.4 (ed. Winterbottom, 141, trans., 78): 'Vero sacerdoti dicitur: "tu es Petrus et super hanc petram aedificabo ecclesiam meum": vos quidem assimilamini "viro stulto

Gildas's thinking can be clarified when he draws on a similar image, again through Cassian as influenced by Christ's Sermon on the Mount (Matthew 5.14), of the holy man as a city placed on a mountain top:

> [Gildas] ut est civibus firmissima forte **in editi montis civitas vertice constituta.**[82]

> [Cassian] sicut euangelica illa **ciuitas in excelsi montis uertice constitutus.**[83]

Gildas, in drawing on this phrase, is also drawing on Cassian's description of the abbot and priest, Piamun. As abbot and priest for a community of anchorites, Piamun had built his divine authority on his virtues, as expressed through miracles witnessed by Cassian himself. This firm foundation, the rock, was literally and metaphorically the coenobium or monastery. For Roman elites, the foundation for service was the classical school featuring the *grammaticus* and the *rhetor*; for Gildas, following Cassian, the foundation for service for Christian elites appears to be the monastery.

Cassian had adjusted Jerome's vision of a clear delineation between the monastic and clerical orders. In bringing the coenobium from the contemplative desert to the active urban environment, he appended the training of both the anchorite and the cleric to the monastery. Significantly, in doing so, he adjusted the solitary life of the anchorite in the desert to a semi-solitary life attached to the monastery. This structure mirrored that of Jerome's connection of monasticism to the Old Testament prophets of Elijah and Elisha and the ascetic communities that supported them, the sons of the prophets.[84] However, whereas Jerome saw the biblical origins of monasticism in the Old Testament and the biblical origins of the clergy in the New Testament, Cassian, again in *Conferences XVIII*, nuanced this inheritance a little further – communal or coenobitic monasticism now had its origins with the apostles and the ascetic communities of the early church. It was anchoritic monasticism that only drew its biblical origins from the Old Testament prophets:

> And so the system of coenobites took its rise in the days of the preaching of the Apostles.[85]

> And of this order [Anchorites] we have heard that the originators were those whom we mentioned just now; viz., Saint Paul and Antony… imitating, to wit, John the Baptist, who passed all his life in the desert, and Elijah and Elisha.[86]

qui aedificavit domum suam super arenam"' [To the true priest is said: 'You are Peter, and on this rock I shall build my church': while you are like 'the foolish man who built his house upon sand'].

82 Gildas, *De excidio*, XCIII.2 (ed. Winterbottom, 133, trans., 70): '**As is a strong city, placed on the peak of a high mountain**, for its citizens.'

83 Cassian, *Collationes*, XVIII.1 (ed. Petschenig, 507): 'For he was **set on the top of a high mountain like that city** in the gospel.'

84 Curiously, Cassian does not mention the sons of the prophets in either the *Institutes* or the *Conferences*, despite Jerome's modelling of communal monasticism on their example. For an expansion on Jerome's and Cassian's approaches to the biblical origins of monasticism, see Joyce, 'Contested Origins', 4–8 and 11–14.

85 Cassian, *Collationes*, XVIII.5 (ed. Petschenig, 509): 'Itaque coenobiotarum disciplina a tempore praedicationis apostolicae sumpsit exordium'.

86 Cassian, *Collationes*, XVIII.6 (ed. Petschenig, 511): 'cuius professionis principes hos quos paulo ante commemorauimus, sanctum scilicet Paulum uel Antonium, nouimus extitisse… ad

For Cassian, then, the monastery was key to reforming a corrupt church. The monastery, as the inheritor of the apostolic communities of the early church, could provide the church with virtuous clerics grounded in Christian traditions; the monastery could also provide, on rare occasions, the supreme monk or anchorite who, granted the powers of prophecy by God, could remind his seniors that to fail their duties would bring the dire judgement of God.[87]

Responding to criticisms of 'rogue' monks and corrupt clerics, Cassian brought a new perspective on integrity to the Gallic church, one that, while affirming the authority and status of the clerical orders, placed a complementary authority within the coenobium. The monastery, as the educational foundation for a Christian life of service, would provide the church with clerics as well as, on rare occasions, the contemplative 'holy man' as *speculator* who would, in the prophetic tradition of the Old Testament, guide clerics away from poor example and bad teaching. It was Cassian's model of authority that allowed the monk Gildas to edify, in the prophetic tradition, the church leaders of Britain. Cassian's model of authority also allowed the deacon Gildas to offer the monastery as a pastoral solution to an uneducated and immoral laity. This model of authority, as expressed by Gildas, was resistant to the authority of the western church fathers and bishops, Hilary, Ambrose, and Augustine of Hippo. To further discern this tradition, we need to examine Augustine and his views on the role of monasticism.

Augustine and monasticism

That Gildas knew about the confrontations between Augustine of Hippo and Pelagius is clear in his use of Jerome's letter to Ctesiphon, addressing the teachings of Pelagius. Despite these confrontations dominating the first half of the fifth century, Gildas chose not to draw on the clerical authority of Augustine in constructing his *De excidio*. This was not a snub to the office of bishop. As noted previously, Gildas was happy to draw on the episcopal examples of the eastern bishops Ignatius, Polycarp, and Basil, and, indeed, he makes it clear in the *De excidio* that he wants to restore the proper order of the church, not usurp it.[88] Nor was it doctrinal differences, since Gildas does not emphasise the debates between Augustine and Pelagius on grace and free will, or their followers' subsequent debates on faith and the role of good works.[89] Gildas's emphasis was on sin, not doctrinal heresy. Clearly, Gildas perceived that the authority of Augustine was not appropriate to those legitimations required to support his criticism of the secular and church leaders of Britain. While it may be, indeed, that he did not have access to Augustine's works, the fact that these works are also missing from the texts that Gildas explicitly cites is significant.

This tradition resistant to the authority of Augustine on matters of grace and original sin is reflected in at least one of Gildas's patristic influences, Salvian.[90] It is also

imitationem scilicet Iohannis Baptistae, qui in heremo tota aetate permansit, Heliae quoque et Helisaei'.

87 For Cassian's view on the rarity of anchoritic perfection see Sheridan, 'John Cassian', 166–70.

88 For instance, Gildas, *De excidio*, XXVI.2 (ed. Winterbottom, 99, trans., 28): 'et ob hoc reges, publici, privati, sacerdotes, ecclesiastici, suum quique ordinem servarunt' [That was why kings, public and private persons, priests and churchmen, kept to their own stations].

89 See Chapter 2, 49–51.

90 See Lambert, 'The Uses of Decay', 129–30.

a tradition revealed in the legacy of Gildas as invoked by Columbanus.[91] Both were monks and both were also profoundly influenced by Cassian.[92] However, Augustine himself took up the ascetic life prior to becoming a cleric and was a keen supporter of the ascetic reform movement. He engaged directly with Jerome and solicited his assistance in the confrontation with Pelagius. The tradition resistant to the authority of Augustine cannot, therefore, be simply about clerical antipathy toward the religious life: it is more about differing interpretations of monasticism itself. In order to discern this ascetic tradition, we need to explore Augustine's position on the origins, order, and purpose of monasticism.

Augustine's presence at a reading of the life of Antony (*ca* 251–356) in Milan in 386 was integral to his conversion from Manichaeism to Nicene Christianity. In 388, inspired by the example of the great desert father, he sold his inheritance and converted his family home in Thagaste in North Africa into an informal Christian community or 'lay monastery', modelled on the early apostolic church as laid out in Acts 2.42–7 and Acts 4.32–35.[93] Drawn into an active life in the church, Augustine was ordained a priest in Hippo in 391 (rising to the bishopric in 395/6), subsequently developing his vision of the apostolic community of Jerusalem as a model for Christian life: in old age he would describe his bishop's house as a monastery for clerics.[94] Augustine, in a sense, 'monasticised' the clerical orders, and one of his first enterprises in clerical office was to develop a rule for a coenobitic community in a clerical context.

Around 401, Augustine focussed his attention on monasticism with his work, *De opere monachorum*. Later, around 426, he reflected on the rationale for the work as follows:

> To write the Book on the Work of Monks, the need which compelled me was this. When at Carthage there had begun to be monasteries, some maintained themselves by their own hands, obeying the Apostle; but others wished so to live on the oblations of the faithful, that doing no work whence they might either have or supply the necessaries of life, they thought and boasted that they did rather fulfil the precept of the Gospel... Add to this, that some of them who were for not working, wore their hair long.[95]

Augustine was objecting not only to a monasticism that relied exclusively on the charitable support of lay communities but, significantly, to those monks who wore their hair long. The wearing of long hair, as Augustine pointed out, was drawing

[91] Kelly, 'Augustine in Hiberno-Latin Literature', 141, notes only two potential citations of Augustine in the writings of Columbanus, both in a letter to Boniface written, in his estimation, at Bobbio in Italy and reflecting access to a continental library.

[92] For Columbanus's use of Cassian, see Stancliffe, 'The Thirteen Sermons', 105. For Cassian's influence on Salvian, see Markus, *The End of Ancient Christianity*, 168–70.

[93] Lawless, *Augustine of Hippo*, 58–9.

[94] Lawless, *Augustine of Hippo*, 62. For a detailed biography of Augustine, see Brown, *Augustine of Hippo*.

[95] Augustine of Hippo, *Retractationum*, II.21 (ed. Mutzenbecher): 'ut de opere monachorum librum scriberem, illa necessitas conpulit quod, cum apud carthaginem monasteria esse coepissent, alii se suis manibus transigebant obtemperantes apostolo, alii uero ita ex oblationibus religiosorum uiuere uolebant, ut nihil operantes, unde necessaria uel haberent uel supplerent, se potius implere praeceptum euangelicum existimarent atque iactarent... huc accedebat quod criniti erant quidam eorum qui operandum non esse dicebant'. Translation comes from the prologue in 'Of the Works of Monks' (trans. Browne). See also Lawless, *Augustine of Hippo*, 160.

on the tradition and authority of the prophets and the sons of the prophets of the Old Testament:

> This then we admonish so holy men, not to be moved by foolish quibblings of vain persons, and imitate in this perversity them whom in all else they are far from resembling. For those persons, hawking about a venal hypocrisy, fear lest shorn sanctity be held cheaper than long-haired; because truly he who sees them shall call to mind those ancients whom we read of, Samuel and the rest who did not cut off their hair.[96]

Augustine appears to have sensed three issues within the monastic movement. The first, influenced by his arguments with Pelagius, was the problematic emphasis on perfection.[97] The second was a monasticism that was unduly dependent on secular society. The third issue was the claim of monasticism to the authority of the Old Testament prophets and the sons of the prophets. This placed monasticism in potential conflict with the apostolic authority of the church and its clerical orders. Responding to those, like Jerome, who claimed Old Testament origins for monasticism, Augustine emphasised the early church as the originator of monasticism, reinforcing the apostles as the inheritors of the prophets and the sons of the prophets:

> These words of the psalm, this lovely sound, this song equally sweet as a melody sung or a message understood, has given birth to monasteries. Brothers and sisters who longed to live as one were awakened by the song; this verse roused them like a trumpet. It rang all around the world, and those who were dispersed came together into one sheepfold... Where did the apostles come from, the apostles who were the sons of the prophets, the children of those shaken out?... All these were from the Jewish race. The first people to live together in unity were those who sold all their possessions and laid the proceeds at the feet of the apostles.[98]

This idea of the apostles as the son of the prophets, clearly prominent in Augustine's mind, had been emphasised in two sermons on the Psalms in early 407.[99]

96 Augustine of Hippo, *De opere monachorum*, XXXI.39 (ed. Zycha, 590): 'hoc ergo admonemus tam sanctos uiros, ne stultis uanorum argumentationibus moueantur et eos in hac peruersitate imitentur, quibus sunt in ceteris longe dissimiles. illi enim uenalem circumferentes hypocrisin timent, ne uilior habeatur tonsa sanctitas quam comata, ut uidelicet qui eos uidet, antiquos illos quos legimus cogitet, samuelem et ceteros, qui non tondebant'. Translations, unless otherwise stated, come from 'Of the Works of Monks' (trans. Browne).

97 See Markus, *The End of Ancient Christianity*, 63–6, for how Augustine's views on monasticism evolved through his conflict with Pelagius.

98 Augustine of Hippo, *Enarrationes in Psalmos*, CXXXII.2 (ed. Dekkers & Fraipont): 'ista enim uerba psalterii, iste dulcis sonus, ista suauis melodia, tam in cantico quam in intellectu, etiam monasteria peperit. ad hunc sonum excitati sunt fratres qui habitare in unum concupierunt; iste uersus fuit tuba ipsorum. sonuit per omnem orbem terrarum, et qui diuisi erant, congregati sunt... et unde apostoli, filii prophetarum, filii excussorum?... omnes inde [iudaei] erant: et ipsi primi habitaverunt in unum, qui omnia quae habebant vendiderunt, rerumque suarum pretia ad pedes apostolorum posuerunt'. Translations, unless otherwise stated, come from *Expositions of the Psalms* (edd. Boulding & Ramsey). For an expansion of Augustine's approach to the biblical origins of monasticism, see Joyce, 'Contested Origins', 8–11.

99 Augustine of Hippo, *Enarrationes in Psalmos*, CXXVI.11 (ed. Dekkers & Fraipont): 'ergo intellego, fratres, quantum possum, filios excussorum fortasse ipsos apostolos dictos, filios prophetarum' [Well now, brothers and sisters, I will tell you as best I can how in this latter sense I understand the apostles themselves to be the children of those shaken out because they are the sons of the prophets]; CXXVII.2 (ed. Dekkers & Fraipont): 'et cum quaereremus qui sint filii

Augustine's model of authority placed communal monasticism under the authority of bishops. This model was drawn from and legitimated by the New Testament and the lives of the apostles and their disciples, and it was the apostles and the clerical orders of the church that inherited the ascetic traditions of the Old Testament. Augustine appeared to have no formal role for the anchorite as *speculator*: in answer to Jerome's question of who could intercede for a fallen priest, Augustine would have simply replied that another priest would intercede.[100]

Cassian, faced with these two differing models of monasticism, those of Jerome and Augustine, clearly fashioned a compromise. While influenced by Jerome's model for monasticism when writing the *Institutes ca* 420, by the time he came to write the *Conferences ca* 426–30, the authority of Augustine had clearly been incorporated into his vision.[101] Coenobitic monasticism now, like Augustine, had its biblical origins in the apostles, allowing the monastery to become a legitimate nursery for clerics. However, influenced by the impact of the desert fathers of the fourth century and the authority of Jerome, Cassian could not dispense with the superior monastic example of the solitary life: he attached the anchorite to the coenobium, at the same time emphasising the enormous difficulty in attaining that rank. In doing so, he left open the possibility, however slim, of monasticism exerting the considerable authority of the biblical prophets. This model resisted Augustine's attempts to institutionalise the *speculator* within the clerical orders alone, and influenced and legitimated Gildas's claim to prophecy.

Conclusion

Gildas's patristic legitimation for his prophetic criticisms of his seniors drew on a model of authority constructed by Jerome and modified by Cassian that allowed the monk, when directed by God, to edify a fallen priesthood. Gildas as a deacon

excussorum, visum esse nobis, suggerente quantum credimus domino, filios excussorum apostolos dictos esse, filios prophetarum' [We wondered what the children of those shaken out might mean, and at the suggestion of the Lord, I like to think, we decided that the apostles, who are the sons of the prophets, were called the children of those shaken out]. These two sermons are dated to 5 January 407 and 14 January 407 respectively. See *Expositions of the Psalms* (edd. Boulding & Ramsey, 83, n. 1, 98, n. 1).

100 On this point, see Chapter 6.

101 We can see in the opening of the *Institutes*, that Cassian follows Jerome's model for the Old Testament origins of the ascetic life. See Cassian, *De institutis*, I.1 (ed. Petschenig, 8): 'itaque monachum ut militem Christi in procinctu semper belli positum accinctis lumbis iugiter oportet incedere. hoc enim habitu etiam illos ambulasse, qui in ueteri testamento professionis huius fundauere primordia, Heliam scilicet et Helisaeum, diuinarum scripturarum auctoritate monstratur: ac deinceps principes auctoresque testamenti noui, Iohannem uidelicet, Petrum et Paulum ceterosque eiusdem ordinis uiros taliter incessisse cognoscimus' [A monk, then, as a soldier of Christ ever ready for battle, ought always to walk with his loins girded. For in this fashion, too, the authority of Holy Scripture shows that they walked who in the Old Testament started the original of this life – I mean Elijah and Elisha; and, moreover, we know that the leaders and authors of the New Testament, viz., John, Peter, and Paul, and the others of the same rank, walked in the same manner]. When we come to the *Conferences*, Cassian has clearly selectively incorporated Augustine's view on the New Testament origins of the ascetic life: Cassian, *Collationes*, XVIII.5 (ed. Petschenig, 509): 'Itaque coenobiotarum disciplina a tempore praedicationis apostolicae sumpsit exordium' [And so the system of coenobites took its rise in the days of the preaching of the Apostles]. See *John Cassian* (ed. Ramsey, 10–11) for a brief discussion of the influence, both positive and negative, of Augustine on Cassian.

could not publicly criticise his seniors. Gildas as a monk, however, could draw on scriptural authority, via the Old Testament prophets, to publicly edify his seniors. The authority on which Gildas drew was monastic not clerical. In writing the *De excidio*, Gildas had, in a sense, made a choice: his hope to become an anchorite was attached to his position within a community of monks. In claiming the role of watchman or *speculator* from within the institution of monasticism, he legitimated its authority to edify the clergy of *Britannia*. Resistance to the authority of Augustine was not a question of doctrine, in this case, but whether monasticism had a formal institutional role in the life of the church. Augustine saw potential conflict between the apostolic succession and monks claiming prophetic authority and argued that monasticism should remain a lay order under the authority of bishops. Gildas, following Cassian and Jerome, saw literal corruption in a clerical order that edified itself, and claimed a complementary authority for monasticism, in the prophetic tradition, as *speculatores*.

But Gildas went one step further. Unlike Augustine, Jerome, or Cassian, he was faced not with Roman imperial authority but anointed Christian kings. In connecting Paul, from the tribe of Benjamin and apostle to the nations, with Jeremiah, also from the tribe of Benjamin and prophet to the nations, Gildas had overlain Cassian's model of authority with a model of authority found in the Old Testament.[102] It was this innovation that allowed Gildas to criticise kings in the prophetic tradition and to offer both a monastic education and the 'holy man' as a solution to a corrupt and immoral Christian kingship. In extending 'the primitive church' from the ascetic communities of the apostles to biblical Israel and, by association, Britain, Gildas offered a new interpretation of an Old Testament model of authority, that of apostles (as priests), ministers (as prophets/monks), and members (as kings):

> This, and much more besides that I have decided to leave out in the interests of brevity, I frequently pondered, my mind bewildered, my heart remorseful. For (I said to myself) when they strayed from the right track the Lord did not spare a people that was peculiarly his own among all nations, a royal stock, a holy race, to whom he had said: 'Israel is my first-born son', or its priests, prophets and kings, over so many centuries the apostle, minister and members of that primitive church. What then will he do with this great black blot on *our* generation?[103]

Kingship, as Gildas related in his *historia*, was not his innovation: it was put in place in *Britannia* at the precise point when the people looked not to Rome or Man but to God, and failed initially because, despite divine favour, the people still looked to sin:

> Now for the first time they inflicted a massacre on [the Scots and Picts], trusting not in man but in God…The enemy retreated from the people, but the people did not retreat from their own sins… Kings were anointed not in God's name, but as being crueller than the rest; before long, they would be killed, with no enquiry into the truth, by those

[102] Via the phrase 'sed redditionem unicuique secundum opera sua verebar'. See above, 57–8.

[103] Gildas, *De excidio*, I.13 (ed. Winterbottom, 88,trans., 15): 'Haec igitur et multo plura quae brevitatis causa omittenda decrevimus cum qualicumque cordis compunctione attonita mente saepius volvens, si, inquam, peculiari ex omnibus nationibus populo, semini regali gentique sanctae, ad quam dixerat: "primogenitus meus Israel", eiusque sacerdotibus, prophetis, regibus, per tot saecula apostolo ministro membrisque illius primitivae ecclesiae dominus non pepercit, cum a recto tramite deviarint, quid tali huius atramento aetatis facturus est?' The phrase *illius primitivae ecclesiae* is an echo of Cassian, *Collationes*, XVII.20, but, significantly, Cassian uses it as a descriptor of the early apostolic church.

> who had anointed them, and others still crueller chosen to replace them. Any king who seemed gentler and rather more inclined to the truth was regarded as the downfall of Britain: everyone directed their hatred and their weapons at him, with no respect.[104]

In his innovative defence of the novelty of kingship, one that looked back to a subsequent golden period chastened by the divine judgement of the *adventus Saxonum*, Gildas never, at any point, looked to pre-Christian or barbarian models. His edification of kingship drew solely from the Bible, as viewed through a shared *romanitas* informed by the monastic authority of Jerome and Cassian.

Gildas, directed by God to edify a fallen kingship and priesthood, had no choice but to draw on and adapt a model of authority that allowed him to do what he did. That he was subsequently held up as an authority in the British Isles reveals the success of the *De excidio* in achieving its aims. Ironically, Gildas's successful claim to prophecy, in turn, legitimated the Cassianic model of monasticism, allowing it to prosper in Britain and Ireland even as it was being modified within a Gallic church increasingly under the influence of bishops sensitive to the teachings of Augustine, such as Caesarius of Arles (*ca* 470–542).[105] Crucially, Gildas's proffering of a monastic education to the classically educated elites of *Britannia* as a solution to corruption and immoral behaviour must place the *De excidio* earlier rather than later, most probably within the last quarter of the fifth century, a context implied by Bede. His profound silence on Germanus now falls into the realm of the unknown rather than the wilful. The publication of Constantius's *Vita Germani* could be a Gallic response reminding Gildas's *Britannia* of the significant role of Roman imperial authority and the clerical orders in its success as an orthodox *natio*, offering a 'tried and tested' New Testament model of authority against Gildas's innovative interpretation and defence of Old Testament kingship.

A few generations later, the Irish *peregrinus* Columbanus arrived on the continent with twelve disciples, mirroring Christ's apostolic mission. Calling directly on the authority of Gildas, Columbanus followed an existing mode of discourse in exerting his role as an edifier of kings and bishops in the tradition of the Old Testament prophets. Elements of the Christian culture of Gaul and Italy, also under the authority of kings and bishops, responded to Columbanus's call for moral reform in ways not reflective of a fundamental exoticism but rather with familiarity. Others, however, responded with suspicion. In order to examine the legacy of Gildas and its potential impact on the continent, we need to examine the tensions at the heart of Columbanus's mission: the issues of schism, simony, and Easter.

[104] Gildas, *De excidio*, XX.3, XXI.4 (ed. Winterbottom, 95–6, trans., 24): 'Et tum primum [inimicis]… agentibus strages dabant, non fidentes in homine, sed in deo… Quievit parumper inimicorum audacia nec tamen nostrorum malitia; recesserunt hostes a civibus nec cives a suis sceleribus… Ungebantur reges non per deum sed qui ceteris crudeliores exstarent, et paulo post ab unctoribus non pro veri examinatione trucidabantur aliis electis trucioribus. Si quis vero eorum mitior et veritati aliquatenus propior videretur, in hunc quasi Britanniae subversorem omnium odia telaque sine respectu contorquebantur'. This precise moment where Gildas describes the anointing of kings post-dates his placement of the letter to Agitius and a miraculous victory against Picts and Scots, and is prior to the *adventus Saxonum*, perhaps placing it somewhere in the second quarter of the fifth century. On this, see Chapter 2, 45.

[105] The authority of Augustine was finally confirmed, in a Gallic context, at the Council of Orange in 529. See Chapter 2, 49.

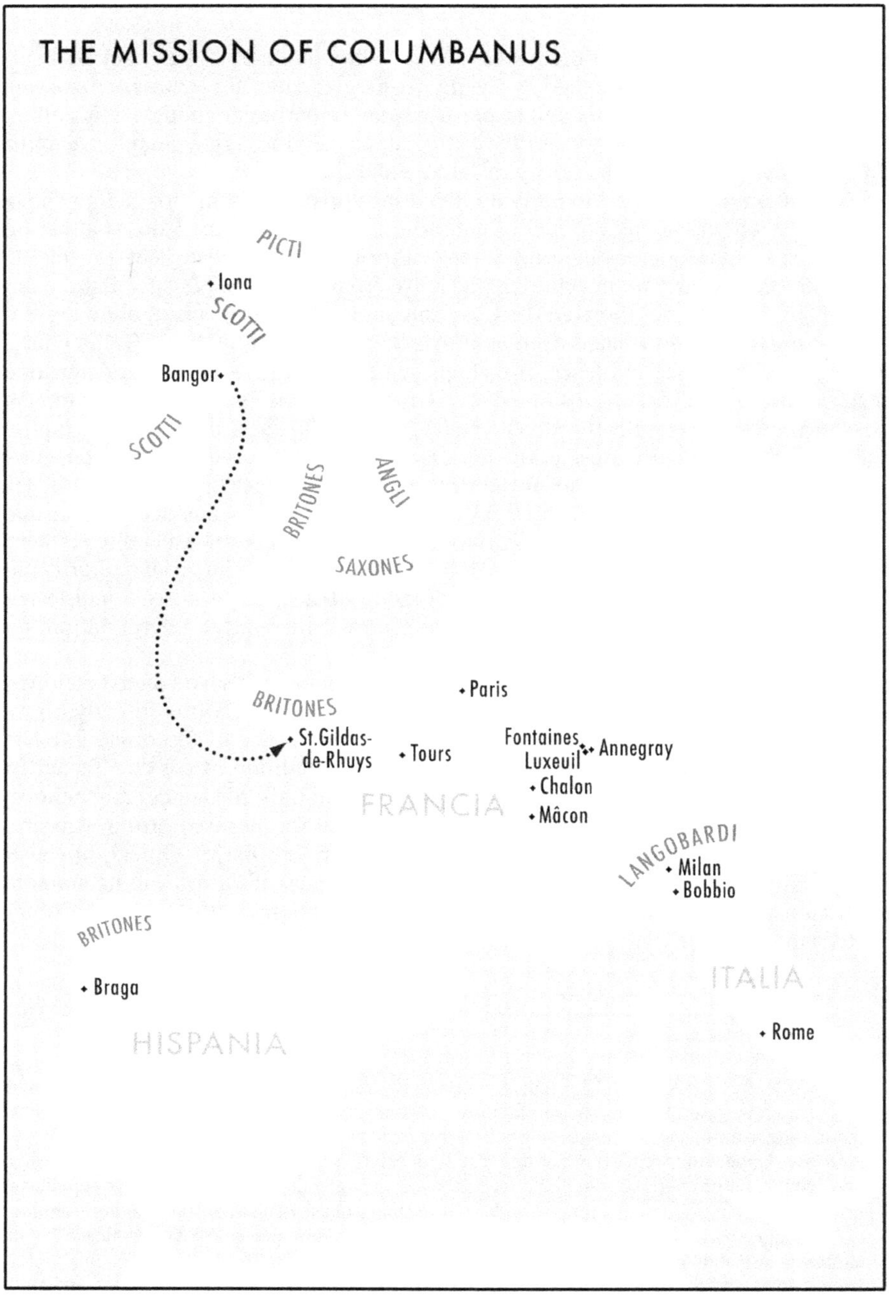

Columbanus's peregrinatio *to the continent.*

4

COLUMBANUS AND GREGORY THE GREAT

An emphasis on Gildas's *De excidio* as a jeremiad has reinforced a perception of the *De excidio* as a failed intervention. Indeed, Gildas begins his letter by invoking the lamentations of Jeremiah over the fall of Jerusalem and the destruction of her temple:

> I read how, because of the sins of men, the voice of the holy prophets rose in complaint, especially Jeremiah's, as he bewailed the ruin of his city in four alphabetic songs. And I could see that in our time too, just as Jeremiah had lamented, 'the city' (that is, the church) 'sat solitary, bereaved; formerly it had been full of peoples, mistress of races, ruler of provinces: now it had become tributary'.[1]

He ends his letter, however, by summoning the more active and reformist 'call to arms' of Jeremiah's contemporary, Ezekiel, whom God had installed as the *speculator* or watchman for his people:

> You are drunk with the practising of constant sins, and shaken by the waves of accumulated crimes that incessantly rush upon you; seek then, as though you had suffered shipwreck, with all the striving of your mind, for the single plank of penitence that can carry you to the land of the living, so that the fury of the Lord may be turned away from you. For in his mercy he said: 'I do not desire the death of a sinner, but that he may turn and live'.[2]

In offering, at the last, a 'plank' to the Christian leaders of *Britannia*, Gildas emphasised his role as a *speculator* within an Old Testament Israel where kings, priests, and prophets shared responsibility for protecting her people. That this model of authority offered in the *De excidio* – where the monastery provided holy men as *speculatores* – was successful in the British Isles is most clearly seen with the pastoral mission of the Irish *peregrinus* Columbanus to the continent at the end of the sixth century. Operating in both Gaul and Italy, Columbanus was confident in his ability to establish monastic foundations in inhospitable regions lacking in ecclesiastical

[1] Gildas, *De excidio*, I.4–5 (ed. Winterbottom, 87, trans., 13–14): 'Legebam… ob peccata hominum querulas sanctorum prophetarum voces et maxime Hieremiae ruinam civitatis suae quadruplici plangentis alphabeto. Videbamque etiam nostro tempore, ut ille defleverat, "solam sedisse urbem viduam, antea populis plenam, gentium dominam, principem provinciarum, sub tributo fuisse factam", id est ecclesiam'. This passage cites Lamentations 1.1.

[2] Gildas, *De excidio*, CX.2 (ed. Winterbottom, 142, trans., 79): 'Multumque nam usu ac frequentia peccatorum inebriati et incessanter irruentibus vobis scelerum cumulatorum ac si undis quassati unam veluti post naufragium in qua ad vivorum terram evadatis paenitentiae tabulam toto animi nisu exquirite, ut avertatur furor domini a vobis misericorditer dicentis: "nolo mortem peccatoris, sed ut convertatur et vivat"'. This passage cites Ezekiel 33.11. The sentiment in also repeated at Ezekiel 3.17–18, where God installs Ezekiel as the *speculator* of Israel.

infrastructure, and in his ability to edify volatile kings and territorial bishops lacking in moral leadership. His confidence in his intervention on the continent drew, in part, on the authority of Gildas, and reflected, in part, that the Christian culture of the British Isles had neither disintegrated nor had it fatally fragmented.

In a letter to Pope Gregory the Great *ca* 600, Columbanus called on the authority of Gildas to clarify the correct approach to simony in the context of a defence of the Insular Easter. In examining Columbanus's letters to the bishops of Rome and Gaul on the issues of schism, simony, and Easter, this chapter outlines his attachment of schism and Easter to the deeper issue of simony, and the degree to which his criticisms of simony drew on Gildas's portrayal of simoniac clerics as the 'wicked shepherd' from Ezekiel and John. Subsequently, I demonstrate that Gregory, the first monk to become pope, shared similar concerns to Columbanus, manifest in his emphasis on clerical discipline via Ezekiel and on the role of the priest as the vocal *bonus pastor* or 'good shepherd' of John and Isaiah. Gregory was the first pope to construct a handbook for priests (as shepherds) – the *Regula pastoralis* – and, significantly, the first pope to emphasise the purchase of clerical office as the heresy of Simon Magus or *simoniaca haeresis* (simony). In exploring how Columbanus used and adapted Gildas's *De excidio* to buttress his vision of the *ordo* of the church, I argue that the legacy of Gildas, as represented by Columbanus, may have influenced Gregory's pastoral mission.

Columbanus and his mission

In the last decades of the sixth century, generally dated to around 590, the Irish abbot and priest, Columbanus (*ca* 543–615), embarked on a religious exile or *peregrinatio* to the continent, perhaps to edify a church he saw as corrupt and torn by schism.[3] The sixth century had been a traumatic time for a church dependent on the continuity and authority of Rome and its apostolic see. The collapse of direct imperial authority in the west in the last quarter of the fifth century saw attempts to assert imperial authority from Constantinople. Efforts to impose this authority on the former Roman province of Italy in the sixth century resulted in a devastating war between the Arian Gothic kings who had risen to power in the late fifth century and Catholic imperial

[3] The issues of corruption and schism are fundamental concerns addressed in his surviving letters. See below for more detail. For a summation of the career of Columbanus, see Bullough, 'The Career of Columbanus'. See also *Sancti Columbani Opera* (ed. Walker, ix–xxxi); Charles-Edwards, *Early Christian Ireland*, 344–90; O'Hara, *Jonas of Bobbio*, 38–46. Details of Columbanus's activities on the continent are contained in Jonas of Bobbio's *Vita Columbani abbatis discipulorumque eius* or *Life of Columbanus and His Disciples*, written a generation or so after the death of Columbanus *ca* 642–3. The edition quoted in this book is Jonas, *Vita Columbani* (ed. Krusch, 61–156). All translations, unless otherwise stated, come from Jonas, *The Life of Columbanus* (trans. O'Hara & Wood, *Jonas of Bobbio*, 85–239). For the dating of the *vita*, see O'Hara & Wood (trans.), *Jonas of Bobbio*, 1–3. The orthodox date of *ca* 590 for Columbanus's arrival in Gaul conflicts with the claim of Jonas, written within living memory of Columbanus, that Columbanus arrived in the reign of King Sigibert (*ob. ca* 575). See *Vita Columbani*, I.6 (ed. Krusch, 72): 'Pervenit ergo fama Columbani Sigiberti regis ad aulum' [At length the fame of Columbanus reached the court of King Sigibert]. For a brief discussion of the problems of synchronising the chronology of Columbanus from the surviving primary sources, see Bullough, 'The Career of Columbanus', 9–11. For further discussion on this point, see below, 99–101.

forces.[4] Further, the patriarch of Constantinople's claim to equivalency with or, indeed, primacy over the bishop of Rome created enormous tensions within the church herself.[5] Imperial interference in papal elections created a tainted, defensive papacy, one that was unable to bring its authority to bear decisively on doctrinal debates. The Council of Constantinople in 553, dominated by imperial authority and the ecclesiastical interests of the imperial capital, created schism via the 'Three Chapters controversy' as well as affirming the Bishop of Constantinople as equal in authority to the Bishop of Rome.[6] Into this tense stand-off came the Arian-influenced Germanic tribe, the Lombards. Practically unopposed, they invaded Italy in 568, subsequently establishing kingdoms in the north and south of the peninsula and subjecting Rome itself to siege, plague, and famine.[7] An isolated Roman papacy, fighting for its primacy and, indeed, for its very existence, was unable to exercise its customary authority over ecclesiastical disputes, as perhaps exemplified by the failure to enforce uniformity on the dating of Easter. The result, in places like Gaul where Columbanus set foot, was an impression of a disjointed clerical order increasingly bound up in the affairs of local secular elites.[8] Columbanus must have been acutely aware of the similarity between the situation he perceived in Gaul and the one criticised by Gildas in his *De excidio.*

Columbanus arrived in Brittany – associated with the Christian culture of the British Isles since the fifth century – with twelve companions or 'apostles', symbolic of Christ's mission on Earth and emblematic of an Irish monastic attachment to *peregrinatio* or pilgrimage to establish monasteries and save souls.[9] His predecessor and

4 For a brief overview of the Gothic War in Italy (535–54) between the imperial forces of Emperor Justinian (*r.* 527–65) and the Ostrogothic forces of the Kingdom of Italy, see Amory, *People and Identity*, 9–12. See also Llewellyn, *Rome in the Dark Ages*, 52–77. For an overview of the Arian heresy in the late antique and early medieval period, see Brennecke, 'Introduction'.

5 For an overview of political and ecclesiastical tensions between Rome and Constantinople in the context of the Acacian Schism (484–519), see Blaudeau, 'Between Petrine Ideology and Realpolitik'.

6 See Richards, *The Popes and the Papacy*, 139–61, for a discussion of the Three Chapters controversy. See also Chazelle & Cubitt (edd.), *The Crisis of the* Oikoumene.

7 See Richards, *The Popes and the Papacy*, 162–80, for a discussion of the Lombardic Crisis. That the tribulations of Italy in the sixth century could have been known in Britain and Ireland, see *Adomnán's Life of Columba*, I.28 (edd. Anderson & Anderson, 54–5): 'Sanctus tum sic profatur: "Sulfurea de caelo flamma super romani iuris ciuitatem intra Italiae terminos sitam hac hora effusa est, triaque ferme milia uirorum excepto matrum puerorumque numero disperierunt. Et antequam praesens finiatur annus gallici nautae de Galliarum prouinciis aduentantes haec eadem tibi enarrabunt". Quae uerba post aliquot menses ueridica fuisse sunt conprobata. Nam idem Lugbeus, simul cum sancto uiro ad caput regionis pergens, nauclerum et nautas aduentantis barcae interrogans, sic omnia illa de ciuitate cum ciuibus ab eis audit enarrata, quemadmodum a praedicabili uiro sunt praedicta' [Then the saint spoke thus: 'In this hour, sulphurous flame has been poured down from heaven upon a city of the Roman dominion within the borders of Italy; close upon three thousand men, not counting the number of women and children, have perished, and before the present year is ended the Gallic sailors arriving from the province of Gaul will tell you the same.' After some months, these words were proved to have been correct. For this Lugbe went, along with the holy man, to the chief place of the district; and he questioned the master and sailors of a ship that arrived, and heard these things about the city and its inhabitants related by them, all precisely as the memorable man had said before].

8 For an overview of the political instability of the Frankish kingdoms of the sixth century, see Wood, *The Merovingian Kingdoms*, 88–101.

9 For the Irish tradition of *peregrinatio*, see Johnston, *Literacy and Identity*, 42–50. For the cultural connections between Brittany and Britain, see Charles-Edwards, *Wales and the Britons*,

namesake, the Irish abbot and priest Columba, had embarked on a *peregrinatio* to northern Britain with twelve companions to establish monasteries and save souls a generation earlier *ca* 563.[10] Columba, himself, came to be perceived as one of the 'twelve apostles' of Ireland under the direction of Finnian, highlighting a tradition of *peregrinatio* within Britain and Ireland going back to at least the first half of the sixth century.[11] Columbanus's claim to both the name Columba (he never referred to himself as Columbanus), and his citing of the authority of Finnian in connection to that of Gildas (see Chapter 5), situated him within this monastic tradition, defined by a sense of exile and mission.[12]

Under the protection of Frankish kings, Columbanus and his disciples eventually settled in the remote district of the Vosges Mountains in Burgundy where they founded three monasteries, Annegray, Luxeuil, and Fontaines.[13] Changes in political fortune with the Frankish kings, probably driven by Columbanus's refusal to tolerate their moral failings, eventually saw Columbanus arrive in north Italy *ca* 612.[14] There, under the protection of Lombard kings, he founded a monastery at Bobbio where he died on 23 November, traditionally thought to be in the year 615.[15] Columbanus's feast day is, perhaps, the only date of which we can be certain: his year of birth is unknown, his year of death drawn from tradition, and the timing of his movements within Europe based on a legacy of personal writings and subsequent hagiographies that often conflict in their detail. Of his surviving attributed writings, only select

56–74. For the twelve companions, see Jonas, *Vita Columbani*, I.4 (ed. Krusch, 70): 'Vicensimum ergo aetatis annum agens, arrepto itinere, cum duodecim comitibus Christo duce ad litus maris accedent' [Columbanus is twenty when he sets out on his journey and under the guidance of Christ makes for the seashore with twelve companions]. Significantly, Ian Wood makes a case from his examination of Jonas's *vita* that Columbanus may have entered Gaul via the monastery of Saint-Gildas-de-Rhuys. See Wood, 'Columbanus', 107–8.

10 For an overview of the career of Columba, see Charles-Edwards, *Early Christian Ireland*, 282–308.

11 Adomnán reports that Columba studied under a Bishop Findbarr/Vinniauus in Ireland. See, for instance, *Adomnán's Life of Columba*, II.1 (edd. Anderson & Anderson, 94–5): 'cum uir uenerandus in Scotia apud sanctum Findbarrum episcopum adhuc iuuenis sapientiam sacrae scripturae addiscens commaneret' [when the venerable man, while still a youth, was living in Ireland with the holy bishop Findbarr, acquiring knowledge of sacred scripture]. This Findbarr/Vinniauus is variously identified as Finnian of Clonard (*ob. ca* 549) or Finnian of Moville (*ob. ca* 579), and is, perhaps, the same Finnian connected to Gildas by Columbanus. For the equation of Findbarr with Finnian, see Dumville, 'Gildas and Uinniau', 208–10.

12 For a sense of *peregrinatio* as mission, see Wood, 'What Is a Mission?'

13 Jonas, *Vita Columbani*, I.6 (ed. Krusch, 72): 'Erat enim tunc vasta heremus Vosacus nomine, in qua castrum dirutum olim, quem antiquorum traditio Anagrates nuncupabant' [There was at that time a vast wilderness called the Vosges in which there was a fortress, long since in ruins, called *Anagrates*]; I.10 (ed. Krusch, 76): '... quo monasterium construxisset... quem Luxovium prisca tempora nuncupabant... aliumque monasterium construit, cui Fontanas nomen indedit' [... in which he might build a monastery... which was known as *Luxovium* since ancient times... and he builds there another monastery, which he names *Fontanas*].

14 Jonas, *Vita Columbani*, I.30 (ed. Krusch, 106): 'Beatus... Columbanus... Italiam ingreditur' [blessed Columbanus... enters Italy].

15 Jonas, *Vita Columbani*, I.30 (ed. Krusch, 106–8): 'ubi ab Agilulfo Langobardorum rege honorifice receptus est... beatus Columbanus... in antedictu caenubio Ebobiensi vita beata functus... VIIII. K1. Decembris' [There he was honourably received by Agilulf, king of the Lombards... blessed Columbanus completed his blessed life in the monastery of Bobbio... On 23 November].

letters can be firmly assigned to Columbanus.[16] Columbanus's legacy was both highly influential and controversial: as a 'holy man' he founded and inspired a network of monastic foundations for the edification of the church of Gaul and Italy; as a 'defender of the faith' he courted controversy with his refusal to obey or condone his seniors in matters of praxis, such as clerical interpretations of the correct dating of Easter, and moral behaviour, such as secular interpretations of the legal rights of children born outside marriage.[17]

Elements of Christian observance that Columbanus introduced to the continent appeared to be different to that found in Gaul and Italy and opened the way for tension with the clerical orders. Columbanus advocated different methods for calculating Easter and practising penance within an orthodox faith he asserted was drawn directly from the apostolic authority of Rome, as outlined in his letter to Pope Boniface.[18] In criticising what he saw as unorthodox approaches to clerical and monastic discipline, he offered, via Gildas and Finnian, Insular approaches to the problems of simony and monastic recreantism, as outlined in his letter to Pope Gregory.[19] Challenging the papacy on praxis and clerical discipline, Columbanus placed himself within the traditions of the Old Testament prophets and called on the authority of

[16] Surviving attributed texts include letters, sermons, poetry, a penitential, and a monastic rule. For the authenticity of the *epistulae*, see Wright, 'Columbanus's *Epistulae*', 29–30.

[17] For Columbanus and Easter, see below, 91–3. For Columbanus's criticisms of Merovingian attempts to ensure succession through children born out of wedlock, see Wood, 'Jonas', 107–12.

[18] Columbanus, *Epistulae*, V.3 (ed. Walker, 38–9): 'Nos enim sanctorum Petri et Pauli et omnium discipulorum divinum canonem spiritu sancto scribentium discipuli sumus, toti Iberi, ultimi habitatores mundi, nihil extra evangelicam et apostolicam doctrinam recipientes; nullus hereticus, nullus Iudaeus, nullus schismaticus fuit; sed fides catholica, sicut a vobis primum, sanctorum videlicet apostolorum successoribus, tradita est, inconcussa tenetur' [For all we Irish, inhabitants of the world's edge, are disciples of Saints Peter and Paul and of all the disciples who wrote the sacred canon by the Holy Ghost, and we accept nothing outside the evangelical and apostolic teaching; none has been a heretic, none a Judaizer, none a schismatic; but the Catholic Faith, as it was delivered by you first, who are the successors of the holy apostles, is maintained unbroken]. For a brief overview of Columbanus and Easter, see Fox, *Power and Religion,* 93. See also Corning, 'Columbanus and the Easter Controversy'. Bullough, 'The Career of Columbanus', 11–13, attributes to Columbanus the introduction into continental Europe of the Irish practice of private and frequent confession, followed by private and reiterated penance. For a caution on attributing innovation in penance to Columbanus in a Gallic context, see Meens, *Penance in Medieval Europe*, 70–8. For Columbanus as a junior comfortable in criticising seniors, see Bracken, 'Authority and Duty'. Tensions over the correct monastic tonsure are not mentioned by Columbanus or his contemporaries during his lifetime, and probably belong to the seventh century: see Chapter 5.

[19] Columbanus, *Epistulae*, I.6 (ed. Walker, 8–9): 'Ceterum de episcopis illis quid iudicas, interrogo, qui contra canones ordinantur, id est quaestu; simoniacos et Gildas auctor pestes scripsit eos. Numquid cum illis communicandum est?' [Concerning those bishops, however, who ordain uncanonically, that is for hire, I ask what you decree; Gildas the writer set them down as simoniacs and plagues]; I.7 (ed. Walker, 8–9): 'quid faciendum est de monachis illis, qui pro Dei intuitu et vitae perfectioris desiderio accensi, contra vota venientes primae conversionis loca relinquunt, et invitis abbatibus, fervore monachorum cogente, aut laxantur aut ad deserta fugiunt. Vennianus auctor Gildam de his interrogavit, et elegantissime ille rescripsit' [what is to be done about those monks who, for the sake of God, and inflamed by the desire for a more perfect life, impugn their vows, leave the places of their first profession, and against their abbots' will, impelled by monastic fervour, either relapse or flee to the deserts. Finnian the writer questioned Gildas about them, and he sent a most polished reply].

Gildas.[20] Written responses from the papacy, if there were any, have not survived. The lack of surviving responses to Columbanus's letters has reinforced a notion of antipathy between the papacy and Columbanus.[21] In order to examine this notion of antipathy as it relates to the model of authority presented by Columbanus, we need to examine the relationship between his surviving letters to the bishops of Rome and Gaul and the model of authority laid out in Gildas's *De excidio*.

The *De excidio* and the letters of Columbanus

Of the works attributed to Columbanus, only five letters can be confidently ascribed to him.[22] The letters, copied in the seventeenth century from a lost Saint Gallen and/or Bobbio codex by Judocus Metzler (1574–1639) and subsequently by Patricius Fleming (1599–1631), perhaps from the same Bobbio codex, were edited in the latter half of the twentieth century by George Walker.[23] Walker's edition contains, amongst other works attributed to Columbanus, six *epistulae*, with the sixth 'letter' drawn from a separate manuscript solely transmitting Columbanus's attributed sermons or *instructiones*.[24] The letters are generally dated from the papacy of Gregory the Great to that of Boniface IV, traditionally covering the years 600–13 and supporting Columbanus's activity on the continent from 590 to 615. Setting aside the contested attribution of *Epistula VI*, Walker's edition has reinforced the following chronology, as supported, for instance, by Wright:

[600]	*Epistula I* to Pope Gregory the Great.
[603]	*Epistula II* to bishops at the Council of Chalon.
[604 or 607]	*Epistula III* to Pope N (Sabinian or Boniface III).
[610]	*Epistula IV* to his disciples (in the context of exile).
[613]	*Epistula V* to Pope Boniface IV.[25]

[20] Columbanus calls directly on his namesake, the Old Testament prophet Jonah. See Columbanus, *Epistulae*, V.16 (ed. Walker, 54–5): 'facienti mihi Ionae hebraice, Peristerae graece, Columbae latine, potius tantum vestrae idiomate linguae nancto, licet prisco utor hebraeo nomine' [I am called Jonah in Hebrew, Peristera in Greek, Columba in Latin, yet so much is my birth-right in the idiom of your language, though I use the ancient Hebrew name of Jonah].

[21] See, for instance, Kelly, 'The Letter of Columbanus'. He sees Columbanus's letter to Gregory as too offensive to warrant a reply.

[22] Wright, 'Columbanus's *Epistulae*', 29–30. Smit, *Studies on the Language*, 25. Stancliffe, 'The Thirteen Sermons', makes a strong argument that the *instructiones* can be assigned to Columbanus, but, for brevity, these will be set aside for the certainty of Columbanus's *epistulae*. Her identification of the author as Columbanus does rely, in part, on supporting the traditional dating of Gildas to the sixth century. See Stancliffe, 'The Thirteen Sermons', 174–86. For a recent overview of Columbanus's surviving works, see O'Hara, *Jonas of Bobbio*, 45–50.

[23] Columbanus, *Epistulae* (transc. Metzler, St. Gall, Stiftsbibliothek, Cod. Sang. 1346): *Epistula IV* (60–70), *Epistula VI* (= *Instructio XIV*) (70–2), *Epistulae III, II, V, I* (74–119); Columbanus, *Epistulae* (ed. Fleming, *Collecteana*, 102–64); Columbanus, *Epistulae* (ed. Walker, 2–59). For a discussion of the manuscript tradition of the letters, see *Sancti Columbani Opera* (ed. Walker, xxxv–xxxix and lxxiv–lxxv); Smit, *Studies on the Language*, 33–8. I would like to thank Dr Cornel Dora of Stiftsbibliothek St Gallen for arranging early access to the digitised version of Metzler's manuscript.

[24] The sixth letter does not contain a conventional epistolary introduction, and is, perhaps, better to be regarded as a short text. See Wright, 'Columbanus's *Epistulae*', 30.

[25] Wright, 'Columbanus's *Epistulae*', 29.

However, this rationalisation of the letters is at odds with the editions of Metzler and Fleming who, in preserving the layout of the lost codex, presented the letters (utilising Walker's numbering) in the order III, II, V, and I, with, in Flemings's case, IV inserted between II and V from a different section of the codex, one also preserving Columbanus's attributed sermons or *instructiones*. The publisher Thomas Sheerin noted in Fleming's edition that *Epistula I* was terribly corrupt, to the extent that Fleming had set it aside from publication.[26] It was Sheerin who restored *Epistula I* (from another source, perhaps Metzler) to the end of Fleming's edition of III, II, IV, and V, a sequence that implied a chronology of 604/607–13, with the placement of IV informed by Columbanus's exile from Gaul, traditionally dated to 610.[27] Walker, in this context, following Wilhelm Gundlach's 1892 edition, moved *Epistula I* to the beginning of Fleming's sequence and prior to the death of Gregory (*ob.* 604) mentioned in *Epistula III*.[28] He also swapped, following Gundlach, II and III on the basis of identifying the Gallic Synod addressed by Columbanus as also occurring prior to the death of Gregory. However, as the original codex may have been preserving a different rationale for ordering, the chronology reinforced by Walker's edition is not certain. Further, the insertion of *Epistula IV* into the sequence by Fleming is itself a rationalisation of the order preserved in the manuscript tradition. Thus, only III, II, V, and I represents a systemisation that predates the seventeenth century. It is possible that the contexts of Columbanus's letters, perhaps even their transcription, have been affected by attempts to harmonise them within later temporal traditions. We shall return to this point at the end of this chapter.

In his letters, Columbanus adopts a prophetic voice similar to that of Gildas in his *De excidio*. This is not surprising as the surviving letters, like Gildas, call on the authority embedded within monasticism for juniors to edify their clerical seniors.[29] Concentrating on the original collation of III, II, V, and I, and setting aside the covering letter to Pope N (III), what we have are three critical letters of which two address the papacy on the issues of schism, corrupt clergy, and Easter (V and I), and one that addresses the bishops of Gaul on corrupt clergy and Easter (II). As

26 See *Collectanea Sacra* (ed. Fleming, 108): 'ex pervetusto, sed mendoso satis Bibliothecae Bobiensis Codice' [from an ancient but quite faulty manuscript from the library of Bobbio]. For the letter to Gregory in particular, see *Collectanea Sacra* (ed. Fleming, 157): 'Caeterum Epistolae, ut hic iacet, sensum in multis evertunt mendae crebrae, et fere inemendabiles nisi collatione melioris MS, quae causa fuisse videtur P. Flemingo eam in sui collectione praetereundi' [The rest of the letter, as it lies here, ruins the sense with numerous errors, almost uncorrectable unless by comparison with a better MS, which seems to have been the reason for P. Fleming setting it aside from his collection]. Translations are my own.

27 *Sancti Columbani Opera* (ed. Walker, lxxiv–lxxv).

28 Columbanus, *Epistulae*, III.2 (ed. Walker, 22–3): 'Idcirco semel et bis satanas impedivit portitores nostrorum ad beatae memoriae papam conscriptorum Gregorium olim apicum in subiectis positorum' [Thus once and again Satan hindered the bearers of our letters once written to Pope Gregory of blessed memory and annexed to this]. For Gundlach's edition, see Columbanus, *Epistolae* (ed. Gundlach).

29 Perhaps best seen at Columbanus, *Epistulae*, V.10 (ed. Walker, 46–9): 'ideo et vestri iudices erunt qui semper orthodoxam fidem servaverunt, quicumque illi fuerint, etiamsi iuniores vestri videantur; ipsi autem orthodoxi et veri catholoci, qui neque hereticos neque suspectos aliquos aliquando receperunt neque defenderunt, sed in zelo verae fidei permanserunt' [thus too shall they be your judges, who have always kept the orthodox faith, whoever these may have been, even if they seem to be your subordinates; but they themselves are the orthodox and true catholics, since they never favoured or supported any heretics or suspect persons, but have remained in eager love of the true faith].

noted previously, Columbanus calls directly on the authority of Gildas in *Epistula I* to Pope Gregory the Great in the context of simoniac bishops. Michael Winterbottom and Neil Wright's work on Columbanus's letters have also noted direct references to Gildas's *De excidio*.[30] Significantly, these references are overwhelmingly placed within the letters to the papacy. *Epistula II* to the Gallic bishops, on the other hand, calls directly on the same authority as Gildas in his *De excidio*, namely Jerome's letters to Heliodorus and Paulinus of Nola, both letters, as we have seen in Chapter 3, emphasising the distinct roles of monasticism and the clerical orders and the importance of monks edifying their clerical seniors.[31] In addressing the bishops of Gaul, Columbanus appears to take on the role of Gildas; in addressing the papacy, Columbanus appears to defer to Gildas.

In appealing to Gildas in his letters to the papacy, Columbanus is presumptuous, not so much in his criticisms, which he considers to be mandated by God, but in the fact that he regards the papacy as being directly aware of Gildas's authority. Further, direct references to phrasing from the *De excidio* imply that Columbanus believed that the papacy had access to that text and that the papacy was aware of the prophetic authority contained in that text. Nearly half of the phrases used by Columbanus that can be assigned to the *De excidio* with certainty come from an accusatory section contrasting the corrupt and indolent clergy of Britain with the active examples of the martyred apostles, James, Peter, and Paul, and the martyred deacon, Stephen. Within this section, Columbanus specifically draws on the example of Peter:

> [Gildas] Quis vestrum, qui **torpetis potius quam sedetis legitime** in sacerdotali sede, eiectus de consilio impiorum, post diversarum plagas virgarum, ut sancti apostoli, quod dignus habitus est pro Christo vero deo contumeliam pati toto corde trinitati gratias egit?... Quis inversis pedibus crucis affixus pro reverentia Christi patibulo, quem non minus morte quam vita honoraturus, ut **clavicularius ille caelorum regni** idoneus, extremum halitum fudit?[32]

> [Columbanus] Nec loci namque nec ordinis est ut magnae tuae auctoritati aliquid quasi discutiendo inrogetur et ridiculose te mei, nimirum Petri cathedram apostoli et **clavicularii legitime insidentem**, occidentales apices de Pascha sollicitent.[33]

30 Winterbottom, 'Gildas and Columbanus'; Wright, 'Columbanus's *Epistulae*', 82–7. These direct references form the basis of the following analysis.

31 See Wright, 'Columbanus's *Epistulae*', 71–2.

32 Gildas, *De excidio*, LXXIII.2–3 (ed. Winterbottom, 123, trans., 58): 'Which of you, who **slouch rather than sit lawfully** in the priestly seat, was cast out of the council of the wicked like the holy apostles and beaten with diverse rods, and then thanked the trinity with whole heart for being judged worthy to suffer insult for Christ, the true God?... Which was fixed feet upwards to the gibbet of a cross for his reverence to Christ, and there breathed his last, honouring Christ in death as in life, like the fit **keeper of the keys of the kingdom of heaven**?' The incidents about Peter are taken from Acts 5.17–41, where Peter leads the apostles against the Sanhedrin, and from Jerome's *De uiris illustribus*, where he describes the crucifixion of Peter. See O'Loughlin, *Gildas and the Scriptures*, 283–4. The only patristic author to use the term *clavicularius* prior to Gildas is Ambrose. Gildas appears to be the first to apply the role of the key-keeper to Peter.

33 Columbanus, *Epistulae*, I.5 (ed. Walker, 6–9): 'For it befits neither place nor station that your great authority should be at all questioned by the appearance of debate, and that you, who indeed **lawfully occupy** the chair of Peter the apostle and **bearer of the keys**, should ludicrously be troubled about Easter by my letters from the West.'

> ad te namque totius exercitus Domini in his regionibus, in campo **potius torpentis quam** pugnantis, et partim, quod lacrimabilius est, adversariis potius manus dantis quam resistentis, periculum pertinent.[34]

> Tam diu enim potestas apud vos erit, quamdiu recta ratio permanserit; **ille** enim certus **regni caelorum clavicularius** est, qui dignis per veram scientiam aperit et indignis claudit; alioquin si contraria fecerit, nec aperire nec claudere poterit.[35]

The legitimacy of the priesthood, as represented by the apostolic seat of Peter, is directly tied to suffering and martyrdom in defence of Christ: torpor and surrender, on the other hand, delegitimise the priesthood in such a way that the incumbents are no longer priests. Columbanus directly follows Gildas in asserting that status is not enough to command spiritual authority, and that suffering and martyrdom in defence of Christ are inherent duties of priestly office. In doing so, he once again draws on the authority of Jerome's letter to Heliodorus to state that the office of the priesthood – the office of the papacy itself – is contingent not just on faith, but faith and deeds:

> [Columbanus] Non sufficit tibi, quod pro te ipso sollicitus sis, qui multorum curam susceptisti; **cui** enim **plus creditur, plus ab eo exigitur**.[36]

> [Jerome] **Cui plus creditur, plus ab eo exigitur**. 'Potentes potenter tormenta patientur'.[37]

Jerome's phrase is itself a unique rendering of the instructions of Christ in Luke 12.48 on the theme of *vigilantia* or watchfulness, a biblical phrase also alluded to in *Epistula I*.[38]

In *Epistula V*, this theme of *vigilantia* is immediately associated by Columbanus with the role of *speculator* or watchman through direct comparison of the role of the papacy with that of the Prophet Isaiah:

> May Isaiah send you to the mountain, who publish good tidings to Zion, rather may God through Isaiah place you on the watch-tower of true contemplation, according to

34 Columbanus, *Epistulae*, V.7 (ed. Walker, 42–5): 'for it is you that are concerned with the danger of the Lord's whole army in these regions, **sleeping rather than** fighting on the field, and partly (which gives even more cause for tears) surrendering rather than opposing the foe'.

35 Columbanus, *Epistulae*, V.11 (ed. Walker, 50–1): 'For power will be in your hands just so long as your principles remain sound; for he is the appointed **key-bearer of the Kingdom of Heaven**, who opens by true knowledge to the worthy and shuts to the unworthy; otherwise if he does the opposite, he shall be able neither to open nor to shut.'

36 Columbanus, *Epistulae*, V.4 (ed. Walker, 40–1): 'It is not enough for you, who have undertaken responsibility for many, to be careful for yourself; for **to whom more is entrusted, from him will more be demanded**.'

37 Jerome, *Epistulae*, 54, XIV.9 (ed. Hilberg, 58): '**To whom God has committed much, of him He will ask the more**. "Mighty men shall be mightily tormented".' The biblical phrase cited is from Wisdom 6.7. Gildas cites Wisdom 6.7 at Gildas, *De excidio*, LXIII.1 (ed. Winterbottom, 117).

38 Luke 12.48: 'Omni autem cui multum datum est, multum quaeretur ab eo: et cui commendaverunt multum, plus petent ab eo' [And unto whomsoever much is given, of him much shall be required: and to whom they have committed much, of him they will demand the more]. Columbanus, *Epistulae*, I.9 (ed. Walker, 10–11): 'Sed et tu magna habes, quia de parvo minus et de multo plus bene scis esse foenerandum' [But you too have large resources, since you know well that from a small stock less must be lent and from a great one more].

> the meaning of your name, and there, as it were placed above all mortals and made near to the heavenlies, may you lift up your voice like a trumpet and proclaim their sins to the people of your Lord, committed to you by Him, and to the house of Jacob their iniquities.[39]

This prophetic role of *speculator* is then associated directly with the theme of the shepherd or *pastor* as ultimately responsible for the fate of his sheep, itself derived from Ezekiel:

> Then, since according to the Lord's warnings the blood of so many will be sought for at the hands of their shepherds, careful watch must be kept, that is, the word of the Lord must be often preached, and preached by the shepherds, by the Church's bishops and teachers, that none may perish through ignorance; for if he perishes through lack of heed, his blood will lie on his own head.[40]

Further, Columbanus equates the role of the *pastor* with that of the *bonus pastor* related by Christ in John 10, whose role as the good shepherd relies on the sheep recognising his voice. In his *Epistula II* to the Gallic bishops, where he significantly relies on the New Testament in addressing his clerical seniors, Columbanus combines the authority of John with the monastic ideal inherited from Gildas to support his right to criticise his seniors for their lack of words and deeds in their role as shepherds:

> I have touched these matters briefly for this reason, that if you are willing for us juniors to teach you fathers, you may ever keep in work and word this saying of the true shepherd, which His sheep know – for they do not hear the voice of strangers, but flee from him whose voice they know not, which, unless it be exemplified in practice, does not agree with the voice of the true shepherd.[41]

39 Columbanus, *Epistulae*, V.5 (ed. Walker, 40–3): 'Mittat te Isaias in montem, qui evangelizas Zion, immo per Isaiam Deus iuxta tui nominis interpretationem in speculam verae contemplationis ponat, in qua quasi cunctis mortalibus altior positus vicinusque caelestium effectus, exaltans quasi tuba vocem tuam annunties populo domini tui, tibi ab eo commisso, peccata eorum et domui Iacob iniquitates eorum'. This passage invokes Isaiah 40.9 and 58.1.

40 Columbanus, *Epistulae*, V.5 (ed. Walker, 42–3): 'Inde quia iuxta minas Domini sanguis tantorum de manibus requirendus erit pastorum, vigilandum est diligenter, id est, praedicandum est frequenter verbum Domini, a pastoribus scilicet, ecclesiae speculatoribus et magistris, ut nullus pereat per ignorantiam; si enim per socordiam perierit, suus sanguis in suum caput reputabitur'. The image of blood on the hands of the watchman is found at Ezekiel 33.6. Columbanus's emphasis on Ezekiel is also noted by Bracken, 'Juniors Teaching Elders', 272–3. Craigie, *Ezekiel*, 243, notes Ezekiel's development of God as the Good Shepherd who actively seeks out his lost sheep. Manning Jr, *Echoes of a Prophet*, 114, confirms this innovation by Ezekiel. See also Smit, *Studies on the Language*, 40–7, for Columbanus's connection of Ezekiel and Isaiah.

41 Columbanus, *Epistulae*, II.4 (ed. Walker, 14–15): 'Haec idcirco breviter tetigi, ut, si volueritis nos inferiores vos patres docere, hanc vocem veri pastoris et in opere et in ore semper habeatis, quam suae agnoscunt oves – non enim audiunt vocem alienorum, sed fugiunt ab eo, cuius vocem non agnoscunt, quae, nisi actualis sit, voci veri non concordat pastoris'. The biblical phrase 'sed fugiunt ab eo' is from John 10.5. *Epistula II*, aside from two allusions to the Psalms, only refers to the New Testament. This has to be a deliberate choice by Columbanus: to use only the words of Christ and his apostles to criticise the clerical orders is surely significant. On John 10, see Bracken, 'Juniors Teaching Elders', 268–9.

Columbanus's connection of the *speculator* with the *bonus pastor*, with Isaiah, Ezekiel, and John, is also found in Gildas's *De excidio*. Columbanus's opening address to the papacy, using a distinct phrasing from the *De excidio*, one that supports the prophetic *tuba* or *vox* rather than silence, alerts us to this connection:

> [Columbanus] Non igitur pro vanitate aut procacitate scribere **vilissimae qualitatis** homunculus tam praecelsis viris praesumo.[42]

> [Gildas] Nam si haec surdis auribus audias, prophetas contemnas, Christum despicias, nosque, licet **vilissimae qualitatis** simus, nullius momenti ducas.[43]

Gildas follows up immediately with Isaiah 58.1, but, as O'Loughlin has noted, it is a rendition that deliberately merges Isaiah with a similar passage from Micah:

> though it is with sincere piety of the mind that I obey the pronouncement of the prophet: 'I shall surely fill my courage with the spirit and virtue of the Lord, to announce to the house of Jacob its sins, and its crimes to the house of Israel'.[44]

What Gildas thinks these sins and crimes might be can be found succinctly described in Micah 3.11, itself reflective of the warning against corrupt shepherds or 'hirelings' in John 10:

> [Micah] Her princes have judged for bribes, and her priests have taught for hire, and her prophets divined for money.[45]

> [John] The good shepherd giveth his life for his sheep. But the hireling, and he that is not the shepherd, whose own the sheep are not, seeth the wolf coming, and leaveth the sheep, and flieth: and the wolf catcheth, and scattereth the sheep: And the hireling flieth, because he is a hireling: and he hath no care for the sheep.[46]

The collusion of the secular leadership and the clerical orders in corrupt practice is a fundamental concern in Gildas's *De excidio*. In his opening complaint directed at the clergy, Gildas calls on the image of the wicked shepherds from both Ezekiel and John:

42 Columbanus, *Epistulae*, V.2 (ed. Walker, 38–9): 'So it is not for vainglory or for impudence that I, a creature **of the meanest station**, dare to write to such exalted men'.

43 Gildas, *De excidio*, XXXVI.4 (ed. Winterbottom, 104, trans., 35): 'You may hear this with deaf ears, spurning the prophets, despising Christ, regarding me, **worthless** as I am, as of no importance.'

44 Gildas, *De excidio*, XXXVI.4 (ed. Winterbottom, 104, trans., 35): 'propheticum illud sincera animi pietate servantes utcumque: "si non ego implevero fortitudinem in spiritu et virtute domini, ut enuntiem domui Iacob peccata eorum et domui Israhel scelera eorum"'. For Gildas's connection of Isaiah 58.1 to Micah 3.8, see O'Loughlin, *Gildas and the Scriptures*, 173–4. For Gildas's approach to Isaiah in general, see Perkins, 'Biblical Allusion'.

45 Micah 3.11: 'Principes ejus in muneribus judicabant, et sacerdotes ejus in mercede docebant, et prophetae ejus in pecunia divinabant'.

46 John 10.11–13: 'Bonus pastor animam suam dat pro ovibus suis. Mercenarius autem, et qui non est pastor, cujus non sunt oves propriae, videt lupum venientem, et dimittit oves, et fugit: et lupus rapit, et dispergit oves; mercenarius autem fugit, quia mercenarius est, et non pertinet ad eum de ovibus'.

> Britain has priests, but they are fools; very many ministers, but they are shameless; clerics, but they are treacherous grabbers. They are called shepherds, but they are wolves all ready to slaughter souls. They do not look to the good of their people, but to the filling of their own bellies.[47]

Gildas, in imitation of the *tuba* of Isaiah and the *vox* of Christ the Good Shepherd, has announced, via Ezekiel and John, the sin of the clergy: that of greed. It is surely no accident that Gildas ends his *De excidio* with the plea of God to Israel through his prophet Ezekiel, 'I do not desire the death of a sinner, but that he may turn and live.'[48] It mirrors his emphasis in his preface on Ezekiel's contemporary Jeremiah, both prophets who predicted the destruction of Jerusalem, both, as Nicholas Cachia notes, rebukers of neglectful leaders and proclaimers of consequences.[49]

In establishing greed as the root cause for the corruption of the clergy, Gildas subsequently describes the purchase of clerical office as a sin passed on from generation to generation:

> For what is so impious and so wicked… for anyone to want to purchase, like Simon Magus, the office of bishop or presbyter for a worldly price, when such office is more fittingly acquired through holiness and right behaviour?… But (alas!) it may well be that those who ordain these candidates for priesthood… were themselves called to the priesthood in just the same way: and do not greatly detest (and even respect) in their sons something which certainly happened in their own case and that of their fathers too.[50]

With this description, he distances himself from the image of the *mercenarius* or 'hireling' from John 10.[51] Instead, with his focus on the structural corruption of the clerical orders as indicative of a corrupted apostolic succession, Gildas appears to have elevated the purchase of clerical office to that of the heresy of Simon Magus.

The purchase of clerical office is one of the core complaints in Columbanus's letters to the papacy and the Gallic bishops. That he interprets Gildas's attitude to the purchase of clerical office as the heresy of simony is set out in his letter to Gregory the Great. As previously noted, he cites Gildas directly on the matter:

47 Gildas, *De excidio*, LXVI.1 (ed. Winterbottom, 118, trans., 52): 'Sacerdotes habet Britannia, sed insipientes; quam plurimos ministros, sed impudentes; clericos, sed raptores subdolos; pastores, ut dicuntur, sed occisioni animarum lupos paratos, quippe non commoda plebi providentes, sed proprii plenitudinem ventris quaerentes'. This section draws from Ezekiel 34 and John 10.12. See O'Loughlin, *Gildas and the Scriptures*, 258.

48 Gildas, *De excidio*, CX.2 (ed. Winterbottom, 142, trans., 79): 'ut avertatur furor domini a vobis misericorditer dicentis: "nolo mortem peccatoris, sed ut convertatur et vivat"' [so that the fury of the Lord may be turned away from you. For in his mercy he said: 'I do not desire the death of a sinner, but that he may turn and live]. As already noted, this passage cites Ezekiel 33.11.

49 Cachia, *The Image of the Good Shepherd*, 51–2.

50 Gildas, *De excidio*, LXVII.1–4 (ed. Winterbottom, 119–20, trans., 53–4): 'Quid enim tam impium tamque scelestum est quam ad similitudinem Simonis magi… episcopatus officium vel presbyterii terreno pretio, quod sanctitate rectisque moribus decentius adquiritur, quempiam velle mercari?… Sed forte (heu!) qui ambitores istos ordinant… eodem modo sacerdotio adsciti sunt: et ideo non magnopere detestantur in filiis, quin immo venerantur, quod similiter ut patribus sibi evenisse certissimum est'.

51 Indeed, the term *mercenarius* does not appear in the *De excidio*.

> Concerning those bishops, however, who ordain uncanonically, that is for hire, I ask what you decree; Gildas the writer set them down as simoniacs and plagues. Are we really to communicate with them?[52]

That Columbanus might regard Gildas's view of the heresy of simony – in this case described by the grecism *simoniacus* – as unknown or not accepted on the continent is seen in his *Epistula II* to the Gallic bishops: Columbanus is careful only to use the word *mercenarius* or 'hireling' for his criticism of the purchase of clerical office. While Thomas O'Loughlin observes that 'the notion of simony as a sin belongs to a period later than Gildas', it is possible, taking into account the witness of Columbanus, that Gildas is one of the earliest authorities to emphasise the purchase of clerical office as that of the heresy of Simon Magus.[53]

This emphasis on Simon Magus by Columbanus via Gildas may also underscore his other fundamental complaints: that the troubles of the church are a direct result of the tainting of papal authority, and that proper authority is attached to the correct date of Easter, itself intimately tied to the fundamental rites of baptism and ordination.[54] That 'false baptism' could also be equated with the falsely ordained heretic, Simon Magus, is seen in Jerome's *Commentary on Ezekiel*:

> This applies not just to heretics but also to some in the church who want the salvific effects of baptism without a full faith. It can be said that they may receive the water but not the [Holy] Spirit. This was the case with Simon Magus, who sought to gain the grace of God for money. Such a one is baptised with water but in no way baptised unto salvation.[55]

For Columbanus, as for Gildas, the church was also corrupted by a simoniacal apostolic succession.

52 Columbanus, *Epistulae*, I.6 (ed. Walker, 8–9): 'Ceterum de episcopis illis quid iudicas, interrogo, qui contra canones ordinantur, id est quaestu; simoniacos et Gildas auctor pestes scripsit eos. Numquid cum illis communicandum est?'

53 O'Loughlin, *Gildas and the Scriptures*, 259. He argues, because of this point, that Gildas is merely utilising the image of Simon Magus because of its direct appeal to his situation.

54 Columbanus, *Epistulae*, V.3 (ed. Walker, 38–9): 'Doleo enim, fateor, de infamia cathedrae sancti Petri' [Indeed I grieve, I confess, for the disgrace of St. Peter's chair]; I.3 (ed. Walker, 4–5): 'Nam qui hac lunae aetate Pascha definiunt possibile celebrari, non solum illud auctoritate divinae scripturae affirmare non possunt, sed et sacrilegii et contumaciae crimen et animarum periculum incurrunt' [For those who determine that Easter can be celebrated at this period of moon, not only cannot maintain this on the authority of holy scripture, but also incur the charge of sacrilege and contumacy, together with the peril of their souls]. The latter citation is from a passage where Columbanus is quoting from a computational tract on Easter authored by Bishop Anatolius of Loadicea (*r.* 268–83). This text is regarded by Walker as an Irish forgery. See 3, n. 4. Recent work argues the text by Anatolius is genuine: see Mc Carthy & Breen, *The Ante-Nicene Christian Pasch*. The early medieval period saw an emphasis on Easter, Pentecost, and the Epiphany for baptism. See Jensen, *Baptismal Imagery*, 132. On the significance of Pentecost (as related to the date of Easter) on clerical ordination, see Reynolds, *Clerical Orders*, XI, 4–5.

55 Jerome, *Commentarii in Ezechielem*, IV.16 (ed. Glorie): 'quod quidem non solum de haereticis, sed et de ecclesiasticis intellegi potest qui non plena fide accipiunt baptismum salutare, de quibus dicendum est quod acceperint aquam sed non acceperint spiritum – sicut et simon ille magus, qui pecunia uolebat redimere gratiam dei, baptizatus quidem est in aqua sed nequaquam baptizatus est in salutem'. For the translation and further comment, see Colish, *Faith, Fiction, and Force*, 104.

That simony and its impact on the papal elections of the sixth century was known within monastic circles can be inferred from Gregory's letter to the anchorite Secundinus in May, 599. Gregory appears to allay Secundinus's concern over the papal succession following Pope Hormisdas (*r.* 514–23) and up to that of Pope Vigilius (*r.* 537–55):

> But concerning the ordinations of pontiffs of the apostolic see, your Charity asks whether anything has been added since the most blessed Hormisdas. But you should recognise that the ordinations of prelates were established right up to the time of Pope Vigilius.[56]

Indeed, all the papal elections from John I (*r.* 523–6) through to Vigilius, who ratified the Council of Constantinople and catalysed the Three Chapters schism, were tainted by simony, political interference, and electoral fraud.[57] It is probable that subsequent papal elections still attracted suspicion. Vigilius's successor Pope Pelagius I (*r.* 556–61), who did much to restore the papacy, still had to deal with a tainted election and distrust over his orthodoxy, and the invasion of Italy by the Lombards in 568 and subsequent sieges of Rome would have brought similar scrutiny of the apostolic succession in the seat of Peter, particularly from those, like Columbanus, who came from a tradition of *praesens iudicium* or 'judgement in the here and now'.[58]

With a tainted succession in the seat of Peter seen to replicate that of Simon Magus's false apostolic succession, we can see that the decisions made by the successive popes from John I to Vigilius might also have been seen to be tainted. The three decisions of note for Columbanus may have been John I's commission of new Easter tables from Dionysius Exiguus (*ob. ca* 544) that continued the 'error' of Victorius of Aquitaine (*fl.* fifth century); Felix IV's (*r.* 526–30) support of the condemnation of 'semi-Pelagianism' at the Council of Orange in 529, which targeted the monastic tradition built around John Cassian; and, of course, Vigilius's ratification of the Council of Constantinople's condemnation of the Three Chapters in 553 which, in amending decisions taken at the Council of Chalcedon and retrospectively condemning fathers of the church, created an alarming precedent and schism. What we have here is a 'perfect storm' targeting the Christian traditions inherited from Jerome and Cassian via Gildas to Columbanus. This storm was manifested by endemic corruption, torpor, and unorthodoxy, and had its origins in 'false baptism' and 'false ordination' as exemplified by Simon Magus and substantiated by an incorrect date for Easter.

Columbanus had adjusted Gildas's observation on the structural corruption of the clerical orders to include the effect of the degradation of the efficacy of the rites of baptism and ordination, a degradation that he intimately attached to the calculation of the date of Easter. Simony was, therefore, at the heart of Columbanus's complaint to the papacy and the Gallic bishops, a heresy built on pretence or idolatry. In support

56 Gregory the Great, *Registrum epistularum*, IX.148 (ed. Norberg): 'De ordinationibus uero apostolicae sedis pontificum, utrum post beatissimum ormisdam aliqua sint addita uestra caritas requirit. Sed usque ad uigilii papae tempora expositas ordinationes praesulum esse cognoscat'. Translation is my own.

57 For an overview of complex secular influences brought to bear of papal succession around the middle of the sixth century, see Richards, *The Popes and the Papacy*, 114–35. See also Moorhead, *The Popes*, 65–99. The *Liber Pontificalis* itself notes irregularities in the papal elections of Boniface II (*r.* 530–2), Silverius (*r.* 536), Vigilius (*r.* 537–55), and Pelagius I (*r.* 556–61). See *The Book of Pontiffs* (trans. Davis, 53–61).

58 Richards, *The Popes and the Papacy*, 159.

of this, Columbanus, like Gildas, drew on Ezekiel and John and the role of the priest as the active and vocal 'good shepherd', but he also stressed, through Ezekiel, the importance of the salvific effects of a correct baptism.

In drawing on Ezekiel and John, Columbanus placed himself in a monastic tradition similar to that of one of his known contacts, Gregory the Great. Gregory, as monk and pope, also drew on the example of Isaiah, John, and Ezekiel, and that of the active and vocal 'good shepherd': one of his first publications in office *ca* 591 was the *Regula pastoralis* or *Rules for Shepherds*, a handbook for priests.[59] A subsequent publication was his *Homiliae in Hiezechihelem prophetam* or *Homilies on the Prophet Ezekiel*, presented publicly *ca* 592–3, and revised *ca* 600.[60] Gregory also emphasised the purchase of clerical office as the heresy of simony. He used the grecism *simoniacus*, a term appearing first in his *Homiliae in euangelia* or *Homilies on the Gospels*, presented publicly *ca* 591–2 and published *ca* 593, and subsequently in his *Registrum epistularum* or *Register of Letters* from October 593.[61] The monastic traditions and world view of Gregory the Great and Columbanus appear to be aligned. In order to discern a potential influence of the legacy of Gildas on that of the pastoral mission of Gregory the Great, we need to examine Gregory's relationship with the heresy of simony.

Gregory and simony

The heresy most consistently tackled by Gregory during his papal reign was the heresy of simony, the buying and selling of clerical office.[62] Gregory, himself, had come from an aristocratic background prominent in the church of Rome: his ancestors had been pope – Felix III (*r.* 483–92) and, perhaps, Agapitus I (*r.* 535–6) – and there was a family tradition of monastic retirement, particularly within the female line.[63] Born *ca* 540 and classically educated, Gregory had begun his career in public service, rising to the position of *praefectus Urbis* or urban prefect by 573, but in 576, on the death of his father, he left public service to found several monasteries and establish a monastic community in his paternal home, one dedicated to the apostle Andrew. His contemplative sojourn was short-lived: in 578 he was ordained a deacon and in 579 he became a papal legate or *apocrisiarius* for Pope Pelagius II (*r.* 579–90)

59 For the *Regula pastoralis*, see Gregory the Great, *Regula pastoralis* (ed. Rommel & Clement).

60 For the *Homiliae in Hiezechielem*, see Gregory the Great, *Homiliae in Hiezechielem* (ed. Adriaen).

61 Gregory the Great, *Homiliae in euangelia*, I.17 (ed. Étaix, 127): 'Hinc est quod sacri canones simoniacam haeresim damnant' [This is why the sacred canons condemn the heresy of simony]. Translation is my own. Gregory the Great, *Registrum epistularum*, IV.13 (ed. Norberg): 'Et siquidem sine datione aliqua ad eundem ordinem uenit, ut in simoniacam haeresem non potuisset incidere, in aliam quamcumque uacantem ecclesiam eum uolumus ordinari' [And if indeed he came to this same rank without any payment, so that he could not have fallen into the heresy of simony, we want him to be consecrated for some other vacant church]. All translations of Gregory's letters, unless otherwise stated, come from *The Letters of Gregory the Great* (trans. Martyn).

62 See *The Letters of Gregory the Great*, I (trans. Martyn, 84). There is a useful list of letters dealing with simony at n. 231. For a general history of simony, see Webber, *A History of Simony*. See also Willis, *Simony*; Leclercq, 'Simoniaca Heresis'; Ryder, *Simony*. A modern overview of the history of simony is sorely needed.

63 Straw, *Gregory the Great*, 5.

in Constantinople, eventually rising to the position of Deacon of Rome *ca* 585.[64] He was elected pope in 590 and remained in office for fourteen years.

Gregory's family, in embracing the monastic life and clerical service, influenced Gregory to hold Cassian's view of the monastery as a provider of clerics grounded in the teachings of Christ.[65] This was evidenced, in a practical sense, by Gregory's favouring of monks for clerical duties on taking office. In a philosophical sense, this desired combination of the contemplative and cloistered life of the monk with the active and worldly life of the cleric was formally emphasised from the outset of taking office. Gregory's synodical letter in February 591 to the church patriarchs of Constantinople, Alexandria, Antioch, and Jerusalem drew on elements that would later appear in his *Regula pastoralis*:

> I consider indeed that one must be vigilant and take all care that a bishop is pure in thought, outstanding in action, discrete in silence, useful with his speech, very close to individuals with compassion, more uplifted in contemplation with others, allied with those doing good through humility, but upright with the zeal of justice against the vices of wrong-doers.[66]

Gregory is clearly emphasising the importance of the integrity of the clerical orders, and is quick to subsequently attach the model life of the monk to the active role of the cleric through the example of the vocal good shepherd, drawing on Ezekiel, John, and Isaiah:

> Again when I turn to consider what works a priest should do, I reflect with what great attention he must take care that he is remarkable in his action, to show his subjects the way of life by his way of living, and so that the flock which follows the shepherd's voice and morality might make better progress through his examples than his words… For that voice penetrates the hearts of listeners more readily which the life of the speaker commends… For this reason the prophet says: 'Go up to the high mountain, Zion, herald of good tidings'.[67]

That the voice of the good shepherd can be undermined by inappropriate silence or careless talk is also drawn from Ezekiel, John, and Isaiah. Silence, in this case, is intimately attached to the purchase of clerical office:

64 For Gregory's career, see *The Letters of Gregory the Great,* I (trans. Martyn, 1–14). An excellent summation can also be found in Davies, 'The "Mouth of Gold"', 250–3.

65 Markus, *Gregory the Great*, 17.

66 Gregory the Great, *Registrum epistularum*, I.24 (ed. Norberg): 'Perpendo quippe quod omni cura uigilandum est, ut rector cogitatione sit mundus, operatione praecipuus, discretus in silentio, utilis in uerbo, singulis compassione proximus, prae cunctis contemplatione suspensus, bene agentibus per humilitatem socius, contra delinquentium uitia per zelum iustitiae erectus'. See also Gregory the Great, *Regula pastoralis*, II.1 (ed. Rommel & Clement).

67 Gregory the Great, *Registrum epistularum*, I.24 (ed. Norberg): 'Rursum cum me ad consideranda debita pastoris opera confero, perpendo quanta intentione curandum est ut sit operatione praecipuus, quatenus uitae uiam subditis uiuendo denuntiet, et grex qui pastoris uocem moresque sequitur per exempla melius quam uerba gradiatur… Illa namque uox libentius auditorum cor penetrat, quam dicentis uita commendat… Hinc enim per prophetam dicitur: "super montem excelsum ascende tu, qui euangelizas syon"'. See also Gregory the Great, *Regula pastoralis*, II.3 (ed. Rommel & Clement). The biblical phrase cited is Isaiah 40.9. This phrase is rarely used by the church fathers: before Gregory it is used only by Jerome. Columbanus also uses this biblical phrase in Columbanus, *Epistulae*, V.5 (ed. Walker, 40).

For, just as a careless remark leads him into error, even so an indiscreet silence leaves in error those who could have been instructed. For often improvident bishops, fearful of losing human favours, are afraid to speak freely about what is right, and by no means do they then look for the protection of their flock according to the voice of Truth, with the endeavour of shepherds, but rather in the manner of hired servants, because they flee as the wolf approaches, while hiding themselves under silence. For this is why the Lord attacks them through the prophet, saying: 'they are all dumb dogs, they cannot bark'.[68]

That Gregory is an ascetic like Columbanus and Gildas when criticising improper behaviour in the clerical orders is clear. Whether they share a common tradition is difficult to discern. What is significant, in this context, is Gregory's approach to the purchase of clerical office. In this synodical letter, Gregory uses the word taken from John and the Hebrew prophets, that of *mercenarius* or 'hireling', appearing to place himself in a clerical tradition, following Augustine of Hippo, that criticised the purchase of clerical office as a sin.[69] This is in keeping with his *Moralia in Iob* and his *Homiliae in euangelia.*[70] However, by October 593, Gregory begins to identify the purchase of clerical office not as a sin but as the heresy of simony.[71] In a letter to Crementius, prelate and bishop of the province of Bizacium in North Africa, he shifts from the term *mercenarius* to that of *simoniaca haeresis*:

[68] Gregory the Great, *Registrum epistularum*, I.24 (ed. Norberg): 'Saepe namque rectores improuidi, humanam amittere gratiam formidantes, loqui libere recta pertimescunt, et iuxta ueritatis uocem nequaquam iam gregis custodiae pastorum studio sed mercennariorum uice deseruiunt, quia ueniente lupo fugiunt, dum se sub silentio abscondunt. Hinc namque eos per prophetam dominus increpat, dicens: canes muti non ualentes latrare'. The biblical phrase cited is Isaiah 56.10. See also Gregory the Great, *Regula pastoralis*, II.4 (ed. Rommel & Clement). Isaiah 56:10 is used rarely by the church fathers: prior to Gregory it is used sparingly by Ignatius, Jerome, Eucherius of Lyon, and Caesarius, and also by Gildas. See Gildas, *De excidio*, XXXVI.4 (ed. Winterbottom, 104).

[69] Augustine relates simony to the purchase of clerical office and uses the Latin form *simonia* for the heresy. See Augustine of Hippo, *De haeresibus*, I (edd. Vander Plaetse & Beukers): 'simoniani a simone mago, qui baptizatus a philippo diacono, sicut in actibus apostolorum legitur, pecunia uoluit a sanctis apostolis emere ut etiam per impositionem manus eius daretur spiritus sanctus' [Simonians from Simon Magus, who was baptised by Phillip the Deacon, just as it is read in the Acts of the Apostles, and who wished to buy with money from the holy apostles the gift of the holy spirit through the imposition of hands]. Translation is my own. However, in his other writings, Augustine refers to the actor engaged in the selling or purchase of clerical office, following the Gospel of John, as a *mercenarius* or 'hireling', avoiding an innate connection between the sin and heresy.

[70] A search of Brepols's *Library of Latin Texts* reveals that Gregory used *mercenarius* or variants thirty-four times: eighteen in *Moralia in Iob*; twelve in *Homliae in euangelia*; one in *Dialogi*; one in *Regula pastoralis*; and two in *Registrum epistularum*.

[71] A search of Brepols's *Library of Latin Texts* reveals that Gregory used *simoniacus* or variants thirty-two times: one in *Homiliae in euangelia*; and thirty-one in *Registrum epistularum*. There is also a *simoniacus* under the entry for Pelagius I (*r.* 556–61) in the *Liber Pontificalis*, I, LXII (ed. Duchesne, 303) 'vos omnes scitis quia simoniacus est' [you all know that is simoniacal]. However, this entry was probably added in the time of Honorius (*r.* 625–38) and, thus, postdates Gregory. See *The Book of Pontiffs* (trans. Davis, xiii). The sole surviving canon from the Council of Constantinople in 459 mentions *simoniacum*, but the surviving signatory letter from the Council does not refer to the grecism. It is perhaps a later construct. On the council, see *A Manual of Councils*, I (ed. Landon, 195).

> And if indeed he came to this rank without payment, so that he could not have fallen into the heresy of simony, we want him to be consecrated for some other vacant church.[72]

Sometime prior to October 593, if we can accept the dating of the letter, Gregory escalated the purchase of clerical office from a sin to the heresy of simony. He did so without argument or fanfare, as might be required with an innovation, but as if it were already attached to a tradition. The tradition that Gregory called on was that of the sacred canons of the church.[73] However, none of the canons that predate Gregory use the specific phrase *simoniaca haeresis*.[74]

The tradition Gregory may have tapped into, that of simony as a heresy related to false apostolic succession, was emphasised by Jerome. Following church fathers such as Irenaeus (*ob. ca* 202), Hippolytus (*ca* 170–235), and Eusebius (*ca* 260–340), Jerome established Simon Magus as the 'spiritual father' of all heresies in his letter to Ctesiphon, substantively dealing with the heresy of Pelagius.[75] There he connected Simon Magus – through anti-apostles such as Nicolas (*fl.* first century), Montanus (*fl.* second century), and Arius (*ca* 256–336) – to Priscillian (*ob. ca* 385), all associated with prostitutes.[76] While scholars such as Alberto Ferreiro have explored a more direct interpretation of Jerome's description of heresies, one highlighting his attitudes toward women, there is also a further allegorical meaning driven by Jerome's use of Ezekiel.[77] Ezekiel 13–16 describes Jerusalem (and, by association, the church) as a prostitute corrupted by false prophets, idolatry, riches, fame, and beauty. The sense is, then, not just of heretics consorting with prostitutes, but heretics turning the

72 Gregory the Great, *Registrum epistularum*, IV.13 (ed. Norberg): 'Et siquidem sine datione aliqua ad eundem ordinem uenit, ut in simoniacam haeresem non potuisset incidere, in aliam quamcumque uacantem ecclesiam eum uolumus ordinari'.

73 Gregory the Great, *Homiliae in euangelia*, I.17 (ed. Étaix, 127): 'Sed Redemptor noster cathedras uendentium columbas euertit, quia talium negotiatorum sacerdotium destruit. Hinc est quod sacri canones simoniacam haeresim damnant, et eos sacerdotio priuari praecipiunt, qui de largiendis ordinibus pretium quaerunt' [But our Redeemer overthrew the temple and the selling of doves because such trade destroys the priesthood. That is why the sacred canons condemn the heresy of simony, and demand that they are to be stripped of the priesthood who seek a price for bestowing orders]. Translation is my own. This idea, equating the selling of doves to Simon Magus, appears to be taken from Augustine of Hippo. However, Augustine uses the term 'mercatores'. See Augustine of Hippo, *In Iohannis Evangelium*, X.6 (ed. Willen): 'fratres mei, qui talia quaerunt, uendunt. nam et simon ille ideo uolebat emere spiritum sanctum, quia uendere uolebat spiritum sanctum; et putabat apostolos mercatores tales esse, quales dominus de templo flagello eiecit. talis enim ipse erat, et quod uenderet emere uolebat; de illis erat qui columbas uendunt' [My brethren, they that seek such things are they that sell. For that Simon too, wished to buy the Holy Ghost, just because he meant to sell the Holy Ghost; and he thought the apostles to be just such traders as they whom the Lord cast out of the temple with a scourge. For such an one he was himself, and desired to buy what he might sell: he was of those who sell doves]. Translations, unless otherwise stated, come from 'St Augustine: Homilies on the Gospel of John' (trans. Gibb & Innes). As the *Homiliae in euangelia* were continually revised through the 590s, dating this use of *simoniacus* is uncertain.

74 It is, of course, possible that Gregory is calling on a Greek canonical tradition from the eastern church. However, I have not been able to find an earlier Greek form of *simoniaca haeresis* or variants. A search of *The Thesaurus Linguae Graecae* implies that *simoniacus* entered Greek from Latin.

75 See Ferreiro, *Simon Magus*, 88.

76 See Jerome, *Epistulae*, 56, CXXXIII.4 (ed. Hilberg, 248).

77 See, for instance, Ferreiro, *Simon Magus*, 85.

church into a consort. The outcome, as seen with Jerome's use of Jeremiah 17, is of a church as a barren woman gathering children and riches that are not truly hers, who, deserted by them, becomes a fool.[78]

Jerome's notion of simony as a heresy related to a false apostolic succession found an early exponent in the monastic authority of Vincent of Lérins (*ob. ca* 445), who also described the heretic Priscillian as a direct successor of Simon Magus.[79] The stipulation of Canon XXII of the Council of Chalcedon in 451 saw a new emphasis on clerical authority (via canon law) that emphasised the purchase of clerical office as a sin, and one remedied by the forfeit of clerical rank, with the cleric, significantly, protected from excommunication.[80] The canon made no mention of Simon Magus. Subsequently, the priest Gennadius of Marseilles, drawing on the monastic tradition represented by Vincent, connected the purchase of clerical office to the image of Simon Magus in his *De ecclesiasticis dogmatibus*, published *ca* 495,

[78] Jerome, *Epistulae*, 56, CXXXIII.4 (ed. Hilberg, 248): 'Duplex sexus utrumque supplantat, ut illud propheticum cogamur adsumere: "clamauit perdix, congregauit quae non peperit, faciens diuitias suas non cum iudicio. In dimidio dierum derelinquent eum, et nouissimum eius erit insipiens"' [Men and women in turn lay snares for each other till we cannot but recall the prophet's words: 'the partridge has cried aloud, she has gathered young which she has not brought forth, she gets riches and not by right; in the midst of her days they shall leave her']. See Ferreiro, *Simon Magus*, 86–7. Translation is a slight amendment.

[79] Vincent of Lérins, *Commonitorium*, XXIV (ed. Demeulenaere): 'Quis ante crudelissimum Nouatianum crudelem deum dixit, eo quod mallet mortem morientis, quam ut reuertatur et uiuat? Quis ante magum Simonem, apostolica districtione percussum, a quo uetus ille turpitudinum gurges usque in nouissimum Priscillianum continua et occulta successione manauit, auctorem malorum, id est scelerum impietatem flagitiorumque nostrorum ausus est dicere creatorem Deum?' [Who before cruellest Novatian represented God as cruel in that He had rather the wicked should die than that he should be converted and live? Who before Simon Magus, who was smitten by the apostle's rebuke, and from whom that ancient sink of every thing vile has flowed by a secret continuous succession even to Priscillian of our own time — who, I say, before this Simon Magus, dared to say that God, the Creator, is the author of evil, that is, of our wickednesses, impieties, flagitiousnesses?]. Translations, unless otherwise stated, are from 'The Commonitory' (trans. Heurtley). Vincent's criticism of Novatian using Ezekiel is reminiscent of Gildas's *De excidio*, which mentions the negative example of the Novatians in a British context and ends in the same plea from Ezekiel.

[80] *Concilium Chalcedonense a. 451*, II (87–8): 'Si quis episcopus ob pecuniam fecerit ordinationem et sub pretio redegerit gratiam, quae non potest venundari, ordinaveritque per pecunias episcopum aut presbyterum seu diaconum vel quemlibet ex his, qui connumerantur in clero, aut promoverit per pecunias dispensatorem aut defensorem vel quemquam, qui subiectus est regulae, pro suo turpissimi lucri commodo: his, cui hoc adtemptanti probatum fuerit, proprii gradus periculo subiacebit, et qui ordinatus est, nihil ex hac ordinatione vel promotione, quae est per negotiationem facta, proficiat. Sed sit alienus ea dignitate vel sollicitudine, quam per pecunias adquisivit. Si quis vero mediator tam turpibus et nefandis datis vel acceptis exstiterit, si quidem clericus fuerit, proprio gradu decidat, si vero laicus aut monachus anathematizatur' [If any Bishop should ordain for money, and put to sale a grace which cannot be sold, and for money ordain a bishop, or chorepiscopus, or presbyters, or deacons, or any other of those who are counted among the clergy; or if through lust of gain he should nominate for money a steward, or advocate, or prosmonarius, or any one whatever who is on the roll of the Church, let him who is convicted of this forfeit his own rank; and let him who is ordained be nothing profited by the purchased ordination or promotion; but let him be removed from the dignity or charge he has obtained for money. And if any one should be found negotiating such shameful and unlawful transactions, let him also, if he is a clergyman, be deposed from his rank, and if he is a layman or monk, let him be anathematized]. Translations, unless otherwise stated, are from 'The Seven Ecumenical Councils' (trans. Percival).

but did not directly comment on heresy or excommunication.[81] The transmission of the initially apocryphal *Canons of the Apostles* from the east to the west in the last quarter of the fifth century, and the subsequent authority given to them by Dionysius Exiguus's collation of church canons, the *Collectio Dionysiana* (compiled in Rome *ca* 500), equated the purchase of clerical office with Simon Magus and described it as an excommunicable offence for the clergy, but did not directly equate the sin with heresy.[82]

The first direct mention of the purchase of clerical office as a heresy in a continental setting appears not to come until the Second Council of Tours in 567, a council attended by Bishop Victorius of Rennes and Bishop Felix of Nantes, both of whose dioceses bordered Brittany.[83] Canon XXVII, reinterpreting Gennadius's *De ecclesiasticis dogmatibus*, directly equates the purchase of clerical office with heresy:

> No bishop may presume to request payment for the ordinations of clerics, because this is not only sacrilegious but heretical. Just as it is said in the *dogmatibus ecclesiasticis*: he should not be ordained a cleric, who through ambition offers money to a priest in the likeness of Simon Magus. On this it is stated: give freely what you have freely received.[84]

The idea of simony as a heresy is first stated on the continent in an area potentially influenced by the Christian culture of the British Isles, and at a time when papal authority in Gaul was weak, perhaps, with the imminent Lombardic crisis, soon to be severely constricted.[85]

81 Gennadius, *Liber Ecclesiasticorum Dogmatum*, XXXVIII (ed. Turner, 96): 'nec illum, qui per ambitionem ad imitationem Simonis magi pecuniam offert' [nor should (that cleric), through ambition to imitate Simon Magus, offer money]. Translation is my own.

82 For Dionysius's *Canones Apostolorum* as they relate to simony, see *Ecclesiae Occidentalis Monumenta Iuris Antiquissima*, I.30 (ed. Turner, 20): 'Si quis episcopus aut presbiter aut diaconus per pecunias hanc optinuerit dignitatem, deiciatur et ipse et ordinator eius et a communione modis omnibus abscidatur, sicut Symon magus a me Petro' [If any bishop, priest, or deacon obtains their office with money, let them and the person who ordained them be deprived of that office; and let them be completely cut off from communion, just as Simon Magus was by me, Peter]; I.31 (ed. Turner, 20–1): 'Si quis episcopus seculi potestatibus usus ecclesiam per ipsos optineat, deponatur et segregetur omnesque qui illi communicant' [If any bishop through the use of secular powers obtains a church for himself, let him be deposed and shunned, and all that communicate with him]. Translations are my own. For the *Apostolic Constitutions* (which included the Canons of the Apostles), see *Les Constitutions Apostoliques* (ed. Metzger). For a general overview on the nature and reception of the *Apostolic Constitutions*, see Ohme, 'Sources of the Greek Canon Law', 28–33. It is, perhaps, these canons that were referred to by Gregory.

83 The council was attended by nine bishops, who signed in the following order: Euphronius of Tours, Praetextus of Rouen, Germanus of Paris, Felix of Nantes, Chaletricus of Chartes, Domitianus of Anjou, Victorius of Rennes, Domnulus of Le Mans, and Leudebaudis of Sagensis, perhaps Seez. See *Concilium Turonense a. 567* (ed. de Clercq, *Concilia*, 194).

84 See *Concilium Turonense a. 567*, XXVII (ed. de Clercq, *Concilia*, 194): 'Nullus episcoporum de ordinationibus clericorum praemia praesumat exigere, quia non solum sacrilegum, sed hereticum est. Sicut in dogmatibus ecclesiasticis habetur insertum, non ordinandum clericum, qui per ambitionem ad imaginem simonis magi pecuniam offert sacerdoti. Et quia dixit: gratis accepistis, gratis date'. Translation is my own.

85 For the weak authority of the papacy in Gaul at this time, see *The Letters of Gregory the Great*, I (trans. Martyn, 51–3). Martin notes that the pallium of Arles had not been confirmed by the papacy since the granting of the pallium to Sapaudus, Bishop of Arles, in 557 by Pelagius I. Communication with Arles was established by Gregory in *Epistula I.45* written in June 591. For

It is into this context that Columbanus arrived. He brought with him a similar tradition of simony as a heresy – one where the purchase of clerical office was intimately linked to the creation of a false apostolic succession – as well as the particular use of the grecism *simoniacus* as laid out in his letter to Gregory. In *Epistula I*, Columbanus assigns both the use of *simoniacus* and the purchase of clerical office as an excommunicable offence to the authority of Gildas. It is this unique term *simoniacus* that Gregory combines with *haeresis* and uses in all his communication from 593, apart from one letter in July 599 where he reverts to *mercenarius*.[86] The evidence points to the possibility that Gregory's view on simony was shaped by the tradition that underpinned that of Columbanus and Gildas.

As noted previously, the lack of surviving papal replies to the letters of Columbanus has reinforced a notion of antipathy between the papacy and the 'arrogance' of Columbanus. However, that the former monk Gregory sought out and valued communication with anchorites or 'holy men' on complex issues is seen in his communication with the anchorite Secundinus (or Secundus), perhaps active in the court of the Lombards *ca* 600.[87] *Epistula 9.148* (May 599) covers such topics as the Three Chapters controversy, the fate of the souls of unbaptised babies, and, as mentioned previously, the papal succession. Further, the dating of Columbanus's activity in Italy post *ca* 612, as supported by Jonas's *vita* and Walker's edition of the *Epistulae Columbani*, has set aside a medieval tradition, still reported in the nineteenth century, of an earlier visit by Columbanus to Italy during the pontificate of Gregory the Great.[88] This medieval tradition is supported by the seventeenth-century Italian Cistercian, Fernando Ughelli, who cites in his *Italia sacra* several medieval manuscripts from the monastery of Bobbio: two charters pertaining to the foundation of Bobbio from Lombard king Agilulf to Columbanus (dated to 598) and from Columbanus to Pope Gregory the Great (dated to 591); and a report describing a meeting between Columbanus and Gregory in 595.[89]

the crisis in papal authority and its impact on papal letters during the Three Chapters controversy, see Eno, 'Papal Damage Control', 52–6. Bronwen Neil notes no surviving papal letters from John III to Benedict I, or from 561–79. See Neil, '*De profundis*', 206–7.

86 Gregory the Great, *Registrum epistularum*, IX.225 (ed. Norberg): 'Quod si ita est, uehementius ingemesco, ne apud omnipotentem dominum, quod absit, mercennarii officium et non pastoris meritum habeatis ... ' [If that is so, I groan all the more strongly, in case before our almighty Lord (Heaven forbid!), you may be holding the office of mercenaries and not the service of pastors].

87 Gregory the Great, *Registrum epistularum*, IX.148 (ed. Norberg). Martyn conjectures Secundinus as the Secundus mentioned in *Epistula XIV.12*. See *The Letters of Gregory the Great*, III (trans. Martyn, 878, n. 43).

88 Stokes, *Six Months in the Apennines*, 125–33. Stoke reports – based on medieval documents preserved at Bobbio in the seventeenth century – that Columbanus was in Milan 595–8, and visited Rome in 599.

89 *Italia sacra*, IV (ed. Ughelli, 950–6). Ughelli preserves a manuscript, attributed to Columbanus's hagiographer Jonas, that records a meeting between Columbanus and Gregory (*Beatus Columbanus*); a confirmation of the charter granted to Bobbio from Columbanus to Gregory (*Chartula qualiter dominus Columbanus tradidit monasterium Bobiense sedi apostolicae*); and the privilege granting Bobbio to Columbanus by King Agilulf (*Privilegium sive prima donatio Flavii Agilulfi, Longobardorum regis, venerabili S. Columbano de territorio Bobiensi per millia quatuor ab omni parte concessum*). The manuscript attributed to Jonas dates the meeting between Gregory and Columbanus to just over a year before his reported death in 596: 'Eodemque itaque tempore dum haec agerentur, contigit sanctissimum Columbanum gratia visitandi limina Apostolorum, ac loquendi summum Pontificem Gregorium Magnum tam sanctissimum virum Romam ire...

This earlier visit to Italy can be supported by other sources: Gregory the Great's surviving *epistulae* collection indicates a possible interest in Ireland in July 592; the presence of a significant *peregrinus*, perhaps an Irish priest, in Rome in March 594; the delivery of Gregory's *Regula pastoralis* to a priest named Columbus under the protection of a bishop in northern Italy in November 594; and a commendation of a priest named Columbus to the abbot of Lérins in Southern Gaul in October 600.[90] That Columbanus had read a version of Gregory's *Regula pastoralis* is affirmed in *Epistula I*.[91] It is possible, as both Roy Flechner and Clare Stancliffe have noted, that *Columbus presbyter* and Columbanus are the same person.[92] James O'Carroll's work on reconciling the hagiography concerning Columbanus also argues that Columbanus arrived in Gaul as early as 573, as supported by Jonas's *vita*, with *Epistula II* written to the bishops at the Second Council of Mâcon in 585, which, unlike the later councils of Sens (601) and Chalon (603), has a surviving legacy of dealing

Qua propter reversus Sanctus Columbanus Bobium transacto anni curriculo, menseque uno, et octo diebus, in antedicto coenobio Bobiensi vita beata functus, anima membris resolute, coelo reddidit spiritum, nono Kalendas Decembris, anno Dominicae Incarnationis 596' [And so, at the same time that this was happening, it befell that the most holy Columbanus went to Rome for the purpose of visiting the house of the apostles and speaking to the highest Pontifex Gregory the Great, such a holy man…. Having returned to Bobbio for this reason, after the passage of a year, a month, and eight days, Saint Columbanus, having completed his blessed life, his soul being separated from the body, gave his spirit back to Heaven in the aforementioned monastery of Bobbio on 23 November 596]. The privilege of Agilulf to Columbanus is among a list of the earliest documents relating to Bobbio compiled by Michael Richter and tentatively dated to *ca* 613 despite it indicating it was written in the eighth year of Agilulf's reign, usually regarded as commencing *ca* 590: see Richter, *Bobbio*, 13–14. The *Chartula qualiter dominus Columbanus* remains relatively understudied: it is included in *Codice Diplomatico*, I (ed. Cipolla, 81–3). Cipolla reports the dating for 591, but is highly sceptical. See *Codice Diplomatico*, I (ed. Cipolla, 81): 'Le note cronologiche dell'offersione… accennano al 591, ma è inutile soggiungere che tutto questo non ha valore alcuno e non è il caso di studiare di quale anno di pontificato si tratti. Ad un documento così disgraziato non è possibile assegnare alcuna data' [The chronological notes of the controversial date… refer to 591, but it is pointless to add that all this has no value and it is not necessary to study which year of the pontificate it is. It is not possible to assign any date to such an unfortunate document]. Translations are my own.

90 John Martyn has listed the potential references in his paper. See Martyn, 'Pope Gregory the Great and the Irish'. They include Gregory's *Epistula II.43* (Martyn conjectures this as an encyclical sent to the Irish church over the Three Chapters controversy); *Epistula IV.18* to Maurus, abbot of Saint Pancras in Rome ('idcirco huius tibi auctoritatis tenore praecipimus ut **peregrinum** illic non desinas adhibere presbyterum' [we accordingly order you with the direction of this authority not to stop employing the **non-Italian** priest there]); *Epistula V.17* to Venantius, Bishop of Luni ('Codicem uero regulae pastoralis domno **columbo presbytero** transmittendum per harum portitores direximus' [We have also directed that those bearing this letter should hand over a copy of our Pastoral Care to the noble **priest, Columban**]); *Epistula XI.9* to Conan, abbot of Lérins ('Filium praeterea nostrum **columbum presbyterum**, qui caritati tuae suis est meritis commendatus, in tua dilectione proficere optamus et ex nostra commendatione' [Besides this, we hope that our son and **priest, Columban**, who has been commended to your Charity through his merits, may prosper in your love and from this commendation of ours]). Emphasis is mine.

91 Columbanus, *Epistulae*, I.9 (ed. Walker, 10–11): 'Legi librum tuum pastorale regimen continentem, stilo brevem, doctrina prolixum, mysteriis refertum' [I have read in your book containing the pastoral rule, brief in style, pregnant in doctrine, replete with sacred lore].

92 Flechner, 'Dagan, Columbanus and the Gregorian Mission', 71–4. Stancliffe, 'Columbanus and Shunning', 118–19. Stancliffe argues that a relationship between Gregory and Columbanus may have begun as early as 594.

with Easter.[93] Canons II and III of this council, notably prescribing regulations for the whole of Gaul, address Easter, a matter made significant by the prominence given to the festival in the ordering of the canons. Canon II instructed the due observation of both Easter and Holy Week.[94] Canon III instructed that the baptism of infants could not take place at any time other than the Easter endorsed by the Gallic church, an assertion of authority potentially correcting those, like Columbanus, who had linked a worldly clergy to a 'false baptism' and 'false ordination' predicated on a 'false Easter'.[95]

Returning to the problematic issue of the ordering of the *epistulae*, there is, perhaps, another way that the letters were bound in the original manuscript: *Epistula III*, written at a time when no pope had been elected, was a covering letter to which were attached older letters sent by Columbanus to Gregory. If the original manuscript had been bound in this way, the letters following *Epistula III* (II, V, and I) may well be those attached letters. These letters would, in this instance, be older than the covering letter, variously placed during the papal elections of 604 or 607. Interpretations of

93 O'Carroll, 'The Chronology of Saint Columban'. O'Carroll takes the view that Jonas of Bobbio's dating of the arrival Columbanus to the continent in the reign of Sigibert (*ob. ca* 575) should be taken seriously. The traditionally accepted arrival date, that of *ca* 590, O'Carroll assigns to the foundation of Luxeuil. While O'Carroll remains an outlier in the debate on dating, the problems he raises with the traditional dating have not been resolved. For a discussion of the chronology, see also Rohr, 'Hagiographie als historische Quelle', 252–6. Albrecht Diem proposes Jonas's inclusion of Sigibert as a literary device. See Diem, 'Monks, Kings', 541–2. The potential attribution of *Epistula II* to the Council of Mâcon is further supported by Columbanus's silence on the term *simoniaca haeresis* – it implies that Columbanus wrote the letter prior to Gregory's elevation of simony to a heresy. Walker's identification of a *Sanctus Gregorius* mentioned in *Epistula II* with Gregory the Great has been ably set aside by Neil Wright, who has identified the figure mentioned as Gregory of Nazianzus (*ca* 329–90). See Wright, 'Columbanus's *Epistulae*', 74. Ian Wood continues to advocate an arrival date of around 590 based on an attribution of *Epistula II* to the Council of Chalon (dated by him to 603/604), but has recently canvassed a slightly earlier date based on his interpretation of Jonas's *vita*. See Wood, 'Columbanus', 106.

94 *Concilium Matisconense a. 585*, II (ed. de Clercq, *Concilia*, 240): 'Pascha itaque nostrum… debemus omnes festissime colere et sedulae obseruationis sinceritate in omnibus uenerari, ut illis sanctissimis sex diebus nullus seruile opus audeat facere' [And therefore we ought to celebrate our Easter most festively and venerate it in all things with the sincerity of assiduous observation, so that for these most holy six days no one should dare to do any servile work]. Translation is my own.

95 *Concilium Matisconense a. 585*, III (ed. de Clercq, *Concilia*, 240): 'Relatione quorumdam fratrum nostrorum comperimus christianos non obseruantes legitimum diem baptismi paene per singulis dies ac natalis martirum filios suos baptizare… Ideoque praesentibus admonitionibus a suis erroribus uel ignorantia reuocati omnes omnino a die quadragensimo cum infantibus suis ad ecclesiam obseruare praecipimus, ut inpositionem manus certis diebus adepti et sacri olei liquore peruncti ligitimi diei festiuitate fruantur et sacro baptismate regenerentur, quo possint et honoribus, si uita comis fuerit, sacerdotalibus fungi et singulares celebrationes solemnitate frui' [We learn from our brothers that Christians are not observing the legitimate days for baptism but are baptising their sons on almost every other day and on the feasts of martyrs… therefore we require all people, in order to be saved from error and superstition, to come to church with their infants from the fortieth day of Lent, so that, in receiving the imposition of hands and being anointed with holy oil, they may enjoy the festivities of the legitimate day and be reborn in holy baptism. Enabled by this honour, if their life is filled with grace, they may become priests and enjoy the singular privilege of celebrating mass]. Translation is my own. Edward Landon states that Canon III appears to suggest that a non-Easter baptism was a bar to admission to holy orders. See *A Manual of Councils*, I (ed. Landon, 358). The Councils of Sens (601) and Chalon (603) do not have surviving acts, so it cannot be known whether they addressed the Easter issue or not. See O'Carroll, 'The Chronology of Saint Columban', 90–2.

Epistula III to Pope N and the naming of the recipient of *Epistula V* as Pope Boniface are the most significant statements against this interpretation:

> Thus once and again Satan hindered the bearers of our letters once written to Pope Gregory of blessed memory and annexed to this.[96]
>
> the Dove dares to write to Pope Boniface.[97]

However, the first statement does not conclusively state that Gregory never received the attached letters forwarded by Columbanus to Pope N. The interpretation that Gregory did not receive or respond to the letters is a circular one, framed by notions of antipathy and the later chronology emphasised by Walker's edition, one drawn from a selective approach to Jonas's *Vita Columbani*. The second statement identifying Boniface (whether III or IV) as the recipient of *Epistula V* must stand. However, an internal pun on the name of the recipient with that of *specula* or watchtower allows for the possibility that *Epistula V* may have been sent to Gregory, whose name is a Greek form of *speculator* or watchman.[98] If this is the case, the naming of Boniface in *Epistula V* may be an interpolation relating to the identity of Pope N. Regardless of this conjecture, *Epistula III* demonstrates that Columbanus's epistolary traditions allowed for the forwarding of previous correspondence when it came to seeking advice on matters of concern. The fluid contexts of his letters are, therefore, a problematic basis for dating his activities. Jonas's report of Columbanus's earlier entry into continental affairs deserves attention.

A combination of literary, historical, and anecdotal evidence suggests that Gregory, shaped in the monastic traditions of Cassian, may have been familiar with the writings of Gildas and Columbanus from early in his papacy, when he began to shift from the passive example of the suffering of Job to the more active image of Isaiah, Ezekiel, and John as the vocal *bonus pastor*.[99] Certainly, Gregory's elevation of the purchase of clerical office, as represented by the term *mercenarius*, to that of the heresy of simony, or *simoniaca haeresis*, implies a debt to the legacy of Gildas.

[96] Columbanus, *Epistulae*, III.2 (ed. Walker, 22–3): 'Idcirco semel et bis satanas impedivit portitores nostrorum ad beatae memoriae papam conscriptorum Gregorium olim apicum in subiectis positorum'.

[97] Columbanus, *Epistulae*, V.1 (ed. Walker, 36–7): 'scribere audet Bonifatio Patri Palumbus'.

[98] Columbanus, *Epistulae*, V.5 (ed. Walker, 40–1): 'Mittat te Isaias in montem, qui evangelizas Zion, immo per Isaiam Deus iuxta tui nominis interpretationem in speculam verae contemplationis ponat' [May Isaiah send you to the mountain, who publish good tidings to Zion, rather may God through Isaiah place you on the watch-tower of true contemplation, according to the meaning of your name]. A pun on the name Boniface – 'fortunate one' – does not appear quite as apt. Walker observes in a note that the pun is on the title of bishop (*episcopus*, as also deriving from a Greek form of *speculator*), and, indeed, this pun is also viable, though, perhaps, more oblique.

[99] Clare Stancliffe has also observed that Gregory's views are closer to those of Columbanus than those of the Gallic episcopate and, as noted previously, has proposed a personal relationship between Columbanus and Gregory beginning as early as 594. See Stancliffe, 'Columbanus and Shunning', 114–23.

Conclusion

Columbanus brought to the continent a Christian tradition that not only profoundly shaped monasticism but possibly clerical authority, as represented by the pastoral mission of Gregory the Great. The prophetic model of authority that Columbanus represented, one where juniors could criticise their seniors, was simultaneously attractive and aggravating to the episcopal and secular elites of Gaul and Italy, causing controversy and, ultimately, modification. Rather than representing exoticism, Columbanus presented to Gregory an ascetic tradition that also described clerical authority as the vocal *bonus pastor* of Ezekiel, Isaiah, and John. Against this was the wicked shepherd of Ezekiel and John, one that could ultimately be attached to the first heretic, Simon Magus. The *auctor* Gildas had described those involved in the structural corruption of the clerical orders as a *simoniacus* or a simoniac, and he did so in a situation where the corrupt collusion of secular and clerical elites had led to the partition and imminent destruction of *Britannia*. Gregory, taking office in a city literally under siege within a similarly partitioned Italy, may have seen in Gildas's *De excidio* a mirror and a solution to his own times. A similar response came soon into his time in office: by 593, Gregory had elevated the purchase of clerical office to the heresy of simony.

Whether Gregory had read the *De excidio* directly is difficult to disentangle from the influence of Gildas on Columbanus. That Gregory may have had an innate understanding of Gildas's prophetic description of a partitioned *Britannia* as the 'unfaithful Judah' and 'faithless Israel' described in Jeremiah is possibly revealed in his letter to Bishop Eulogia of Alexandria in July 598. In describing his mission to convert the English, Gregory appears to relate the English to Jeremiah's prophecy as divined by Gildas:

> [Gregory] quia, dum gens anglorum in mundi angulo posita in **cultu lignorum ac lapidum perfida** nuncusque remaneret, ex uestrae mihi orationis adiutorio placuit ut ad eam monasterii mei monachum in praedicatione transmittere deo auctore debuissem.[100]

> [Jeremiah] et facilitate fornicationis suae contaminavit terram, et **moechata est cum lapide et ligno**.[101]

It is, perhaps, in Gregory's mission to the English that we can see the biggest impact of Columbanus. Indeed, it appears to have been designed, initially at least, on monastic lines similar to that of a *peregrinatio*, in contrast to previous papal missions to Ireland and Britain as represented by bishops Palladius and Germanus. It was Augustine's subsequent rise to the episcopate – a rise possibly influenced by the ambitions of Frankish bishops – and subsequent accusations of arrogance that arguably led to his failure to reinstate the diocese of *Britannia*.[102] *Peregrinatio*, after Gildas and

[100] Gregory the Great, *Registrum epistularum*, VIII.29 (ed. Norberg): 'For while the English race, who live in a corner of the world, still remain **faithless in their worship of trees and rocks**, thanks to your support you gave me with your prayer, I have decided to send over a monk of my monastery to preach to them.'

[101] Jeremiah 3.9: 'And by the facility of her fornication she defiled the land, and **played the harlot with stones and with stocks**.'

[102] See Gregory's *Epistula XI.36* for his warnings to Augustine against arrogance and pride. The chronology of Augustine's mission, and when and where he was ordained a bishop, is a matter

Columbanus, was intimately structured on a model of authority that placed authority in the hands of juniors.

After the death of Gregory, the term *simoniaca haeresis* was quietly dropped from papal discourse.[103] Instead, with the return of secular clerics to the papacy and a shift in emphasis from clerical discipline to clerical authority, the image of Simon Magus came to be associated, not with the purchase of clerical office, but with the distinct tonsure of the British Isles. As the Insular Easter controversy, now tied to the Insular tonsure controversy, came to dominate ecclesiastical tensions in the seventh century, so the legacy of Gildas appeared to radically change. With Columban monasticism, as represented by Columba and Columbanus, under attack, both in a continental and an Insular context, attention switched from Gildas's *De excidio* to Gildas's letter to Finnian.

of debate: we can be certain that he was not ordained by Gregory prior to the commencement of the mission. See Markus, 'The Chronology of the Gregorian Mission'. For potential legal issues with this mission in terms of canon law, one that might have encouraged Gregory to initially maintain Augustine's status as a monk, see Flechner, 'Pope Gregory and the British'.

[103] Indeed, the term *simonica haeresis* does not reappear in a significant sense until the papacy of Gregory VII (*r.* 1073–85). For an investigation into how Gregory's reputation was retrospectively reconstructed, see Lathama, 'Inventing Gregory "the Great"'. For a hostile response to Gregory's legacy in Rome on his death, see Mews & Renkin, 'The Legacy of Gregory the Great', 318–19.

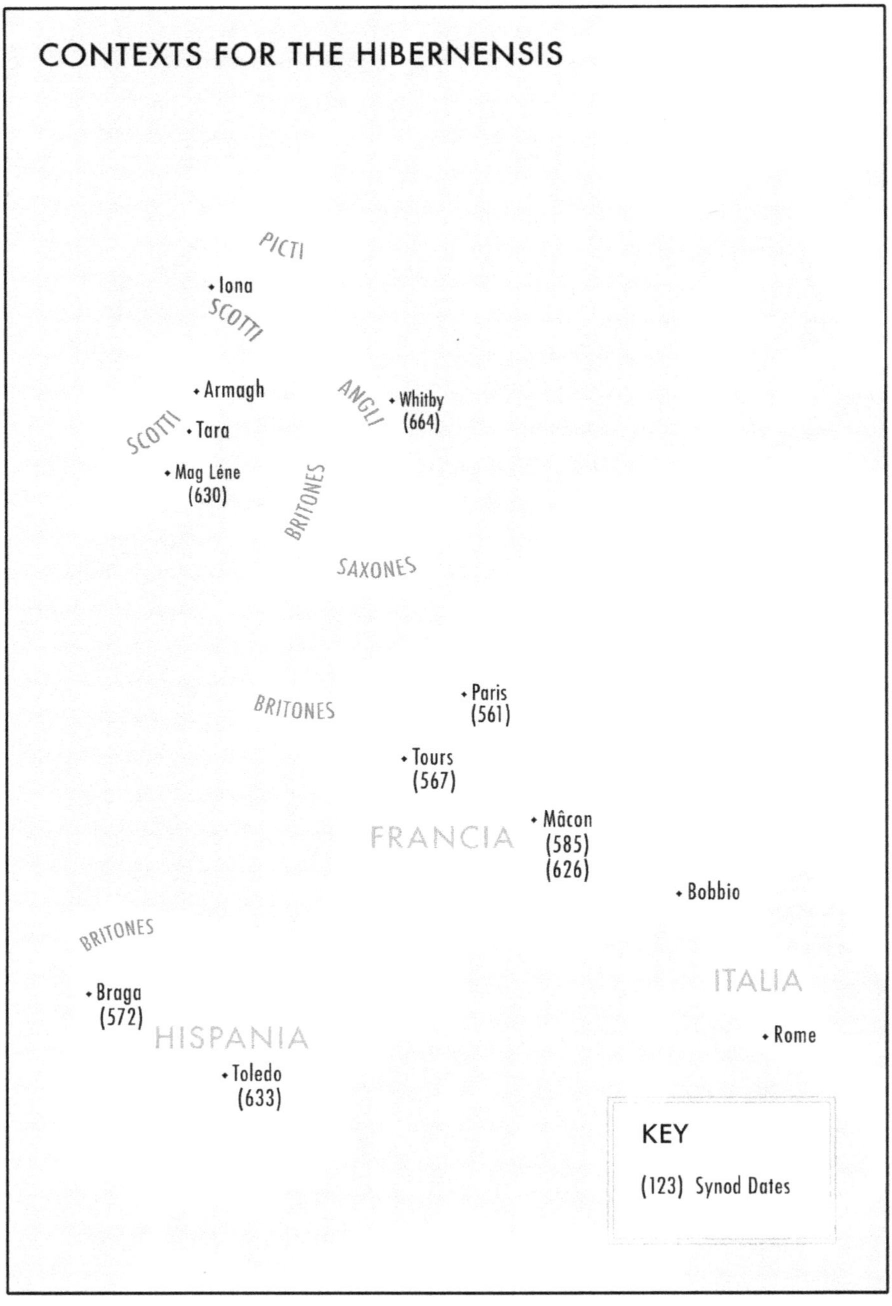

Select synodal attempts to assert uniform religious practice in the sixth and seventh centuries.

5

GILDAS AND THE *HIBERNENSIS*

Gildas's inclusive approach to resolving the spiritual and political crisis in his *Britannia* is demonstrated in his final appeal to the proclamation of the watchman Ezekiel: that God did not desire the death of sinners, but that they should turn back and live.[1] This inclusive attitude is reinforced by Gildas's subsequent approach to church discipline as represented by elements of his letter to Finnian, preserved as fragments within the *Collectio canonum Hibernensis* as well as in certain earlier versions of this hugely influential canon collection.[2] Here, Gildas laid out his view that religious zeal and excessive censure should be eschewed in favour of moderation, that a Christian community should be tolerant and connected rather than judgmental and fragmented:

> Noah did not wish to keep his son Ham, teacher of the magic art, away from the ark or from sharing his table. Abraham did not shrink from Aner and Eschcol when he was warring with the five kings. Lot did not curse the banquets of the Sodomites... Moses, too, lodged and banqueted in peace with Jethro. Our Lord Jesus Christ did not avoid eating with publicans, so as to save all sinners and whores.[3]

At the same time, Gildas stressed the proper structuring of a Christian community to maintain stability, recalling the model of authority put forward in his *De excidio*:

> 'Let each in God stay where he is called': so that the chief should not be changed except at the choice of his subjects, nor the subject obtain the place of his superior without the advice of an elder... Therefore it is quite proper for bishops and abbots to judge those beneath them, for their blood will be required at their hands by the Lord if they do not rule them well. But those who disobey their fathers shall be as the heathen and publicans.[4]

1 Ezekiel 33.11. This chapter draws on material already published: see Joyce, 'Memories of Gildas'. I would like to thank the Sydney University Press for permission.

2 The earlier versions examined in this book are the *Incipiunt capitula canonica* and the *Collectio canonum Turonensis*. See 112–14 for more details.

3 Gildas, *Fragmenta*, I (ed. Winterbottom, 143, trans, 80): 'Non Noe Cham filium suum magicae artis scribam aut arca aut mensae communione voluit arcere. Non Abraham Aner et Heschol in debellatione quinque regum exhorruit. Non Loth Sodomitarum convivia execratus est... Nec non Moyses simul cum Iethro hospitium et convivium pacificum init. Non dominus noster Iesus Christus publicanorum convivia devitabat, ut omnes peccatores et meretrices salvaret'. See also *The Hibernensis*, XXXIX.4 (ed. Flechner, 301).

4 Gildas, *Fragmenta*, VI (ed. Winterbottom, 145, trans., 82): '"Unusquisque permaneat in eo in quo vocatus est apud deum", ut nec primarius nisi voluntate mutetur subiectorum neque subiectus sine senioris consilio locum prioris obtineat... Iudicare ergo satis salubre est subiectos episcopis abbatibusque, quorum sanguinem, si eos non bene regnant, de manibus requiret dominus:

The acceptance of Gildas as a spiritual master on church discipline reveals an understanding that his criticisms of the secular and church leaders of *Britannia* in his *De excidio* were not polemical but constructive. It also implies that contemporaneous political and church structures may have been restored on the lines of Gildas's intervention, granting a stability that would make Columbanus's intervention on the continent both practically possible and confident in its message.

The Irish *peregrinus* Columbanus is our earliest witness to the importance given to Gildas's letter to Finnian as a canonical contribution to maintaining discipline in a Christian community. In his letter to Pope Gregory, he called on the authority of Gildas's letter to offer an Insular approach to the problem of monks who broke their communal vows without the permission of their abbots. Elements of this letter were subsequently cited in the *Hibernensis*, a canon collection which also emphasised, among many church fathers, the local authority of Patrick. Curiously, Gildas is named here solely in connection with this letter to Finnian. He is not named in connection to his more famous text, the *De excidio*. In examining how Gildas was remembered in Ireland, I argue that between the mission of Columbanus and the compilation of the *Hibernensis*, the image of Gildas was transmuted from that of an edifier of kings and bishops in the prophetic tradition to that of a respected monastic figure supportive of the authority of bishops to edify kings, as represented by Patrick.

Gildas and Ireland

While the legacy of Gildas had been invoked by Columbanus in continental Europe, he was also remembered as an authority in Ireland. Sometime in the decades around 700, a collection of canon law – the *Collectio canonum Hibernensis* – was assembled in Ireland that cited Gildas in the same breath as Augustine of Hippo, Jerome, Gregory the Great, and Isidore of Seville, as well as that of the apostle to Ireland, Patrick.[5] This collection was distinct from equivalent canon collections on the continent. Aside from stressing the authority of local synods and significant local church figures such as Patrick, Gildas, and Finnian, the *Hibernensis* was unusual in its emphasis on the Latin church fathers and the Bible rather than on papal decretals and conciliar canons as on the continent.[6] It further distinguished itself by eschewing the chronological systemisation of continental canon collections for one based on a thematic arrangement of regulations as they related to the proper lives of Christians – whether clerical, monastic, or lay – within the church.[7] This distinctiveness was both influential and divisive: by the eleventh century, the *Hibernensis* would profoundly influence the structure of continental canon collections, but in the ninth century it attracted suspicion from Gallic and Roman perspectives.[8]

inoboedientes vero patribus sint sicut gentiles et publicani'. The biblical passage directly cited is I Corinthians 7.24. See also *The Hibernensis*, XXXVI.32 (ed. Flechner, 272).

5 Flechner dates the *Hibernensis* conservatively to 669–748, with a historical argument for 716–47. See *The Hibernensis* (ed. Flechner, 61*).

6 For its distinctiveness see *The Hibernensis* (ed. Flechner, 47*–51*); Elliot, *Canon Law Collections*, 138–40. Gildas is named in the *Hibernensis* fifteen times; Patrick is named thirty-five times; Finnian is named once.

7 See Richter, *Ireland and Her Neighbours*, 217.

8 Reynolds, 'Unity and Diversity', 101–2, describes early ninth-century attacks on the *Hibernensis* from Gallic and Roman perspectives. Richter, *Ireland and Her Neighbours*, 217, describes the

The citation of Gildas in the *Hibernensis* is not surprising. In the *Catalogue of the Saints of Ireland*, Gildas was not only connected to significant early Irish saints, he was also held to be one of the three saints that brought the liturgy to Ireland:

> [The second order of saints] accepted their ritual of the Mass from holy men of Britain: St David and St Gildas and St Doc. And their names are: Finnian, Énda, Colmán, Comgal, Áed, Ciarán, Columba, Brendan, Brichin, Cainnech, Cóemgen, Laisren, Lugid, Barra, and many others who were of the second ranks of saints.[9]

The second order of saints in Ireland, following the first order represented by Patrick, intimately connected Gildas to the teachers of Columba and Columbanus: Finnian and Comgall (*ob. ca* 602). The earliest surviving confirmation of this relationship of Gildas to Ireland is Columbanus's critical letter to Pope Gregory the Great *ca* 600, which acted as a direct witness to an exchange of letters between Gildas and Finnian on a matter of monastic discipline:

> What is to be done about those monks who, for the sake of God, and inflamed by the desire for a more perfect life, impugn their vows, leave the places of their first profession, and against their abbots' will, impelled by monastic fervour, either relapse or flee to the deserts? Finnian the writer questioned Gildas about them, and he sent a most polished reply.[10]

Both Gildas and Finnian subsequently appear as authorities in the *Hibernensis*, with the *Hibernensis* preserving excerpts of Gildas's letter to Finnian also known as the *fragmenta Gildae.*

In the *Hibernensis*, Gildas is quoted solely from his letter to Finnian, primarily concerned, as Richard Sharpe has argued, with monastic discipline.[11] He is not mentioned in relation to his *De excidio*. As Thomas Charles-Edwards notes, the fundamental role of the *Hibernensis* was not simply to regulate the church but 'to create a Christian law for a Christian society', as seen in its attempts to regulate secular matters including kingship and its unusual merging of rules relating to the clergy and laity.[12] Not referring to Gildas's *De excidio* in the context of kingship or episcopal authority is a notable omission, particularly in light of Columbanus's invocation

standardisation of the *Hibernensis* systemisation in continental Europe in the eleventh century.

9 *Catalogus sanctorum Hiberniae* (ed. Grosjean, 206): '[Secundus vero ordo sanctorum] ritum celebrandi missam acceperunt a sanctis viris de Britannia, scilicet a sancto David et sancto Gilda et a sancto Doco. Et horum nomina sunt hec, scilicet Finnianus, Endeus, Colmanus, Comgallus, Aedeus, Queranus, Columba, Brandanus, Brichinus, Caynecus, Caymginus, Laysreus, Lugeus, Barrideus, et alii multi qui erant de secundo gradu sanctorum'. For the translation, see de Paor, *Saint Patrick's World*, 225–6. For the dating of this text to the eighth century, see Chapter 2.

10 Columbanus, *Epistulae*, I.7 (ed. Walker, 8–9): 'quid faciendum est de monachis illis, qui pro Dei intuitu et vitae perfectioris desiderio accensi, contra vota venientes primae conversionis loca relinquunt, et invitis abbatibus, fervore monachorum cogente, aut laxantur aut ad deserta fugiunt. Vennianus auctor Gildam de his interrogavit, et elegantissime ille rescripsit'. As already noted, Sharpe, 'Gildas as a Father of the Church', argues that fragments of writings attributed to Gildas in the *Hibernensis* come from this letter to Finnian.

11 Sharpe, 'Gildas as a Father of the Church,' 197. However, I will argue that Gildas's letter to Finnian was advice on the proper exercise of episcopal authority in matters of church discipline. See below, 116. For Gildas's approach to excommunication in his letter to Finnian, see Appendix. See also Joyce, 'Attitudes to Excommunication'.

12 Charles-Edwards, 'Early Irish Law', 353.

of Gildas's opposition to simony, a heresy intimately associated with secular and clerical elites.[13] Rather than the issue of simony, the *Hibernensis* includes a passage, attributed to Gildas, that connects him to the controversy over the correct tonsure, an issue not mentioned by Gildas or Columbanus.[14] This suggests that between the mission of Columbanus and the compilation of the *Hibernensis*, interpretations of the image of Gildas in Ireland altered from that of a judge of kings and bishops in the prophetic tradition to that of a respected monk promoting unity and uniformity in ecclesiastical law and religious practice under the authority of bishops. This shift was shadowed by an emphasis away from Bishop Palladius as apostle to Ireland – as alluded to by Columbanus – to an emphasis on Bishop Patrick as apostle to Ireland, upon whom Columbanus is silent.[15]

This shift in attitude toward Gildas in Ireland in the seventh century reflects a shift in papal attitudes toward Ireland herself. The papacy of Gregory the Great (*ob.* 604) and its legacy, possibly sensitive, as we have seen in Chapter 4, to the religious traditions of Ireland and Britain as represented by Columbanus and Gildas, ended, after a period of vacillation, with the papacy of Boniface IV in 615 and the rise of the papacies of Adeodatus I (*r.* 615–18), Boniface V (*r.* 619–25), Honorius I (*r.* 625–38), Severinus (*r.* 640), and John IV (*r.* 640–2), all sensitive, in different ways, to the authority of the clerical orders.[16] The effect was to emphasise clerical authority rather than clerical discipline, reflected in the disappearance of Gregory's innovation, *simoniaca haeresis,* from papal discourse. The impact on Ireland was immediate and direct. Honorius's granting of a unique privilege to Columbanus's foundation of Bobbio in 628 ushered in a period of significant papal pressure on the Irish church to conform on the question of Easter.[17] Papal accusations of heresy and threats of excommunication saw a contentious split in the Irish church, reinforced by the failure of the Synod of Mag Léne (*ca* 630) to enforce consensus in favour of

[13] The *Hibernensis* is more enigmatic on this issue, preferring to merely cite Acts 8.20. See *The Hibernensis*, II.13 (ed. Flechner, 26, trans., 495): 'Lucas in actibus apostolorum: Phetrus ad Simonem magum dicit: Pecunia tua tecum sit in perditionem; existimasti enim donum Dei pretio mercari' [Luke in the Acts of the Apostles: Peter says to Simon Magus: let your money be with you unto perdition; for you reckoned that the gift of God might be purchased with money]. See also *The Hibernensis*, XXXVI.26 (ed. Flechner, 270, trans., 674): 'In actibus apostolorum Petrus ad Simonem magum dixit: Pecunia tua tecum sit in perditionem; existimasti enim donum Dei pretio mercari' [In the Acts of the Apostles Peter said to Simon Magus: Let your money be with you unto perdition; for you thought that the gift of God may be purchased with money].

[14] *The Hibernensis*, LI (ed. Flechner, 409–10). See below, 124–8, for an analysis.

[15] As mentioned in Chapter 1, Prosper records a papal mission to Ireland by Bishop Palladius in the year 431 and Columbanus alludes to this mission in one of his letters. See Prosper, *Epitoma Chronicorum* (ed. Mommsen, *Chronica*, I, 473); Columbanus, *Epistulae*, V.3 (ed. Walker, 38).

[16] While Adeodatus I (or Deusdedit), Boniface V, Severinus, and John IV were active supporters of the clergy, Honorius I followed Gregory the Great in maintaining a significant connection with monasticism. However, he was conscious of the need to protect and project clerical authority through reforms of clerical education and an ambitious program of church building and renovation. See Richards, *The Popes*, 261–5. See also Llewellyn, 'The Roman Church'.

[17] The issue of Easter in Ireland begins with this papal privilege to Bobbio (and Bobbio's acceptance of the Roman Easter); followed by a letter of Pope Honorius to Ireland in 629; followed by the failure of the Synod of Mag Léne to enforce a consensus on Easter *ca* 630; followed by a letter by Cummian to recalcitrant representatives of Columban monasticism *ca* 632; followed by the acceptance of the Roman Easter in a south Irish context *ca* 633. On the papal bull placing Bobbio under the jurisdiction of the papacy, see Richter, *Bobbio*, 59–62. See also Wood, 'Jonas', 118–19.

Rome.[18] Resistance by the episcopal and monastic centres of Armagh and Iona on Easter lasted until *ca* 688 and *ca* 716 respectively, a resistance that created three generations of significant political and ecclesiastical instability in Ireland. Within this highly contested transition in Ireland, the religious practices defended by Columban monasticism gave way to a standardisation of religious practice as influenced by the apostolic authority of Rome. In order to examine this radical readjustment of the image of Gildas as it relates to authority in Ireland, we need to examine the way the *Hibernensis* utilised his letter to Finnian.

The *Hibernensis* and the *fragmenta Gildae*

The origins of the *Hibernensis* are obscure. As a collection of canon law drawing on a range of older Insular and continental sources, it was probably compiled in Ireland prior to the middle of the eighth century, a context noted by Roy Flechner as the latest possible date of composition as preserved in the surviving manuscript tradition.[19] From a continental perspective, the *Hibernensis*'s use of the Bible, church fathers, papal decretals, and synodal canons, while suggesting a desire to preserve traditions, is idiosyncratic for a seventh- or eighth-century text. The latest continental church synod to be cited is that of the Council of Orléans in 511, with a significant source of canons concerned with ordination and clerical discipline coming from the *Statuta ecclesiae antiqua*, dated to the last quarter of the fifth century and attributed to Gennadius of Marseilles.[20] A second significant source of canons, predominantly from the eastern church, was mined from the *Dionysiana*, collated in Rome in the first quarter of the sixth century by Dionysius Exiguus (*ca* 470–544).[21] Local canons are assigned to Patrick (with elements preserved elsewhere as the *Synodus I Patricii* or the *First Synod of Patrick*) or to local synods, identified here as the *Synodus Romana* (with elements preserved elsewhere as the *Synodus II Patricii* or the *Second Synod of Patrick*), and the *Synodus Hibernensis*.[22] The canons attributed to Patrick in the *Synodus I Patricii* appear to represent an Irish church prior to the seventh century, while

18 For the letter of Honorius to Ireland on the Easter question and the resultant controversy in Ireland, see Richter, *Ireland and Her Neighbours*, 209; Charles-Edwards, *Early Christian Ireland*, 364–5. The reluctance of supporters of Columban monasticism to accept the Roman Easter was subsequently attached to judaising and Pelagianism by a letter from Pope-elect John in 640. See *Bede: The Reckoning of Time* (trans. Wallis, lxi).

19 On the issue of an Irish origin, Flechner is decisive, see *The Hibernensis* (ed. Flechner, 50*). However, others still argue for a possible Breton origin: see Elliot, *Canon Law Collections*, 138; see also Davies, 'The "Mouth of Gold"', 249. This chapter seeks to situate the *Hibernensis* as a text arising from tensions both on the continent and in the British Isles but compiled in Ireland.

20 See Davies, '*Statuta ecclesiae antiqua*'. Only one continental manuscript of the *Hibernensis* – Ms Cologne, Dombibl., 210 – cites subsequent Gallic councils up to 540. *The Hibernensis* (ed. Flechner, 75*–6*) notes a potential echo of the Council of Marseilles in 533. For a list of the councils cited in the *Hibernensis*, see *The Hibernensis* (ed. Flechner, 985–7).

21 For a brief assessment of the relationship between the *Hibernensis* and the *Dionysiana*, see Flechner, *Making Laws for a Christian Society*, 29.

22 For an analysis of the canons of the *First Synod of Patrick* and the *Second Synod of Patrick* in the *Hibernensis*, see Breen, 'The Date, Provenance and Authorship'. An edition and translation of the *Second Synod of Patrick* is in the same article, at 112–21. The attribution of these canons to Patrick post-dates the publication of the *Hibernensis*, where elements are referred to as being from the *Synodus Romana*. For an edition and translation of the *First Synod of Patrick*, see *Synodus I S. Patricii* (ed. Bieler, 54–9).

canons attributed to other Insular synods may represent the seventh-century Roman liturgical reform movement, known as that of the *Romani* and reflecting similar and highly contested reform in Britain.[23] The *Hibernensis* appears to combine conciliar perspectives significant to the continental church in the early sixth century with those significant to the Insular church in seventh-century Ireland.[24]

These perspectives are, perhaps, also reflected in the choice of patristic authorities: fourth- and fifth-century fathers of the church such as Ambrose, Jerome, and Augustine of Hippo are largely complemented by late sixth- and early seventh-century authorities such as Gregory the Great and Isidore of Seville, with the latest authority cited being that of Theodore of Canterbury (*ob. ca* 690).[25] The ambivalence towards continental authority in the sixth century appears, initially at least, to reflect that implied in the letters of Columbanus. However, neither Columbanus nor Columba is cited in the *Hibernensis*.[26] While the *Hibernensis* clearly emphasises episcopal and synodal authority, its distinctive use of scripture, the patristic fathers, and its unique systemisation appears to betray continuing respect for local practices. This position is perhaps reflected in the contemporaneous attitude of the English scholar, Bede, who makes no mention of the *Hibernensis* nor of earlier versions of this influential canon collection.

The use of the *fragmenta Gildae* within the *Hibernensis* appears to support an evolving interest in connecting Gildas to the liturgical reform movement of the *Romani*, an interest not necessarily isolated to Ireland. A version of the *Hibernensis* containing more complete versions of the *fragmenta* is found within a ninth-century Insular codex preserved at Tours (now Cambridge, Corpus Christi College, MS 279), a codex also containing the sole witness to the *Synodus I Patricii*.[27] Tours exerted an often contested, metropolitan authority over an Insular-influenced church in Brittany.[28] Another version of the *Hibernensis*, also preserving more complete elements of the *fragmenta*, is found within two early ninth-century Carolingian manuscripts along with an unattributed version of the *Synodus II Patricii*.[29] This version

23 Richter, 'Dating the Irish Synods', 71. See also Charles-Edwards, *Early Christian Ireland*, 245–50 for a discussion of the dating of the First Synod of Patrick. He prefers a dating no later than the middle of the sixth century. For an overview of the contested Roman liturgical reform in Britain from an Irish perspective, see 429–38. On a potentially earlier context for the *Second Synod of Patrick*, see Hughes, 'Synodus II S. Patricii'. See also Joyce, 'Attitudes to Excommunication'.

24 On Insular perspectives in the seventh century, see 113–16.

25 *The Hibernensis* (ed. Flechner, 60*, 982–1000). Bishop Caesarius of Arles (*r.* 502–42) is, perhaps, the only notable authority from the sixth century, but he is not named, and his authority is often given to Augustine of Hippo. Pope Symmachus (*r.* 498–514) and Cassiodorus (*ca* 485–585) are cited once, but not named; Benedict of Nursia (*ca* 480–547) is named and cited once, but, of course, his authority derives from that given to him by Gregory the Great.

26 Flechner notes one potential use of Columbanus, but it is a biblical quote from Deuteronomy 32.7, also used by Cummian among others. See *The Hibernensis*, XIX (ed. Flechner, 111).

27 Elliot, *Canon Law Collections*, 104–5, details Cambridge, Corpus Christi College, MS 279 (CCCC 279): ninth or tenth century, Tours; contains *Collectio canonum Hibernensis* (excerpts), *Synodus I Patricii*, *Liber ex lege Moysi*, and the *Iudicia Theodori versio discipuli Umbrensis* (excerpts). Flechner argues that CCCC 279 was copied from a Breton exemplar. See Flechner, 'Aspects of the Breton Transmission', 28.

28 Indeed, when the Second Council of Tours in 567 asserts its authority over Brittany, no Breton bishop is in attendance. See Chapter 4, 98.

29 Breen, 'The Date, Provenance and Authorship', 96–7, details the manuscript tradition underpinning his edition of the *Synodus II Patricii*, based on two early ninth-century manuscripts of south German (Carolingian) provenance (Munich, Bayerische Staatsbibliothek, Clm 14468; Vienna,

is included alongside canons of Braga in the diocese of Galicia in north-west Spain in the late sixth century, itself exerting metropolitan authority over an Insular-influenced church in *Britonia*.[30] These sources point to a regional interest in Gildas as author of the letter to Finnian as linked to the image of Patrick.[31]

The fragments of Gildas's letter to Finnian are preserved in their most complete form in Cambridge, Corpus Christi College, MS 279, a version termed by Michael Elliot as the *Collectio canonum Turonensis* (*Turonensis*) due to its association with Tours.[32] This version, systemised by both source and topic, contains eight of the ten fragments as published in Winterbottom's edition.[33] All of the fragments, except fragment eight, are found together as a continuous text under a heading on Christian sayings, emphasising the themes of excommunication, fasting, the last days, and monks.[34] This version, quoting more complete sections of Gildas's letter to Finnian, is not a derivative of the *Hibernensis* as previously thought but rather a major source for the *Hibernensis*.[35] The latest citation appears to be from the epilogue to a penitential perhaps authored by the noted Irish scholar, Cummian (*ob. ca* 661).[36] The

Österreichische Nationalbibliothek, Lat. 2232), and containing a number of texts in common: a series of epitomes of conciliar statutes of Gallic and African origin (under the nominal title *Incipiunt sententiae de canonibus expressae*); a section entitled *Incipiunt capitula canonica* containing the canons of the *Synodus II Patricii* (without authorial attribution); and a number of excerpts from Augustine of Hippo, Gregory the Great, Jerome, Gildas, and early Gallic councils very similar to CCCC 279. I would like to thank Dr Sven Meeder for access to a copy of Vienna, Österreichische Nationalbibliothek, Lat. 2232.

30 A point picked up by Maasen, who connects canons associated with a *Sancto Martiano* to Bishop Martin of Braga (*ca* 520–80). See Maasen, *Geschichte der Quellen*, 665–6. On closer examination canons 5–35 relate directly to canons XXXVIII–LXXXIV from a series of Greek canons translated into Latin by Martin of Braga and presented to the Second Council of Braga (*ca* 572) and the associated Synod of Lugo in the same year. For the canons, see *Concilium Bracarense II* (ed. Bruns, *Canones*, 43–59). The Synod of Lugo was attended by the British bishop of *Britonia*, Mailoc. For Mailoc, see Charles-Edwards, *Wales and the Britons*, 93. For contact between Spain and Ireland in the seventh century, see Hillgarth, 'Ireland and Spain'. The presence of a canon collection translated by Martin of Braga and presented to a British bishop, along with the inclusion of the *Synodus II Patricii*, along with the citation of both Gildas and Augustine of Hippo as authorities adds significant interest to these Carolingian manuscripts as preserving a potential fusion of Insular and continental traditions.

31 This connection is supported by other Gallic and Spanish influences on the *Hibernensis*. See Davies, '*Statuta ecclesiae antiqua*'.

32 Elliot, *Canon Law Collections*, 161–6. His Latin edition of the *Turonensis* is at 691–728, and is the edition used in this book.

33 Elliot, *Canon Law Collections*, 163–4. Gildas occurs at *Turonensis 42* and *Turonensis 82–94*. See 691–2 for a list of sources for the *Turonensis*. The other two fragments are drawn from the *Hibernensis*. For more on this, see Joyce, 'Attitudes to Excommunication', 12–15.

34 *Turonensis*, XLII (ed. Elliot, 704): 'DE UERITATE PRAEDICANDA MULTI SANCTI LOQUUNTUR'. *Turonensis*, LXXXII–XCIV (ed. Elliot, 709–13): 'DE CHRISTIANIS LOQUITUR QUOD INUICTI SUNT'; 'DE EXCOMMONICATIONE'; 'DE ABSTINENTIA CIBORUM'; 'DE NOUISSIMIS DIEBUS'; 'DE MONACHIS'.

35 Elliot, *Canon Law Collections*, 162, invoking Sharpe, 'Gildas as a Father of the Church', 196. Sharpe argues convincingly against a scholarly tradition that perceived the *Turonensis* as a derivative of the *Hibernensis*.

36 The penitential of Cummian is cited at *Turonensis*, CXXIII (ed. Elliot, 719): 'sed in omni penitentia solenter inquirendum est' [but one shall enquire carefully into all matters of penance]. Translation is my own. See *Paenitentiale Cummeani* (ed. Bieler, 132): 'Sed hoc in omni paenitentia solerter intuendum est'.

relative lack of emphasis on the authority of Gregory the Great and Isidore of Seville, together with a construction prior to the diffusion of Gregory's *Dialogi*, point to a compilation of the *Turonensis* sometime prior to the middle of the seventh century, most probably following the failure of the Synod of Mag Léne (*ca* 630) and the first recorded mention of Patrick by Cummian (*ca* 632).[37] The single citation attributed to Patrick in the *Turonensis*, following immediately after the quotes from Gildas and taken together with the presence in the codex of the *Synodus I Patricii*, reveals early efforts to combine the authority of Gildas with that of Patrick.[38]

A potentially earlier canon collection with influence on the *Hibernensis* survives in two Carolingian manuscripts from Germany, manuscripts which, as Aidan Breen notes, contain an unattributed version of the *Synodus II Patricii* along with elements of the *fragmenta Gildae* and the *Turonensis* under the title *Incipiunt capitula canonica* (see Appendix).[39] The *fragmenta* used (fragments one and seven) are connected to the authority of Augustine of Hippo. The latest patristic author cited is Gregory the Great, specifically his early works *Homilies on the Gospels* and *Homilies on Ezekiel*. This, and the notable absence of the authority of Isidore of Seville, suggests a composition prior to the *Turonensis*, perhaps as early as the first quarter of the seventh century.[40]

These precursors to the *Hibernensis*, preserved in a continental context, point to an active dialogue between the British Isles and the continent on the development of canon law in the sixth and early seventh centuries, a position supported by the presence of Bishop Samson at the Council of Paris (*ca* 561), and the synodal invitation issued to Columbanus (and declined) by Gallic bishops, possibly to the Second Council of Mâcon (*ca* 585) as discussed in Chapter 4.[41] This is supported by other

37 While Elliot conservatively dates the *Turonensis* from the middle of the seventh century to the first quarter of the eighth century, this merely duplicates Flechner's dating for the *Hibernensis*. See Elliot, *Canon Law Collections*, 161. On 164, he argues for a date in the second half of the seventh century, perhaps even earlier, based on the citation from the penitential of Cummian. Cummian's letter on the Paschal controversy, dated *ca* 632, is the earliest datable source to mention Patrick in an Insular context. For the letter, see Ó Cróinín & Walsh (edd.), *Cummian's Letter*. Clarke, *The 'Gregorian' Dialogues,* 260–74, charts the diffusion of Gregory's *Dialogi*. He argues that the historical record does not record the *Dialogi* until the second half of the seventh century. I set aside his argument about the authorship of the *Dialogi*. On the first reception of Isidore in early medieval Ireland, see Herren, 'On the Earliest Irish Acquaintance'. Herren inclines to a date around the middle of the seventh century. Smyth, 'Isidorian Texts in Seventh-Century Ireland', cautions against this early reception, preferring the latter half of the seventh century. Smyth acknowledges, however, that a proto-version of the *Hibernensis* and its notable use of Isidore can be dated 669–700. In this context, sources for the *Hibernensis* such as the *Turonensis* could conceivably be compiled prior to *ca* 650.

38 *Turonensis*, XCV (ed. Elliot, 713): 'PATRICIUS DE UNITATE ET SUBDITORUM: Quis ergo audet scindere unitatem quam nemo hominum soluere uel repraehendere potest' [PATRICK CONCERNING UNITY OF SUBJECTS: Who therefore dares to rend unity, which no man can loosen or fault]. Translation is my own. The source for this quote of Patrick is unidentified by Elliot. However, Breen has identified the influence of Cyprian. See below.

39 For the manuscript tradition, see n. 29, above. For Breen's Latin edition of the *Incipiunt capitula canonica*, see Breen, 'The Date, Provenance and Authorship', 121–5. The phrase above appears in the *Incipiunt capitula canonica* and is identified by Breen as being influenced by Cyprian. See Breen, 'The Date, Provenance and Authorship', 122. Following directly on from Gildas's *fragmenta*, this expression may be from Gildas's letter to Finnian.

40 See Breen, 'The Date, Provenance and Authorship', 121–5.

41 *Concilium Parisiense a. 556–573* (ed. de Clercq, *Concilia*, 210): 'Samson subscripsi et consensi in nomine christi' [Samson subscribes and consents in the name of Christ]. Translation is my

sources. As also seen in Chapter 4, the Second Council of Tours in 567 appears to have been the first instance where simony was designated specifically as a heresy in a continental context.[42] This early condemnation of simony echoes that of Gildas as recalled by Columbanus. These potential connections are further supported by an echo of the letter to Finnian in the canons from the same council, as supported by the *Turonensis*. The *Hibernensis*'s use of a rarely cited passage from Deuteronomy 27.16–26 is reflected in Canon XXI of the Second Council of Tours, an element of which is, in turn, assigned by the *Turonensis* to the *fragmenta Gildae*:

> [Tours/*Hibernensis*] **Maledictus, qui transfert terminos proximi sui**, et dicit omnis populus amen.[43]
>
> [*Turonensis*/*Fragmenta*] **Maledictus qui transfert terminos** suos **uel proximi sui**.[44]

The direct citation of scripture in the canons of the Second Council of Tours is unusual in a continental context and in the same style as that of the *Hibernensis*.

The Second Council of Tours alerts us to tensions as well as influences. Canon IX reflects anxiety over the impact of charismatic clerics from Britain in Gaul (as potentially represented by Samson) in the second half of the sixth century:

> We also add that no one should presume to ordain a Briton or Roman in Armorica without the consent or letters from the metropolitan or the bishops of the province. If anyone should try to act contrary to this, let him observe the decree laid out in previous canons and recognise that he will be removed from our confraternity until the greater synod, because they who scorn the statutes of the fathers are rightly removed from our charity and our churches.[45]

This dialogue over canon law emphasises two influential Insular perspectives in Gaul in the sixth century: one emphasising the importance of episcopal and synodal authority, as represented by Samson; the other emphasising the authority of scripture, as represented by Columbanus.

Drawing on divisive debates in the later sixth century over uniform religious practice, such as the correct calculation for the date of Easter, what we see in these seventh- and eighth-century Insular canon collections is an evolving emphasis on Gildas's letter to Finnian as it relates to the communion or unity of the church. This evolving emphasis begins with Gildas's warning against excessive excommunication;

own. Ian Wood makes a case for dating this synod to 561: see Wood, 'Columbanus', 104–5. For Columbanus, see Chapter 4, 100–1.

42 See Chapter 4, 98.

43 *Concilium Turonense a. 567*, XXI (ed. de Clercq, 189); *The Hibernensis*, LX.6 (ed. Flechner, 443–4, trans., 806): '**Cursed be he who moves his neighbour's landmarks,** and all the people shall say: Amen'.

44 *Turonensis*, XC (ed. Elliot, 712); Gildas, *Fragmenta*, VI (ed. Winterbottom, 145, trans., 82): '**Cursed is he who removes boundary stones, particularly those of his neighbour**'.

45 *Concilium Turonense a. 567*, IX (ed. de Clercq, 178): 'Adicimus etiam, ne quis brittanum aut romanum in armorico sine metropolis aut comprouincialium uoluntate uel literis episcopum ordinare praesumat. Quod si quis contraire temptauerit, sententiam in anterioribus canonibus prolatam obseruet et a nostra caritate usque ad maiorem synodum se cognoscat esse remotum, quia merito a caritate nostra uel nostris ecclesiis segregantur, qui patrum statuta contemnunt'. Translation is my own.

subsequently expanding with his warnings against excessive excommunication, extreme asceticism, and judgementalism; and finally, utilising his warnings against excessive excommunication, extreme asceticism, judgementalism, and fastidious criticism. The focus on moderation in excommunication as it applies to secular leadership, a power inherent in episcopal authority, alerts us to the possibility that Gildas's letter to Finnian was not concerned with advice on monastic discipline but rather with advice relating to the proper exercise of episcopal authority.[46] The attitude of Gildas to excommunication, as related in his letter to Finnian, appears to be contrary to that of Patrick as expressed in his *Epistola* (see Appendix).[47] It is significant, in the context of the omission of the *De excidio*, that the *Hibernensis* also omits direct citations from Patrick's *Confessio* and *Epistola*, rather attaching his episcopal image to synodal authority via the *Synodus I Patricii*.[48]

The criticism of simony represented by Columbanus's appeal to Gildas's *De excidio* in his letter to Gregory is also not reflected in the *Hibernensis*. Whereas Columbanus knew both the clerical and secular criticisms of the *De excidio* and the warnings against fastidious criticisms of the letter to Finnian, the *Hibernensis* only refers to the letter to Finnian. While the placing of Gildas's fragments into sections of the *Hibernensis* on bishops and kings appears to support a continued memory of Gildas as the author of the *De excidio*, the lack of directly attributed citations from that text is significant. That the *De excidio* still exerted influence in an Insular context is certain. The *Leiden Glossary*, reflecting the teaching of Theodore and Hadrian in the last decades of the seventh century, notes the presence of the *De excidio* in the library in Canterbury.[49] Theodore is the latest authority quoted in the *Hibernensis*.[50] Gildas, as author of the *De excidio*, was clearly not relevant to the authorial intentions of the compilers of the *Hibernensis*.

That the works of Gildas seem to have been approached selectively by the compilers of the *Hibernensis* can be seen in the attribution of one of Gildas's *fragmenta*. The fragment at *Hibernensis 36.31* is attributed to Jeremiah, when it is, in fact, a Gildasian version of II Timothy 3.1–5, a biblical citation also found in the *De excidio*:

> [*Hibernensis*] 'Heremias dicit: **Nouissimis diebus instabunt tempora pessima. Et erunt homines sui amatores, auarii, adrogantes, superbi, blasfemii, parentibus inobedientes, ingrati, inpurii, sine affectione, sine pace, accusatores, intemperantes, crudeles, odio habentes bonum, proditores magis quam amatores Dei, habentes formam pietatis, uirtutem eius abnegantes**'[51]

[46] The penitential of Finnian, possibly by the same figure, may also have been written by a bishop. On this, see Mews & Joyce, 'The Preface of Gildas', 92.

[47] This is also examined in more detail in Joyce, 'Attitudes to Excommunication'.

[48] Flechner has detected five possible allusions to Patrick's *Epistola*, but there are no direct citations of his personally authored works. See *The Hibernensis* (ed. Flechner, 996). The *Synodus I Patricii*, on the other hand, is directly cited thirteen times. See *The Hibernensis* (ed. Flechner, 999).

[49] On this, see Hardison, 'Words, Meanings, and Readings'.

[50] *The Hibernensis* (ed. Flechner, 60*).

[51] *The Hibernensis*, XXXVI.31 (ed. Flechner, 271–2, 675): 'Jeremiah says: **In the last days shall come the worst times. Men shall be lovers of themselves, covetous, arrogant, proud, blasphemers, disobedient to parents, ungrateful, impure, without affection, without peace, slanderers, incontinent, cruel, hating of what is good, traitors rather than lovers of God, having an appearance of piety, but denying the power thereof**'.

> [*Fragmenta/Turonensis*] Gildas in epistolis suis de **novissimis diebus: 'Instabunt tempora pessima** et **erunt homines sui amatores, avari, adrogantes, superbi, blasphemi, parentibus inoboedientes, ingrati, inpuri, sine adfectione, sine pace, accussatores, intemperantes, crudeles, odio habentes bonum, proditores**, temerarii, inflati, voluptatum **amatores magis quam dei, habentes formam pietatis** et **virtutem eius abnegantes**.[52]

This selective approach to the influence of the *De excidio* and its critical attitude toward bishops and kings alerts us to the fact that the authority of Gildas may have been modified. In order to identify how Gildas's authority was modified, we need to discern whether elements of the *De excidio* survive unattributed in the *Hibernensis*.

The *De excidio* and the *Hibernensis*

Gildas's emphasis in his *De excidio* on God's exacting requirements for *speculatores* or watchmen is a tradition we explored in Chapter 4. Curiously, however, any direct reference to the *De excidio* and its position on the duties of *speculatores* is missing from the *Hibernensis*, with only the *fragmenta* being attributed directly to Gildas. An emphasis on monasticism is seen with the select use of his letter to Finnian but also one of leadership (*De principatu*), a core theme in the *De excidio*. However, on leadership, as with monastic discipline, Gildas is not used as a strident critic, but as a mediator advocating forgiveness for trifling faults, the importance of stability, and the need to avoid bad leaders until the appropriate penance has been enacted:

> Gildas: Mary was punished by leprosy for siding with Aaron in blaming Moses on account of his Ethiopian wife. We, who disparage good *principes* for trivial faults, must be afraid of this example.[53]

> Gildas: Let every man, wherein he was called, therein abide [with God], so that the leader may not be removed except by the will of his subjects, nor the subject obtain the place of his superior without the recommendation of an elder.[54]

> Gildas: Unless they perform correct penance, we should ban those whom we know without doubt to be fornicators from the peace, and mass, and the table of whichever

52 Gildas, *Fragmenta*, III (ed. Winterbottom, 143, trans., 80): '**On the last days** Gildas says in his letters: '**The worst of times will come: men will be conceited, avaricious, arrogant, proud, blasphemous, disobedient to parents, ungrateful, unclean, without affection, without peace, accusers, intemperate, cruel, haters of the good, traitors,** rash, puffed up, **lovers of** pleasure **rather than God: possessing the form of piety but denying its virtue**'. Here, Gildas is closer to the version in the prologue of Jerome's *Commentary on the Book of Zephaniah*. The version in the *De excidio* is closer to the Vulgate version. See Gildas, *De excidio*, CIV.1 (ed. Winterbottom, 138).

53 *The Hibernensis*, XXXVI.5 (ed. Flechner, 259, trans., 665); 'Gildas: En adsentiente Aron in culpando Moise propter uxorem Etiopisam, lepra Maria damnatur. Quod nobis timendum, qui bonis principibus detrahimus propter mediocres culpas'. See also Gildas, *Fragmenta*, IX (ed. Winterbottom, 82).

54 *The Hibernensis*, XXXVI.32 (ed. Flechner, 272, trans., 675): 'Gildas: Vnusquisque in quo uocatus est, in eo permaneat, ut nec primarius nisi uoluntate motetur subiectorum, nec subiectus nisi senioris consilio locum prioris obteneat'. See also Gildas, *Fragmenta*, VI (ed. Winterbottom, 82).

order they belong to, according to this rule: If any man who is named a brother, while being a fornicator, etc.[55]

As has been noted above, a more strident Gildas from the letter to Finnian, one quoting Paul on the Last Days, has been attributed by the compilers to Jeremiah. To this we can add a rare citation from Jeremiah 23.1, quoted in the *De excidio* and in the *Hibernensis* and *Turonensis*, suggesting that the *Turonensis* also had an ambivalence in directly assigning authority to the *De excidio*:

> [*Hibernensis*] Hieremias: **Ve** uobis **pastoribus qui disperdunt et lacerant gregem pascuae meae, dicit Dominus**.[56]

> [*Turonensis*] Hieremias: **Uae pastoribus** israhel **qui disperdunt et delacerant gregem pascuae meae dicit dominus**.[57]

> [*De excidio*] Et iterum: '**Vae pastoribus qui disperdunt et dilacerant gregem pascuae meae, dicit dominus**'.[58]

Gildas's highly original use of scripture in the *De excidio*, where his criticisms of secular and church leaders are drawn directly from two sequential scans through the Bible, contributes to his use of rarely cited scriptural phrases. The reference to shepherds and sheep in Jeremiah 23.1 within *Hibernensis 36.4*, a subsection also quoting Isaiah and Ezekiel on the same theme and placed just prior to the use of Gildas's letter to Finnian at *Hibernensis 36.5*, alerts us to the fact that the tradition embedded in the *De excidio* – that of Isaiah, Ezekiel, and John on the role of the *speculator* – is also in the *Hibernensis*. This can also be seen in *Hibernensis 36.22*: this section recalls the *De excidio* and its citation of Isaiah 56.10, Ezekiel 33.1–9, and Jerome's letter to Heliodorus (attributed to Paul in the *Hibernensis*), a tradition also reflected in the *fragmenta*:

> [*Hibernensis*] Isaias dicit: Sacerdotes eorum non proderunt eis. **Canes muti non possunt latrare**. Vos demulgitis lac ouium et comedetis eas. Ego uindicabo sanguinem earum de manibus uestris, dicit Dominus omnipotens. Dominus ait: Nisi renuntiaueris iniquo **iniquitatem suam, sanguinem eius requiram de manu tua**.

> Gregorius: **Sanguis morientis de manu speculatoris requiritur**, quia peccatum subditi culpe prepositi deputatur, si tacuerit. Vnde quoque hic additur: Si autem tu nuntiaueris et ille non fuerit conuersus ab impiaetate sua et **a uia sua impia, ipse quoque in iniquitate sua moritur. Tu autem animam tuam** saluasti.

[55] *The Hibernensis*, XXXVI.37 (ed. Flechner, 276, trans., 678): 'Gildas: Quos scimus sine ulla dubitatione esse fornicatores, nisi legitimo ordine peniteant, a pace, et missa et mensa cuiuscumque ordinis fuerint, arceamus, ut est illud: Si quis frater nominatur ut est fornicator, et reliqua'. See also Gildas, *Fragmenta*, VII (ed. Winterbottom, 82).

[56] *The Hibernensis*, XXXVI.4 (ed. Flechner, 258, trans., 664): 'Jeremiah: **Woe to the pastors who destroy and tear the sheep of my pasture, says the Lord**'.

[57] *Turonensis*, LXXIV (ed. Elliot, 708–9): 'Jeremiah: **Woe to the shepherds** of Israel **who destroy and tear apart the flock in my pasture, says the Lord'**. Translation is my own.

[58] Gildas, *De excidio*, LXXXII.1 (ed. Winterbottom, 128, trans., 63): 'And again: "**Woe to the shepherds who destroy and tear apart the flock in my pasture says the Lord**".'

Vt Paulus ait: Non omnes aepiscopi, aepiscopi habentur. Adtendis **Petrum**, sed **Iudam** consideras. **Stefanum** aspicis, sed **Nicolaum** aspice.[59]

[*De excidio*] ne simus '**canes muti non valentes latrare**'.[60]

Et speculator si viderit gladium venientem et non significaverit tuba et populus non observaverit, et veniens gladius acceperit ex eis animam, et ipsa propter **iniquitatem suam capta est et sanguinem de manu speculatoris requiram.** Et tu, fili hominis, speculatorem te dedi domui Israel et audies ex ore meo verbum, cum dicam peccatori: morte morieris, et non loqueris, ut avertat se a via sua impius, et ipse **iniquus in iniquitate sua morietur, sanguinem autem eius de manu tua requiram**. Tu vero si praedixeris impio viam eius, ut avertat se ab ea, et non se averterit a **via sua, hic sua impietate morietur et tu animam tuam** eripuisti.[61]

merito beatissimum dicebam **Petrum** ob Christi integram confessionem, at **Iudam** infelicissimum propter cupiditatis amorem, **Stephanum** gloriosum ob martyrii palmam, sed **Nicolaum** miserum propter immundae haeresos notam.[62]

[*Turonensis*/*Fragmenta*] Iudicare ergo satis salubre est subiectos episcopis abbatibusque quorum **sanguinem** si eos non bene regnant **de manibus requiret dominus**. Inoboedientes uero patribus sint sicut gentiles et publicani.[63]

59 *The Hibernensis*, XXXVI.22 (ed. Flechner, 267, trans., 671–2): 'Isaiah says: Their priests were of no benefit to them. **Dumb dogs are not able to bark**. You milk your sheep and eat them. I shall avenge their blood from your hands, says the almighty Lord. The Lord said: Unless you proclaim **his wickedness** to the wicked man, **I will require his blood at your hand**. Gregory: **The blood of a dying man is required at the hand of the one watching over him**, for the sin of a dependant is imputed to the guilt of the superior, if he remained silent. Whence also the following is added: If you have admonished him, and he has not reformed his impiety **and his impious way, he dies in his iniquity. You, however, have saved your soul**... As Paul said: Not all bishops are considered true bishops. You think of **Peter**, but reflect also on **Judas**. You observe **Stephen**, but observe also **Nicolas**'.

60 Gildas, *De excidio*, XXXVI.4 (ed. Winterbottom, 104, trans., 35): 'To avoid being one of the **"dogs that are dumb and cannot bark"**'.

61 Gildas, *De excidio*, XCI.3 (ed. Winterbottom, 132–3, trans., 69): 'But if the watchman sees the sword coming and does not give the signal with the trumpet and the people does not take heed, and the sword comes and takes a life from them, **that life is taken because of its wickedness, and I shall demand blood from the hand of the watchman**. So, son of man, I have set you as a watchman for the house of Israel. You will hear the word from my mouth when you say to the sinner: You will die the death. If you do not speak, so that the wicked man can turn from his way, **the wicked man will die for his wickedness: but I shall demand recompense from your hand for his blood**. But if you tell the wicked man of his ways in good time, so that he can turn from his way, **but he fails to turn, he will die for his wickedness: but you will have got away with your life**'.

62 Gildas, *De excidio*, I.11 (ed. Winterbottom, 88, trans., 14): 'I used to say it was right that **Peter** was most blessed because he wholly confessed Christ, **Judas** most wretched because he loved greed: **Stephen** glorious because of his martyr's palm, **Nicolas** unhappy because of the stain of his foul heresy'. See Jerome, *Epistulae*, 54, XIV.9 (ed. Hilberg, 57): 'attendis petrum, sed et iudam considera; stephanum suscipis, sed nicolaum respice' [You consider Peter; mark Judas as well. You notice Stephen; look also on Nicolas]. See also Gildas, *De excidio*, LXVII.4 (ed. Winterbottom, 119–20, trans., 54): 'Iudam quodammodo in Petri cathedra... ac Nicolaum in loco Stephani martyris statuunt' [in sense, placing Judas... in the seat of Peter, and... Nicolas, in the place of the martyr Stephen].

63 *Turonensis*, XCII (ed. Elliot, 712); trans., Gildas, *Fragmenta*, VI (ed. Winterbottom, 82): 'Therefore it is quite proper for bishops and abbots to judge those beneath them, **for their blood will be**

Another scriptural passage in this section on leadership in the *Hibernensis* also reflects the influence of the *De excidio*. The rarely cited verse of I Timothy 3.5 at *Hibernensis 36.26* reflects *De excidio 109.1*:

> [*Hibernensis*] Item: Quicumque **domui sue bene praeesse nescit, quomodo aeclesie Dei** potest habere regimina?[64]

> [*De excidio*] Si quis autem **domui suae praeesse nescit, quomodo ecclesiae dei** diligentiam adhibebit?[65]

The effect is to turn the section in the *Hibernensis* on leadership from three attributed subsections referring to Gildas's letter to Finnian (36.5, 36.32, 36.37) to seven subsections (four unattributed) referring to Gildas's letter to Finnian and the *De excidio* (36.4, 36.5, 36.22, 36.26, 36.31, 36.32, 36.37). While the citations in the *Hibernensis* are often poorly attributed, as we can see above with the attribution of Jerome's letter to Paul, there appears to be an awareness when compiling the *Hibernensis* of placing selected elements of Gildas's letter to Finnian within sections influenced by Gildas's *De excidio*.[66] The compilers were intimate with both works of Gildas.

The *De excidio*, with its emphasis on the role of kings and bishops as *speculatores*, as the vocal good shepherds described by Isaiah, Ezekiel, and John, clearly influenced the compilation of the *Hibernensis*. However, it appears not to have been part of the compilers' vision to cite Gildas directly on the duties attached to these roles. In reference to bishops, this is understandable, as Gregory the Great also drew on the good shepherd in his works and, as above in *Hibernensis 36.22*, Gregory is the preferred authority, rightly in the sense of seniority, for commenting on the role of the *speculator* in a clerical context. Gildas is directly quoted only once on the role of the bishop, a position drawn from the letter to Finnian, one that, at best, alludes to the strident prophetic criticism in the *De excidio*:

> Gildas said: Indeed, [priests] and bishops have a terrible judge, to whom it belongs, and not to us, to judge them in both worlds.

> Likewise: It is better not to judge fellow bishops and fellow abbots and fellow subjects.[67]

This allusion is supported by the compilers' use of I Timothy 3.1 at *Hibernensis 1.1* and *Hibernensis 1.7*, again reflecting Gildas's use of I Timothy 3.1 in the *De excidio*.[68]

required at their hands by the Lord if they do not rule them well. But those who disobey their fathers shall be as the heathen and publicans'.

64 *The Hibernensis*, XXXVI.26 (ed. Flechner, 270, trans., 673): 'Likewise: Anyone **does not know how to govern his house well**, **how** can he govern **the church of God?**'

65 Gildas, *De excidio*, CIX.1 (ed. Winterbottom, 140–1, trans., 78): 'But if a man **does not know how to govern his own house**, **how** can he give due attention to **the church of God**?'

66 For the high level of poorly attributed citations in the *Hibernensis*, see Gorman, 'Patristic and Pseudo-Patristic Citations', 20.

67 *The Hibernensis*, I.16 (ed. Flechner, 15, trans., 488): 'Gildas ait: Habent quippe sacerdotes et episcopi terribilem iudicem, cui pertinet et non nobis, de illis in utroque seculo iudicare. Item: Conepiscopus et coabbates nec non consubiectos non iudicare melius est'. See also Gildas, *Fragmenta*, V (ed. Winterbottom, 145); VII (ed. Winterbottom, 145).

68 *The Hibernensis*, I.1 (ed. Flechner, 4, trans., 481): 'Paulus: Qui desiderat episcopatum, bonum opus desiderat' [Paul: He who desires the office of bishop, desires good work]. *The Hibernensis*,

It is, however, on the role of kings in *Hibernensis 24* that the absence of Gildas is at its most profound. While Gildas's criticisms of clerics could be replaced by the more senior authority of Gregory the Great, his criticisms of kings in the prophetic tradition in his *De excidio* remained relatively unique in an Insular, perhaps even a continental, context.[69] Thus, when the compilers put together the section on kings, *De regno*, they led with Wisdom 6.2–7, a biblical citation reinforcing the severity of divine punishment on sinful kings directly informed by the *De excidio*:

> [*Hibernensis*] De increpatione regum. Liber Salamonis sapientiae: **Audite** ergo **reges et intelligite, discite iudices finium terre, prebete aurem uos qui continetis multitudinem et placetis uobis in turbis nationum. Quoniam a Deo data est potestas et uirtus ab altissimo, qui interrogabit opera uestra et cogitationes uestras scrutabitur. Quoniam cum essetis ministri regni eius, non recte iudicastis neque custodistis legem iustiti neque secundum uoluntatem eius ambulastis. Horrende et celeriter apparebit uobis, quoniam iudicium durissimum in his qui presunt fiat. Exiguo enim** {eis} **concedetur missericordia.** Salamon: **Potentes enim potenter tormenta** sustinebunt.[70]

> [*De excidio*] Sed transeamus ad cetera: '**audite**', inquit, 'omnes **reges et intellegite, discite, iudices finium terrae: praebete aures vos, qui continetis multitudines et placetis vobis in turbis nationum. Quoniam data est a deo potestas vobis et virtus ab altissimo, qui interrogabit opera vestra et cogitationes scrutabitur: quoniam cum essetis ministri regni illius, non recte iudicastis neque custodistis legem iustitiae neque secundum voluntatem eius ambulastis: horrende et celeriter apparebit vobis, quoniam iudicium durissimum his qui praesunt fiet. Exiguis enim conceditur misericordia, potentes autem potenter tormenta patientur**'.[71]

I.7 (ed. Flechner, 8, trans., 483): 'Paulus: Si quis episcopatum cupit, bonum opus desiderat' [Paul: If someone desires the office of bishop, he desires good work]. Gildas, *De excidio*, CVIII.3 (ed. Winterbottom, 140, trans., 77): 'Si quis episcopatum cupit, bonum opus desiderat' [If anyone desires a bishopric, he desires a good work].

69 This can be seen with the influence of the *De excidio* on the Irish text *De XII abusivis saeculi*, a critique of the secular and clerical orders also drawing on a prophetic tradition and possibly dating to the second quarter of the seventh century. Like Gildas, it draws on Ezekiel in its criticisms of negligent bishops in *Caput X*, and its criticism of wicked kings in *Caput IX*, echoes the sins assigned to the five kings by Gildas in *De excidio XXVII* (*peiuriantes*, *parricidis*, *adulteris*, *impius*, *iniusta*). For the dating and prophetic stance of *De XII abusivis saeculi*, see Breen, 'The Evidence of Antique Irish Exegesis', 76. For more on the *De XII abusivis saeculi*, see below, 122–3.

70 *The Hibernensis*, XXIV.1 (ed. Flechner, 145–6, 581): 'The book of Solomon's Wisdom: **Hear** therefore, **o kings, and understand; learn, o judges of the ends of the earth; give ear, you who rule the multitude and who please yourselves in masses of nations. For power is given you by God, and strength by the most high, who will examine your works and inspect your thoughts. For when you were ministers of his kingdom, you have not judged rightly, nor kept the law of justice, nor went by his will. Horribly and speedily will he appear to you, for a most severe judgement shall be for them who bear rule. For to him who is little, mercy is granted.** Solomon: **The mighty shall be mightily tormented.**'

71 Gildas, *De excidio*, LXIII (ed. Winterbottom, 117, trans., 51): 'But let us go on to what remains; "**Hear**, all **you kings, and understand, learn, you judges of the ends of the earth; give ear you who control multitudes, and have your way among the thronging nations. God gave you your power; your virtue is from the most high. He will enquire into what you do, and scrutinise your thoughts. You were servants of his kingdom, yet you did not judge aright, or keep the law of justice, or walk according to his will; swiftly and dreadfully shall he come upon you, for those who rule will receive the harshest judgement. Pity is granted to the**

The prophetic voice was taken from Gildas, as the originator of the scriptural citation in the context of a criticism of kingship, and given back to the Bible, in this case, Solomon.

This tactic by the compilers is further reinforced by another original use of scripture in Gildas's criticism of kings, that of II Kings 24.12–15, this time used in section 26 of the *Hibernensis* dedicated to sin and punishment (*De sceleribus et uindictis eorum*):

> [*Hibernensis*] In Regum libro ad Dauid dicitur: **Trium tibi optio datur, elige unum**: utrum III-bus **annis ueniet tibi famis aut tribus mensibus fugies aduersarios tuos aut certe III diebus erit pestilentia in** terminis **tuis**. Dauid dicit: Melius est, ut **incidam in manus Domini, quam hominum**. Et **moriuntur** de **populo** a Dan usque Bersabe **LXX milia** uirorum eo quod **numerauit Dauid populum** suum.[72]

> [*De excidio*] Quid **David numerando populum** evenit? dicente ad eum propheta Gaad: 'Haec dicit dominus: **trium tibi optio datur: elige unum** quod volueris ex his ut faciam tibi. Aut septem **annis veniet tibi fames**, **aut tribus mensibus fugies adversarios tuos** et illi te persequentur, **aut certe tribus diebus erit pestilentia in** terra **tua**'. Nam artatus tali condicione et volens magis **incidere in manus** misericordis **dei quam hominum**, **LXX milium populi** sui **strage** humiliator.[73]

Once again, the authority of Gildas – as the originator of the biblical citation in the context of a prophetic criticism of kingship – is referred back to the authority of the Bible alone.

The intentions of the compilers in collating this section on kings in the *Hibernensis* can be adduced when we move a little further to sections 24.3 and 24.4 on recognising good and bad kings from their works (*De eo quod malorum regum opera distruant*; *De eo quod bonorum regum opera aedificentur*). Both sections – alluding to the *De excidio*'s prophetic emphasis on judgment according to deeds but taken from an anonymous seventh-century Irish text criticising abuses of authority, *De XII abusivis saeculi* – are attributed to Patrick.[74] Significantly, *De XII abusivis saeculi*

small; but the powerful shall suffer powerful torments".' Wisdom 6.2–7 is rarely cited in full prior to Gildas.

72 *The Hibernensis*, XXVI.18 (ed. Flechner, 178, trans., 604): 'In the book of Kings, David is told: **A choice of three things is given you; choose one**: **either** three **years of famine shall come to you, or you shall flee three months before your adversaries, or for three days there shall be a pestilence in your land**. David says: It is better **that I should fall into the hands of the Lord**, than of men. And there **died of the people** from Dan to Bersabee **seventy thousand** men, because **David counted the people**.'

73 Gildas, *De excidio*, XXXIX.2–3 (ed. Winterbottom, 106, trans., 37): 'What happened to **David** when he **numbered his people**? The prophet Gad said to him: "The Lord says this: **You have a choice between three things. Choose** which you want me to do to you. **Either famine will come upon you for** seven **years**, **or you will flee from your enemies for three months** and they will pursue you, **or there will be pestilence in your land for three days**". Under the constraint of these choices, **and wishing to fall into the hands of a merciful God** rather than men, David was laid low by the **death of seventy thousand of his people.**' The incident referred to in II Kings 24.12–15 is rarely cited prior to Gildas: only Jerome and Ambrose appear to draw on it.

74 The *Hibernensis* accords sections of the *De XII abusivis saeculi* to Patrick. Authorship is usually attributed to Augustine of Hippo or Cyprian. *The Hibernensis*, XXIV.3–4 (ed. Flechner, 147–9, trans., 583): 'Patricius: Nonus abusionis gradus est rex iniquus… Patricius: Iusticia uero regis iusti haec est…' [Patrick: The ninth grade of abuse is the iniquitous king… Patrick: This is, therefore, the justice of a just king…]. Breen notes that these are not garbled versions of *De XII*

places the role of bishop at the apex of both secular and clerical orders, equal to or above that of kingship.[75] The authority of Gildas, reflecting his letter to Finnian, is now one of a monastic advisor to bishops; the role of the critic has been given to Patrick. The effect intended by the compilers was to place the prophetic role of the edification of kingship within the apostolic succession. This change is reflected in the attention given to simony: the *Hibernensis* avoids a direct association of the purchase of clerical office with heresy, a position complemented by a lack of reference to simony in the *Turonensis*.[76]

The use of the letter to Finnian and the *De excidio* in the *Hibernensis* alerts us to one of the ways clerical authority was being reasserted. There is one distinct citation of Gildas in the *Hibernensis* set aside from the most recent edition of the *fragmenta*, that of Gildas on the theme of the tonsure:

> Gildas said: The Britons are in opposition to the whole world, enemies of Roman customs, not only in respect to mass, but also to tonsure, together with the Jews they worship the shadows of future things more than truth. They celebrate Easter with the Jews on the fourteenth moon.[77]

This reference to Gildas's opinion on the Insular tonsure, one that also alludes to his opinion on the Easter controversy, is not replicated in the *De excidio* nor in reference to Gildas by any other author prior to the compilation of the *Hibernensis*.[78] It is possible, therefore, that the compilers of the *Hibernensis* deliberately attached Gildas's authority to this issue. Curiously, this allusion to the *quartodeciman* heresy is the only time that the dating of Easter is mentioned in the *Hibernensis*.[79] This silence on the issue of the Insular Easter controversy at a time when the correct calculation of Easter was hotly contested – arguably from Columbanus in the last quarter of the sixth century through to Iona's acceptance of the Roman Easter in the first quarter of the eighth century – is also curious.[80] Scholars have used this silence to date the compilation of the *Hibernensis* to after Iona's acceptance of the Roman Easter in 716.[81] However, this interpretation of the silence on Easter, while attractive, cannot provide a definite context. The emphasis on the correct tonsure, on which the *Hibernensis* devotes an entire section including the attribution to Gildas, may provide an

abusivis saeculi but a deliberate synopsis and recasting of the original, perhaps taken from an intermediate source such as a synod. See Breen, 'The Date, Provenance and Authorship', 107–8. For more on the *De XII abusivis saeculi*, see Mews, 'The *De xii abusivis saeculi*'.

75 For the potential of a bishop to be placed higher in status to that of a king in an Irish context, see Grigg, 'The Just King', 46–8.

76 See below, 124. The *Turonensis* makes no mention of Simon Magus or simony.

77 *The Hibernensis*, LI.6 (ed. Flechner, 409–10, trans., 781): 'De tonsura Britonum et solemnitate et missa. Gildas ait: Britones toto mundo contrarii, moribus Romanis inimici, non solum in missa, sed etiam in tonsura, cum Iudeis umbrae futurorum seruientes, quam ueritati. Pascha cum Iudaeis XIIII luna celebrantes'.

78 Though the notion of Britons as contrary and morally weak is emphasised in Gildas, *De excidio*, IV–VI (ed. Winterbottom, 90–1).

79 *Quartodeciman*, in this context, may be those who celebrate Easter within a lunar period beginning with the fourteenth moon rather than always on the fourteenth moon, as with the Jewish Passover.

80 This silence on the Easter controversy is also replicated in the *Turonensis*.

81 See, for instance, Hughes, *The Church in Early Irish Society*, 133, n. 3.

insight into the context for both the construction of the *Hibernensis* and the shaping of Gildas's authority.

The *Hibernensis* and the tonsure

Section 51 of the *Hibernensis* (*De tonsura*) is primarily devoted to the issue of the correct tonsure for clerics. A small final section citing the reasons women should not cut their hair indicates that this section is also addressing the tonsure outside a clerical context. Unlike simony, which is not emphasised as an issue of concern in the *Hibernensis*, an incorrect tonsure is clearly regarded as an excommunicable offence.[82] Further, the incorrect tonsure is also associated with Simon Magus:

> The *Romani* say: They say that their tonsure originated with Simon Magus, whose tonsure extended from ear to ear, standing for the excellence of the tonsure of the magi, by which only the foremost part of the forehead used to be covered.[83]

The correct tonsure cited in the *Hibernensis* is the Petrine tonsure, and the patristic authorities cited in support of this correct tonsure are quite specific: Isidore of Seville, Gildas, Patrick, and, perhaps representing the seventh-century Insular Roman liturgical reform movement, the *Romani*. Isidore, following Augustine, is used to skilfully define the tonsure as of Nazarite (or Jewish) origin, but one remade into a Christian tradition as defined by the Petrine tonsure.[84] Gildas, as seen above, is used to define the incorrect tonsure as having an origin with the Britons, one contrary to Roman practice and attached to judaising.[85] The *Romani* are cited as emphasising the connection of this incorrect tonsure to Simon Magus and to the pagan, possibly druidic, high king, Lóegaire mac Néill, a bitter enemy of Patrick who ultimately became the first of the Uí Néill dynasty to submit to Patrick's authority and convert to Christianity.[86] Patrick, himself, is quoted to emphasise that the wearing of any tonsure other than the Petrine tonsure by a cleric is an excommunicable offence.[87]

82 For example, *The Hibernensis*, LI.7 (ed. Flechner, 410, trans., 781): 'De excommonicandis clericis qui non tondentur tonsura Romana' [That clerics who are not tonsured in the Roman manner must be excommunicated].

83 *The Hibernensis*, LI.6 (ed. Flechner, 410, trans., 781): 'Romani dicunt: Quorum tonsura a Simone mago sumsisse exordium tradunt, cuius tonsura de aure ad aurem tantum contingebat, pro excellentia ipsa magorum tonsura, qua sola frons anterior tegi solebat'. Bertram Colgrave notes the Celtic tonsure as shorn at the front from ear to ear. See *Felix's Life of Saint Guthlac* (ed. Colgrave, 179).

84 Isidore writes on the tonsure in his *De ecclesiasticis officiis* (written *ca* 598–618) and is quoted directly in the *Hibernensis: The Hibernensis*, LI.1 (ed. Flechner, 407), from *De ecclesiasticis officiis*, II.4.1–2; *The Hibernensis*, LI.4 (ed. Flechner, 409), from *De ecclesiasticis officiis*, II.4.3. Augustine was suspicious of monastic tonsures that recalled the Nazarite tradition and the authority of the Old Testament. See Chapter 3. For the dating of *De ecclesiasticis officiis*, see Isidore, *De Ecclesiasticis Officiis* (trans. Knoebel, 5).

85 *The Hibernensis*, LI.6 (ed. Flechner, 409–10).

86 *The Hibernensis*, LI.3 (ed. Flechner, 408); LI.6 (ed. Flechner, 410). Patrick converts Lóegaire in Muirchú's *Life of Patrick*. See de Paor, *Saint Patrick's World*, 187. In Tirechàn's *Life of Patrick*, Patrick converts Lóegaire's two daughters, but not Lóegaire himself. See de Paor, *Saint Patrick's World*, 165.

87 *The Hibernensis*, LI.7 (ed. Flechner, 410). This canon comes from Canon VI of the *First Synod of Patrick*. See *Synodus I S. Patricii* (ed. Bieler, 54–5): 'Quicumque clericus… non more

The logic is quite clear: the Insular tonsure is associated with an anti-clerical and pagan past, and a judaising present tainted by that past.

That this controversy over the correct tonsure – whether Peter's (the corona), Paul's (completely shaved), John's (triangular), or Simon Magus's (shaved from ear to ear) – was not a purely Insular issue can be seen with the earliest continental synods regulating for the correct tonsure. The first was at the Fourth Council of Mâcon in Gaul in 626/627, significantly in the context of the legacy of Columbanus.[88] Subsequent to this was Canon XLI at the Fourth Council of Toledo in 633, significantly in the context of the clerical orders:

> All clerics and readers, just like Levites and the priests, should have the top of the whole head shorn to leave only an encircling crown of hair. Not as those readers in parts of Galicia seem to do currently, who, with long hair like the laity, shave only a small circle at a spot on the head. For that was the rite of heretics in Spain up till now. Therefore, in order to excise scandal from the churches, this disgraceful sign ought to be removed, and there should be one tonsure or habit, just as is the use of all Spain. He who does not guard this sign of the Catholic faith will be a sinner.[89]

As with the *Hibernensis*, not only was the Petrine tonsure defined as the correct tonsure in a clerical context, failure to adhere to the correct tonsure was heretical. Significantly, the canon was directed, in part, at the province of Galicia in north-western Spain, itself connected to the Christian culture of the British Isles. These continental attempts to control the tonsure stand in marked contrast to those taken on Columbanus's entry into continental affairs, a period complemented, in part, by the monastic sympathies of Pope Gregory the Great. Columbanus, a controversial critic of bishops and kings in Gaul and Italy, made no issue of the tonsure nor did his clerical and secular enemies.

The focus on the tonsure as an indicator of heresy implies a greater concern for uniformity after 615, one intimately connected to the controversy over Easter. The Council of Toledo of 633, overseen by Isidore of Seville, was notably concerned with diocesan affairs, prescribing regulations for the whole of Spain that touched upon kingship, the clerical orders, monks, and the laity.[90] Aside from confirming an unusual stance on the non-hereditary nature of sacral kingship, the Council also took a notably anti-Jewish stance, confirming but regulating the savage persecution launched against the Jews by King Sisebut (*r.* 612–21), where failure to convert led to expulsion.[91] This policy of forced conversion signified a departure from the papal

Romano capilli eius sint… ab ecclesia separentur' [Any cleric… whose hair is not shorn after the Roman custom… shall… be removed from the church].

88 For the Fourth Council of Mâcon, see Charles-Edwards, *Early Christian Ireland*, 364–5. Targeted at this synod, as reported by Jonas, was Eustasius, abbot of Luxeuil. See Jonas, *Vita Columbani*, II.9 (ed. Krusch, 123–6). On the doctrinal attack on Eustasius, see O'Hara, *Jonas of Bobbio*, 68–86.

89 *Concilium Toletanum*, XLI (ed. Vives, *Concilios*, 206): 'Omnes clericos vel lectores sicut levitae et sacerdotes detonso superius toto capite inferius solam circuli coronam relinquant. Non sicut hucusque in Gallitiae partibus facere lectores videntur, qui prolixis ut laici comis in solo capitis apice modicum circulum tondunt. Ritus enim iste in Spaniis hucusque hereticorum fuit. Unde oportet ut pro amputando ab ecclesiis scandalo, hoc signum dedecoris auferatur, et sit una tonsura vel habitus, sicut totius Spaniae est usus, qui autem hoc non custodierit fidei catholicae, reus erit'. Translation is my own.

90 See Stocking, *Bishops, Councils, and Consensus*, 148–9.

91 Stocking, *Bishops, Councils, and Consensus*, 155–6.

policy of Gregory the Great, who notably criticised a Gallic bishop for attempting to forcibly convert Jews within the diocese of Marseilles.[92] One of the contexts for the move to enforce the Petrine tonsure was, as subsequently emphasised in the *Hibernensis*, as a reaction against suspected judaisers. That the accusation of judaising was known to Columbanus can be seen in his letter, nominally to Pope Boniface IV, defending against the charge:

> For all we Irish, inhabitants of the world's edge, are disciples of Saints Peter and Paul and of all of the disciples who wrote the sacred canon by the Holy Ghost, and we accept nothing outside the evangelical and apostolic teaching; none has been a heretic, none a Judaizer, none a schismatic; but the Catholic Faith, as it was delivered by you first, who are the successors of the holy apostles, is maintained unbroken.[93]

Clearly, even outside the tonsure issue, the Christian culture of the British Isles, with its emphasis on Mosaic Law and prophetic authority, was vulnerable to accusations of judaising. That Spain and Britain may have been in contact over problems concerning Jews and judaisers is seen with a letter from Bishop Julian of Toledo (*ob. ca* 690) to Hadrian in Canterbury *ca* 690, now lost, that alerted Canterbury to Jewish computistic refutations of the divinity of Christ. This warning may have led to a subsequent accusation of heresy against Bede in 708.[94]

While the question of Easter appears in an Insular context in the second quarter of the seventh century, concerns about the tonsure do not appear in the British Isles until a reassertion of Roman observance in an English context with the Synod of Whitby held in Northumbria *ca* 664 (which decided on the date of Easter and the tonsure in favour of Rome), and the restoration of the Canterbury mission under Theodore and Hadrian in 669.[95] Indeed, Theodore had to delay his arrival until he had adjusted his tonsure from the Pauline to the Petrine. Post 669, the first evidence of friction over the tonsure issue appears in a letter from Aldhelm (*ob. ca* 709) to Geraint (*ob. ca* 710), the British king of Dumnonia (modern-day Devon and Cornwall), probably written in the last decades of the seventh century:

> A rumour hostile to the faith of the Church has bruited it about far and wide that there are in your province certain bishops and clerics who obstinately refuse the tonsure of St Peter, Prince of the Apostles.[96]

92 Neusner, *A History of the Jews*, 122–4, briefly describes Jewish rebellions from the second half of the sixth century to the first half of the seventh century in Palestine. A pogrom was initiated in Antioch 608–9. They were held complicit in the fall of Jerusalem to the Persians in 614, and to the Muslims in 636. Gregory's *Plurimi Iudaice* was addressed to the Archbishop of Arles and the Bishop of Marseilles in June 591. See Gregory, *Registrum epistolarum*, I.45 (ed. Norberg).

93 Columbanus, *Epistulae*, V.3 (ed. Walker, 38–9): 'Nos enim sanctorum Petri et Pauli et omnium discipulorum divinum canonem spiritu sancto scribentium discipuli sumus, toti Iberi, ultimi habitatores mundi, nihil extra evangelicam et apostolicam doctrinam recipientes; nullus hereticus, nullus Iudaeus, nullus schismaticus fuit; sed fides catholica, sicut a vobis primum, sanctorum videlicet apostolorum successoribus, tradita est, inconcussa tenetur'.

94 See Chapter 6, 133–4.

95 For an overview of the impact of the Synod of Whitby, see Stancliffe, 'The Irish Tradition in Northumbria', 20–30. For the impact of the mission of Theodore and Hadrian, see Bischoff & Lapidge (edd.), *Biblical Commentaries*, 133–89.

96 *Aldhelmi Opera* (ed. Ehwald, 482): 'Denique rumor ecclesiae fidei contrarius longe lateque percrebruit, quod sint in provincia vestra quidam sacerdotes et clerici tonsuram sancti Petri, apostolorum principis, pertinaciter refutantes'. Translations, unless otherwise stated, come from

The tonsure as an issue thus only appears in an Insular context in the seventh century. Gildas's attachment to this issue must be seen as a sleight of hand. Both Patrick and Gildas's role in emphasising the Petrine tonsure in the *Hibernensis*, one embellished by the more recent patristic authority of Isidore of Seville, alerts us to the compilers' intention. As the earliest evangelisers of Ireland from Britain – representative of the first and second orders as outlined in the *Catalogus sanctorum Hiberniae* – Patrick and Gildas are used to criticise the authority of Columban monasticism, as representative of the third order.[97] The compilers of the *Hibernensis* had subverted the image of Simon Magus as it related to corrupt clerical authority. Instead, the image of Simon Magus was now attached to an independent monasticism.

This awkward inversion of the legacy of Gildas, from one drawn on by Columbanus in his criticisms of clerical authority to one critical, in an apocryphal sense, of Columban monasticism as seen in the *Hibernensis*, alerts us to the possibility that the *Hibernensis* was compiled under duress. This is further reflected in the extraordinary number of what Michael Gorman terms 'bogus citations' contained in the *Hibernensis*, not only patristic, but also biblical.[98] The sheer prevalence of poorly attributed citations is a remarkable break with the precision of Gildas and Columbanus. While Gorman has proposed that the compilers may have worked from existing miscellanies rather than the original works, the lack of rigour is significant. It might be explained by a crisis not only in authority but, in a practical sense, in both time and available resources. The compilers' emphasis on Patrick indicates a need to assert episcopal authority in an Insular context. The lack of rigour indicates an immediate need to create or, indeed, recreate, a legal code. The use of Gildas and Patrick to affirm tonsural conformity and the lack of emphasis on Paschal conformity indicates a context when the Easter question was resolved but the tonsure question was still ongoing.

The context of the *Hibernensis* and its emphasis on the authority of Patrick is possibly shaped, not by reference to Iona's acceptance of the Roman Easter and tonsure in 716, but by Armagh's acceptance of the Roman Easter *ca* 688 and its assertions of episcopal primacy (through its association with Patrick) in the last decades of the seventh century.[99] This profound shift was perhaps influenced by the catastrophic and eschatologically significant raid of Ecgfrith of Northumbria on Ireland in 684, a raid that targeted the centre of secular authority in Ireland – Tara – and its surrounding spiritual centres such as Kells (founded by Columba).[100] This raid not only saw a dramatic demonstration of Northumbrian secular power under the auspices of a church that favoured Roman liturgical traditions, its threat to the sovereignty of Ireland

Aldhelm: The Prose Works (trans. Lapidge & Herren). See also Grimmer, 'Saxon Bishop and Celtic King'. For further dating of the letter to Geraint, see Lapidge, 'The Career of Aldhelm', 66–9. He dates the letter to *ca* 682–706.

97 See the *Catalogus sanctorum Hiberniae* (ed. Grosjean). Patrick represents the first order of saints, while Gildas sanctioned the liturgy for the second order of saints, of which Finnian was representative. The third order appears to have 'abandoned' pastoral care for the solitary life, and is, perhaps, contemporaneous with the contests over authority that led to the compilation of the *Hibernensis*. See de Paor, *Saint Patrick's World*, 225–6.

98 Gorman, 'Patristic and Pseudo-Patristic Citations', 20.

99 On Armagh's exertion of archiepiscopal claims over Ireland in the seventh century, see Charles-Edwards, *Early Christian Ireland*, 426–40. See also Ó Cróinín, *Early Medieval Ireland*, 172–8.

100 For Armagh and Easter, see Charles-Edwards, *Early Christian Ireland*, 428–9. For Ecgfrith's raid and the resultant alarm in Ireland, see 435–8.

herself, along with the death and kidnap of elites and the devastation of important spiritual centres and their libraries, formed a context that may have contributed to the drafting of the *Hibernensis*: the final impetus in a highly contested debate for the realignment of Irish secular and spiritual power away from Columban monasticism and toward clerical authority. Within this context, the compilers of the *Hibernensis* drew on elements of Gildas's authority in order to construct a compromise legal document, one that gave ground to the *Romani* on religious practice but also gave weight to complex sovereignty issues as represented by the long-held familial connections between Columban monasticism and secular authority.[101]

The compilers harked back to Patrick and Gildas to affirm the authority of bishops to confirm and edify the high kings and lesser kings of Ireland in the tradition of the Old Testament *speculator*. The image of Gildas as a respected father of the Irish church was utilised to address a fundamental change in authority in Ireland, one that took the edification of sacral kingship from monasticism and returned it to the apostolic succession.

Conclusion

The *Hibernensis*, a collection of canon law compiled in Ireland perhaps in the last decade of the seventh century, was itself drawn from a series of Insular canon collections responding to tensions in the sixth and seventh centuries in the British Isles and on the continent over the role of bishops and 'holy men' in the shaping of ecclesiastical law. These broader debates, represented by the presence of Samson and Columbanus in Gaul, and set against a context of a papacy weakened by schism and war, drew on Gildas's letter to Finnian to emphasise inclusivity and unity rather than criticism and schism. Subsequent to the end of the papacies sensitive to the traditions of Columban monasticism, as seen with Gregory the Great, and the recalibration of Columban monasticism on the continent, as seen with the papal 'takeover' of Columbanus's foundation at Bobbio, papal authority was asserted directly over Ireland, accelerating the already existing tensions and resulting in the compilation of the *Hibernensis*.

The *Hibernensis* emphasised the importance of episcopal and synodal authority in imposing uniformity over the diverse and problematic interpretation of scriptural law by 'holy men' within a variety of communities. As such, it modified the authority of Gildas to legitimise the reconstructed authority of Patrick. The readjustment of Gildas, from an edifier of kings and bishops in the prophetic tradition to a respected monastic voice emphasising tolerance and moderation in the judgement of kings and bishops, allowed the compilers to emphasise Patrick, and thus the apostolic succession, as the *speculator*. Within this readjustment, the compilers recast elements of Gildas's *De excidio* as a Patrician construct and lent Gildas's authority to the issue of the tonsure – not one of Gildas's own concerns. Created under political and ecclesiastical stress, the *Hibernensis* was elusive in merging Roman clerical authority with Insular monastic traditions. Its hasty attempts to create an ambitious 'national' legal

[101] For example, the notable Irish dynasty, the Uí Néill, dominating the high kingship of Ireland in the period under study, provided significant authority to Columban monasticism through direct family attachments. Columba himself was related to the Uí Néill. For an overview of the Uí Néill, see Charles-Edwards, *Early Christian Ireland*, 441–68. For Columba's relationship to the Uí Néill, see 282.

code through doubtful attributions and a fusion of antipathetic patristic authorities such as Augustine of Hippo and Pelagius and, at an Insular level, Patrick and Gildas (see Appendix), made for an apocryphal conciliar collection vulnerable to criticism. A generation or so later, the great scholar Bede would write a history of the English church from a Northumbrian and Roman perspective. At no point would he mention the *Hibernensis* or Patrick. He would draw on a different aspect of the legacy of Gildas: not the letter to Finnian, but the *De excidio*.

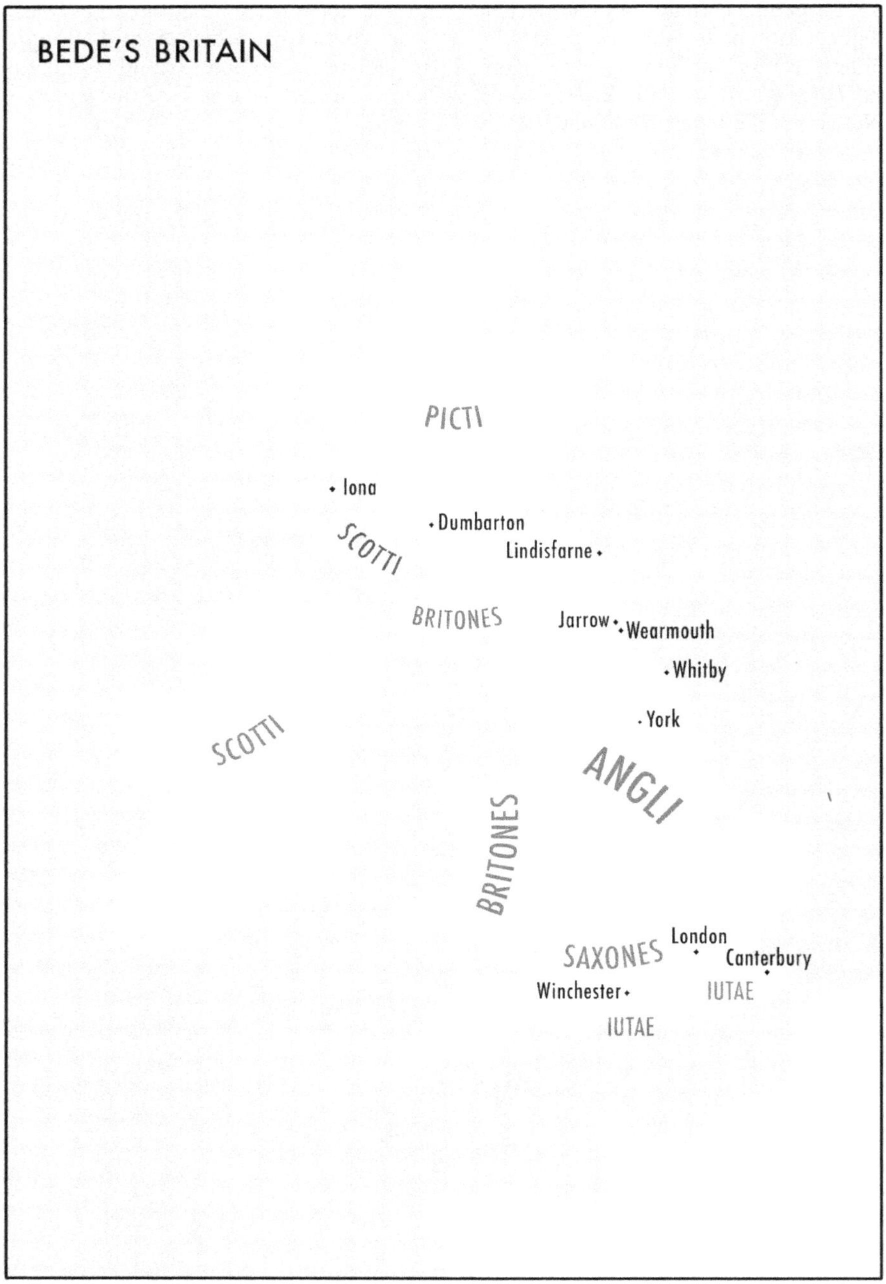

A select view of Britain from the perspective of Bede.

6

BEDE AND GILDAS

While the compilers of the *Hibernensis* had drawn on Gildas's letter to Finnian to support an episcopal approach to exhorting moral behaviour and reinforcing church discipline in an Irish context, a different perspective on Gildas was evolving in Britain. This perspective shared a common approach to the issues of Easter and the tonsure but did not draw on the image of Gildas as a contributor to canon law. Rather, it focussed on a specific aspect of his prophetic authority as expressed in the *De excidio*, that of the providential historian. The advocate of this distinct image of Gildas was the English scholar, Bede (*ca* 673–735).

Bede was aware that of those few writers who had touched on the history of Britain prior to his own time, none was more important than Gildas. As he moved toward the end of his life and compiling his *Historia ecclesiastica*, Bede increasingly turned his attention to what Gildas had to say, not only about that most singular moment from an English perspective, the *adventus Anglorum sive Saxonum*, but also about the role of history and its relation to providence. In constructing a new vision of the history of Britain, Bede, as we saw in Chapter 1, referred to Gildas's admonitions in the *De excidio* to shade the legitimacy of the Christian culture of the British Isles prior to the arrival of Augustine of Canterbury with uncertainty.

Bede's pointed reference to the *De excidio* has often been seen to stress Gildas's criticisms of the secular and ecclesiastical failings of the *Britones*, emphasising a terminal decline in the Christian culture of the British Isles prior to the triumphant conversion of the English to continental orthodoxy. The present exploration, however, will highlight Bede's evolving understanding of the *De excidio* as an intervention in the eschatological landscape. In constructing a providential history of Britain, Gildas created an image of an ordered, tolerant, and exclusive *Britannia* (based on a single chosen people) as a bulwark against sin and divine punishment. This understanding of Gildas's reaction to crisis in Britain encouraged Bede to also construct his *Historia ecclesiastica* as an intervention in the eschatological landscape. However, Bede chose instead to create an ordered, tolerant, and inclusive image of a greater *Britannia* consisting of many chosen peoples – English, Scots, Picts, Britons, and Romans. In doing so, he constructed a new vision for Britain and a new handbook for her kings and bishops, effectively replacing the *De excidio*. Subsequently, in an analysis of Bede's only instance of public criticism – his letter to Bishop Ecgbert – I argue that he not only appropriated Gildas's eschatological vision of national unity, but he reclaimed the prophetic authority to edify seniors reserved within monasticism, rather making it the apostolic duty of all clerics as advocated by Augustine of Hippo.

Bede and the end of times

Bede was a significant scholar both within his lifetime and after his death. Living in the kingdom of Northumbria at the double-sited monastery of Wearmouth (founded in 674) and Jarrow (founded in 681), he produced a diverse array of scholarly works, well beyond that of any contemporary Insular author and hugely influential both in the British Isles as well as on the continent.[1] Some ten years after his death, the English missionary to Germany, Bishop Boniface (*ca* 675–754), described Bede as a 'candle of the church'.[2] What little we know about Bede can only be gleaned from his own works: he is not named in any surviving text except for one letter.[3] Bede reports he was dedicated as an oblate to the monastery at the age of seven.[4] He was ordained a deacon at the relatively young age of nineteen and ordained to the priesthood at the canonical age of thirty, an ordination that appears to coincide with his first major publications, *Expositio Apocalypseos*, his first biblical commentary (significantly on the Book of Revelation), and *De temporibus*, his first attempt at a work on time.[5] Subsequent to these publications, Bede embarked on a generation of literary activity from biblical commentaries and hagiographies to complex 'scientific' works examining time, nature, and history through the lens of orthodox Roman Christianity.

Bede's work on time and how the past, the present, and the future fitted in with God's plan for humanity thematically underscored his literary output.[6] His ordination as a priest coincided with a crisis in sacral kingship that forced him to take into account the impact of protracted conflict within the church on the secular orders. At the centre of this crisis was the power to make and unmake kings: the prophetic authority embedded in the Irish church, as represented by Columba and Columbanus, had allowed for prophets (in a monastic context) to confirm royal succession.[7] The

1 Higham, *(Re-)Reading Bede*, 5. For a recent overview of Bede's life and works, see Brown, 'Bede's Life in Context'. See also Brown, *A Companion to Bede*, 1–16.

2 *Bonifatii et Lulli Epistolae* (ed. Tangl, *Epistolae Selectae*, I, 158–9): 'candellae aecclesiastice'.

3 Higham, *(Re-)Reading Bede*, 6.

4 Bede, *Historia ecclesiastica*, V.24 (edd. Colgrave & Mynors, 566–7): 'Baeda famulus Christi et presbyter monasterii beatorum apostolorum Petri et Pauli, quod est ad Uiuraemuda et Ingyruum. Qui natus in territorio eiusdem monasterii, cum essem annorum VII, cura propinquorum datus sum educandus reuerentissimo abbati Benedicto, ac deinde Ceolfrido' [I, Bede, servant of Christ and priest of the monastery of St. Peter and St. Paul which is at Wearmouth and Jarrow,… was born in the territory of this monastery. When I was seven years of age I was, by the care of my kinsman, put into the charge of the reverend Abbot Benedict and then of Ceolfrith, to be educated].

5 Bede, *Historia ecclesiastica*, V.24 (edd. Colgrave & Mynors, 566–7): 'Nono decimo autem uitae meae anno diaconatum, tricesimo gradum presbyteratus, utrumque per ministerium reuerentissimi episcopi Iohannis, iubente Ceolfrido abbate, suscepi' [At the age of nineteen I was ordained deacon and at the age of thirty, priest, both times through the ministration of the reverend Bishop John on the direction of Abbot Ceolfrith]. See Higham, *(Re-)Reading Bede*, 7–10; Darby, *Bede and the End of Time*, 1–2, for brief accounts of Bede's early life. For the dating of the *De temporibus* see Darby, *Bede and the End of Time*, 18. On 19–21, Darby argues for the pairing of *De temporibus* with another of Bede's early works, *De natura rerum*.

6 Darby, *Bede and the End of Time*, 1–2, a position reiterated in Darby & Wallis (edd.), *Bede and the Future*, 2.

7 For Adomnán's positioning of Columba as an edifier of kings, see Enright, *Iona, Tara, and Soissons*, 59.

Roman response to this, as represented by Bishop Wilfrid (*ca* 633–709), was to claim this power for the clerical orders.[8] The result was enormous tension between Irish-influenced and Roman-influenced elements within the Northumbrian church over kingship and succession. This tension is seen, most notably, in Bede's involvement in the contestations over authority evident within an extraordinary series of saints' lives produced *ca* 697–720. These followed, amongst others, the examples of the sixth-century Irish abbot and priest, Columba (as promoted by the abbot of Iona, Adomnán), the Northumbrian abbot and bishop, Cuthbert (*ca* 634–87, as promoted by Bede), and the aforementioned secular bishop, Wilfrid (as promoted by the monk, Stephen of Ripon (*fl. ca* 700)).[9] The subsequent weakening of the authority of kingship contributed to a climate of anxiety and instability that fed into eschatological anxieties about the Last Judgement.

These anxieties embedded themselves in Bede's mental landscape; first as a reaction against the societal dangers of eschatological speculation, then as an increased embracing of genuine eschatological anxiety, and finally as an 'intervention' in the eschatological landscape.[10] This movement within Bede revolved around three personal crises. The first was the charge of heresy laid against him in 708 over his *De temporibus*, where Bede had recomputed the age of the world in order to avert eschatological speculation.[11] The second was the personal crisis precipitated by the sudden and unusual departure of his abbot, Ceolfrith (*ca* 642–716), to Rome in 716, provoked by political uncertainty in Northumbria and perhaps informed by reports of the destruction of the Christian kingdom of Spain by the heretic Saracens. This caused Bede to pause his commentary on Hebrew kings, *In primam partem Samuelis*, and subsequently produce a new work on time, *De temporum ratione* (*ca* 725).[12] The third crisis was engendered by the appearance of the 'two comets' of 729 and the associated eschatological reactions, both Insular and continental.[13] This led to Bede's most famous work, his *Historia ecclesiastica gentis Anglorum* (*ca* 731), a work that cast the English within providential history.[14]

8 For a brief discussion of Bishop Wilfrid's influence on the succession crisis of 705, see Goffart, *The Narrators of Barbarian History*, 270–2.

9 For a brief overview, see Stancliffe, 'Cuthbert', 22–4. Stancliffe proposes Cuthbert as a figure of unity between the Irish and Roman traditions. Barbara Yorke also sees Bede as supportive of aspects of the Irish tradition in this contest. See Yorke, 'Bede's Preferential Treatment of the Irish'.

10 Darby, *Bede and the End of Time*, 186–214, charts Bede's evolving eschatological perspective in detail.

11 Darby, *Bede and the End of Time*, 42–51. This charge may have originated in Canterbury. Darby, 42, notes the Jews of Toledo using *annus mundi* to refute Jesus as the Messiah *ca* 690. For potential contact between Hadrian of Canterbury and Julian of Toledo, see Bischoff & Lapidge (edd.), *Biblical Commentaries*, 189, n. 236. For more on Bede's response to the accusation, see Darby, 'Heresy and Authority'.

12 Darby, *Bede and the End of Time*, 5. Darby, 175–85, notes that Books I and II of Bede's commentary on I Samuel are eschatologically unremarkable; Books III and IV, however, are strongly eschatological. See also DeGregorio, 'Bede's Midlife Crisis'. For a brief description of the political uncertainties in Northumbria, as represented by contestations over royal succession in the late seventh and early eighth centuries, see Campbell, 'Secular and Political Contexts', 28–9. For an overview of the destruction of the Visigothic kingdom in Spain by the 'Arabs' *ca* 710–13, see Collins, *Visigothic Spain*, 130–43.

13 The 'two comets' were, in fact, an optical illusion relating to one comet.

14 Darby, *Bede and the End of Time*, 95 and 211–2, notes comets had strong eschatological connotations for Bede. Higham, *(Re-)Reading Bede*, 199–200, relates Bede's repeated reference to the

We can see, perhaps, three phases in Bede's thinking. The failed charge of heresy increased Bede's stature: building on the authority of Augustine of Hippo, Bede enjoyed a period of enormous confidence in the handling of eschatological expectations.[15] The subsequent personal crisis of 716 ushered in a period where personal anxieties were dominated by the thinking of Gregory the Great, whose pastoral reforms were shaped by the potential imminence of the Last Judgement.[16] In the final third phase post 729, Bede, facing a real possibility of an imminent Last Judgement, chose to fashion an 'intervention' that laid the fate of the covenant on the active choices of his people, the English. In moving from time and chronology to history, Bede moved from the abstract and the 'scientific' to the Old Testament concept of history as providing moral examples. In doing so, he increasingly made use of that other exponent of history as shaped by moral example, Gildas.

While Columbanus had drawn on Gildas to support a prophetic approach to exhorting moral behaviour and reinforcing church discipline, Bede appeared to chart a different course with his use of Gildas.[17] This can be seen in his emphasis on simony. Whereas Columbanus followed both Gildas and Gregory the Great in stressing simony as a clerical heresy, Bede's emphasis on simony as a clerical issue was muted. He had touched briefly on simony as a clerical heresy in his earlier works on the New Testament, a position drawn directly from Gregory the Great.[18] However, when he came to compiling his *Historia ecclesiastica*, Bede described simony not in relation to a corrupt clergy, but following the pattern established in the seventh century within Britain and Ireland and the continent by the Roman church, in relation to the correct tonsure:

> But as for the tonsure which Simon Magus is said to have worn, what believer, I ask you, will not, at the very sight of it, detest and reject it together with his magic? And rightly so. In the front of the forehead it does seem to bear the resemblance to a crown, but when you come to look at the neck, you will find that the crown which you expected to see is cut short; so that you recognize this as a fitting fashion for simoniacs but not Christians. For in this present life those whom they deceived thought that they were worthy of the glory of the everlasting crown; but in the life to come they are not only deprived of any hope of a crown but moreover are condemned to eternal punishment.[19]

twin comets to his unease with the contemporary political situation in Northumbria.

15 Darby, *Bede and the End of Time*, 82–6, notes Bede's views on the concept of time post 708 are buttressed by Augustine.

16 Darby, *Bede and the End of Time*, 147, notes while Bede opposes any kind of eschatological speculation, he, like Gregory, appears to waver between no concern and immediate concern. For an overview of Gregory's eschatological anxieties, see Baun, 'Gregory's Eschatology'.

17 Bede was aware of Columbanus. See Bede, *Historia ecclesiastica*, II.4 (edd. Colgrave & Mynors, 146–7): 'et Columbanum abbatem in Gallis uenientem' [and… Abbot Columban when he came to Gaul]. However, there is no evidence that he used or had access to his works.

18 For Bede's earlier use of Gregory's innovation of simony as a heresy, see, for instance, Bede, *In Marci euangelium expositio*, III.11 (ed. Hurst): 'Hinc est quod sacri canones simoniacam heresim damnant et eos sacerdotio priuari praecipiunt qui de largiendis ordinibus pretium quaerunt' [That is why the sacred canons condemn the heresy of simony, and demand that they are to be stripped of the priesthood who seek a price for bestowing orders]. Translation is my own. This is taken word for word from Gregory the Great, *Homiliae in euangelia*, I.17 (ed. Étaix, 127).

19 Bede, *Historia ecclesiastica*, V.21 (ed. Colgrave & Mynors, 548–9): 'Ceterum tonsuram eam, quam magum ferunt habuisse Simonem, quis rogo fidelium non statim cum ipsa magia primo detestetur et merito exsufflet aspectu? Quae in frontis quidem superficie coronae uidetur speciem

In highlighting Abbot Ceolfrith's description of the tonsure of Adomnán, abbot of Iona, as representing the heresy of Simon Magus, Bede defined simony as a public departure from Petrine authority and the practice of the continental church, significantly remembered as a recent situation in an influential Irish monastic foundation.

True conversion, as represented by adherence to Petrine authority, clearly had an impact on Bede's eschatological vision. Bede's view of the last times, dominated by the agreed narrative of the complete conversion of the gentiles leading to the final conversion of the Jews and the coming of the Anti-Christ, placed enormous significance on the British Isles (as Ultima-Thule) as the last gentile nations within the in-gathering of nations.[20] Gildas's prophetic vision of *Britannia* as *praesens Israel* was replicated in Bede's eschatological vision, and the importance of the eschatological roles of the Christian peoples of Britain, rather than the subjection of Britain by any one Christian people, came to dominate his thinking. In attempting to make eschatological sense of the providential role of the peoples of *Britannia* as well as that of his own people in his *Historia ecclesiastica*, Bede relied on Gildas, as we still do today, as a rare witness to the *adventus* of the English (as *Saxones*) to Britain.

Bede, Gildas, and the *Historia ecclesiastica*

In constructing a providential history of the English, Bede incorporated the *adventus Anglorum sive Saxonum* – the coming of the Anglo-Saxons to Britain – into his eschatological vision of the past. It was a curious decision for a providential history. Gildas had started his history of the Britons with the coming of Christianity to Britain, as represented by the Romans. In Gildas's mind, history began with conversion, and, to an extent, Bede shared this vision.[21] His *Historia ecclesiastica* effectively begins with the arrival of Gregory the Great's apostolic mission, as represented by Augustine of Canterbury, reported by Bede for the year 596.[22] However, it is an event that is delayed until Chapter 23 of Book I. While some scholars see this extended prelude describing the belligerent arrival of the pagan Anglo-Saxons as part of Bede's interpretation of the divine plan, a 'foreknowing' of the English, this emphasis on the *adventus* is, perhaps, not his major intention.[23] Bede rarely describes the Anglo-Saxons of the *adventus* in any context except as described by Gildas, with

praeferre, sed ubi ad ceruicem considerando perueneris, decurtatam eam, quam te uidere putabas, inuenies coronam, ut merito talem simoniacis et non Christianis habitum conuenire cognoscas; qui in praesenti quidem uita a deceptis hominibus putabantur digni perpetuae gloria coronae, sed in ea quae hanc sequitur uitam non solum omni spe coronae priuati sed aeterna insuper sunt poena damnati'.

[20] See Thacker, 'Bede and the Ordering of Understanding', 60–2.

[21] Higham, *(Re-)Reading Bede*, 75.

[22] Indeed, Higham suggests this event as the potential beginning of Book II, rather than its current position at the end of Book I. Higham, *(Re-)Reading Bede*, 109.

[23] Higham emphasises both the *adventus* and the conversion as central to Bede's providential history. See Higham, *(Re-)Reading Bede*, 149–50. Other scholars, such as Ian Wood, regard Bede's *Historia ecclesiastica* as functioning as a history of conversion or mission. See Wood, *The Missionary Life*, 42. The context of the English as a chosen people is contested. Samuel Cardwell, following Patrick Wormald, makes a case for Bede describing the English as enjoying a special relationship with God, one that replaces that of the Britons. See Cardwell, '"The People Whom He Foreknew"'. For Patrick Wormald, see Wormald, 'The Venerable Bede and the "Church of the English"'. Against this special divine relationship, and for Bede emphasising a more generic

some emendations to Gildas's narrative from other sources.[24] He is mostly silent on any details of Anglo-Saxon history after the fall of the Roman empire and prior to the arrival of Augustine.[25] His account of the *adventus* appears to be driven, not by an emphasis on the 'foreknown' English, but on the *excidium*, the 'cutting off' of the Britons from God's favour. Bede builds on Gildas's history in order to emphasise the historical outcome of a people who failed, and were continuing to fail, their covenant with God.

This use of Gildas in the *Historia ecclesiastica* appears to be a part of the evolution in Bede's eschatological thinking. In the *Chronica minora* attached to his first work on time, *De temporibus*, Bede used Gildas to affirm and date the *adventus* to between the Council of Chalcedon (451) and the beginning of the reign of the east Roman emperor, Leo I (*r.* 457–74). This dating was predicated on his reading Gildas as relating the *adventus* to the third consulship of Aetius (446–54):[26]

> [451] The Council of Chalcedon is conducted.
>
> The English people come into Britain.
>
> [457] Leo the Great [reigns] 17 years.[27]

The emphasis for Bede in his *De temporibus* in 703 was thus on simply establishing the *adventus*, suggesting a cursory use of Gildas's *De excidio* and its concept of *Britannia*.

Subsequent to his personal crisis in 716 and the construction of a new chronicle, the *Chronica maiora* (as attached to a new work on time, *De temporibus ratione*), Bede expanded on his use of Gildas. As Molly Miller notes, Bede made substantial use of Gildas in his post-Roman section of the *Chronica maiora*, entries that formed the backbone of his subsequent history in Book I of the *Historia ecclesiastica* (specifically Chapters 12–16 and 22).[28] In his use of Gildas, Bede emphasised *Britannia* as a site of struggle for supremacy between the competing peoples of the Picts, Scots, Britons, Romans, and Anglo-Saxons, with the *adventus* once again dated prior to the death of Aetius in 454:

relationship of a Christian people with God, is Molyneaux, 'Did the English Really Think They Were God's Elect?' This chapter will tend to support Molyneaux's position.

24 For instance, Bede amends Gildas's narrative concerning the *adventus* of the Saxons with elements sourced from Constantius's *Vita Germani*. See Miller, 'Bede's Use of Gildas', 252–9. He also adds at Bede, *Historia ecclesiastica*, I.15 (edd. Colgrave & Mynors, 50), an 'English' perspective to Gildas's description of the *adventus* from an unknown Insular source, including origin myths for the Angles, Saxons, and Jutes, and the 'English' commanders at the time of the *adventus*, Hengist and Horsa. Miller, 'Bede's Use of Gildas', 254, describes this source as Kentish dynastic propaganda. It is probable that this source came from Canterbury.

25 The exception is Bede's Kentish regnal genealogy and his 'overking' list in Bede, *Historia ecclesiastica*, II.5 (ed. Colgrave & Mynors, 148, 150), which offers some named Anglo-Saxon kings from the fifth and/or sixth centuries, and one entry in his recapitulation, Bede, *Historia ecclesiastica*, V.24 (ed. Colgrave & Mynors, 562). These are probably from the same Kentish source as above.

26 For Bede's reading of Gildas on Aetius, see Chapter 2, 45–7.

27 Bede, *De temporibus liber*, XXII (edd. Mommsen & Jones): 'Calcidonense concilium geritur; Anglorum gens in brittaniam uenit; Leo maior ann. xvii'. Translation is my own.

28 Miller, 'Bede's Use of Gildas', 241–2.

[450] Marcian and Valentinian [ruled for] 7 years.

> The people of the Angles or of the Saxons were conveyed to Britain in three longships. When their voyage turned out to be a success, news of them was carried back home. A stronger army set out, which, joined to the previous one, first of all drove away the enemies [the Scots and the Picts] they were seeking.
>
> Then they turned their arms on their allies, and subjugated almost the entire island by fire or the sword, from the eastern shore as far as the western one, on the trumped-up excuse that the Britons had given them a less than adequate stipend for their military services...
>
> [The bishops of Gaul] stemmed the campaign of the Saxons and Picts against the Britons by divine power. With Germanus himself as their general, the brutal enemy was put to flight, not by the sound of the trumpet, but by the voice of the whole army in a shout of "Alleluia" to the stars...
>
> [454] The patrician Aetius, the great salvation of the Western empire and once terror of King Attila, is killed by Valentinian; with him fell the Western realm, and to this day it has not had the strength to be revived.[29]

The fact that Bede had to reuse this material of Gildas in his construction of the *Historia ecclesiastica* indicates that his detailed interpretation of the eventual subjection of *Britannia* by his *gens Anglorum* within a universal providential history in a chronological form did not have sufficient traction to meet the new eschatological anxieties of 729, as shaped by the appearance of the 'comets'. In this regard, Bede returned to the primary literary genre of Book I of the *De excidio*, that of *historia* or history, and, to all appearances, a deeper respect for Gildas.[30] It is significant that Bede uses the term *historicus* for Gildas in his *Historia ecclesiastica*. It is a title that he otherwise only reserves for himself:

> Qui inter alia inenarrabilium scelerum facta, quae **historicus** eorum Gildas flebili sermone describit.[31]

[29] Bede, *De temporum ratione liber*, LXVI (ed. Jones): 'Marcianus et valentinianus an. vii. Gens anglorum siue saxonum britaniam tribus longis nauibus aduehitur, quibus dum iter prosperatum domi fama referret, mittitur exercitus fortior, qui iunctus prioribus primo hostes quos petebatur abigit. Deinde in socios arma uertens totam prope insulam ab orientali eius plaga usque ad occidentalem igni uel ense subigit conficta occasione, quod pro se militantibus brittones minus sufficienter stipendia darent... Sed et bellum saxonum pictorumque aduersus brittones eo tempore iunctis uiribus susceptum diuina uirtute retundunt, cum germanus ipse dux belli factus, non tubae clangore sed clamore alleluiae totius exercitus uoce ad sidera leuato, hostes in fugam uertit inmanes... Aetius patricius, magna occidentalis rei publicae salus et regi quondam attile terror, a valentiniano occiditur, cum quo hesperium cecidit regnum neque hactenus ualuit releuari'. The translation is a slight amendment of *Bede: The Reckoning of Time* (trans., Wallis, 221–2).

[30] Miller, 'Bede's Use of Gildas', 242, notes that Bede moved from a position where he regarded Gildas as exaggerating facts in his *Chronica maiora* to a belief in his *Historia ecclesiastica* that Gildas, when corrected, did not.

[31] Bede, *Historia ecclesiastica*, I.22 (edd. Colgrave & Mynors, 68–9): 'To other unspeakable crimes, which Gildas their own **historian** describes in doleful words.'

immo hoc multum detestans, sicut in libro quem de Temporibus conposui manifestissime probaui; sed quasi uerax **historicus** simpliciter ea, quae de illo siue per illum sunt gesta, describens.[32]

Bede's respect for Gildas was, perhaps, influenced by a similar context. Like Gildas, Bede also faced an immediate crisis in sacral kingship, a situation he related directly to the appearance of the 'two comets' in 729, the loss of two significant church and secular leaders, Egbert and Osric, and the rise to power of a flawed king, Ceolwulf, to whom the *Historia ecclesiastica* was dedicated:

> In the year of our Lord 729 two comets appeared around the sun, striking great terror into all beholders… In the same year the holy man of God, Egbert, went to be with the Lord on Easter Day as has already been described; and soon after Easter, on 9 May, Osric, king of the Northumbrians, departed this life when he had reigned eleven years, after appointing Ceolwulf, brother of his predecessor Cenred, as his successor. Both the beginning and course of his reign have been filled with so many and such serious commotions and setbacks that it is as yet impossible to know what to say about them or to guess what the outcome will be.[33]

Parallels between this crisis and the one faced by Gildas were clearly on Bede's mind when he came to write his opening account of the Britons in Book I of the *Historia ecclesiastica*. In doing so, Bede also returned to the two sources for Gildas's account in Book I of the *De excidio*, that of Rufinus's translation and update of Eusebius's *Historia ecclesiastica* (published *ca* 402) and Orosius's *Historiarum adversum paganos* (published *ca* 416).[34] Both these works, in different ways, connected divine will to the positive development of a Christian society. This development relied on an active relationship between aristocratic and apostolic succession. However, as Bede clearly realised, Gildas's *De excidio* and the prophetic warnings of *excidium* for failures in secular and spiritual leadership had no traction amongst his contemporaries and could not address the eschatological crisis of 729. Gildas's aim to inspire by threat or fear was a rhetorical strategy that no longer had any impact in the age of Bede.[35]

Bede also faced a different *Britannia* from that faced by Gildas, who defined his 'island' of *Britannia* as peopled by the Britons and demarcated in the north by the deep intrusion of the sea at the Clyde and Forth estuaries, intrusions extended by their

[32] Bede, *Historia ecclesiastica*, III.17 (edd. Colgrave & Mynors, 264–6): 'indeed I heartily detest it, as I have clearly shown in the book which I wrote called *De Temporibus*, but, as a truthful **historian**, I have described in a straightforward manner those things which were done by him or through him'.

[33] Bede, *Historia ecclesiastica*, V.23 (edd. Colgrave & Mynors, 556–9): 'Anno dominicae incarnationis DCCXXVIIII apparuerunt cometae duae circa solem, multum intuentibus terrorem incutientes… Quo anno sanctus uir Domini Ecgberct, ut supra commemorauimus, ipso die paschae migrauit ad Dominum; et mox, peracto pascha, hoc est septima iduum Maiarum die, Osric rex Nordanhymbrorum uita decessit, cum ipse regni (quod XI annis gubernabat) successorem fore Ceoluulfum decreuisset, fratrem illius qui ante se regnauerat Coenredi regis, cuius regni et principia et processus tot ac tantis redundauere rerum aduersantium motibus ut, quid de his scribi debeat quemue habitura sint finem singula, necdum sciri ualeat'.

[34] Higham, *(Re-)Reading Bede*, 73–5. See also Gunn, *Bede's Historiae*, 96 and 99–100.

[35] Gunn, *Bede's Historiae*, 105–6.

connected river systems and reinforced by the Roman structure, the Antonine Wall.[36] Gildas constructed a history of a single Christian *gens*, the *Britones*, defending this island of *Britannia* from the pagan incursions of the Scots (from Ireland), the Picts (from the north of Britain), and, subsequently, the Saxons (from the continent).[37] Bede extended Gildas's concept of *Britannia* to include the whole island of Britain, thus including the English (as Saxons), the Picts, and the mainland Scots.[38]

Britain was, thus, legitimately populated by many peoples at different 'levels' of Christianity, levels defined, in a sense, by their continued attachment to 'primitive' religious traditions such as celebrating Easter on the Jewish Passover. The Picts and Scots (as the good Jews) had only recently (re)assented to Petrine authority; the Britons (as the bad Jews) refused to (re)assent to Petrine authority; the *gens Anglorum* (as Angles, Saxons, and Jutes), the newest of the Christian peoples, had assented to Petrine authority; and finally, the Romans as the representatives of Petrine authority itself.[39] Bede's description in his *Historia ecclesiastica* was, therefore, not framed by

[36] Gildas describes *Britannia* as an island, and the Scots and Picts as overseas peoples. See Gildas, *De excidio*, III.1 (ed. Winterbottom, 89, trans., 16): 'Brittannia insula in extremo ferme orbis limite circium occidentemque' [The island of Britain lies virtually at the end of the world, towards the west and north-west]; XIV (ed. Winterbottom, 93, trans., 21): 'et omnis belli usus ignara penitus, duabus primum gentibus transmarinis vehementer saevis, Scotorum a circione, Pictorum ab aquilone calcabilis, multos stupet gemitque annos' [Quite ignorant of the ways of war, she groaned aghast for many years, trodden under foot by two exceedingly savage overseas nations, the Scots from the north-west and the Picts from the north]. The implication is that the island of Britain was regarded as two islands in the early medieval period as defined by the Clyde and Forth estuaries and the Antonine Wall, an image that survived into the medieval period. For example, see 'Matthew Paris's Map of Great Britain. St Albans, c.1250', in British Library, Cotton MS Claudius D.vi, f. 12v. Bede also supports Gildas's sense of a *Britannia* bound in the north by the Clyde and Forth estuaries and the Antonine Wall, but moves away from the concept of northern Pictland as an island. See Bede, *Historia ecclesiastica*, I.12 (edd. Colgrave & Mynors, 40–1): 'Transmarinas autem dicimus has gentes non quod extra Brittaniam essent positae, sed quia a parte Brettonum erant remotae, duobus sinibus maris interiacentibus' [We call them races from over the waters, not because they dwelt outside Britain but because they were separated from the Britons by two wide and long arms of the sea]. This implies that Bede thought the Scots were resident in the north of the island of Britain at the time Gildas was writing. On this, see Miller, 'Bede's Use of Gildas', 242–3.

[37] Though Gildas does refer to distinct *gentes* within the overarching *gens* or *natio* of the *Britones*, such as the *Demetae* and the *Damnonii*, something that surely would not be lost on Bede. See Gildas, *De excidio*, XXVIII (ed. Winterbotton, 99); XXXI (ed. Winterbottom, 101).

[38] See n. 40, below. Indeed, there is some evidence, with Bede's inclusion of a 'biblical' description of Ireland and his alternate title of 'Historia ecclesiastica Britanniarum, et maxime gentis Anglorum', that he had extended Gildas's *Britannia* to a greater *Britanniae*, a concept inclusive of Ireland. This may be a subtle reaction to the evolution of an 'independent' Irish church in his lifetime. For the 'biblical' description of Ireland, see Bede, *Historia ecclesiastica*, I.1 (edd. Colgrave & Mynors, 18–21). For the alternate title, see Bede, *Historia ecclesiastica*, V.24 (edd. Colgrave & Mynors, 566–7): 'Haec de historia ecclesiastica Brittaniarum, et maxime gentis Anglorum' [this account of the Church of Britain and of the English people in particular].

[39] Bede's works, post the personal crisis of 716, are intimately involved in positioning the Jews in eschatology. See Thacker, 'Bede and the Ordering of Understanding', 55–6. See also Darby, *Bede and the End of Time*, 105–9. Apart from the Romans who literally represent Peter, Bede gives all the peoples of *Britannia* an initial papal or Roman mission that authorises their right to being a Christian people: the Britons have King Lucius's request to Pope Eleutherus (Bede, *Historia ecclesiastica*, I.4 [edd. Colgrave & Mynors, 24]); the Irish have Palladius, sent by Pope Celestine (Bede, *Historia ecclesiastica*, I.13 [edd. Colgrave & Mynors, 46]); the (southern) Picts have Ninian, instructed in Rome, completed by the (non-Roman) Columban mission to the northern Picts (Bede, *Historia ecclesiastica*, III.4 [edd. Colgrave & Mynors, 220–2]); the

struggle or subjection, but by how these various Christian peoples, at different levels of Christianity, might join peaceably together as members of the universal church, thus ushering in the first part of the eschatological narrative for the Last Judgement. The focus for Bede was no longer on the domination of a single Christian *gens*, but on many Christian *gentes* as one fully converted Christian *populus*, who would subsequently join the *populus Romanorum* and usher in the end of times. When Bede came to sum up the present situation at the end of his *Historia ecclesiastica*, he did so by describing the current state of *Britannia*:

> The Picts now have a treaty of peace with the English and rejoice to share in the catholic peace and truth of the Church universal. The Irish who live in Britain are content with their own territories and devise no plots or treachery against the English. Though, for the most part, the Britons oppose the English through their inbred hatred, and the whole state of the catholic Church by their incorrect Easter and their evil customs, yet being opposed by the power of God and man alike, they cannot obtain what they want in either respect. For although they are partly their own masters, yet they have also been brought partly under the rule of the English.[40]

Bede had evolved Gildas's concept of a Christian *Britannia* to include all the peoples of the island of Britain.

In repurposing Gildas's definition of *Britannia*, Bede allowed himself to omit and adjust, both stylistically and interpretively, elements of Gildas's narrative of British Christianity.[41] The most notable adjustments were Bede's expansion on Gildas's description of the martyr Alban (*fl. ca* 300), and the inclusion of three significant narratives missing from the *De excidio*, that of the Roman mission of Ninian (*fl. ca* 400) to the Picts, the papal mission of Bishop Palladius *ca* 431 to the Irish (as *Scotti*), and Bishop Germanus of Auxerre's two sanctioned missions (*ca* 429 and *ca* 437–48) to combat the heresy of Pelagianism in Britain, as recorded in Constantius's *Vita Germani*.[42] These significant adjustments, particularly the addition of the Germanus narrative, have seen arguments that Bede's intention was to highlight the Britons in an even more negative light than Gildas in order to emphasise them as a failed people prior to the history of the English as a chosen people.[43] Walter Goffart, following Robert Hanning, regards the inclusion of the Germanus narrative – a narrative that describes Gallic assistance to the British church – as reinforcing Bede's criticism of

English, of course, have Gregory the Great, as represented by Augustine of Canterbury (Bede, *Historia ecclesiastica*, I.23 [edd. Colgrave & Mynors, 68]).

40 Bede, *Historia ecclesiastica*, V.23 (edd. Colgrave & Mynors, 560–1): 'Pictorum quoque natio tempore hoc et foedus pacis cum gente habet Anglorum, et catholicae pacis ac ueritatis cum uniuersali ecclesia particeps existere gaudet. Scotti qui Brittaniam incolunt, suis contenti finibus, nil contra gentem Anglorum insidiarum moliuntur aut fraudium. Brettones, quamuis et maxima ex parte domestico sibi odio gentem Anglorum, et totius catholicae ecclesiae statum pascha minus recto moribusque inprobis inpugnent, tamen et diuina sibi et humana prorsus resistente uirtute in neutro cupitum possunt obtinere propositum, quippe qui, quamuis ex parte sui sint iuris, nonnulla tamen ex parte Anglorum sunt seruitio mancipati'.

41 Miller, 'Bede's Use of Gildas', 242–3.

42 For Alban, See Bede, *Historia ecclesiastica* I.7 (edd. Colgrave & Mynors, 28–35). For Palladius, see Bede, *Historia ecclesiastica*, I.13 (edd. Colgrave & Mynors, 46); V.24 (edd. Colgrave & Mynors, 562). For Germanus, see Bede, *Historia ecclesiastica*, I.17–21 (edd. Colgrave & Mynors, 54–67).

43 See n. 39, above.

a British Church that refused to preach to the pagan Anglo-Saxons.[44] However, Vicky Gunn has shown that Bede is, in fact, more positive about the Britons than Gildas, following the general pattern in the *Historia ecclesiastica* in emphasising positive role models.[45] This emphasis on a more positive description of the Britons, and, therefore, one more sympathetic to his readers, underscores Bede's purpose in building on Gildas's history of the Britons. The purpose was not to replace the Britons as a failed people with the English as a chosen people, but to highlight that, as 'Britannic' peoples who each legitimately share *Britannia*, the English stood at exactly the same eschatological threshold in Bede's time as that faced by the Britons in Gildas's time.

As Peter Darby notes, when Bede sums up the present state of Britain and the English nation at the end of Book V, he links it to his description of Gildas's Britons in Book I, just prior to the introduction of Gregory the Great's mission to convert the English:[46]

> [V.23] Qua adridente pace ac **serenitate temporum**, plures in gente Nordanhymbrorum, **tam nobiles quam priuati**, se suosque liberos depositis armis satagunt magis, accepta tonsura, monasterialibus adscribere uotis quam bellicis exercere studiis. Quae res quem sit habitura finem, **posterior aetas** uidebit.[47]

> [I.22] Attamen recente adhuc memoria calamitatis et cladis inflictae seruabant utcumque reges, sacerdotes, **priuati et optimates** suum quique ordinem. At illis decedentibus, cum **successisset aetas** tempestatis illius nescia et **praesentis** solum **serenitatis** statum experta, ita cuncta ueritatis ac iustitiae moderamina concussa ac subuersa sunt, ut earum non dicam uestigium sed ne memoria quidem praeter in paucis, et ualde paucis, ulla appareret.[48]

In addition, unnoticed by Darby, Bede's description of the Britons is drawn directly from Gildas's description of the present state of *Britannia* just prior to launching into his complaint against her kings and clergy:

> [Bede] Attamen recente adhuc memoria calamitatis et cladis inflictae seruabant utcumque **reges, sacerdotes, priuati et optimates suum quique ordinem. At illis decedentibus, cum successisset aetas tempestatis illius nescia et praesentis solum serenitatis statum experta, ita cuncta ueritatis ac iustitiae moderamina concussa**

44 Hanning, *The Vision of History*, 77–9. Goffart, *The Narrators of Barbarian History*, 302–3.

45 Gunn, *Bede's Historiae*, 103–5.

46 Darby, *Bede and the End of Time*, 213–14.

47 Bede, *Historia ecclesiastica*, V.23 (edd. Colgrave & Mynors, 560–1): 'In these favourable times of peace and prosperity, many of the Northumbrian race, both noble and simple, have laid aside their weapons and taken the tonsure, preferring that they and their children should take monastic vows rather than train themselves in the art of war. What the result will be, a later generation will discover.'

48 Bede, *Historia ecclesiastica*, I.22 (edd. Colgrave & Mynors, 66–9): 'Nevertheless, so long as the memory of the calamity and bloodshed was still fresh, somehow the kings, priests, **nobles, and private citizens** kept within bounds. But, when they died, **a generation succeeded** which knew nothing of all these troubles and was used only to **the present state of peace**. Then all restraints of truth and justice were so utterly destroyed and abandoned that, not merely was there no trace of them to be found, but only a small, a very small minority even remembered their existence.'

> **ac subuersa sunt, ut earum non dicam uestigium sed ne memoria quidem** praeter **in paucis, et ualde paucis,** ulla **appareret.**[49]

> [Gildas] Haesit etenim tam desperati insulae excidii insperatique mentio auxilii memoriae eorum qui utriusque miraculi testes extitere; et ob hoc **reges, publici, privati, sacerdotes, ecclesiastici, suum quique ordinem servarunt. At illis decedentibus cum successisset aetas tempestatis illius nescia et praesentis tantum serenitatis experta, ita cuncta veritatis ac iustitiae moderamina concussa ac subversa sunt ut earum non dicam vestigium sed ne monimentum quidem** in supra dictis propemodum ordinibus **appareat**, exceptis **paucis et valde paucis**.[50]

Bede is not highlighting the wickedness of the Britons in order to legitimate the English as their replacement, but rather subtly alerting the reader to the repetition of a significant eschatological moment in providential history, though with one fundamental difference. At the precise point of *serenitas* where Gildas chooses to criticise the secular and church leaders of *Britannia*, Bede, consigning the crimes of the Britons and, through allusion, the crimes of the English to a brief aside, embarks on a positive providential history of conversion.[51] The emphasis for teaching, for avoiding judgement, is not on threats or fear but on positive example. The outcome for not acting on Bede's positive example lies in another text and the history of another people, Gildas's *De excidio* and the former sole inhabitants of *Britannia*, the Britons.

As Darby has also noted, Bede's use of *serenitas* as the 'peace among sinners' – in a sense a 'false *serenitas*' – is drawn from I Thessalonians 5.2–3: 'For yourselves know perfectly, that the day of the Lord shall so come, as a thief in the night. For when they shall say, peace and security; then shall sudden destruction come upon them.'[52] This notion of the Last Judgement coming as a 'thief in the night', is, itself,

[49] Bede, *Historia ecclesiastica*, I.22 (edd. Colgrave & Mynors, 66–9): 'Nevertheless, so long as the memory of the calamity and bloodshed was still fresh, somehow the **kings, priests, nobles, and private citizens kept within bounds. But, when they died, a generation succeeded which knew nothing of all these troubles and was used only to the present state of peace. Then all restraints of truth and justice were so utterly destroyed and abandoned that, not merely was there no trace of them to be found,** but **only a small, a very small minority even remembered their existence**.'

[50] Gildas, *De excidio*, XXVI.2–3 (ed. Winterbottom, 98–9, trans., 28): 'For the remembrance of so desperate a blow to the island and of such unlooked for recovery stuck in the minds of those who witnessed both wonders. That was why **kings, public and private persons, priests and churchmen, kept to their own stations. But they died; and an age succeeded them that is ignorant of that storm and has experience only of the calm of the present. All the controls of truth and justice have been shaken and overthrown, leaving no trace, not even a memory,** among the orders I have mentioned; **with the exception of a few, a very few**.'

[51] Bede, *Historia ecclesiastica*, I.22 (edd. Colgrave & Mynors, 68–9): 'Qui inter alia inenarrabilium scelerum facta, quae historicus eorum Gildas flebili sermone describit' [To other unspeakable crimes, which Gildas their own historian describes in doleful words]. Bede's image of Gildas as a 'doleful historian' is drawn from Gildas: see Gildas, *De excidio*, XXXVII (ed. Winterbottom, 105, trans., 36): 'Hic sane vel antea concludenda erat… tam flebilis haec querulaque malorum aevi huius historia' [Here, or even earlier, I should have finished this tearful history, this complaint of the evils of the age]. This image emphasises the point of departure between Bede and Gildas.

[52] I Thessalonians 5.2–3: 'quia dies Domini, sicut fur in nocte, ita veniet: cum enim dixerint, Pax et securitas: tunc repentinus eis superveniet interitus'. For Darby's observation, see Darby, *Bede and the End of Time*, 213–14.

drawn from Matthew 24.[53] Gildas, too, emphasises phrases and images from Matthew 24. Gildas not only refers directly to Matthew 24 in his *De excidio*, he alludes to its images in a linked series of salvific and condemnatory texts in his *praefatio*.[54] In this enigmatic section revolving around Christ's sayings taken from Matthew 7, 8, 15, 25, Luke 23, and Mark 16, Gildas contrasts Christ's salvific role in the Last Judgement with Christ's condemnatory role as the Judge. He draws on a series of images of Christ's gathering of his sheep and his casting out of hypocrites that, for the discerning reader, intimately connects these chapters to Matthew 24, itself intimately concerned with the Last Judgement.[55]

While it is clear that Bede respected and followed Gildas's *historia* in his construction of the *Historia ecclesiastica*, it is important to consider whether Bede was influenced by Gildas's subsequent criticisms of the secular and clerical orders in the prophetic tradition. The purpose of the *Historia ecclesiastica* was to build on history as positive example, a purpose shaped by the avoidance of direct criticism. The criticism discerned in the *Historia ecclesiastica* has been largely based on interpretation, from a modern perspective, of Bede's occasional enigmatic statements.[56] These interpretations have largely been drawn from the one overtly critical work that has survived, Bede's letter to Bishop Ecgbert of York (*r.* 734–66). In this letter, following Gildas and Columbanus, Bede publicly criticises his seniors. In order to discern whether Bede drew on the legacy of Gildas in ways other than the providential and eschatological, we need to examine this letter.

Bede and criticism

In the last year of his life, Bede, faced with rapidly deteriorating health, composed a letter to the new bishop of York, Ecgbert, cousin to King Ceolwulf and intimately involved in the crisis over sacral kingship ignited within Northumbria by the

[53] Matthew 24.42–44: 'Vigilate ergo, quia nescitis qua hora Dominus vester venturus sit. Illud autem scitote, quoniam si sciret paterfamilias qua hora fur venturus esset, vigilaret utique, et non sineret perfodi domum suam. Ideo et vos estote parati: quia qua nescitis hora Filius hominis venturus est' [Watch ye therefore, because ye know not what hour your Lord will come. But know this ye, that if the goodman of the house knew at what hour the thief would come, he would certainly watch, and would not suffer his house to be broken open. Wherefore be you also ready, because at what hour you know not the Son of man will come].

[54] For direct citations of Matthew 24, see Gildas, *De excidio*, XXXI.2 (ed. Winterbottom, 101); XCVI.3 (ed. Winterbottom, 135). For allusions to Matthew 24, see Gildas, *De excidio*, LXVIII.2 (ed. Winterbottom, 120); XCII.2 (ed. Winterbottom, 133). For these allusions, see O'Loughlin, *Gildas and the Scriptures*, 262 and 318–19.

[55] Matthew 15.24 (The lost sheep of Israel will be saved); against this, Matthew 8.12 (The subjects of Israel will not be saved). Matthew 15.26 (faith will save); against this, Matthew 15.7 (lip service will not). Matthew 8.11 (many gentiles will be saved); against this, Matthew 7.23 (those who claim to be Jesus's kin but do not obey God's law will not). Luke 23.29 (wise virgins will be saved); against this, Matthew 25.10–12 (foolish virgins will not). Mark 16.16 (he who believes will be saved/he who does not believe will not) is both salvific and condemnatory. The paraphrasing of these biblical citations is mine. Images of hypocrites (as false teachers and false prophets) underscore Matthew 24. For Gildas's use of these biblical citations, see Gildas, *De excidio*, I.8–10 (ed. Winterbottom, 88). O'Loughlin notes Gildas's originality at this point. See O'Loughlin, *Gildas and the Scriptures*, 131.

[56] Higham, *(Re-)Reading Bede*, 56.

appearance of the 'comets' in 729.[57] That Bede would compose a letter to a bishop critical of clerical authority was an extraordinary turnaround in his world view, representative, perhaps, of a fourth and final crisis as he faced his own death. In 716, faced with the personal crisis of the sudden departure of Abbot Ceolfrith to Rome, Bede had emphasised that it was wrong to criticise the clerical orders:

> so also we, following the example of blessed Samuel, should behave discreetly towards them and not expose them, even though we are in no doubt that they are beyond correction and already likely to be condemned by divine judgment, especially if we have recognised that they are marked out as belonging to some ecclesiastical rank.

> it teaches us how much reverence should be shown to divine sacraments, even when administered by the hand of evil men, how much honour should be accorded persons bound to the service of the holy altar, how much anyone's presumption should be restrained from harming such persons, however evil their manner of living, on account of the distinction of their rank… We should be wary of presuming to abuse or dishonour the reputation of bishops, priests, deacons anywhere.[58]

This view of avoiding criticism of the clerical orders had coalesced in an initial, probably limited, publication of the *Historia ecclesiastica* in 731, the immediate impact and success of which saw Bede return to the *Historia ecclesiastica* with a preface dedicated to Ceolwulf, one that positioned him as a benefactor to the king, and a recapitulation that highlighted the depth and breadth of his scholarship.[59]

While Nicholas Higham has seen a defensive quality to the preface and the recapitulation, these additions can also be seen as an assertion of authority, additions perhaps influenced by the literary traditions of continental historians such as Gregory of Tours.[60] The timing of these additions may tie in with Bede's enigmatic account of Islamic incursions on the continent, an account best interpreted as being readjusted after the decisive and eschatologically significant victory by Charles Martel over Islamic forces at the Battle of Poitiers in 732:

57 The letter is dated to 5 November 734. Bede dies on 26 May 735. Higham, *(Re-)Reading Bede*, 200, notes that Ecgbert probably played a significant role in Ceolwulf's survival of the political crisis of 731; on Bede's deteriorating health towards the end of his life, see 8 and 40.

58 An observation made by Campbell, 'Bede', 177. He cites the quotes from Bede's *Commentary on I Samuel* there. Bede, *In primam partem Samuelis*, II.15 (on I Samuel 15.30–31): 'nos quoque in exemplum beati Samuhelis erga tales modeste agere neque eos traducere oportet quos incorrigibiles et divino iam iudicio non dubitamus esse damnandos, maxime si hos aliquo gradu ecclesiastico'; IV.26 (on I Samuel 26.9–11): 'docet quanta reverentia sit divinis adhibenda sacramentis quamvis per malorum manum dispensatis, quantus personis sacri altaris officio mancipatis honor impendendus, quantum ab harum laesione quamlibet male viventium propter insigne gradus sit cuiuslibet temperanda praesumptio… Cavendum ergo ne episcoporum, presbiterorum, diaconorum famam passim lacerare et attaminare praesumamus'. For the translations, see *Bede: On First Samuel* (trans. DeGregorio & Love, 316 and 482).

59 See Higham, *(Re-)Reading Bede*, 10–11, on Bede establishing himself as a benefactor to the king in his preface. Higham proposes Chapter 24 as a recapitulation at 82–95.

60 For Higham's view of the defensive nature of the preface and the recapitulation, see Higham, *(Re-) Reading Bede*, 93–5; for the potential influence of Gregory of Tours on Bede, see 10–11.

> At this time a terrible plague of Saracens ravaged Gaul with cruel bloodshed and not long afterwards they received the due reward of their treachery in the same kingdom.[61]

The success of Bede's *Historia ecclesiastica* as an 'intervention' in the eschatological landscape of Northumbria and more widely in Britain and Ireland – perhaps 'rebadged' for dissemination to the continent – may have allowed Bede to finally accept the prophetic voice. Having the prophetic voice and being heard, however, is the essential problem faced by prophets.

The letter to Ecgbert raises the question whether Bede, dependent through ill health on active engagement by others, may have been isolated in the last year of his life. This isolation may not just have been physical but political. The return of Ceolwulf to the throne in 732, if we accept the reference to the Battle of Poitiers in the *Historia ecclesiastica*, coincided with the exile of Bede's long-time supporter, Bishop Acca of Hexham.[62] The opening of Bede's letter to Ecgbert is replete in frustration at being isolated from influence:

> I remember that last year… you said that you also wanted to invite me this year… to a discussion with you… If by God's will this could have happened, there would have been no need to send these pages to you in writing, since speaking more freely face to face I would have been able to put to you whatever I considered I had to say in a private conversation. As you know a sudden attack of physical weakness has prevented me from doing this, so that it could not happen; but nevertheless I have taken care to do what I could in response to your concern for me… by sending in writing what I could not convey in conversation by coming in person.[63]

This frustration is of itself understandable for a man of Bede's status, but subsequent to this apologetic introduction, Bede launches immediately into a criticism of the Northumbrian church and a denunciation of the failure of its clerics to fulfil their duties. The dislocation between this letter and his *Historia ecclesiastica* could not be more pronounced. Further, the preservation of this letter is witness to the fact that Bede was aware that his criticism of clerical authority might become public.

In embarking on a critical assessment of the Northumbrian church, Bede addressed his perceived issues in a direct way, offering both criticism and advice. Pointing to poor teaching, poor example, corruption, and a lack of clerics, Bede effectively targeted the generation of ecclesiastical activity that coincided with his life as a priest and scholar.[64] He also targeted corrupt monastic practice and the

61 Bede, *Historia ecclesiastica*, V.23 (edd. Colgrave & Mynors, 556–7): 'Quo tempore grauissima Sarracenorum lues Gallias misera caede uastabat, et ipsi non multo post in eadem prouincia dignas suae perfidiae poenas luebant'. Goffart, *The Narrators of Barbarian History*, 242, supports this reading.

62 For a discussion of the relationship between Bede and Bishop Acca, see Stancliffe, 'Bede and Bishop Acca'.

63 Bede, *Epistola ad Ecgbertvm*, I (edd. Grocock & Wood, 124–5): 'Memini te hesterno dixisse anno… quod hoc etiam anno uelles… me quoque… ad tuum accipere colloquium. Quod si ita Deo uolente posset impleri, non opus esset tibi haec per litteras scripta dirigere; cum possem liberius ore ad os loquens quaequae uelim siue necessaria ducerem secreta tibi allocutione suggerere. Verum quia hoc, ne fieret, superueniens ut nosti corporis mei ualitudo prohibuit agere, tamen quod potui… intuiti curaui, mittendo uidelicet per litteras quod corporaliter ueniendo per collocutionem nequiueram'.

64 Bede, *Epistola ad Ecgbertvm*, XIII (edd. Grocock & Wood, 148–9): 'Sic per annos circiter triginta, hoc est ex quo Aldfrid rex humanis rebus ablatus est' [So for about thirty years, since King

active collusion of aristocratic families in monastic foundations to avoid fiscal and feudal responsibilities to the institution of sacral kingship.[65] The advice given was extraordinarily forward for a priest to a bishop. Not only was there a general call for good teaching and example, as illustrated by Bede's emphasis on Gregory the Great's *Regula pastoralis* as a handbook for priestly behaviour, but there was also specific administrative advice.[66] This included an investigation into the legitimacy of all monastic foundations in the diocese, as well as a radical reorganisation of the diocese itself along the lines of Gregory the Great's recommendations in his letter to Augustine of Canterbury, a radical reorganisation predicated on the suggested creation of a monastic episcopacy.[67]

At the core of Bede's fears for the Northumbrian church was what would happen to its failed clerics on Judgement Day. Echoing the sentiment expressed by Jerome on the eschatological dangers inherent in the burden of clerical office, Bede, right from the very outset, repeatedly refers to the severity of divine punishment for failure in clerical duties:

> But if any one – perish the thought! – has accepted the office of bishop and yet does not bother to preserve either himself from evil actions by living a good life, or the people placed under him by rebuking and warning them, the statement in the gospels clearly shows what will happen to this man when the Lord comes at an hour he does not expect, in which it is said to the useless slave, 'throw him into the outer darkness there, there will be weeping and gnashing of teeth'.[68]

Each mention of the 'unprofitable servant' introduces a thematic charge against the clerical orders. The first, directly following on from the previous quote, is poor teaching:

Aldfrith was taken from the world of men].

65 Bede, *Epistola ad Ecgbertvm*, XIII (edd. Grocock & Wood, 148–9): 'prouincia nostra uesano illo errore dementata est ut nullus paene exinde praefectorum extiterit qui non huiusmodi sibi monasterium in diebus suae praefecturae comparauerit suamque simul coniugem pari reatu nociui mercatus astrinxerit' [our province has been driven mad by the lunatic policy that has resulted in there being almost none of the local rulers who has not acquired a monastery of this kind for himself during his period of office, and at the same time has bound his wife in just the same kind of guilt-ridden crooked business].

66 Bede, *Epistola ad Ecgbertvm*, III (edd. Grocock & Wood, 126–7): 'sed in uerbis sanctissimi papae Gregorii... in libro Regulae Pastoralis' [also the words of the most holy Pope Gregory... in the book of Pastoral Care].

67 On this, see Bede, *Epistola ad Ecgbertvm*, IX–X (edd. Grocock & Wood, 140–1): 'Nam et sanctus papa Gregorius... ad beatissimum archiepiscopum Augustinum missis litteras disputaret... Quapropter commodum duxerim habito maiori concilio et consensus pontificali simul et regali edicto prospiciatur locus aliquis monasteriorum ubi sedes fiat episcopalis' [And when the holy Pope Gregory... in letters sent to the most blessed Archbishop Augustine... decreed... Because of this, I had thought it advisable that with the agreement of a great council and by decree of both bishop and king, some monastic location should be identified as a likely episcopal see].

68 Bede, *Epistola ad Ecgbertvm*, II (edd. Grocock & Wood, 126–7): 'Si quis uero – quod absit – gradu episcopatus accepto nec seipsum a malis actibus bene uiuendo nec subditam sibi plebem castigando uel ammonendo corrigere curat, quid huic ueniente Domino hora qua non sperat euenturum sit euangelica manifeste sententia declarat, qua dicitur ad inutilem seruum: "Eicite in tenebras exteriores, ibi erit fletus et stridor dentium"'.

> Above all then I urge you, holy father, to keep yourself away from storytelling, gossip, and other plagues of an unbridled tongue, in conduct proper for a bishop.[69]

The second is simony:

> Just as on the other hand, if you have carried out the business entrusted to you by the Lord less carefully, you are destined in the future age to receive a share with the worthless and idle servant for hiding your talent… If therefore he ordered them to preach the gospel without payment and did not allow them to accept either gold or silver or any kind of earthly money from those to whom they preached, what kind of peril, I ask, threatens those who do exactly the opposite?[70]

This subtle linking of quotes from Matthew 25.30 with the Last Judgement described in Matthew 24 follows that of Gildas in his preface to the *De excidio*, as does the connection between the 'unprofitable servant' and that of the priest or bishop who fails their clerical duties. Gildas makes this allusion explicit when he refers directly to Matthew 24 when citing the New Testament to criticise irregular priests:

> 'The lord of that servant will come on a day when he does not expect him and at an hour when he does not know, and separate him' (that is, from the holy priests) 'and place his portion with the hypocrites' (that is, no doubt, those who hide a deal of wickedness under the cloak of priesthood), 'and there will be wailing and gnashing of teeth' for those to whom that rarely happens in this life despite the daily calamities suffered by the sons of the mother church and the losses occurred by the kingdom of heaven.[71]

Bede's criticisms of the Northumbrian church echo those of Gildas. In much the same way as Gildas, Bede primarily targets poor teaching and corruption within the clerical orders. He differs from Gildas in that, following on from the *Historia ecclesiastica*, Bede continues to set aside simony as a clerical heresy, rather, like Augustine of Hippo, emphasising the buying and selling of clerical office as a sin.[72] In doing so, Bede reverts to the term *mercenarius* or 'hireling':

> And yet I must earnestly beg and beseech you in the Lord zealously to protect the flock committed to you from the wickedness of wolves that rush in, to remember that you have been appointed as shepherd and **not as hireling** and should display the love of the great Shepherd, ever concerned with feeding his sheep, and be ready to lay

69 Bede, *Epistola ad Ecgbertvm*, III (edd. Grocock & Wood, 126–7): 'Ante omnia sane tuae sanctae paternitati suadeo, ut ab otiosis te confabulationibus obtrectationibus ceterisque linguae indomitae contagiis pontificali dignitate coerceas'.

70 Bede, *Epistola ad Ecgbertvm*, VI (edd. Grocock & Wood, 134–5): 'Sicut e contrario, si commissum tibi a Domino negotium minus diligenter compleueris, pro retentione talenti cum seruo nequam et pigro partem es recepturus in futuro… Si ergo illos gratis euangelium praedicare iussit, neque aurum uel argentum, uel aliquid pecuniae temporalis ab eis, quibis praedicabant, accipere permisit; quid, rogo, illis qui his contraria gerunt, periculi immineat?'

71 Gildas, *De excidio*, XCVI.3 (ed. Winterbottom, 135, trans., 71–2): '"Veniet ergo", inquit, "dominus servi illius in die qua non sperat, et hora qua ignorat, et dividet eum", a sanctis scilicet sacerdotibus, "partemque eius ponet cum hypocritis", cum eis certe qui sub sacerdotali tegmine multum obumbrant nequitiae, "illic", inquiens, "erit fletus et stridor dentium", quibus in hac vita non crebro evenit ob cotidianas ecclesiae matris ruinas filiorum vel desideria regni caelorum'.

72 See Chapter 4, 95–6.

down your life for these selfsame sheep like the blessed prince of the apostles did if circumstances demand it.[73]

These failures in clerical duties – poor teaching and corruption – make up the two of the three sections of Bede's letter to Ecgbert. In the third section, Bede targets 'false monasteries'. While Gildas alludes to the secular corruption of monasticism, he does not emphasise it in his *De excidio*, preferring to concentrate on kings and clerics.[74] Bede's attack on 'false monasticism', on the other hand, is aimed more broadly at the corruption of the secular orders, and the impact of this corruption on effective and stable secular leadership.[75]

Bede's attachment of 'false monasteries' to the corruption of sacral kingship is reinforced by his perception of the role of these institutions in the weakening of internal political and military cohesion. The monasteries are false, but Bede does not concentrate on rogue monks, rather rogue laics avoiding secular, particularly military duties. In calling on the example of the Kings of Judah, both good and bad, Bede emphasised the proper roles of the secular orders and the importance of stable succession in the maintenance of political and military prowess. Sinful kings and worldly bishops need not lead to a permanent corruption of the secular orders because subsequent righteous kings, as aided by holy bishops, would set aside their unjust decrees:

> Following this example it behoves your holiness with the pious king of our people to rip up the impious and evil deeds and writings of earlier leaders, and to watch over those things in our province which are valuable either in the sight of God or in the sight of the world, so that in our day, when faith is failing and the love and fear of him who sees into our hearts is being forsaken, and when the forces of worldly soldiery are fading away, there should not be a dearth of men who can protect our borders from barbarian raiding.[76]

In doing so, Bede, like Gildas, draws on the link between military strength and spiritual strength and reinforces the importance of every man keeping to his station. However, unlike Gildas who stresses worldly kings corrupting the church, Bede inverts the criticism, emphasising a church actively weakening the secular, particularly the military, authority of kingship. For Bede, kingship had become a consort to the church.

[73] Bede, *Epistola ad Ecgbertvm*, XIV (edd. Grocock & Wood, 150–1): 'Et iam iamque te multum deprecor atque obtestor in Domino ut commissum tibi gregem sedulus ab irruentium luporum improbitate tuearis, teque **non mercenarium** sed pastorem constitutem esse memineris, qui amorem summi Pastoris sollerti ouium ipsius pastione demonstres proque eisdem ouibus, si ita res poposcerit, cum beato apostolorum principe animam ponere paratus sis'. Emphasis is mine.

[74] Gildas refers to the tyrant Constantine committing murder in the robes of an abbot at *De excidio XXVIII*, and that Maglocunus was a monk prior to becoming a tyrant at *De excidio XXXIV*.

[75] Bede's criticisms of false monasteries are explored in *Abbots of Wearmouth and Jarrow* (edd. Grocock & Woods, li–lvi).

[76] Bede, *Epistola ad Ecgbertvm*, XI (edd. Grocock & Wood, 144–5): 'Quo exemplo tuam quoque sanctitatem decet cum religioso rege nostrae gentis irreligiosa et iniqua priorum gesta atque scripta conuellere, et ea quae prouinciae nostrae siue secundum Deum siue secundum seculum sint utilia prospicere, ne nostris temporibus uel religione cessante amor timorque interni deseratur inspectoris, uel rarescente copia militiae secularis absint qui fines nostros a barbarica incursione tueantur'.

While Bede appears to be sounding a similar prophetic *tuba* to Gildas, he is careful not to call on his authority. There is no direct reference to the *De excidio* in his letter to Ecgbert. That Bede has an intimate understanding of the *De excidio* is seen with his use of scripture – Bede and Gildas are the only early medieval authors to directly quote I Samuel 12.2–4 in the context of a corrupt priesthood:

> [Gildas] Quis... ut **Samuel**, valedicturus **populo** astabit hoc modo dicens: '**Ecce praesto sum, loquimini coram domino et Christo eius, utrum bovem cuiusquam tulerim an asinum, si quempiam calumniatus sum, si oppressi aliquem, si de manu cuiusquam munus accepi?'** Cui a populo responsum est **dicente: 'non es calumniatus nos neque oppressisti neque tulisti de manu alicuius quippiam'**.[77]

> [Bede] cum Deo dilectus pontifex **Samuel** longe aliter fecisse omni **populo** teste legatur: 'Itaque conuersatus', inquit, 'coram uobis ab adolescentia mea usque ad diem hanc, **ecce praesto sum, loquimini** de me **coram Domino et** coram **Christo eius, utrum bouem alicuius tulerim, an asinum, si quempiam calumniatus sum, si oppressi aliquem, si de manu cuiusquam munus accepi;** et contempnam illud hodie restituamque uobis'. Et **dixerunt: 'Non es calumpniatus nos neque oppressisti neque tulisti de manu alicuius quippiam'**.[78]

This potential influence of the legacy of Gildas on Bede's view of clerical corruption can be seen in further scriptural phrases used by Bede and also found in the section of the *De excidio* relating to Gildas's criticisms of the clerical orders. These phrases, drawn from Matthew 15:14, Ephesians 5.5 (alluding to I Corinthians 5.9–11), and Acts 5.29, appear to indicate that Bede, in the last year of his life, drew on monastic authority (in the prophetic tradition, as with Gildas and Columbanus) to criticise his seniors.[79] This view is reinforced by Bede's apparent paraphrasing of Jerome,

77 Gildas, *De excidio*, LXXI.2 (ed. Winterbottom, 122, trans., 56): 'And which, like **Samuel**, when he has to say farewell to **his people**, will stand up and say: "**Behold, I am here; speak in the presence of the Lord and his anointed, say whether I have taken any man's ox or ass, if I have slandered any man, oppressed any man, received a bribe from any man's hand?' The** people's **reply was: 'You have not slandered us, or oppressed us, or taken anything from the hand of any man**".'

78 Bede, *Epistola ad Ecgbertvm*, VII (edd. Grocock & Wood, 136–7): 'For it is said that the priest Samuel, beloved of God, behaved far differently, with all **the people** as witness: "I have behaved thus towards you", he said, "from my youth right up to this day; **see, here I am; speak of me in the presence of the Lord and in the presence of his anointed, whether I have taken anyone's ox, or their ass, if I have slandered anyone, if I have oppressed anyone, if I have received any gift from anyone's hand and I will condemn it today and will restore it to you". And they said "you have not slandered us, nor have you oppressed us, nor have you received anything from the hands of anyone**".' Bede differs from Gildas in emphasising Samuel's role as clerical (*pontifex*). Patrick also makes a notable allusion to this rarely cited biblical passage in the context of a defence against accusations of clerical corruption. See Patrick, *Confessio*, IIII (ed. Howlett, 84–7): 'Forte autem quando baptizaui tot milia hominum sperauerim ab aliquo illorum uel dimidio scriptulae? Dicite mihi et reddam uobis. Aut quando ordinauit ubique Dominus clericos per modicitatem meam et ministerium gratis distribui illis, si poposci ab aliquo illorum uel pretium uel calciamenti mei, dicite aduersus me et reddam uobis' [Perhaps moreover when I baptized so many thousands of men I would have hoped for even half a scruple from any of them. Tell me and I will give it back to you. Or when the Lord ordained clerics everywhere through my littleness and I distributed the ministry to them free, if I asked for even the price even of my shoe from any of them, tell it to my face and I will give more back to you].

79 For Matthew 15:14, see Gildas, *De excidio*, XCV.4 (ed. Winterbottom, 134); Bede, *Epistola ad Ecgbertvm*, XIII (edd. Grocock & Wood, 150); for I Corinthians 5:9–11/Ephesians 5.5, see

as seen above, that asked, but rhetorically did not answer, who could intercede for a fallen priest:

> [Jerome] who will intercede for a fallen priest?[80]
>
> [Bede] what kind of peril, I ask, threatens those who do exactly the opposite?[81]

Bede, however, appears to be more subtle than this. While the notion of juniors criticising their seniors became embedded within a monastic tradition represented by Gildas and drawn from Jerome, Bede, prior to his deliberate elision of Ephesians 5.5 with I Corinthians 5.9–11 (itself recalling Thessalonians 5.5), visits the debate between Augustine of Hippo and Jerome over the controversial moment in Galatians 2.11–14 where Paul chastised Peter:

> Or perhaps we think that the apostle made a mistake or wrote down a falsehood when he said for our instruction 'brothers, do not err', and then immediately added 'neither greedy, nor drunken, nor thieving men will possess the kingdom of heaven'.[82]

Jerome favoured a traditional patristic interpretation that Paul had told a 'white lie' rather than support an interpretation that saw Paul, as Peter's junior, publicly criticising his senior for judaising.[83] Augustine corrected Jerome, arguing that this interpretation undermined the divine truth inherent in the Bible:

> Is it really better to believe that the Apostle Paul wrote something untrue than that the Apostle Peter did something unrighteous? If it were, then we could (God forbid!) go on and say that it is better to believe that the Gospel lies than that Christ was denied by Peter; and that the Book of Kings lies [in saying] that a great prophet [like King David], so eminently chosen by the Lord God, committed adultery by coveting and seducing another man's wife, and was guilty of a revolting murder by killing her husband.[84]

Gildas, *De excidio*, C.3 (ed. Winterbottom, 136–7); *Epistola ad Ecgbertvm*, XVI (edd. Grococh & Wood, 156); for Acts 5.29, see Gildas, *De excidio* LXXV.3 (ed. Winterbottom, 125); *Epistola ad Ecgbertvm*, XVI (edd. Grocock & Wood, 154].

80 Jerome, *Epistulae*, 54, XIV.9 (ed. Hilberg, 59): 'pro sacerdotis lapsu quis rogaturus est?'

81 Bede, *Epistola ad Ecgbertvm*, VI (edd. Grocock & Wood, 134–5): 'quid rogo illis qui his contraria gerunt, periculi immineat?'

82 Bede, *Epistola ad Ecgbertvm*, XVI (edd. Grocock & Wood, 156–7): 'An forte errasse ac mendacium scripsisse putamus apostolum cum nos ammonens dicebat: "Fratres, nolite errare", statimque subtexuit "neque auari, neque ebriosi, neque rapaces regnum Dei possidebunt"'.

83 Jerome, *Ad Galatas*, I.2.14a (ed. Raspanti, *Commentarii*, 57): 'unde et paulus eadem arte qua ille simulabat, ei restitit in faciem, et loquitur coram omnibus; non tam ut petrum arguat, quam ut hi, quorum causa petrus simulauerat, corrigantur' [Paul likewise employed the same pretense as Peter and confronted him and spoke in front of everyone, not so much to rebuke Peter as to correct those for whose sake Peter had engaged in simulation]. Translation, Cain, *St. Jerome*, 110.

84 Augustine of Hippo, *Epistulae*, 34.2, LXXXII (ed. Goldbacher, 355): 'at enim satius est credere apostolum paulum aliquid non uere scripsisse, quam apostolum petrum non recte aliquid egisse. hoc si ita est, dicamus, quod absit, satius esse credere mentiri euangelium, quam negatum esse a petro christum, et mentiri regnorum librum, quam tantum prophetam a domino deo tam excellenter electum et in concupiscenda atque abducenda uxore aliena commisisse adulterium et in marito eius necando tam horrendum homicidium'. For the translation, see *Augustine in His Own Words* (trans. Harmless, 189).

Bede called directly on the authority of Augustine, in a passage that reinforced that even apostles could be unrighteous and that great kings (as prophets) could commit capital sins. As a monk and priest of a monastery dedicated to Peter and Paul, Bede drew on clerical authority in order to criticise his senior, a position laid out by Augustine in the same letter to Jerome:

> Therein Peter left to those that came after him an example, that, if at any time they deviated from the right path, they should not think it beneath them to accept correction from those who were their juniors – an example more rare, and requiring greater piety, than that which Paul's conduct on the same occasion left us, that those who are younger should have courage even to withstand their seniors if the defence of evangelical truth required it, yet in such a way as to preserve unbroken brotherly love.[85]

Bede had transformed Gildas's prophetic voice in his *Historia ecclesiastica*, moving from fear of judgement and abandonment to the importance of good example and pastoral care. In the last year of his life, Bede reframed the authority that underpinned Gildas's prophetic voice – the monastic authority to criticise seniors ultimately drawn from Jerome – and placed it back within the clerical authority of Augustine of Hippo. Bede had come full circle on Gildas and his legacy, from a cursory acknowledgement of the 'old-fashioned', through to an innate understanding of the power of historical *exempla*, through to a complete understanding of the underlying tradition that allowed juniors to publicly criticise their seniors. Prophecy, as Gildas understood it, had been drawn back by Bede into the clerical orders.

Conclusion

At the tender age of seven, Bede was offered as an oblate to Abbot Benedict Biscop (*ca* 628–89), perhaps at the founding of the monastery of Jarrow in 681.[86] Benedict, like his fellow Northumbrian, Bishop Wilfrid (*ca* 633–709), had responded to the renewal of papal interest in the mission to convert the English through the reconstitution of the authority of Canterbury in the 660s with the arrival of Theodore and Hadrian.[87] From this mission, and his own visits to Rome, Benedict had drawn the authority of Augustine of Hippo northwards to Northumbria, as represented by the establishment of his writings in monastic libraries and a selective implementation of the monastic rule of Benedict of Nursia (*ca* 480–547).[88] With an Augustinian emphasis on love rather than a Cassianic emphasis on obedience, Northumbria was increasingly a Roman bulwark against the powerful founding influence of the Irish

[85] Augustinus of Hippo, *Epistulae*, 34.2, LXXXII (ed. Goldbacher, 374): '[Petrus] atque ita rarius et sanctius exemplum posteris praebuit, quo non dedignarentur, sicubi forte recti tramitem reliquissent, etiam a posterioribus corrigi, quam paulus, quo fidenter auderent etiam minores maioribus pro defendenda euangelica ueritate salua fraterna caritate resistere'. For the translation, see 'The Letters of St Augustin' (trans. Cunningham, 357).

[86] Thacker conjectures that Bede may have been related to Benedict Biscop. See Thacker, 'Bede and the Ordering of Understanding', 41.

[87] Indeed, Biscop and the mission of Theodore and Hadrian to Canterbury are intimately connected. See Gunn, *Bede's Historiae*, 48. On Biscop's second trip to Rome (*ca* 665), Theodore was placed in the care of Biscop, with Biscop becoming abbot at the monastery of St Peter in Canterbury.

[88] On the potential influence of the *Rule of Benedict* on Northumbria, see DeGregorio, 'Bede and Benedict of Nursia'.

church. Bede, thus, was one of the first generation of Northumbrian monastic clerics to be inculcated with the works of Augustine, and the responsibility of embedding Augustine's authority within a potent tradition resistant to that authority was something that Bede appeared to take to heart.

The difficulty of implementing radical changes in a tradition reliant on immutability was not lost on Bede. His initial response was simply to draw on Augustine's allegorical and, essentially, apocalyptic approaches to eschatology to set about tempering the Irish (and Old Testament) emphasis on *praesens iudicium* or 'judgment in the here and now' and its tendency toward eschatological speculation. The innovative nature of Bede's work, and the subsequent charge of heresy, was handled expertly by reinforcing the authority of Augustine. Within this perspective, 'old fashioned' works representing the patristic traditions of the Irish church, such as Gildas's *De excidio*, received only cursory attention. The personal and political crisis of 716, followed by the eschatological crisis of 729, alerted Bede that this approach was not enough. Using Gregory the Great as a guiding light into the ascetic and eschatological perspectives that underpinned authority within the Irish church, Bede set about reworking Augustine within the Irish tradition as represented by Gildas. The apocalyptic eschatology of his early works, of God transforming history – most notably his commentary on Revelation – made room for the prophetic eschatology found in works such as Gildas's *De excidio* where God acted within history. Gildas's prophetic understanding of *Britannia* as *praesens Israel* was utilised and built on by Bede in his most successful work, the *Historia ecclesiastica*. Here he presented the English as a chosen people among the chosen peoples of Britain, attaching the eventual conversion of all her peoples to orthodoxy to the eschatological timetable that ushered in the Last Judgement. Reversals of fortune in this scheme were no longer necessarily apocalyptic triggers or divine judgements, but rather the continuing journey of the *populus* under God's guidance, a journey dependent on actively keeping the covenant.

Bede divined that Gildas had addressed a providential moment in time with an eschatological intervention, a moment that was replicated in Bede's present. Conscious of the need for a similar eschatological intervention, Bede constructed his *Historia ecclesiastica* as a response to a crisis in the secular orders. The emphasis was on Christian communities sharing *Britannia*, of the clerical, monastic, and secular orders fulfilling their proper roles within these communities, and of the proper relationship between these orders, particularly those of bishops and kings. Bede's *Historia ecclesiastica*, as a model for the interrelationship between apostolic and aristocratic succession, eschewed criticisms and threats in favour of good example and pastoral care. Through restoring kingship as a complementary authority to that of bishops, it became an influential handbook for kings and bishops both in the British Isles and on the continent.

At the end of his life, Bede drew on Gildas once more. In finally accepting and asserting the right expressed by Gildas of juniors criticising their seniors, Bede subtly incorporated Gildas's prophetic authority – drawn from the monasticism of Jerome and Cassian – within his own clerical authority. In doing so, Bede answered Jerome's rhetorical question on who could intercede for a fallen priest with the authority of Augustine: another cleric would intercede. In sounding the *tuba* once more with the laments of Gildas, Bede reclaimed the prophetic authority to criticise seniors embedded within monasticism for the clerical orders.

CONCLUSION: THE LEGACY OF GILDAS

We have explored the evolving images of the authority of Gildas from the fifth to the eighth centuries. At times, the space given to the complex issues that shaped this early medieval period both in the British Isles and on the continent has resulted in contexts that may appear overly brief or 'quaint' in their description. There has not been enough space to flesh out the extraordinarily convoluted debates behind the controversial theologian, Pelagius, the Three Chapters controversy, or the Easter controversy, for example. The conceptual framework, as laid out at the very start, has been to follow the direct citation of Gildas up to the second quarter of the eighth century.

This framing has resulted in some new approaches to the limited material. Chapter 1 identified Bede's construction of a 'dark age' in the British Isles *ca* 450–600 as buttressed solely by Gildas's immediate descriptions of sin and civil war, an observation that nuances a dependence on Bede's vision of the past. Chapter 2 clarified the way in which multiple images of Gildas were developed by competing 'national' conceptions of authority in Britain and Ireland in the early medieval period, positioning Gildas (as the author of the *De excidio*) as a figure active in debates over authority in the second half of the fifth century. Chapter 3 explored the monastic model of authority put forward in the *De excidio*, emphasising the *De excidio* not as a failed intervention, but as an innovative *speculum principum* defining the roles of Christian kings and bishops, the emerging polity of the medieval West. Chapter 4 established Columbanus and Gregory the Great, often regarded as antagonists, within similar monastic traditions, and offered evidence that Gregory actively drew on the authority of Gildas (via Columbanus) in the development of his pastoral mission. Chapter 5 examined the way the moderating influence of Gildas (via his letter to Finnian) was adapted to support ecclesiastical and political unity in Ireland via the *Hibernensis*, a highly influential collection of canon law that emphasised episcopal and synodal authority over that of the 'holy man'. Chapter 6 revealed Bede's abiding respect for Gildas and the significant influence of Gildas on his providential construction of an inclusive Britain in his *Historia ecclesiastica*, a national construct that is still relevant to this day. A common theme in these observations is the active projection and fusion of the Christian culture of the British Isles with that of the continent, one that goes against notions of a fragmented and disorganised church dependent on continental intervention and correction.

The book began with a discussion of the problematic respect accorded to Bede's account of British history as related in his *Historia ecclesiastica*. Bede's providential construction of a dark age *ca* 450–600 – from the *adventus Saxonum* to the *adventus* of Augustine of Canterbury – has profoundly shaped our conceptions of the past. Characterised by depictions of isolation and insularity and drawing on Gildas's descriptions of fragmentation and ruin, his dark age created an image of the British Isles where the church no longer functioned effectively. The rare surviving literary sources for this church, as we saw, became tangled in Bede's vision: decontextualised by darkness, they floated away from their loose moorings, often to the edge of his dark age or beyond into the seventh century, creating an intrinsic archaism that reinforced this sense of isolation and insularity. The result became uncertainty about these sources and their authors, such that the contexts of Gildas and Patrick, as prime examples, were continually debated but never really resolved. The problem of tackling this uncertainty became clouded by an acceptance that nothing more could be seen through our most reliable lens, the eyes of Bede.

Viewed more broadly, this has meant the development of a historiography built around two core approaches to Bede. On the one hand, Bede is seen as correct in his emphasis on ecclesiastical fragmentation and disorganisation in the British Isles, and wayward British, Irish, and Pictish churches restored and corrected by the English as agents of Rome (the 'English perspective'). On the other, Bede is understood as deliberately neglecting the continuity, connectedness, and agency represented by an organised Insular church active in the British Isles and Europe (the 'Irish perspective'). In a modern context, these ideas have evolved to a broader position, a 'European perspective' that denies agency and innovation to local entities such as the English and the Irish, rather subsuming them within a universal vision emanating from Rome. National and international agendas seeking to negotiate identities within competing political frameworks continue to shape narratives for their inception as a Christian people. Gildas, as we have seen, is a unique foil in this regard, for his authority was drawn on by all sides of these debates in the early medieval period. In following his legacy, we have seen that the reification of Bede's vision of the English church, the subsequent reification of an Insular 'Celtic' church, and more recent attempts to marginalise these debates altogether have not been helpful to the historian.

Following the legacy of Gildas, this book has dismissed Bede's caricature of isolation as a cause for fragmentation and disorganisation. The Christian culture of Britain and Ireland was clearly in contact with the continent in the early medieval period on religious matters, and while there may have been periods where contact was muted, there is no evidence for disconnection. Actors like Samson and Columbanus are indicative of a profound connectivity, as is continued influence in Brittany and Galicia. Insularity, as defined by Bede, is a little more difficult. However, we have seen with the *peregrinatio* of Columbanus and his connection to the monastic perspectives of Gregory the Great that debates often seen to be both insular and Insular are, in fact, also continental. Given that Gregory's pontificate was controversial in Rome after his death, we cannot draw a distinction between a defence of Insular practices in debates within seventh-century Britain and Ireland, and a perceived defence of the authority of Gregory the Great, a figure significant to both the English and Irish churches. Innovation, and what to do with it, is, after all, an issue common to the universal church and not strictly an Insular problem. What we see in figures such as Cassian, Gildas, Gregory the Great, and Bede are, rather, attempts to fuse traditions with innovations to the benefit of a concordant universal church. The Christian culture of the British Isles is no different from the continent in this respect.

Returning to Gildas, we can see that interpretation of his *De excidio* has also been affected by Bede's reconstruction of the past. Framed as a retrospective lament detailing the disintegration and fragmentation of *Britannia*, the *De excidio* came to be read as an intervention that failed, despite memories (particularly Irish memories) of a successful intervention that raised Gildas to the status of a *sapiens* who made a significant contribution to canon law. Bede's presentation of Gildas did not invoke this image, rather describing him as a historian. The impact, as we have seen, was to emphasise the providential history of the *De excidio* over and above Gildas's novel defence of Christian kingship and his subsequent contributions to maintaining unity as represented by his letter to Finnian. It also muddied Gildas's context, catalysing the creation of multiple images that further obfuscated attempts to build a narrative for the events he described.

The patristic authority on which Gildas drew to successfully intervene in the Christian culture of *Britannia* was primarily the monastic authority of Jerome and Cassian. The monastery as an institution was key to Gildas's intervention in the corruption assailing his partitioned *patria*. It could provide both educational and pastoral correction to all the orders of Britain, whether aristocratic, clerical, or lay. The model that Gildas provided was drawn from the authority of Cassian, who had, in turn, mediated a compromise between the authority of Augustine of Hippo and Jerome. The twist that elevates Gildas to potentially being one of the most significant political theorists of the Middle Ages was his attaching of Cassian's monastery to a political system based on the sacral orders – that of kings, priests, and prophets – as found in the Old Testament and the kingdoms of Judah and Israel. While Gildas's rhetorical and theological innovations – constructing the first history of a former Roman province and equating its people with the chosen people of God – have been noted by Edward Thompson, Michael Jones, David Howlett, and Thomas O'Loughlin among others, his interpretation and defence of Christian kingship – neglected by the academy – is an innovation that, regardless of the question of his date, makes him a significant contributor to the development of the medieval polity.[1] Given the ongoing and profound transition from Roman Christian imperial authority to Christian kingship taking place during his lifetime, it is unlikely that the political innovations in the *De excidio* went unnoticed on the continent.

The significance of Gildas as one of the first medieval political theorists has broader implications. Gildas's *De excidio* implies that Christian kingship was developed as a divinely inspired political model drawn from the Bible within a Roman Christian ascetic and/or monastic setting: he never refers to pre-Christian or barbarian kings as a source of inspiration. In fact, he implicitly rejects them. The *De excidio* also implies that, given Gildas's defence of an earlier innovation of kingship in a British context around the second quarter of the fifth century, that *Britannia* may have been the first province to formally embrace Christian kingship, perhaps at the same time as it embraced the teachings represented by Pelagius. The reaction against Pelagius now takes on a deeper meaning, both theological and political. The 'unusual' way that Britain achieved independence from Roman imperial authority, as related to the aspirational 'peasant' movement of the *bagaudae* by Neil Faulkner, opens up the question of whether Christianity, drawing on disenchantments with Roman imperial authority, actively developed competing political models that, themselves, shaped Roman imperial authority – as can be seen with the persecutions of Diocletian and the rise of Constantine the Great – prior to replacing these imperial institutions altogether.[2] While scholars studying the origins of medieval kingship, framed by the

1 As mentioned in Introduction, 4, nn. 17–18: Thompson, 'Gildas and the History of Britain', 208, notes that Gildas was 'the first man in the entire west to write a provincial history'; Jones, *The End of Roman Britain*, 123, observes that this 'must have been a conscious rhetorical innovation'; Howlett, *Insular Inscriptions*, 29, notes that 'No-one before Gildas had identified a single Christian people as *praesens Israel*'; O'Loughlin, *Gildas and the Scriptures*, 25, observes that the 'perception of his people as a distinct baptised nation marks an important break in the history of theology'.

2 Faulkner, 'Gildas: The Red Monk'. This point is also picked up in Dumville, 'The Idea of Government in Sub-Roman Britain', 190; Thompson, *Saint Germanus of Auxerre*, 34–5. For

paradigm of the 'fall of the Roman empire', often look to a 'political vacuum' for the development of medieval kingship, we can see in Gildas's interpretation and defence of Christian kingship an active approach to political reform, one that implies that medieval kingship was not born in a post-Roman vacuum, but was, rather, developed by Roman Christians and embraced by Roman Christians.

It is through Columbanus that we can see that Gildas's model of authority did have an impact on the continent. In addressing Gregory the Great, Columbanus introduced us to the *De excidio* and the letter to Finnian in a way that also implied Gregory's awareness of these texts. Columbanus, as we have seen, brought to the continent a monastic tradition that had much in common with that of Gregory's. Regarding him as distinctly Insular and estranged from Petrine authority in this context does not carry any weight. In contrast, it appears that the authority of Gildas, as mediated by Columbanus, may have influenced Gregory's pastoral mission. Gildas's innovation of the term *simoniacus* in the context of excommunication appears to be integral to Gregory's innovation of *simoniaca haeresis*. Columbanus's role as a *peregrinus* appears to be influential, initially at least, on the design of Gregory's mission to the English, as led by Augustine of Canterbury. As we have seen, the tensions in this period, often attached to the controversy over Easter, lie, rather, in an outcome derived from Gildas's model for Christian governance: that of the prophetic role of the *speculator* or watchman and its relationship to bishops and kings. It is clearly this issue – the tensions between the king, the bishop, and the 'holy man' institutionalised within monasticism – that dominates the sixth, seventh, and early eighth centuries, both on the continent and in the British Isles. The tension over Easter and the tonsure, rather than being the *cause célèbre*, is symptomatic of deeper arguments over authority within the church and between the monastery and the clerical and secular orders. This is best seen, perhaps, in the tension between biblical law as interpreted by the *sapiens* against that of canon law as authorised by a synod of bishops.

In attaching the edification of both the clerical and secular orders to political reform intimately attached to the monastery, Gildas had created an enduring problem – a crisis in the authority and stability of the clerical orders, one that, arguably, reached its apex with Gregory's elevation of simony to a heresy. It is clear that after the 'monastic' papacies of Gregory (*r.* 590–604) and Boniface IV (*r.* 608–15), the experiment in Rome in elevating monks to the papacy drew to a close, as did an emphasis on the heresy of simony as relating to the purchase of clerical office. Rather, in keeping with this reassertion of clerical authority, simony was attached to the non-Petrine tonsures, regarded as indicative of a heretical independence from Petrine authority. Within this context, the image of Gildas, as reflected in his advice to Finnian on the proper exercise of episcopal authority, was transmuted to that of an advisor to bishops on canon law. We can see in an Irish context, via the *Hibernensis*, a move away from the prophetic criticisms in the *De excidio* and toward the pragmatism expressed by the letter to Finnian, a move that connected Gildas to the emerging and senior authority of Patrick despite contrasting attitudes to excommunication (see Appendix). Gildas's model of authority was placed under the authority of the apostolic succession, an adjustment that allowed bishops to reassert their authority as *speculatores* over church discipline and the edification of kings.

an overview of the *bagaudae*, see Drinkwater, 'The Bacaudae of Fifth-Century Gaul'. In this interpretation, the *bagaudae* would not be based on 'class' but on a broad coalition of, perhaps, ascetically minded Christians inspired by political models drawn from the Old Testament.

Earlier sources for the *Hibernensis* – the *Incipiunt capitula canonica* and the *Turonensis* – imply that this process was not strictly Insular but drew on regional tensions. These tensions, perhaps brought to the fore by the attack on Ireland by the Northumbrians *ca* 684, culminated in an ambitious and revolutionary attempt to implement unity by placing all the orders under one Christian law, a unification of the secular and ecclesiastical spheres, perhaps under the authority of bishops, that implied a profound change in the consciousness of the Irish church and, indeed, in Ireland herself. While Thomas Charles-Edwards has noted an ecclesiastical dependence of the Irish church on the British church up to *ca* 560, it is, perhaps, only with the construction of the *Hibernensis*, the reconstruction of the image of Patrick, and the negotiations over the location of an Irish metropolitan that we finally see a fully independent church in Ireland.[3] The adaptation rather than the rejection of the authority of Gildas in this profound transition speaks volumes to the continued importance attached to Gildas, but reinforces that aspects of his authority had become problematic.

The reassertion of episcopal authority over the monastery and sacral kingship created enormous anxiety, as seen in an Insular context by the failures of the Synods of Mag Léne and Whitby to win complete acceptance in Ireland and Northumbria in the seventh century. However, in the context of Christian Europe as a whole, this reassertion of clerical authority was clearly informed by the crisis engendered by the elimination of the apostolic succession in the new heresy of the Ishmaelites (Islam). This crisis was fundamental to Bede's world view, writing in the context of the Islamic destruction of the Visigothic Christian kingdom in Spain and subsequent incursions deep into Frankish territories. However, Bede discerned that this crisis was, in part, created by assertive bishops dominating and destabilising the secular power and military prowess of kings. Bede, despite being influenced by the Irish tradition, did not look to the image of Patrick as the *speculator* and the associated image of Gildas *Sapiens*. Bede's image of Gildas as a historian was entirely providential: history was the guide to the correct structuring of authority and the consequences brought about by internal conflict between the orders. Public criticism had created a crisis that could only be solved by the moral *exempla* of history.

Crucially, in creating his providential history, Bede drew on Gildas's representations of the past to forge a narrative that framed his creation of an inclusive Britain and the legitimacy of all its Christian peoples. In constructing his dark age, Bede deliberately passed over the legitimate grievances of the past to focus on the future, one where internal conflict was set aside in order to face external threats, both physical and spiritual. In doing so, Bede adjusted the monastic emphasis on the external edification of the secular and clerical orders by divinely inspired juniors in the manner of the Old Testament prophets. Rather, following Augustine of Hippo, he emphasised the edification of the clerical orders as the responsibility of all clerics, drawing the role of the Old Testament prophet back into the clerical orders in a way that defused the impact of external public denunciation on the authority of the apostolic succession.

In opening Bede's dark age to historical criticism, this book has also, by way of the journey, offered evidence that questions contexts framed by his dark age, evidence that repopulates this period with the actors and sources under scrutiny. While there is a temptation to offer an alternate chronology for the entire period under

[3] Thomas Charles-Edwards notes a dependence of the Irish church on the jurisdiction of the British church up to a period *ca* 490–560. Charles-Edwards, 'Britons in Ireland', 16–17.

investigation, it is not the intention of this book to make such detailed claims, rather to offer a view that the period from *ca* 450–600, in the context of both the British Isles and the continent, needs to be 'refreshed'. As a potential contribution to new narratives, I simply offer a revision of Dumville's chronology for Gildas (as the author of the *De excidio* and the letter to Finnian), one that appears, from my perspective, to contextualise Gildas within all the relevant evidence:

ca 426x429	The *miserae reliquae* appeal by letter to Agitius-Aëtius, subsequently identified as *ter consul*.
ca 440x442	*Britanniae... saxonum rediguntur*, as reported in the Gallic chronicles of 452 and 511.[4] Gildas's birth.
ca 483x485	Battle of Mount Badon, *novissimae*. Slaughter of the Saxons. Gildas's lifetime. Up to his 44th year, that of writing.[5]

This fits in with the date of 512 given for Gildas's death by William of Malmesbury, and implies that the date of *ca* 570 given in the Irish and Welsh annals could be based on a mistaken assumption about a different person with the same name, or on a retrospective adjustment or creation of an annal entry post-dating Bede's *Historia ecclesiastica* (*ca* 731). In drawing Gildas back into the fifth century, other contexts must follow, particularly our understanding of the relationships between the *De excidio* and letter to Finnian, Patrick's *Confessio* and *Epistola*, and Constantius's *Vita Germani*.

The consideration given to Gildas by all sides of the debates over authority in early medieval Britain and Ireland confirms his importance in an Insular context, and Richard Sharpe was right to call him a 'father of the church' in the context of the 'Celtic Churches'.[6] While Sharpe focused on the ascetic perspective of Gildas's letter to Finnian, this letter also had implications for the wider church. It deserves more study for its contribution to reframing ecclesiastical culture in the early medieval period, in particular through its emphasis on avoiding excommunication except in the most extreme cases. In his *De excidio*, Gildas also formulated expectations on how kings should behave, a model of authority that would again have influence in the twelfth century when the image of King Arthur would attract new attention. It is surely not too brazen, in the context of these considerations, to restore Gildas as a significant contributor to the Christian culture of the British Isles and, more broadly, to that of the medieval West.

[4] *Chronica Gallica a. CCCCLII* (ed. Mommsen, *Chronica*, I, 660): year XVIII, 'Britanniae usque hoc tempus variis cladibus eventibus latae in dicionem saxonum rediguntur' [Britain, suffering up to this time from various disasters and torments, is reduced to the authority of the Saxons]; *Chronica Gallica a. DXI* (ed. Mommsen, *Chronica*, I, 661): year XVI, 'Britanniae a Romanis amissae in dicionem Saxonum cedunt' [Britain, lost to the Romans, falls into the hands of the Saxons]. Translations are my own. See Chapter 1, 15–16, for further discussion.

[5] In this context, Gildas, *De excidio*, XXVI.1 (ed. Winterbottom, 98, trans., 28): 'Ex eo tempore' [From then on] may relate to Gildas, *De excidio*, XXV.3 (ed. Winterbottom, 98, trans., 28): 'tantae tempestatis collisione' [the shock of this notable storm].

[6] Sharpe, 'Gildas as a Father of the Church', 201–2.

APPENDIX: *DE COMMUNICATIONE GILDAS*

As noted in Chapters 2 and 5, fragments one and seven of Gildas's letter to Finnian are connected thematically by excommunication. This connection is further buttressed by the citing of both fragments as a continuous text in two early ninth-century Carolingian manuscripts – Vienna, Österreichische Nationalbibliothek, Lat. 2232 (*V*), and Munich, Bayerische Staatsbibliothek, Clm 14468 (*B*) – manuscripts used by Aidan Breen to compile his edition of the *Incipiunt capitula canonica* (as containing his edition of the *Synodus II Patricii*). This appendix combines the witness of the manuscript tradition (including that of Cambridge, Corpus Christi College, MS 279) with Flechner's edition of the *Hibernensis*, Elliot's edition of the *Turonensis*, and Breen's edition of the *Incipiunt capitula canonica* to merge and extend fragments one and seven into a new edition (and translation) concerning Gildas's approach to the unity of the Church – *De communicatione Gildas*.

Gildas's methodology in *De communicatione* follows that of the *De excidio*: a sequential scan for examples in the Old Testament (in this case, Genesis and Exodus), followed by parallel situations in the New Testament (in this case, Matthew and I Corinthians). Three new sources are identified as being part of Gildas's library: Ps-Clemens, *Recognitiones* (perhaps fourth century); *Epistola Innocentii ad Exuperium Episcopum Tolosanum* (*ca* 405); and Cyprian, *De unitate* (*ca* 250). For the purpose of this edition, *Hibernensis* and *Turonensis* are shortened to *Hib* and *Tur* respectively.

This new edition of the fragment from Gildas's letter to Finnian emphasises his criticism of those *negantes* in the church (potentially, as per Innocent, *negantes veniam* or Novatians) who excommunicate rather than denounce, particularly in the circumstances where guilt is not proven and where the crime is not a capital sin. It reveals an inclusive attitude to dealing with sin and penance, with the exclusion of a sinner only utilised as a last resort and in proven cases of major crimes.

This attitude on caution in the use of excommunication as laid out in this section of the letter to Finnian, as supported by the *De excidio* (where Gildas never calls for excommunication), stands in contrast to the active dependence on the disciplining powers of excommunication laid out in the *Synodus I Patricii* (sixteen of the thirty-four canons prescribe excommunication for a variety of non-capital transgressions), and in Patrick's *Epistola* (where Coroticus and his followers are excommunicated wholesale, without attention to individual guilt or innocence). It implies that Gildas's attitude to excommunication was developed in response to those attitudes exemplified by Patrick and the *Synodus I Patricii*. The *Synodus II Patricii*, on the other hand, does not appear to follow the approach to excommunication expressed in the *Synodus I Patricii*. It does not detail the transgressions that mandate excommunication (and subsequent penances), but rather how to inclusively deal with 'the fallen', reflecting a similar approach to Gildas. More work needs to be done unpacking the significance of these contrary approaches to excommunication.

DE COMMUNICATIONE[1] GILDAS

Gen. 7.13; Ps-Clemens, Recognitiones 4.27.2	Non Noe Cham[2] filium suum magice artis scribam reptorem[3] aut arce[4] aut[5] mensae uoluit arcere communione.
Gen. 14	Non Abraham Aner[6] et Ezcol[7] in debellatione quinque[8] regum[9] exorruit[10].
Gen. 13.12–13; Gen. 14.12	Non Loth sodomitarum[11] conuiuia[12] execratur.
Gen. 26.26–30	Non[13] Isaac[14] mensae participationem Abimelech et Ocazat[15] et Pichol[16] duci[17] militum[18] negat[19], sed post cibum et[20] potum[21] iurauerunt sibi mutuo[22].
Gen. 42.1–4	Non Iacob extimuit communicari filiis suis[23] quos nouit uenerari idola.
Gen. 41	Non Ioseph rennuit Pharaoni[24] mensae et scipho[25] participari.
Ex. 18.12	Non Aaron sacerdotis idolorum Madian[26] mensam reppulit, nec non[27] Moyses simul cum Iethro[28] ospitium[29] et conuiuium pacificum iniuit.[30]
Matt. 9.10	Non dominus[31] noster[32] iesus[33] christus publicanorum[34] conuiuia deuitabat[35] ut omnes peccatores[36] et[37] meretrices[38] saluaret[39].
Innocentii ad Exuperium IV / sinodus Romana (*Hib*)	Item[40]: Uirorum[41] latente enim[42] commisso non facile ex suspitionibus separatur[43]; qui utique submouebitur si eius flagitium[44] detegitur[45]. Cum[46] ergo par causa[47] sit interdum probatione enim[48] cessante, uindictae ratio conquiescit[49].
Innocentii ad Exuperium II	Negantes[50] uero alicui[51] nequam famam[52] putare[53] nullo modo ad integrum[54] sine[55] probationibus[56] arguant, sed leniter increpent[57] cum omni[58] patientia: quos pro conscientia si[59] possint[60] debent quasi suspectos[61] uitare nec tamen ut reos ueros excommunicare uel mensa uel pace arcere cum ratio aliqua necessitatis aut conuentus uel[62] locutionis[63] exigerit, sed illis denuntietur quod non recte agant[64], quia non possumus eos pro hoc damnare dum commonicant illi indigne forte nos per cogitationes malas daemonibus communicamus[65].
I Cor. 10.21	Quos uero[66] scimus sine ulla dubitatione esse fornicatores nisi ligitimo[67] ordine peniteant, a pace et mensa cuiuscumque ordinis ligitime[68] fuerint arcemus. Ut est illud : *Si quis frater nominatur* et[69] *est fornicator* et reliqua[70].
I Cor. 5.11	Et[71] praeter[72] principalium uitiorum causas evidenter prolatas[73], nulla alia ratione debemus fratres a commonicatione[74] altaris uel mensae cum tempus poposcerit arcere.
Cyprianus, De unitate 8.23 / Matt. 16.19, 18.18 / Sinodus (*Hib*) / Patricius (*Tur*)	Quis enim[75] audet scindere unitatem quam nemo hominum solvere uel reprehendere[76] poterit[77].

1 excommonicatione dicit *Tur*; comunicatione *V*

2 om. *B V*

3 om. *Tur Hib*

4 arche *V*; arca *Tur*; ab archa *Hib*

5 ut *B*

6 Aner *Vulg*; Neel *B V Tur*; Anel *Hib*

7 Ezcol *Vulg*; Escol *B Tur*; Ezcol *V*; Hescol *Hib*

8 .V. *Tur*

9 secum *B V*

10 exhorruit *B*

11 sodomorum *Hib*

12 conuiui ea *V*

13 nec *V*

14 Isac *Tur*

15 Ocazat *Vulg*; Choz *B V*; Ocasat *Tur*; Ochaz *Hib*

16 Pichol *B V*; Picus *Tur*; Pichol *Hib*

17 om. *B V*

18 om. *B V*

19 necat *B*

20 om. *B*

21 om. *B*

22 motuo *Tur Hib*

23 om. *Hib*

24 pharaonis *B Hib*; farao *V*; faraoni *Tur*

25 cibo *B V*; scipha *Tur*

26 Midian *Vulg*

27 nonne *B V*; nec *Tur*

28 ietrho *V*; ethor *Tur*

29 hostias *B V Tur*

30 ibit *V*; init *Tur*

31 om. *Hib*

32 om. *Hib*

33 om. *Hib*

34 paganorum *Hib*

35 diuitabat *Tur*

36 om. *B V*

37 om. *B V*

38 om. *B V*

39 saluaret aliquis *V*

40 Ita *B*

41 Uirorum *Innocentius*; om. *B V Tur*; Latente commisso uirorum *Hib*

42 om. *Hib*

43 superatur *B*; seperandus *Hib*; abstinetur *Innocentius*

44 flagitimum *V*

45 detegatur *Hib*; om. Uirorum… detegitur *Tur*

46 Cur *Innocentius*

47 causam *B Tur*

48 om. *B*

49 om. Cum… conquiescent *Hib*

50 foetentes *Tur* (*Tur* appears to be corrupt at this point. It is probable that the section Conepiscopos… melius est (om. *B V)* belongs to Fragment 6); Negantes *B V*

51 aliquis *V*; alicuius *Tur*

52 famem *B V*; fama *Tur*

53 om. *B V*

54 intigrum *Tur*

55 om. *Tur*

56 om. *Tur*

57 increpant *V*

58 om. *Tur*

59 ut *Tur*

60 possunt *B*

61 susceptos *Tur*

62 om. *B V*

63 om. *B V*

64 agunt *B V*

65 om. dum… communicamus *B V Hib*

66 om. *Hib*

67 legitimo *Hib*

68 om. *Hib*

69 ut *Hib*

70 om. Quos… reliqua *B V*

71 om. *B V*

72 propter *V Tur*

73 probatas *Tur*

74 communione *B V*

75 ergo *Tur*; om. *Hib*

76 repraehendere *Hib*; uel repraehendere om. *B V*

77 potest *Tur*; potest anathema sit *Hib*

GILDAS CONCERNING COMMUNION

Gen. 7.13; Ps-Clemens, Recognitiones 4.27.2	Noah did not want to forbid his son Cham, the crawling scribe of magical art, from the communion of the Ark or of the table.
Gen. 14	Abraham did not shrink from Aner and Ezcol in ending the war with the five kings.
Gen. 13.12; Gen. 14.12	Lot did not condemn the gatherings of the Sodomites.
Gen. 26.26–30	Isaac did not deny Abimelech, Ocazat, and Pichol, leader of the army, participation at the table, but they swore mutual oaths to each other after food and drink.
Gen. 42.1	Jacob did not fear to communicate with his sons even though he knew they worshipped idols.
Gen. 41	Joseph did not refuse to partake of Pharaoh's table and cup.
Ex. 18.12	Aaron did not reject the table of the priests of the idols of Midian, nor did Moses refrain from entering into a meal of reconciliation with Jethro.
Matt. 9.10	Our Lord Jesus Christ did not shun feasts with publicans so that he might save all sinners and prostitutes.
Innocentii ad Exuperium IV / sinodus Romana (*Hib*)	Again: For when the criminal act of men is hidden, [a man] is not easily excluded based on suspicions; certainly he will be removed if his misdeed is uncovered. When, therefore, the case is equal while the proof is lacking, the argument for punishment rests.
Innocentii ad Exuperium II	Naysayers, believing a wicked rumour about someone, should not wholly condemn without proofs, rather they should chide gently with all patience. They, for their own conscience, ought to avoid such people as suspect, but not, however, excommunicate them as truly guilty and prohibit them from the table or the peace when reason of necessity demands a meeting or a conversation. What these people do must be denounced to them if they do not act rightly because we cannot damn them for this, for while they commune, though unworthily, we commune with demons through bad thoughts.
I Cor. 10.21	Those whom we know, without doubt, to be fornicators, unless they do penance in a legitimate way, we banish them from the peace and the table to which they legitimately belonged thus far. As it is said: 'If any brother is named as a fornicator', etc.
I Cor 5.11	And when the time demands, we ought not exclude brothers from the communion of the altar or the table for any other reason except the cases of the main vices clearly put forward.
Cyprianus, De unitate 8.23/ Sinodus (*Hib*) / Patricius (*Tur*)	For who dares to rend unity, which no man can loosen or fault.

BIBLIOGRAPHY

Manuscripts

Avranches, Bibliothèque Municipale, Ms 162
Cambridge, Corpus Christi College, MS 279
Cambridge, University Library, Dd.I.17
Cambridge, University Library, Ff.I.27
Cologne, Dombibliothek, Ms 210
Copenhagen, Det Kongelige Bibliotek, Courtenaykompendiet, 2011/5
London, British Library, Cotton MS Claudius D.vi
London, British Library, Cotton Vitellius A.VI
Munich, Bayerische Staatsbibliothek, Clm 14468
Paris, Bibliothèque Nationale de France, lat. 6235
Reims, Bibliothèque Carnegie, Ms 414
St Gall, Stiftsbibliothek, Cod. Sang. 1346 (transc. Judocus Metzler)
Vienna, Österreichische Nationalbibliothek, Lat. 2232

Printed works

ADRIAEN, Marc (ed.) *Gregorius Magnus – Homiliae in Hiezechielem prophetam, CCSL* 142 (Turnhout 1971).

ALBERIGIO, J. *et al.* (edd.) 'Concilium Chalcedonense a. 451 (translatio latina)', in *Conciliorum Oecumenicorum Decreta* (Turnhout 1973) 77–103.

AMORY, Patrick *People and Identity in Ostrogothic Italy, 489–554*, Cambridge Studies in Medieval Life and Thought 33 (Cambridge 1997).

ANDERSON, Alan Orr & ANDERSON, Marjorie Ogilvie (edd. & trans.) *Adomnán's Life of Columba* (2nd edn, Oxford 1991).

AUSENDA, G. (ed.) *After Empire: Towards an Ethnology of Europe's Barbarians*, Studies in Historical Archaeoethnology 1 (San Marino, CA 1995).

AVALON MARSHES 'Earliest monastery in the British Isles discovered' (Glastonbury 2017) avalonmarshes.org/earliest-monastery-in-the-british-isles-discovered/.

BAILEY, Lisa Kaaren *Religious Worlds of the Laity in Late Antique Gaul*, Bloomsbury Classical Studies Monographs (London 2016).

BAMMESBERGER, Alfred & WOLLMANN, Alfred (edd.) *Britain 400–600: Language and History*, Anglistische Forschungen 205 (Heidelberg 1990).

BANNERMAN, John 'Notes on the Scottish Entries in the Early Irish Annals', *Scottish Gaelic Studies* 11 (1968) 149–70.

BARLEY, M. W. & HANSON, R. P. C. (edd.) *Christianity in Britain, 300–700* (Leicester 1968).

BARTRUM, P. C. (ed.) *Early Welsh Genealogical Tracts* (Cardiff 1966).

BAUN, Jane 'Gregory's Eschatology', in *A Companion to Gregory the Great* edd. Neil & Dal Santo 157–76.

BAXTER, Stephen *et al.* (edd.) *Early Medieval Studies in Memory of Patrick Wormald*, Studies in Early Medieval Britain (Farnham 2009).

BECHER, M. & JARNUT, J. (edd.) *Der Dynastieweschel von 751: Vorgenschichte, Legitimationsstrategien und Erinnerung* (Munich 2004).

BERNDT, Guido M. & STEINACHER, Roland (edd.) *Arianism: Roman Heresy and Barbarian Creed* (Farnham 2014).
BIELER, Ludwig (ed. & trans.) *The Irish Penitentials*, Scriptores Latini Hiberniae 5 (Dublin 1975).
BISCHOFF, Bernhard & LAPIDGE, Michael (edd.) *Biblical Commentaries from the Canterbury School of Theodore and Hadrian*, Cambridge Studies in Anglo-Saxon England 10 (Cambridge 1994).
BLAUDEAU, Philippe 'Between Petrine Ideology and Realpolitik: The See of Constantinople in Roman Geo-Ecclesiology (449–536)', in *Two Romes* edd. Grig & Kelly 364–84.
BLUME, Clemens & DREVES, Guido M. (edd.) *Analecta Hymnica Medii Aevi XLVIII* (New York 1961).
BLUMENTHAL, Uta-Renate (ed.) *Carolingian Essays: Andrew W. Mellon Lectures in Early Christian Studies* (Washington, DC 1983).
BONNER, Alison *The Myth of Pelagianism* (Oxford 2018).
BONNER, Alison 'Was Patrick Influenced by the Teaching of Pelagius', *The Journal of Theological Studies* 63.2 (2012) 572–607.
BONNER, Gerald *et al.* (edd.) *St. Cuthbert, His Cult and His Community to AD 1200* (Woodbridge 1989).
BORIUS, René (ed. & trans.) *Constance de Lyon. Vie de St. Germain d'Auxerre, SC* 112 (Paris 1965).
BOUGET, Hélène & COUMERT, Magali (edd.) *Histoires des Bretagnes 5: En marge* (Brest 2015).
BOULDING, M. & RAMSEY, B. (edd. & trans.) *Expositions of the Psalms 121–150*, The Works of Saint Augustine: A Translation for the 21st Century III/20 (New York 2004).
BRACKEN, Damian 'Authority and Duty: Columbanus and the Primacy of Rome', *Peritia*, 16 (2002) 168–213.
BRACKEN, Damian 'Juniors Teaching Elders: Columbanus, Rome and Spiritual Authority', in *Roma felix* edd. Ó Carragáin & Neuman de Vegvar 253–76.
BRADLEY, Ian *Celtic Christianity: Making Myths and Chasing Dreams* (Edinburgh 1999).
BREEN, Aidan 'The Date, Provenance and Authorship of the Pseudo-Patrician Canonical Materials', *Zeitschrift der Savigny-Stiftung für Rechtsgeschichte: Kanonistische Abteilung* 81 (1995) 83–129.
BREEN, Aidan 'The Evidence of Antique Irish Exegesis in Pseudo-Cyprian, *De Duodecim Abusivis Saeculi*', *Proceedings of the Royal Irish Academy* 87 (1987) 71–106.
BREEZE, Andrew C. 'Where was Gildas Born?', *Northern History* 45 (2008) 347–50.
BRENNECKE, Hanns Christof 'Introduction: Framing the Historical and Theological Problems', in *Arianism* edd. Berndt & Steinacher 1–19.
BROOKS, Dodie A. 'Gildas's *De excidio*: Its Revolutionary Meaning and Purpose', *Studia Celtica* 18/19 (1983–84) 1–10.
BROWN, George Hardin *A Companion to Bede*, Anglo-Saxon Studies 12 (Woodbridge 2009).
BROWN, Michelle P. 'Bede's Life in Context', in *The Cambridge Companion to Bede* ed. DeGregorio 3–24.
BROWN, Peter *Augustine of Hippo: A Biography* (2nd edn, Berkeley, CA 2000).
BROWN, Peter 'The Myth of Pelagianism?', *Peritia* 29 (2018) 233–246.
BROWN, Peter 'The Rise and Function of the Holy Man in Late Antiquity', *Journal of Roman Studies* 61 (1971) 80–101.
BROWN, Peter *The Rise of Western Christendom: Triumph and Diversity, AD 200–1000*, The Making of Europe Series (2nd edn, Oxford 2003).
BROWNE, H. (trans.) 'Of the Works of Monks (Augustine)', in *A Select Library* III ed. Schaff 503–24.
BRUCE, James *Prophecy, Miracles, Angels, and Heavenly Light: The Eschatology, Pneumatology and Missiology of Adomnán's Life of Columba*, Studies in Christian History and Thought (Carlisle 2004).
BRUNS, Hermann Theodor (ed.) *Canones Apostolorum et Conciliorum: Saeculorum IV. V. VI. VII.* (Berlin 1839).

BULLOUGH, Donald 'The Career of Columbanus', in *Columbanus* ed. Lapidge 1–28.

BURGESS, R. W. 'The Gallic Chronicle of 452: A New Critical Edition with Brief Introduction', in *Society and Culture* edd. Mathisen & Shanzer 52–84.

BURGESS, R. W. 'The Gallic Chronicle of 511: A New Critical Edition with Brief Introduction', in *Society and Culture* edd. Mathisen & Shanzer 85–100.

BUTLER, Alban *The Lives of the Fathers, Martyrs, and Principal Saints* (12 vols, Dublin 1866).

CACHIA, Nicholas *The Image of the Good Shepherd as a Source for the Spirituality of the Ministerial Priesthood*, Tesi Gregoriana Serie Spiritualità 4 (Rome 1997).

CAIN, Andrew *The Letters of Jerome: Asceticism, Biblical Exegesis, and the Construction of Christian Authority in Late Antiquity*, Oxford Early Christian Studies (Oxford 2009).

CAIN, Andrew (trans.) *St. Jerome: Commentary on Galatians*, The Fathers of the Church 121 (Washington, DC 2010).

CAMPBELL, James 'Bede', in *Latin Historians* ed. Dorey 159–190.

CAMPBELL, James 'Secular and Political Contexts', in *The Cambridge Companion to Bede,* ed. DeGregorio 25–39.

CAMPLANI, A. & FILORAMO, G. (edd.) *Foundations of Power and Conflicts of Authority in Late-Antique Monasticism: Proceedings of the International Seminar Turin, December 2–4, 2004*, Orientalia Loveniensia Analecta 157 (Leuven 2006).

CANNING, Joseph *A History of Medieval Political Thought, 300–1450* (London 1996).

CARDWELL, Samuel '"The People Whom He Foreknew": The English as a Chosen People in Bede's *Historia Ecclesiastica*', *Journal of the Australian Early Medieval Association* 11 (2015) 41–66.

CAREY, John *et al.* (edd.) *Ildánach Ildírech: A Festschrift for Proinsias Mac Cana*, Celtic Studies Publications 4 (Andover 1999).

CARTWRIGHT, Jane (ed.) *Celtic Hagiography and Saints' Cults* (Cardiff 2003).

CASSIDAY, A. M. C. *Tradition and Theology in St John Cassian*, Oxford Early Christian Studies (Oxford 2007).

CHADWICK, Nora K. *The Age of the Saints in the Early Celtic Church*, Riddell Memorial Lectures 32 (London 1961).

CHADWICK, Owen 'Gildas and the Monastic Order', *Journal of Theological Studies* 5 (1954) 78–81.

CHARLES-EDWARDS, T. M. 'Britons in Ireland, c. 550–800', in *Ildánach Ildírech* edd. Carey *et al.* 15–26.

CHARLES-EDWARDS, T. M. (trans.) *The Chronicle of Ireland*, Translated Texts for Historians 44 (Liverpool 2006).

CHARLES-EDWARDS, T. M. *Early Christian Ireland* (Cambridge 2000).

CHARLES-EDWARDS, T. M. 'Early Irish Law', in *A New History of Ireland* ed. Ó Cróinín 331–70.

CHARLES-EDWARDS, T. M. 'The Northern Lectionary: A Source for the *Codex Salmanticensis*?', in *Celtic Hagiography and Saints' Cults* ed. Cartwright 148–60.

CHARLES-EDWARDS, T. M. *Wales and the Britons, 350–1064*, History of Wales Series (Oxford 2012).

CHAZELLE, Celia & CUBITT, Catherine (edd.) *The Crisis of the* Oikoumene*: The Three Chapters and the Failed Quest for Unity in the Sixth-Century Mediterranean*, Studies in the Early Middle Ages 14 (Turnhout 2007).

CIPOLLA, Carlo (ed.) *Codice Diplomatico del monastero di S. Colombano di Bobbio* (3 vols, Rome 1918).

CLARK, E. A. *The Origenist Controversy: The Cultural Construction of an Early Christian Debate* (Princeton, NJ 1992).

CLARKE, Francis *The 'Gregorian' Dialogues and the Origins of Benedictine Monasticism*, Studies in the History of Christian Thought 108 (Leiden 2003).

COLGRAVE, Bertram (ed. & trans.) *Felix's Life of Saint Guthlac: Texts, Translation and Notes* (Cambridge 1956).

COLGRAVE, Bertram & MYNORS, R. A. B. (edd. & trans.) *Bede's Ecclesiastical History of the English People* (Oxford 1969).

COLISH, Marcia L. *Faith, Fiction, and Force in Medieval Baptismal Debates* (Washington, DC 2014).

COLLINS, Roger *Visigothic Spain, 409–711*, History of Spain Series (Oxford 2004).

CORNING, Caitlin 'Columbanus and the Easter Controversy: Theological, Social and Political Contexts', in *The Irish in Early Medieval Europe* edd. Flechner & Meeder 101–15.

COUMERT, Magali 'Gildas', in *Medieval Historical Writing* edd. Jahner *et al.* 19–34.

CRAIGIE, Peter C. *Ezekiel*, The Daily Study Bible Series (Philadelphia, PA 1983).

CUNNINGHAM, J. G. (trans.) 'The Letters of St Augustin', in *A Select Library I* ed. Schaff 219–593.

DARBY, Peter *Bede and the End of Time*, Studies in Early Medieval Britain (Farnham 2012).

DARBY, Peter 'Heresy and Authority in Bede's *Letter to Plegwine*', in *Cities, Saints, and Communities* edd. DeGregorio & Kershaw 145–169.

DARBY, Peter & WALLIS, Faith (edd.) *Bede and the Future*, Studies in Early Medieval Britain and Ireland (London 2016).

DARK, Ken R. *Britain and the End of the Roman Empire* (Stroud 2000).

DAVIES, Luned Mair 'The "Mouth of Gold": Gregorian Texts in the *Collectio Canonum Hibernensis*', in *Ireland and Europe in the Early Middle Ages* edd. Ní Chatháin & Richter 249–67.

DAVIES, Luned Mair '*Statuta ecclesiae antiqua* and the Gallic Councils in the *Hibernensis*', *Peritia* 14 (2000) 85–110.

DAVIES, Wendy 'The Myth of the Celtic Church', in *The Early Church in Wales and the West* edd. Edwards & Lane 12–21.

DAVIES, W. H. 'The Church in Wales', in *Christianity in Britain* edd. Barley & Hanson 131–50.

DAVIS, Raymond (trans.) *The Book of Pontiffs* (Liber Pontificalis)*: The ancient biographies of the first ninety Roman bishops to AD 715*, Translated Texts for Historians 6 (2nd edn, Liverpool 2000).

DAVIS, R. H. C. & WALLACE-HADRILL, J. M. (edd.) *The Writing of History in the Middle Ages: Essays Presented to Richard William Southern* (Oxford 1981).

DE CLERCQ, C. (ed.) *Concilia Galliae 511–695, CCSL* 148A (Turnhout 1963).

DEGREGORIO, Scott 'Bede and Benedict of Nursia', in *Early Medieval Studies* edd. Baxter *et al.* 149–64.

DEGREGORIO, Scott 'Bede's Midlife Crisis: The Commentary on First Samuel', in *Cities, Saints, and Communities* edd. DeGregorio & Kershaw 241–63.

DEGREGORIO, Scott (ed.) *The Cambridge Companion to Bede*, Cambridge Companions to Literature (Cambridge 2010).

DEGREGORIO, Scott (ed.) *Innovation and Tradition in the Writings of the Venerable Bede*, Medieval European Studies 7 (Morgantown, VA 2006).

DEGREGORIO, Scott & KERSHAW, Paul (edd.) *Cities, Saints, and Communities in Early Medieval Europe: Essays in Honour of Alan Thacker*, Studies in Early Medieval Europe 46 (Turnhout 2020).

DEGREGORIO, Scott & LOVE, Rosalind (trans.) *Bede: On First Samuel*, Translated Texts for Historians 70 (Liverpool 2019).

DEKKERS, E. & FRAIPONT, J. (edd.) *Augustinus Hipponensis – Enarrationes in Psalmos CCSL* 40 (Turnhout 1956).

DE LA BORDERIE, Arthur (ed.) *Cartulaire de l'abbaye Landévennec* (Rennes 1888).

DEMACOPOULOS, George E. *The Invention of Peter: Apostolic Discourse and Papal Authority in Late Antiquity*, Divinations: Rereading Late Ancient Religion (Philadelphia, PA 2013).

DEMEULENAERE, R. (ed.) *Uincentius Lerinensis – Commonitorium, CCSL* 64 (Turnhout 1985).

DE PAOR, Liam *Saint Patrick's World: The Christian Culture of Ireland's Apostolic Age* (Dublin 1993).

DIEM, Albrecht 'Monks, Kings, and the Transformation of Sanctity: Jonas of Bobbio and the End of the Holy Man', *Speculum* 82 (2007) 521–59.

DIMOCK, James F. (ed.) *Giraldi Cambrensis Opera, Vol. VI* (London 1868).

DOREY, T. A. (ed.) *Latin Historians*, Studies in Latin Literature and Its Influences (London 1966).

DRINKWATER, John F. 'The Bacaudae of Fifth-Century Gaul', in *Fifth-Century Gaul* edd. Drinkwater & Elton 208–17.

DRINKWATER, John F. & ELTON, Hugh (edd.) *Fifth-Century Gaul: A Crisis of Identity?* (Cambridge 2002).

DUCHESNE, L. (ed.) *Le Liber Pontificalis, Texte, Introduction et Commentaire* (2 vols, Paris 1886–92).

DÜMMLER, Ernst *Epistolae Karolini Aevi II, MGH Epistolae IV* (Berlin 1895).

DUMVILLE, David N. 'The Chronology of *De Excidio Britanniae*, Book I', in *Gildas* edd. Lapidge & Dumville 61–84.

DUMVILLE, David N. 'The Colophon of "The Penitential of Uinniau"', in *Corona Monastica* edd. Lemoine & Merdrignac 167–78.

DUMVILLE, David N. 'Gildas and Maelgwn: Problems of Dating', in *Gildas* edd. Lapidge & Dumville 51–60.

DUMVILLE, David N. 'Gildas and Uinniau', in *Gildas* edd. Lapidge & Dumville 207–14.

DUMVILLE, David N. (ed.) *The Historia Brittonum, Vol. 3: The 'Vatican' Recension* (Cambridge 1985).

DUMVILLE, David N. 'The Idea of Government in Sub-Roman Britain', in *After Empire* ed. Ausenda 177–205.

DUMVILLE, David N. '"Nennius" and the *Historia Brittonum*', *Studia Celtica* 10–11 (1975–76) 78–95.

DUMVILLE, David N. *Saint David of Wales*, Kathleen Hughes Memorial Lectures on Medieval Welsh History 1 (Cambridge 2001).

DUMVILLE, David N. *et al Saint Patrick 493–1993*, Studies in Celtic History 13 (Woodbridge 1993).

DUNCAN, Archibald A. M. 'Bede, Iona, and the Picts', in *The Writing of History in the Middle Ages* edd. Davis & Wallace-Hadrill 1–42.

DUNN, Geoffrey 'Cassian in Syria?: The Evidence of Innocent I', *Vigiliae Christianae* 69 (2015) 3–17.

DUNN, Marilyn *The Emergence of Monasticism: From the Desert Fathers to the Early Middle Ages* (Oxford 2000).

DUNN, Marilyn 'Paradigms of Penance', *The Journal of Medieval Monastic Studies* 1 (2012) 17–39.

ÉCOLE FRANÇAISE DE ROME (ed.) *Gregorio Magno e il suo tempo: XIX Incontro di studiosi dellàntichità cristiana in collaborazione con l'Ecole Française de Rome, Roma, Roma, 9–12 maggio 1990*, Studia Ephemeridis Augustinianum 34 (Rome 1991).

EDWARDS, Nancy 'Perspectives on Conversion in Wales', in *The Introduction of Christianity* edd. Flechner & Ní Mhaonaigh 93–107.

EDWARDS, N. & LANE, A. *The Early Church in Wales and the West: Recent Work in Early Christian Archaeology, History and Place Names*, Oxbow Monograph 16 (Oxford 1992).

EHWALD, Rudolf (ed.) *Aldhelmi Opera, MGH AA* 15 (Berlin 1919).

ELLIOT, Michael 'Canon Law Collections in England ca 600–1066: The Manuscript Evidence' (doctoral thesis, University of Toronto 2013).

ENGELBRECHT, A. (ed.) *Faustus Reiensis – Epistolae, CSEL* 21 (Turnhout 1891) 161–207.

ENO, Robert B. 'Papal Damage Control in the Aftermath of the Three Chapters Controversy', in *Papers Presented to the 10th International Conference on Patristic Studies* ed. Livingstone 52–56.

ENRIGHT, Michael J. *Iona, Tara, and Soissons: The Origin of the Royal Anointing Ritual*, Arbeiten zur Frühmittelalterforschung 17 (New York 1985).

ENRIGHT, Michael J *Prophecy and Kingship in Adomnán's Life of Saint Columba* (Dublin 2013).

ESCALONA, Julio 'Un futuro innombrable: La cronología de Beda frente al augurio anglosajón de Gildas', *Territorio, Sociedad Y Poder* 2 (2007) 155–80.

ÉTAIX, Raymond (ed.) *Gregorius Magnus – Homiliae in euangelia, CCSL* 141 (Turnhout 1999).

ETCHINGHAM, Colmán *Church Organisation in Ireland, A.D. 650 to 1000* (Maynooth 1999).

EVANS, J. G. & RHYS, J. (edd.) *The Text of the Book of Llan Dâv: Reproduced from the Gwynsaney Manuscript* (Oxford 1893).

EVANS, J. Wyn & WOODING, Jonathan M. (edd.) *Saint David of Wales: Cult, Church, Nation*, Studies in Celtic History 24 (Woodbridge 2007).

EVANS, Nicholas *The Present and the Past in Medieval Irish Chronicles*, Studies in Celtic History 27 (Woodbridge 2010).

FARNELL, F. David 'The Current Debate about New Testament Prophecy', *Bibliotecha Sacra* 595 (1992) 277–303.

FAULKNER, Neil 'Gildas: The Red Monk of the First Peasants' Revolt', in *AD 410* ed. Haarer 36–42.

FEAR, Andrew & WOOD, Jamie (edd.) *Isidore of Seville and his Reception in the Early Middle Ages: Transmitting and Transforming Knowledge*, Late Antique and Early Medieval Iberia (Amsterdam 2016).

FERREIRO, Alberto *Simon Magus in Patristic, Medieval, and Early Modern Traditions*, Studies in the History of Christian Traditions 125 (Leiden 2005).

FIELD, P. J. C. 'Gildas and the City of Legions', *The Heroic Age: A Journal of Early Medieval Northwestern Europe* 1 (1999) www.heroicage.org/issues/1/hagcl.htm.

FLECHNER, Roy 'Aspects of the Breton Transmission of the *Hibernensis*', *Pecia* 12 (2008) 27–44.

FLECHNER, Roy 'The Chronicle of Ireland: Then and Now', *Early Medieval Europe* 21 (2013) 422–54.

FLECHNER, Roy 'Conversion in Ireland: State of the Art', in *The Introduction of Christianity* edd. Flechner & Ní Mhaonaigh 41–55.

FLECHNER, Roy 'Dagan, Columbanus and the Gregorian Mission', *Peritia* 19 (2005) 65–90.

FLECHNER, Roy (ed.) *The Hibernensis*, Studies in Medieval and Early Modern Canon Law 17 (2 vols, Washington, DC 2019).

FLECHNER, Roy *Making Laws for a Christian Society: The* Hibernensis *and the Beginnings of Church Law in Ireland and Britain*, Studies in Early Medieval Britain and Ireland (Abingdon 2021).

FLECHNER, Roy 'Pope Gregory and the British: Mission as a Canonical Problem', in *Histoires des Bretagnes 5* edd. Bouget & Coumert 47–65.

FLECHNER, Roy *Saint Patrick Retold: The Legend and History of Ireland's Patron Saint* (Princeton, NJ 2020).

FLECHNER, Roy & MEEDER, Sven (edd.) *The Irish in Early Medieval Europe: Identity, Culture and Religion* (London 2016).

FLECHNER, Roy & NÍ MHAONAIGH, Máire (edd.) *The Introduction of Christianity Into the Early Medieval Insular World: Converting the Isles I*, Cultural Encounters in Late Antiquity and the Middle Ages 19 (Turnhout 2017).

FLEMING, P. (ed.) *Collectanea Sacra Seu S. Columbanis Hiberni Abbatis* (Louvain 1667).

FLOBERT, Pierre (ed. & trans.) *La Vie ancienne de saint Samson de Dol*, Sources d'Histoire Médiévale (Paris 2002).

FLOOD, Victoria *Prophecy, Politics and Place in Medieval England: From Geoffrey of Monmouth to Thomas of Erceldoune* (Cambridge 2016).

FOLLETT, Westley *Céli Dé in Ireland: Monastic Writing and Identity in the Early Middle Ages*, Studies in Celtic History 23 (Woodbridge 2006).

FOX, Yaniv *Power and Religion in Merovingian Gaul: Columbanian Monasticism and the Frankish Elites*, Cambridge Studies in Medieval Life and Thought 98 (Cambridge 2014).

FREMANTLE, W. H. *et al.* (trans.) 'Letters of St. Jerome', in *A Select Library* VI edd. Schaff & Wace.

FREND, W. H. C. '*Ecclesia Britannica*: Prelude or Dead End?', *The Journal of Ecclesiastical History* 30 (1979) 129–44.

GALE, Thomas *Historiae Britannicae, Saxonicae, Anglo-Danicae Scriptores XV* (Oxford 1691).

GAMESON, Richard (ed.) *The Lindisfarne Gospels: New Perspectives*, The Manuscript World 9 (Leiden 2017).

GEERTZ, Clifford 'Thick Description: Toward an Interpretive Theory of Culture', in *The Interpretation of Cultures: Selected Essays* (New York 1973) 3–30.

GEORGE, Karen *Gildas's* De Excidio Britonum *and the Early British Church*, Studies in Celtic History 26 (Woodbridge 2009).

GIBB, Rev. John & INNES, Rev. James 'St. Augustine: Homilies on the Gospel of John', in *A Select Library* VII, ed. Schaff.

GIBSON, C. S. (trans.) 'The Conferences (John Cassian)', in *A Select Library* XI edd. Schaff & Wace 291–545.

GILLETT, Andrew *Envoys and Political Communication in the Late Antique West, 411–533*, Cambridge Studies in Medieval Life and Thought 55 (Cambridge 2003).

GLORIE, F. (ed.) *Hieronymus – Commentarii in Ezechielem, CCSL* 75 (Turnhout 1964).

GOFFART, Walter A. 'Bede's History in a Harsher Climate', in *Innovation and Tradition* ed. DeGregorio 203–26.

GOFFART, Walter A. *The Narrators of Barbarian History (A.D. 550–800): Jordanes, Gregory of Tours, Bede, and Paul the Deacon* (Notre Dame, IN 2005).

GOLDBACHER, A. (ed.) *Augustinus Hipponensis – Epistulae, CSEL* 34.1, 34.2, 44, 57, 58 (Vienna 1895–98).

GOOSMAN, Erik 'The Long-haired Kings of the Franks: "Like So Many Samsons?"', *Early Medieval Europe* 20.3 (2012) 233–59.

GORMAN, Michael M. 'Patristic and Pseudo-Patristic Citations in the *Collectio Hibernensis*', *Revue Bénédictine* 121 (2011) 18–93.

GOUGH-COOPER, Henry W. (transcr.) *Annales Cambriae: The A Text, from British Library, Harley MS 3859, ff. 190r–193r* (Bangor 2015) croniclau.bangor.ac.uk/documents/AC A first edition.pdf.

GOUGH-COOPER, Henry W. (transcr.) *Annales Cambriae: The B Text, from London, National Archives, MS E164/1, pp. 2–26* (Bangor 2015) croniclau.bangor.ac.uk/documents/AC B first edition.pdf.

GOUGH-COOPER, Henry W. (transcr.) *Annales Cambriae: The C Text, from London, British Library, Cotton MS Domitian A. i, ff. 138r–155r* (Bangor 2015) croniclau.bangor.ac.uk/documents/AC C first edition.pdf.

GOUGH-COOPER, Henry W. 'Meet the Ancestors? Evidence for Antecedent Texts in the Late Thirteenth-Century Welsh Latin Chronicles', in *The Chronicles of Medieval Wales* edd. Guy *et al.* 107–37.

GRAFF, Eric 'A Note on the Divisions of Time in the Catalogue of the Saints of Ireland', in *Early Medieval Ireland and Europe* edd. Moran & Warntjes 99–117.

GRIG, Lucy & KELLY, Gavin (edd.) *Two Romes: Rome and Constantinople in Late Antiquity*, Oxford Studies in Late Antiquity (Oxford 2012).

GRIGG, Julianna, 'The Just King and *De Duodecim Abusiuis Saeculi*', *Parergon* 27 (2010) 27–51.

GRIMMER, Martin, 'Saxon Bishop and Celtic King: Interactions between Aldhelm of Wessex and Geraint of Dumnonia', *The Heroic Age: A Journal of Early Medieval Northwestern Europe* 4 (2001) www.heroicage.org/issues/4/Grimmer.html.

GROCOCK, Christopher & WOOD, I. N. (edd. & trans.) *Abbots of Wearmouth and Jarrow: Bede's Homily i. 13 on Benedict Biscop; Bede's History of the Abbots of Wearmouth and Jarrow; The Anonymous Life of Ceolfrith; Bede's Letter to Ecgbert, Bishop of York*, Oxford Medieval Texts (Oxford 2013).

GROSJEAN, Paul (ed.) 'Edition et commentaire du catalogus sanctorum hiberniae secundum diversa tempora ou de tribus ordinibus sanctorum hiberniae', *Analecta Bollandiana* 73 (1955) 197–210, 289–322.

GRUDEM, Wayne A. *The Gift of Prophecy in the New Testament and Today* (Westchester, IL 1988).

GUNDLACH, W. (ed.) 'Columbae sive Columbani abbatis Luxoviensis et Bobbiensis epistolae', in *Epistolae Merowingici et Karolini aevi I*, *MGH* Epistolae III (Berlin 1892).

GUNN, Vicky *Bede's* Historiae*: Genre, Rhetoric and the Construction of the Anglo-Saxon Church History* (Woodbridge 2009).

GUY, Ben *et al.* (edd.) *The Chronicles of Medieval Wales and the March: New Contexts, Studies, and Texts*, Medieval Texts and Cultures of Northern Europe 31 (Turnhout 2020).

GUY, Ben 'The Origins of the Compilation of Welsh Historical Texts in Harley 3859', *Studia Celtica* 49 (2015) 21–56.

HAARER, F. K. (ed.) *AD 410: The History and Archaeology of Late and Post-Roman Britain* (London 2014).

HADDAN, Arthur West & STUBBS William (edd.) *Councils and Ecclesiastical Documents Relating to Great Britain and Ireland* (3 vols, Oxford 1869–78).

HALSALL, Guy *Barbarian Migrations and the Roman West, 376–568*, Cambridge Medieval Textbooks (Cambridge 2008).

HALSALL, Guy *Worlds of Arthur: Facts and Fictions of the Dark Ages* (Oxford 2013).

HANNING, Robert W. *The Vision of History in Early Britain: From Gildas to Geoffrey of Monmouth* (New York 1966).

HARDISON, Brian C. 'Words, Meanings, and Readings: Reconstructing the Use of Gildas's *De excidio Britanniae* at the Canterbury School', *Viator* 47 (2015) 1–22.

HÄRKE, Heinrich 'Anglo-Saxon Immigration and Ethnogenesis', *Medieval Archaeology* 55 (2011), 1–27.

HARMLESS, William (ed.) *Augustine in His Own Words* (Washington, DC 2010).

HARRIES, Jill 'E. A. Thompson, Saint Germanus of Auxerre and the End of Roman Britain', *Journal of Roman Studies* 76 (1984) 315–16.

HARTMANN, W. & PENNINGTON, K. (edd.) *The History of Byzantine and Eastern Canon Law*, History of Medieval Canon Law Series (Washington, DC 2012).

HEIST, W. W. *Vitae Sanctorum Hiberniae ex Codice olim Salmanticensi nunc Bruxellensi*, Subsidia Hagiographica 28 (Brussels 1965).

HEN, Yitzhak 'The Christianisation of Kingship', in *Der Dynastieweschel von 751* edd. Becher & Jarnut 163–77.

HERREN, Michael W. 'Gildas and Early British Monasticism', in *Britain 400–600* edd. Bammesberger & Wollmann 65–78.

HERREN, Michael W. (ed.) *The Hisperica Famina II: Related Poems*, Studies and Texts 85 (Toronto 1987).

HERREN, Michael W. 'On the earliest Irish acquaintance with Isidore of Seville', in *Visigothic Spain* ed. James 243–50.

HERREN, Michael W. & BROWN, Shirley Ann *Christ in Celtic Christianity: Britain and Ireland from the Fifth to the Tenth Century*, Studies in Celtic History 20 (Woodbridge 2002).

HEURTLEY, C. A. 'The Commonitory of St Vincent of Lérins', in *A Select Library XI* edd. Schaff & Wace 123–59.

HIGHAM, N. J. 'Constantius, Germanus, and Fifth-Century Britain', *Early Medieval Europe* 22.2 (2014) 113–37.

HIGHAM, N. J. *The English Conquest: Gildas and Britain in the Fifth Century* (Manchester 1994).

HIGHAM, N. J. *(Re-)Reading Bede: The Ecclesiastical History in Context* (Abingdon 2006).

HILBERG, I. (ed.) *Hieronymus – Epistulae*, *CSEL* 54, 55, 56 (Turnhout 1996).

HILLGARTH, J. N. 'Ireland and Spain in the Seventh Century', *Peritia* 3 (1984) 1–16.

HINGLEY, Richard *Hadrian's Wall: A Life* (Oxford 2012).

HOARE, F. R. (trans.) 'Constantius of Lyon: The Life of Saint Germanus of Auxerre', in *Soldiers of Christ* edd. Noble & Head 75–106.

HOWARD-JOHNSON, James & ANTONY, Paul (edd.) *The Cult of Saints in Late Antiquity and the Middle Ages: Essays on the Contribution of Peter Brown* (Oxford 1999).

HOWLETT, D. R. (ed. & trans.) *Liber Epistolarum Sancti Patricii Episcopi = The Book of Letters of Saint Patrick the Bishop*, Celtic Studies (Dublin 1994).
HOWLETT, D. R. *The Celtic Latin Tradition of Biblical Style* (Dublin 1995).
HOWLETT, D. R. *Insular Inscriptions* (Dublin 2005).
HOWLETT, D. R. 'The Prophecy of Saxon Occupation in Gildas's *De excidio Britanniae*', *Peritia* 16 (2002) 156–60.
HUGHES, Kathleen *The Church in Early Irish Society* (London 1966).
HUGHES, Kathleen 'The Historical Value of the Lives of St Finnian of Clonard', *The English Historical Review* 69 (1954) 353–72.
HUGHES, Kathleen 'Synodus II S. Patricii', in *Latin Script and Letters* edd. O'Meara & Naumann 141–7.
HURST, D. (ed.) *Beda Uenerabilis – In Marci euangelium expositio*, *CCSL* 120 (Turnhout 1960) 431–648.
HVIDT, Niels Christian *Christian Prophecy: The Post-Biblical Tradition* (New York 2007).
HWANG, Alexander Y. *et al.* (edd.) *Grace for Grace: The Debates After Augustine and Pelagius* (Washington, DC 2014).
JACKSON, Kenneth *Language and History in Early Britain: A Chronological Survey of the Brittonic Languages, 1st to 12th c. A.D.* (Edinburgh 1953).
JAHNER, Jennifer *et al.* (edd.) *Medieval Historical Writing: Britain and Ireland, 500–1500* (Cambridge 2019).
JANKULAK, Karen & WOODING, Jonathan 'The Cult of Saint Gildas', in *Colloque saint Gildas* edd. Merdrignac & Provost 25–42.
JAMES, Edward (ed.) *Visigothic Spain: New Approaches: Papers Read at the Visigothic Colloquy, Held in University College, Dublin, between 14 and 17 May 1975* (Oxford 1980).
JARITZ, Gerhard & MORENO-RIANO, Gerson (edd.) *Time and Eternity: The Medieval Discourse*, International Medieval Congress 9 (Turnhout 2003).
JENSEN, Robin M. *Baptismal Imagery in Early Christianity: Ritual, Visual, and Theological Dimensions* (Grand Rapids, MI 2012).
JOHNSTON, Elva *Literacy and Identity in Early Medieval Ireland*, Studies in Celtic History 33 (Woodbridge 2013).
JONES, C. W. (ed.) *Beda Uenerabilis – De temporum ratione liber*, *CCSL* 123B (Turnhout 1977) 263–544.
JONES, Michael E. 'The Appeal to Aetius in Gildas', *Nottingham Medieval Studies* 32 (1988) 141–55.
JONES, Michael E. *The End of Roman Britain* (London 1996).
JONES, W. R. 'England Against the Celtic Fringe: A Study in Cultural Stereotypes', *Journal of World History* 13 (1971) 155–71.
JOYCE, Stephen J. 'Attitudes to Excommunication in the Early Insular Church: Returning to Gildas's Letter to Finnian', *Journal of Medieval Monastic Studies* 9 (2020) 9–30.
JOYCE, Stephen J. 'Contested Origins of Monasticism: Divergent Models of Authority', *Journal of the Australian Early Medieval Association* 11 (2015) 1–16.
JOYCE, Stephen J. 'Gildas: A Contextual Analysis' (honours thesis, Monash University 2011).
JOYCE, Stephen J. 'Gildas and His Prophecy for Britain', *Journal of the Australian Early Medieval Association* 9 (2013) 39–59.
JOYCE, Stephen J. 'Memories of Gildas: Gildas and the *Collectio canonum Hibernensis*', in *Memory, Fate, and Memory* edd. Wooding & Olson 149–70.
JOYCE, Stephen J. 'A New Source for *mons Badonicus*: Returning to the Irish Life of Finnian of Clonard', *Journal of the Australian Early Medieval Association* 15 (2019) 31–46.
KELLY, Joseph E. 'The Letter of Columbanus to Gregory the Great', in *Gregorio Magno e il suo tempo* ed. École Française de Rome 213–23.
KELLY, J. F. 'Augustine in Hiberno-Latin Literature', *Augustinian Studies* 8 (1977) 139–49.
KELLY, J. N. D. *Jerome: His Life, Writings and Controversies* (London 1975).
KELLY, Rev. Matthew (ed.) *Calendar of Irish Saints, the Martyrology of Tallagh: With Notices of the Patron Saints of Ireland and Select Poems and Hymns* (Dublin 1857).

KERLOUÉGAN, F. *Le De excidio Britanniae de Gildas: Les destinées de la culture latine dans l'île de Bretagne au VIe siècle* (Paris 1987).

KERLOUÉGAN, F. 'Gildas [St Gildas] (fl. 5th–6th cent.)', in *The Oxford Dictionary of National Biography* (Oxford 2007).

KERLOUÉGAN, F. 'Le Latin du De Excidio Britanniae de Gildas', in *Christianity in Britain 300–700* edd. Barley & Hanson 151–76.

KLINGSHIRN, W. E. & VESSEY, M. (edd.) *The Limits of Ancient Christianity: Essays on Late Antique Thought and Culture in Honor of R. A. Markus*, Later Latin Texts and Contexts (Ann Arbor, MI 1999).

KNOEBEL, Thomas Louis (trans.) *De Ecclesiasticis Officiis By Saint Isidore (of Seville)* (New York 2008).

KOHLER, CHARLES 'Inventaire de la bibliothèque de Saint-Gildas en Berry', *Bibliothèque de l'école des chartes* 47 (1886) 98–105.

KRUSCH, Bruno (ed.) 'Vitae Columbani abbatis discipulorumque eius', in *Passiones vitaeque sanctorum aevi Merovingici ii, MGH SRM* 4 (Hanover & Leipzig 1902) 61–156.

LAGARRIGUE, G. (ed.) *Saluianus Massiliensis – De gubernatione Dei, SC* 220 (Turnhout 1975).

LAMBERT, David 'The Uses of Decay: History in Salvian's *De gubernatione dei*', *Augustinian Studies* 30 (1999) 115–30.

LANDON, Rev. Edward H. *A Manual of Councils of the Holy Catholic Church* (2 vols, Edinburgh 1909).

LAPIDGE, Michael 'The Career of Aldhelm', *Anglo-Saxon England* 36 (2007) 15–69.

LAPIDGE, Michael (ed.) *Columbanus: Studies on the Latin Writings*, Studies in Celtic History 17 (Woodbridge 1997).

LAPIDGE, Michael 'Gildas's Education and the Latin Culture of Sub-Roman Britain', in *Gildas* edd. Lapidge & Dumville 27–50.

LAPIDGE, Michael (ed.) & CHIESA, Paolo (trans.) *Beda: Storia degli Inglesi*, Scrittori greci e latini (2 vols, Rome 2008–10).

LAPIDGE, Michael & DUMVILLE, David N. (edd.) *Gildas: New Approaches*, Studies in Celtic History 5 (Woodbridge 1984).

LAPIDGE, Michael & HERREN, Michael (trans.) *Aldhelm: The Prose Works* (Cambridge 1979).

LAPIDGE, Michael & SHARPE, Richard *A Bibliography of Celtic-Latin Literature, 400–1200*, Royal Irish Academy dictionary of medieval Latin from Celtic sources: Ancillary publications 4 (Dublin 1985).

LARPI, Luca *Prolegomena to a New Edition of Gildas Sapiens 'De Excidio Britanniae'*, Opuscoli Seconda 8 (Florence 2012).

LATHAMA, Jacob A. 'Inventing Gregory "the Great": Memory, Authority, and the Afterlives of the *Letania Septiformis*', *Church History* 84.1 (2015) 1–31.

LAURENT, C. & DAVIS, H. (edd.) *Irlande et Bretagne: Vingt siècles d'histoire: Actes du colloque de Rennes, 29–31 Mars 1993*, Essais (Rennes 1994).

LAWLESS, George *Augustine of Hippo and His Monastic Rule* (Oxford 1987).

LECLERCQ, Jean 'Simoniaca Heresis', *Studi Gregoriani* 1 (1947) 523–30.

LEMOINE, Louis & MERDRIGNAC, Bernard (edd.) *Corona Monastica: Mélanges offerts au père Marc Simon*, Britannia Monastica 8 (Rennes 2004).

LEWIS, Barry J. '*Bonedd y Saint*, *Brenhinedd y Saesson*, and Historical Scholarship at Valle Crucis Abbey', in *The Chronicles of Medieval Wales* edd. Guy *et al.* 139–54.

LEYSER, Conrad *Authority and Asceticism from Augustine to Gregory the Great*, Oxford Historical Monographs (Oxford 2000).

LEYSER, Conrad '"This Sainted Isle": Panegyric, Nostalgia, and the Invention of Lerinian Monasticism', in *The Limits of Ancient Christianity* edd. Klingshirn & Vessey 188–208.

LIONARONS, Joyce Tally *The Homiletic Writings of Archbishop Wulfstan: A Critical Study*, Anglo-Saxon Studies (Cambridge 2010).

LIVINGSTONE, Elizabeth (ed.) *Papers Presented to the 10th International Conference on Patristic Studies Held in Oxford, 1987: Historica, Theologica, Gnostica, Biblica, et Apocrypha*, Studia Patristica 19–23 (Leuven 1989).

LLEWELLYN, P. A. B. 'The Roman Church in the Seventh Century: The Legacy of Gregory I', *The Journal of Ecclesiastical History* 25.4 (1974) 363–80.

LLEWELLYN, Peter *Rome in the Dark Ages* (London 1971).

LOT, Ferdinand 'Mélanges d'histoire bretonne: Gildae vita et translatio', *Annales de Bretagne* 25.2–3 (1909) 346–65, 493–519.

MAASEN, Friedrich *Geschichte der Quellen und der Literatur des canonischen Rechts im Abendlaude bis zum Ausgange des Mittelalters* (Graz 1870).

MAC AIRT, Seán (ed.) *The Annals of Inisfallen* (Dublin 1944).

MAC AIRT, Seán & MAC NIOCAILL, Gearóid (edd.) *The Annals of Ulster, AD 431–1201* (Dublin 1983).

MANNING JR, Gary T. *Echoes of a Prophet: The Use of Ezekiel in the Gospel of John and in Literature of the Second Temple Period*, Journal for the Study of the New Testament 270 (London 2004).

MÁRKUS, G 'Pelagianism and the "Common Celtic Church"', *Innes Review* 56.2 (2005) 165–213.

MARKUS, R. A. 'The Chronology of the Gregorian Mission to England: Bede's Narrative and Gregory's Correspondence', *Journal of Ecclesiastical History* 14 (1963) 16–30.

MARKUS, R. A. *The End of Ancient Christianity* (Cambridge 1990).

MARKUS, R. A. *Gregory the Great and His World* (Cambridge 1997).

MARKUS, R. A. 'The Legacy of Pelagius: Orthodoxy, Heresy and Conciliation', in *The Making of Orthodoxy* ed. Williams 214–34.

MARTYN, John R. C. (trans.) *The Letters of Gregory the Great*, Mediaeval Sources in Translation 40 (3 vols, Toronto 2004).

MARTYN, John R. C., 'Pope Gregory the Great and the Irish', *Journal of the Australian Early Medieval Association* 1 (2005) 65–83.

MATHISEN, Ralph W. 'Caesarius of Arles, Prevenient Grace, and the Second Council of Orange', in *Grace for Grace* edd. Hwang *et al.* 208–34.

MATHISEN, Ralph W. *Ecclesiastical Factionalism and Religious Controversy in Fifth-Century Gaul* (Washington, DC 1989).

MATHISEN, Ralph W. & SHANZER, Danuta *Society and Culture in Late Antique Gaul: Revisiting the Sources* (Aldershot 2001).

MC CARTHY, Daniel P. *Chronological Synchronisation of the Irish Annals* (4th edn, Dublin 2005) www.scss.tcd.ie/misc/kronos/chronology/synchronisms/annals-chron.htm.

MC CARTHY, Daniel P. 'The Origin of the Latercus Paschal Cycle of the Insular Celtic Churches', *Cambrian Medieval Celtic Studies* 28 (1994) 25–49.

MC CARTHY, Daniel P. & BREEN, Aidan *The Ante-Nicene Christian Pasch* De ratione paschali*: The Paschal Tract of Anatolius, Bishop of Leodicea* (Dublin, 2003).

MCCONE, K. R. & SIMM, K. (edd.) Progress in Medieval Irish Studies (Maynooth 1996).

MCKEE, Ian 'Gildas: Lessons from History', *Cambrian Medieval Celtic Studies* 51 (2006) 1–36.

MEENS, Rob *Penance in Medieval Europe, 600–1200* (Cambridge 2014).

MERDRIGNAC, Bernard & PROVOST, Georges (edd.) *Colloque saint Gildas de Saint-Gildas de Rhuys 30–31 janvier 2009*, Culture et Patrimoine du Morbihan 56 (Gourin 2011).

MERRILS, A. H. *History and Geography in Late Antiquity* (Cambridge 2005).

METZGER, M. (ed. & trans.) *Les Constitutions Apostoliques* (3 vols, Paris 1987).

MEWS, Constant J. 'The *De xii abusivis saeculi* and Prophetic Tradition in Seventh-Century Ireland', in *Prophecy, Fate, and Memory* edd. Wooding & Olson 125–48.

MEWS, Constant J. & JOYCE, Stephen J. 'The Preface of Gildas, the Book of David, and the British Church in the Sixth Century', *Peritia* 29 (2018) 81–100.

MEWS, Constant J. & RENKIN, Claire 'The Legacy of Gregory the Great in the Latin West', in *A Companion to Gregory the Great*, edd. Neil & Dal Santo 315–42.

MEYER, W. (ed.) 'Gildae oratio rythmica', in *Nachrichten der Königlichen Gesellschaft der Wissenschaften zu Göttingen: Philologisch-historische Klasse 1912* (Göttingen 1912) 48–108.
MIGNE, J.-P. (ed.) *Aliud chronicon S. Michaelis*, *PL* 202 (Paris 1855) 1323C.
MIGNE, J.-P. (ed.) *Prosper Aquitanus – De gratia Dei et libero arbitrio contra Collatorem*, *PL* 51 (Paris 1846).
MILLER, M. 'Bede's Use of Gildas', *The English Historical Review* 90 (1975) 241–61.
MOLYNEAUX, George 'Did the English Really Think They Were God's Elect in the Anglo-Saxon Period?', *The Journal of Ecclesiastical History* 65.4 (2014) 721–37.
MOMMSEN, Theodor (ed.) *Chronica Minora Saec., IV, V, VI, VII*, I, *MGH AA* 9 (Berlin 1892).
MOMMSEN, Theodor (ed.) *Chronica Minora Saec., IV, V, VI, VII*, III, *MGH AA* 13 (Berlin 1898).
MOMMSEN, T. & JONES, C. W. (edd.) *Beda Uenerabilis – De temporibus liber*, *CCSL* 123C (Turnhout 1980) 585–611.
MOORHEAD, John *The Popes and the Church of Rome in Late Antiquity*, Routledge Studies in Ancient History 8 (Abingdon 2015).
MORAN, Pádraic & WARNTJES, Immo (edd.) *Early Medieval Ireland and Europe: Chronology, Contacts, Scholarship: Festschrift for Dáibhí Ó Cróinín*, Traditionis Theologiae 14 (Turnhout 2015).
MORRIS, John *The Age of Arthur: A History of the British Isles from 350 to 650* (London 1973).
MORRIS, John 'The Dates of the Celtic Saints', *Journal of Theological Studies* 17 (1966) 342–91.
MORRIS, John 'Pelagian Literature', *Journal of Theological Studies* 16 (1965) 26–60.
MORRIS, John *Nennius: British History and the Welsh Annals*, Arthurian Period Sources 8 (Chichester 1980).
MUHLBERGER, Steven 'Looking Back from Mid-Century: The Gallic Chronicler of 452 and the Crisis of Honorius's Reign', in *Fifth-Century Gaul* edd. Drinkwater & Elton 28–37.
MUIR, Bernard James (ed.) *A Pre-Conquest English Prayer-Book (BL MSS Cotton Galba A.XIV and Nero A.II (ff. 3–13))*, Henry Bradshaw Society 103 (Woodbridge 1988).
MUNIER, C. (ed.) *Concilia Africae 345–525*, *CCSL* 149 (Turnhout 1974).
MURRAY, Alexander Callander (ed.) *After Rome's Fall: Narrators and Sources of Early Medieval History: Essays Presented to Walter Goffart* (Toronto 1998).
MUTZENBECHER, A. (ed.) *Augustinus Hipponensis* – Retractationum libri duo, *CCSL* 57 (Turnhout 1984).
MYERS, Henry A. *Medieval Kingship* (Chicago, IL 1982).
MYNORS, R. A. B. *et al.* (edd. & trans) *William of Malmesbury.* Gesta Regum Anglorum (2 vols, Oxford 1998–99).
NASH-WILLIAMS, V. E. *The Early Christian Monuments of Wales* (Cardiff 1950).
NEIL, Bronwen '*De profundis*: The Letters and Archives of Pelagius I of Rome (556–561)', in *Collecting Early Christian Letters* edd. Neil & Allen 206–20.
NEIL, Bronwen & ALLEN, Pauline (edd.) *Collecting Early Christian Letters: From the Apostle Paul to Late Antiquity* (Cambridge 2015).
NEIL, Bronwen & DAL SANTO, Matthew (edd.) *A Companion to Gregory the Great*, Brill's Companions to the Christian Tradition 47 (Leiden 2016).
NEUSNER, Jacob *A History of the Jews in Babylonia, V: Later Sasanian Times*, Studia Post Biblica 15 (Leiden 1970).
NÍ CHATHÁIN, Próinséas & RICHTER, Michael (edd.) *Ireland and Europe in the Early Middle Ages: Texts and Transmission/Irland und Europa im früheren Mittelalter: Texte und Überlieferung* (Dublin 2002).
NOBLE, Thomas F. X. & HEAD, Thomas *Soldiers of Christ: Saints and Saints Lives from Late Antiquity and the Early Middle Ages* (University Park, PA 1995).
NORBERG, Dag (ed.) *Gregorius Magnus – Registrum epistularum*, *CCSL* 140, 140A (Turnhout 1982).

OAKLEY, Francis *Empty Bottles of Gentilism: Kingship and the Divine in Late Antiquity and the Early Middle Ages (to 1050)*, Emergence of Western Political Thought in the Latin Middle Ages 1 (London 2010).

Ó CARRAGÁIN, Éamonn & NEUMAN DE VEGVAR, Carol (edd.) *Roma felix: Formation and Reflections of Medieval Rome*, Church, Faith and Culture in the Medieval West (Aldershot 2007).

O'CARROLL, James 'The Chronology of Saint Columban', *Irish Theological Quarterly* 24 (1957) 76–95.

Ó CRÓINÍN, Dáibhí *Early Medieval Ireland, 400–1200* (2nd edn, New York 2017).

Ó CRÓINÍN, Dáibhí 'The Irish Provenance of Bede's computus', *Peritia* 2 (1983) 229–47.

Ó CRÓINÍN, Dáibhí (ed.) *A New History of Ireland, vol. 1: Prehistoric and Early Ireland* (Oxford 2005).

Ó CRÓINÍN, Dáibhí 'Review of Church Organisation in Ireland A.D. 650–1000, by Colmán Etchingham', *Peritia* 15 (2001) 413–20.

Ó CRÓINÍN, D. & WALSH, M. (edd.) *Cummian's Letter 'De Controversia Paschali' and the 'De Ratione Computandi'*, Studies and Texts 86 (Toronto 1988).

O'HARA, Alexander (ed.) *Columbanus and the Peoples of Post-Roman Europe*, Oxford Studies in Late Antiquity (New York 2018).

O'HARA, Alexander *Jonas of Bobbio and the Legacy of Columbanus: Sanctity and Community in the Seventh Century*, Oxford Studies in Late Antiquity (New York 2018).

O'HARA, Alexander '17.03.08, Flechner and Meeder, eds., The Irish in Early Medieval Europe', *The Medieval Review* (Bloomington, IN 2017).

O'HARA, Alexander & WOOD, Ian (trans.) *Jonas of Bobbio: Life of Columbanus, Life of John of Réomé, and Life of Vedast*, Translated Texts for Historians 64 (Liverpool 2017).

OHASHI, Masako '"Sexta aetas continet annos praeteritos DCCVIIII" (Bede, *De temporibus*, 22): A Scribal Error?', in *Time and Eternity* edd. Jaritz & Moreno-Riano 55–61.

OHME, Heinz, 'Sources of the Greek Canon Law to Quinisext Council (691/2): Councils and Church Fathers', in *The History of Byzantine and Eastern Canon Law* edd. Hartmann & Pennington 24–114.

O'LOUGHLIN, Thomas *Gildas and the Scriptures*, Studia Traditionis Theologiae 12 (Turnhout 2012).

O'LOUGHLIN, Thomas 'The Latin Sources of Medieval Latin Culture: A Partial *status quaestionis*', in Progress in Medieval Irish Studies, edd. McCone & Simm 91–105.

OLSON, Lynette (ed.) *St Samson of Dol and the Earliest History of Brittany, Cornwall and Wales*, Studies in Celtic History 37 (Woodbridge 2017).

O'MEARA, J. J. & NAUMANN, B. (edd.) *Latin Script and Letters A.D. 400–900: Festschrift presented to Ludwig Bieler on the Occasion of his 70th Birthday* (Leiden 1976).

OOSTHUIZEN, Susan *The Emergence of the English*, Past Imperfect (Leeds 2019).

Ó RIAIN, Pádraig *Dictionary of Irish Saints* (Dublin 2011).

Ó RIAIN, Pádraig 'Finnio and Winniau: A Return to the Subject', in *Ildánach Ildírech* edd. Carey *et al.* 187–202.

Ó RIAIN, Pádraig 'Gildas: A Solution to His Enigmatic Name?', in *Irlande et Bretagne* edd. Laurent & Davis 32–9.

O'SULLIVAN, Thomas *The* De Excidio *of Gildas: Its Authenticity and Date*, Columbia Studies in the Classical Tradition 7 (Leiden 1978).

PERCIVAL, Henry R. 'The Seven Ecumenical Councils', in *A Select Library* XIV edd. Schaff & Wace.

PERKINS, Nicholas 'Biblical Allusion and Prophetic Authority in Gildas's *De excidio Britanniae*', *The Journal of Medieval Latin* 20 (2010) 78–112.

PETSCHENIG, M. (ed.) *Iohannes Cassianus – Collationes xxiiii, CSEL* 13 (Vienna 1886).

PETSCHENIG, M. (ed.) *Iohannes Cassianus – De institutis coenobiorum et de octo principalium uitiorum remediis, CSEL* 17 (Vienna 1888) 3–231.

PLAINE, R. P. (ed.) 'Vita S. Pauli Episcopi Leonensis in Britannia Minori Auctore Wormonoco', *Analecta Bollandiana* 1 (1882) 208–58.

PLUMMER, Charles (ed.) *Vitae Sanctorum Hiberniae* (2 vols, 2nd edn, Oxford 1968).

POLLARD, Richard M. 'The *De Excidio* of "Hegesippus" and the Reception of Josephus in the Early Middle Ages', *Viator* 46.2 (2015) 65–100.

PRICE, Ira M. 'The Schools of the Sons of the Prophets', *The Old Testament Student* 8 (1889) 244–9.

RADFORD, C. A. R. 'Christian Origins in Britain', *Medieval Archaeology* 15 (1971) 1–12.

RAMSEY, Boniface (trans.) *John Cassian: The Conferences*, Ancient Christian Writers 57 (New York 1997).

RAPP, Claudia *Holy Bishops in Late Antiquity: The Nature of Christian Leadership in an Age of Transition*, Transformation of the Classical Heritage 37 (Berkeley, CA 2005).

RASPANTI, G. (ed.) *Hieronymus – Commentarii in iu epistulas Paulinas*, *CCSL* 77C (Turnhout 2006).

REES, B. R. *Pelagius: Life and Letters* (Woodbridge 1998).

REEVE, Michael D. & WRIGHT, Neil (ed. & trans.) *The History of the Kings of Britain: An Edition and Translation of* De gestis Britonum [Historia Regum Britanniae], Arthurian Studies 69 (Woodbridge 2007).

REYNOLDS, Roger E. *Clerical Orders in the Early Middle Ages: Duties and Ordination*, Collected Studies Series 670 (Aldershot 1999).

REYNOLDS, Roger E. 'Unity and Diversity in Carolingian Canon Law Collections: The Case of the *Collectio Hibernensis* and Its Derivatives', in *Carolingian Essays* ed. Blumenthal 99–136.

RICHARDS, Jeffrey *The Popes and the Papacy in the Early Middle Ages, 476–752* (London 1979).

RICHARDSON, E. (trans.) '*De Viris Illustribus* (Jerome)', in *A Select Library* III edd. Schaff & Wace 359–84.

RICHARDSON, E. (ed.) *Gennadius Massiliensis – De uiris illustribus*, in *Texte und Untersuchungen zur Geschichte der Altchristlichen Literatur*, 14 1a (Leipzig 1896) 57–97.

RICHARDSON, E. (ed.) *Hieronymus – De uiris illustribus*, in *Texte und Untersuchungen zur Geschichte der Altchristlichen Literatur*, 14 1a (Leipzig 1896) 1–56.

RICHTER, Michael *Bobbio in the Early Middle Ages: The Abiding Legacy of Columbanus* (Dublin 2008).

RICHTER, Michael 'Dating the Irish synods in the *Collectio canonum Hibernensis*', *Peritia* 14 (2000) 70–84.

RICHTER, Michael *Ireland and Her Neighbours in the Seventh Century* (Dublin 1999).

ROHR, Christian 'Hagiographie als historische Quelle: Ereignisgeschichte und Wunderberichte in der Vita Columbani des Ionas von Bobbio', *Mitteilungen des Instituts fur Östrereichische Geschichtsforschung* 103 (1995) 229–64.

ROMMEL, F. & CLEMENT, R. W. (edd.) *Gregorius Magnus – Regula pastoralis*, *CCSL* 141 (Turnhout 1953).

ROUSSEAU, Philip *Ascetics, Authority and the Church in the Age of Jerome and Cassian* (2nd edn, Notre Dame, IN 2010).

ROWELL, Geoffrey (ed.) *The English Religious Tradition and the Genius of Anglicanism* (Wantage 1992).

RYDER, Raymond A. *Simony: An Historical Synopsis and Commentary*, Canon Law Studies 65 (Washington, DC 1931).

SANFORD, Eva M. (trans.) *Salvian: On the Government of God* (New York 1930).

SAWYER, P. H. & WOOD, I. N. (edd.) *Early Medieval Kingship* (Leeds 1977).

SCHAFF, Philip (ed.) *A Select Library of the Nicene and Post-Nicene Fathers of the Christian Church* (First Series, Buffalo, NY 1887).

SCHAFF, Philip & WACE, Henry (edd.) *A Select Library of the Nicene and Post-Nicene Fathers of the Christian Church* (Second Series, Buffalo, NY 1892).

SCHECK, Thomas P. *Origen and the History of Justification: The Legacy of Origen's Commentary on Romans* (Notre Dame, IN 2008).

SCHWARTZ, E. (ed.) *Acta Conciliorum Oecumenicorum Vol. 1* (Berlin 1925; repr. 1963).

SCOTT, John (ed. & trans.) *The Early History of Glastonbury: An Edition, Translation, and Study of William of Malmesbury's* De Antiquitate Glastonie Ecclesiae (Woodbridge 1981).

SESSA, Kristina *The Formation of Papal Authority in Late Antique Italy: Roman Bishops and the Domestic Sphere* (Cambridge 2012).
SHARPE, Richard 'Gildas as a Father of the Church', in *Gildas* edd. Lapidge & Dumville 193–205.
SHARPE, Richard *A Handlist of the Latin Writers of Great Britain and Ireland before 1540*, Publications of the Journal of Medieval Latin 1 (Turnhout 1997; repr. 2001).
SHARPE, Richard 'Martyrs and Local Saints in Late Antique Britain', in *Local Saints and Local Churches* edd. Thacker & Sharpe 75–154.
SHARPE, Richard *Medieval Irish Saints' Lives: An Introduction to* Vitae Sanctorum Hiberniae (Oxford 1991).
SHARPE, Richard 'Some Problems Concerning the Organization of the Church in Early Medieval Ireland', *Peritia* 3 (1984) 230–70.
SHARPE, Richard & DAVIS, John Reuben (edd. & trans.) 'Rhygyfarch's Life of St David', in *Saint David of Wales* edd. Evans & Wooding 107–55.
SHERIDAN, Mark 'John Cassian and the Formation of Authoritative Tradition', in *Foundations of Power* edd. Camplani & Filoramo 157–75.
SMIT, Johannes Wilhemus *Studies on the Language and Style of Columba the Younger (Columbanus)* (Amsterdam 1971).
SMITH, Joshua Byron 'Introduction and Biography', in *A Companion to Geoffrey of Monmouth* edd. Smith & Henley 1–28.
SMITH, Joshua Byron & HENLEY, Georgia (edd.), *A Companion to Geoffrey of Monmouth*, Brill's Companions to European History 22 (Leiden 2020).
SMYTH, A. P. 'The Earliest Irish Annals: Their First Contemporary Entries, and the Earliest Centres of Recording', *Proceedings of the Royal Irish Academy* 72 (1972) 1–48.
SMYTH Marina 'Isidorian Texts in Seventh-Century Ireland', in *Isidore of Seville* edd. Fear & Wood 111–130.
SNYDER, Christopher A. *The Britons*, Peoples of Europe Series (Oxford 2003).
STANCLIFFE, Clare 'Bede and Bishop Acca', in *Cities, Saints, and Communities* edd. DeGregorio & Kershaw 171–94.
STANCLIFFE, Clare 'Columbanus and Shunning', in *Columbanus* ed. O'Hara 113–42.
STANCLIFFE, Clare 'Cuthbert and the Polarity between Pastor and Solitary', in *St. Cuthbert* edd. Bonner *et al.* 21–44.
STANCLIFFE, Clare 'The Irish Tradition in Northumbria after the Synod of Whitby', in *The Lindisfarne Gospels* ed. Gameson 20–42.
STANCLIFFE, Clare 'The Thirteen Sermons Attributed to Columbanus and the Question of Their Authorship', in *Columbanus* ed. Lapidge 93–202.
STEWART, Columba *Cassian the Monk*, Oxford Studies in Historical Theology (Oxford 1998).
STOCKING, Rachel L. *Bishops, Councils, and Consensus in the Visigothic Kingdom, 589–633*, History, Languages, and Cultures of the Spanish and Portuguese Worlds Series (Ann Arbor, MI 2000).
STOKES, Margaret *Six Months in the Apennines: Or a Pilgrimage in Search of Vestiges of the Irish Saints in Italy* (London 1892).
STOKES, Whitley (ed.) *The Tripartite Life of Patrick with Other Documents Relating to that Saint* (2 vols, London 1887).
STOKES, Whitley (ed. & trans.) 'The Annals of Tigernach', *Revue Celtique* 16 (1895) 374–419.
STOKES, Whitley (ed.) *Lives of the Saints from the Book of Lismore* (Oxford 1890).
STOKES, Whitley (ed.) *The Martyrology of Oengus the Culdee* (London 1905).
STOREY, Joanna 'The Frankish Annals of Lindisfarne and Kent', *Anglo-Saxon England* 34 (2005) 59–110.
STRAW, Carole *Gregory the Great: Perfection in Imperfection*, Transformation of the Classical Heritage 14 (Berkeley, CA 1988).
SWAN, William Declan *The Experience of God in the Writings of Saint Patrick: Reworking a Faith Received*, Tesi Gregoriana Serie Teologia 201 (Rome 2013).
TANGL, M. S. (ed.) *Bonifatii et Lulli Epistolae*, *MGH Epistolae Selectae* I (Berlin 1916) 1–289.

THACKER, Alan & SHARPE, Richard (edd.) *Local Saints and Local Churches in the Early Medieval West* (Oxford 2002).
THACKER, Alan 'Bede and the Ordering of Understanding', in *Innovation and Tradition* ed. DeGregorio 37–63.
THOMAS, Charles *Britain and Ireland in Early Christian Times: A.D. 400–800*, Library of Medieval Civilization (London 1971).
THOMAS, Charles *Christianity in Roman Britain to AD 500* (Berkeley, CA 1981).
THOMPSON, E. A. 'Gildas and the History of Britain', *Britannia* 10 (1979) 203–26.
THOMPSON, E. A. *Saint Germanus of Auxerre and the end of Roman Britain*, Studies in Celtic History 6 (Woodbridge 1984).
THORNTON, David E. *Kings, Chronologies, and Genealogies: Studies in the Political History of Early Medieval Ireland and Wales*, Prosopographica et Genealogica 10 (Oxford 2003).
TOYNBEE, J. M. C. 'Christianity in Roman Britain', *Journal of Archaeological Association* 16 (1953) 1–24.
TURNER, C. H. (ed.) *Ecclesiae Occidentalis Monumenta Iuris Antiquissima* (2 vols, Oxford 1899).
TURNER, C. H. (ed.) 'The *Liber Ecclesiasticorum Dogmatum* Attributed to Gennadius', *The Journal of Theological Studies* 7 (1906) 78–99.
UGHELLI, Ferdinando (ed.) *Italia sacra sive de Episcopis Italiae, et insularum adjacentium* (10 vols, 2nd edn, Venice 1719).
VANDER PLAETSE, R. & BEUKERS, C. (edd.) *Augustinus Hipponensis – De haeresibus*, *CCSL* 46 (Turnhout 1969).
VIVES, J. (ed.) *Concilios Visigóticos e Hispano-Romanos* (Barcelona and Madrid 1963).
WADE-EVANS, A. W. & LLOYD, Scott (edd. & trans.) *Vitae Sanctorum Britanniae et Genealogiae: The Lives and Genealogies of the Welsh Saints* (2nd edn, Cardiff 2013).
WALLACE-HADRILL, J. M. *Bede's Ecclesiastical History of the English People: A Historical Commentary*, Oxford Medieval Texts Series (Oxford 1988).
WALKER, G. S. M. (ed. & trans.) *Sancti Columbani Opera*, Scriptores Hiberniae Latini 2 (Dublin 1957, repr. 1970).
WALLIS, Faith (trans.) *Bede: The Reckoning of Time*, Translated Texts for Historians 29 (Liverpool 1999).
WALSH, P. G. & Kennedy, M. J. (edd. & trans.) *William of Newburgh: The History of English Affairs* (3 vols, Warminster 1988).
WARNER, George (ed.) *The Stowe Missal: MS. D. II. 3 in the Library of the Royal Irish Academy* (London 1915).
WATTS, Dorothy *Christians and Pagans in Roman Britain* (London 1991).
WATTS, Dorothy *Religion in Late Roman Britain: Forces of Change* (London 1998).
WEAVER, Rebecca Harden *Divine Grace and Human Agency: A Study of the Semi-Pelagian Controversy*, Patristic Monograph 15 (Macon, GA 1996).
WEBBER, Rev. N. A. *A History of Simony in the Christian Church: From the Beginning to the Death of Charlemagne (814)* (Baltimore, MD 1909).
WILLEN, Radbodus (ed.) *Augustinus Hipponensis – In Iohannis euangelium tractatis*, *CCSL* 36 (Turnhout 1954).
WILLIAMS, Hugh *Christianity in Early Britain* (Oxford 1912).
WILLIAMS, Hugh (ed. & trans.) *Gildas: The Ruin of Britain, Fragments from Lost Letters, the Penitential Together with the Lorica of Gildas*, Cymmrodorion Record Series 3 (London 1899).
WILLIAMS, Hugh 'Some Aspects of the Christian Church in Wales during the Fifth and Sixth Centuries', *Transactions of the Honourable Society of the Cymmrodorian* (1893–94) 55–132.
WILLIAMS, Hugh (trans.) *Two Lives of Gildas by a Monk of Ruys and Caradoc of Llancarfan* (London 1899; repr. Felinfach 1990).
WILLIAMS, Rowan (ed.) *The Making of Orthodoxy: Essays in Honour of Henry Chadwick* (Cambridge 1989).
WILLIS, William Downes *Simony: Its History and Effects* (London 1865).

WILSON, H. A. (ed.) *The Calendar of Willibrord, From MS Paris Lat. 10837: Facsimile with Transcription, Introduction, and Notes* (London 1918).

WINTERBOTTOM, Michael 'Gildas and Columbanus', *Vigiliae Christianae* 30 (1976) 310–17.

WINTERBOTTOM, Michael (ed. & trans.) *Gildas: The Ruin of Britain and Other Works*, Arthurian Period Sources 7 (London 1978).

WINTERBOTTOM, Michael 'The Preface of Gildas' *De Excidio*', *The Transactions of the Honourable Society of Cymmrodorion* (1974–75), 277–87.

WOOD, Ian N. 'Columbanus, the Britons, and the Merovingian Church', in *St Samson of Dol* ed. Olson 103–14.

WOOD, Ian N. 'Continuity or Calamity?: The Constraints of Literary Models', in *Fifth-Century Gaul* edd. Drinkwater & Elton 9–18.

WOOD, Ian N. 'The End of Roman Britain: Continental Evidence and Parallels', in *Gildas* edd. Lapidge & Dumville 1–25.

WOOD, Ian N. 'Jonas, the Merovingians, and Pope Honorius: *Diplomata* and the *Vita Columbani*', in *After Rome's Fall* ed. Murray 99–120.

WOOD, Ian N. *The Merovingian Kingdoms, 450–751* (London 1994).

WOOD, Ian N. *The Missionary Life: Saints and the Evangelisation of Europe, 400–1050*, Medieval World Series (Harlow 2001).

WOOD, Ian N. 'What is a Mission?', in *The Introduction of Christianity* edd. Flechner & Ní Mhaonaigh 135–53.

WOODING, Jonathan M. 'The Representation of Early British Monasticism and *Peregrinatio* in *Vita Prima S. Samsonis*', in *St Samson of Dol* ed. Olson 137–61.

WOODING, Jonathan M. & OLSON, Lynette (edd.) *Prophecy, Fate, and Memory in the Early and Medieval Celtic World*, Sydney Series in Celtic Studies 18 (Sydney 2020).

WOOLF, Alex 'An Interpolation in the Text of Gildas's *De Excidio Britanniae*', *Peritia* 16 (2002) 161–7.

WORMALD, Patrick 'The Venerable Bede and the "Church of the English"', in *The English Religious Tradition and the Genius of Anglicanism* ed. Rowell 13–32.

WRIGHT, Neil 'Columbanus's *Epistulae*', in *Columbanus* ed. Lapidge 29–92.

WRIGHT, Neil 'Did Gildas Read Orosius?', *Cambridge Medieval Celtic Studies* 9 (1985) 31–42.

WRIGHT, Neil 'Gildas's Prose Style and Its Origins', in *Gildas* edd. Lapidge & Dumville 107–28.

WRIGHT, Neil 'Gildas's Reading: A Survey', *Sacris Erudiri* 32 (1991) 121–62.

WRIGHT, Neil *History and Literature in Late Antiquity and the Early Medieval West: Studies in Intertextuality*, Collected Studies Series 495 (Aldershot 1995).

YORKE, Barbara 'Bede's Preferential Treatment of the Irish', in *Cities, Saints, and Communities* edd. DeGregorio & Kershaw 223–40.

YORKE, Barbara *The Conversion of Britain: Religion, Politics and Society c. 600–800*, Religion, Politics, and Society in Britain Series (Harlow 2006).

ZAHORA, Tomas *et al.* 'Deconstructing Bricolage: Interactive Online Analysis of Compiled Texts with Factotum', *Digital Humanities Quarterly* 9.1 (2015).

ZIMMER, Heinrich *The Celtic Church in Britain and Ireland* (London 1902).

ZYCHA, J. (ed.) *Augustinus Hipponensis – De opere monachorum, CSEL* 41 (Vienna 1900).

INDEX

STUDIES IN CELTIC HISTORY

Already published

XXIV · ST DAVID OF WALES: CULT, CHURCH AND NATION
J. Wyn Evans and Jonathan M. Wooding (eds)

XXV · SAINTS' CULTS IN THE CELTIC WORLD
Steve Boardman, John Reuben Davies and Eila Williamson (eds)

XXVI · GILDAS'S *DE EXCIDIO BRITONUM* AND THE EARLY BRITISH CHURCH
Karen George

XXVII · THE PRESENT AND THE PAST IN MEDIEVAL IRISH CHRONICLES
Nicholas Evans

XXVIII · THE CULT OF SAINTS AND THE VIRGIN MARY IN MEDIEVAL SCOTLAND
Steve Boardman and Eila Williamson (eds)

XXIX · THE TRANSFORMATION OF THE IRISH CHURCH IN THE TWELFTH CENTURY
Marie Therese Flanagan

XXX · HEROIC SAGA AND CLASSICAL EPIC IN MEDIEVAL IRELAND
Brent Miles

XXXI · TOME: STUDIES IN MEDIEVAL CELTIC HISTORY AND LAW IN HONOUR OF THOMAS CHARLES-EDWARDS
Fiona Edmonds and Paul Russell (eds)

XXXII · NEW PERSPECTIVES ON MEDIEVAL SCOTLAND, 1093–1286
Matthew Hammond (ed.)

XXXIII · LITERACY AND IDENTITY IN EARLY MEDIEVAL IRELAND
Elva Johnston

XXXIV · CLASSICAL LITERATURE AND LEARNING IN MEDIEVAL IRISH NARRATIVE
Ralph O'Connor (ed.)

XXXV · MEDIEVAL POWYS: KINGDOM, PRINCIPALITY AND LORDSHIPS, 1132–1293
David Stephenson

XXXVI · PERCEPTIONS OF FEMININITY IN EARLY IRISH SOCIETY
Helen Oxenham

XXXVII · ST SAMSON OF DOL AND THE EARLIEST HISTORY OF BRITTANY, CORNWALL AND WALES
Lynette Olson (ed.)

XXXVIII · THE BOOK OF LLANDAF AS A HISTORICAL SOURCE
Patrick Sims-Williams

XXXIX · PERSONAL NAMES AND NAMING PRACTICES IN MEDIEVAL SCOTLAND
Matthew Hammond (ed.)

XL · GAELIC INFLUENCE IN THE NORTHUMBRIAN KINGDOM: THE GOLDEN AGE AND THE VIKING AGE
Fiona Edmonds

XLI · READING AND SHAPING MEDIEVAL CARTULARIES: MULTI-SCRIBE MANUSCRIPTS AND THEIR PATTERNS OF GROWTH. A STUDY OF THE EARLIEST CARTULARIES OF GLASGOW CATHEDRAL AND LINDORES ABBEY
Joanna Tucker

XLII · MEDIEVAL WELSH GENEALOGY: AN INTRODUCTION AND TEXTUAL STUDY
Ben Guy

XLIII · THE LEGACY OF GILDAS: CONSTRUCTIONS OF AUTHORITY IN THE EARLY MEDIEVAL WEST
Stephen J. Joyce

XLIV · HISTORY AND IDENTITY IN EARLY MEDIEVAL WALES
Rebecca Thomas

XLV · THE GROWTH OF LAW IN MEDIEVAL WALES, c.1100–c.1500
Sara Elin Roberts

XLVI · THE MEDIEVAL WELSH 'ENGLYNION Y BEDDAU': THE 'STANZAS OF THE GRAVES', OR 'GRAVES OF THE WARRIORS OF THE ISLAND OF BRITAIN', ATTRIBUTED TO TALIESIN
Patrick Sims-Williams (ed.)

XLVII · STORYTELLING IN GAELIC FROM AD 700 TO THE PRESENT: TRUTH, TRADITION AND TRANSLATION
Alice R. Taylor-Griffiths and Seosamh Mac Cárthaigh (eds)

XLVIII · VIKINGS IN EARLY MEDIEVAL IRELAND: CHURCH-RAIDING, POLITICS AND KINGSHIP
Colmán Etchingham

XLIX · CLASSICAL MYTH IN MEDIEVAL IRELAND
Brigid Ehrmantraut

www.ingramcontent.com/pod-product-compliance
Lightning Source LLC
LaVergne TN
LVHW011030160826
845780LV00026B/213
* 9 7 8 1 8 3 7 6 5 3 8 2 9 *